Writing in a Technological World

Writing in a Technological World explores how to think rhetorically, act multimodally, and be sensitive to diverse audiences while writing in technological contexts such as social media, websites, podcasts, and mobile technologies.

Claire Lutkewitte includes a wealth of assignments, activities, and discussion questions to apply theory to practice in the development of writing skills. Featuring real-world examples from professionals who write using a wide range of technologies, each chapter provides practical suggestions for writing for a variety of purposes and a variety of audiences. By looking at technologies of the past to discover how meanings have evolved over time and applying the present technology to current working contexts, readers will be prepared to meet the writing and technological challenges of the future.

This is the ideal text for undergraduate and graduate courses in composition, writing with technologies, and professional/business writing.

A supplementary guide for instructors is available at www.routledge.com/9781138580985

Claire Lutkewitte, PhD, is an associate professor of writing at Nova Southeastern University where she teaches undergraduate and graduate writing courses. She has published several books, chapters, and articles related to the teaching of writing. Her current research interests include writing pedagogy, writing with and for technologies, and document design.

Writing in a Technological World

Claire Lutkewitte

Taylor & Francis Group
NEW YORK AND LONDON

First published 2020
by Routledge
52 Vanderbilt Avenue, New York, NY 10017

and by Routledge
2 Park Square, Milton Park, Abingdon, Oxon, OX14 4RN

Routledge is an imprint of the Taylor & Francis Group, an informa business

© 2020 Taylor & Francis

The right of Claire Lutkewitte to be identified as author of this work has been asserted by her in accordance with sections 77 and 78 of the Copyright, Designs and Patents Act 1988.

All rights reserved. No part of this book may be reprinted or reproduced or utilised in any form or by any electronic, mechanical, or other means, now known or hereafter invented, including photocopying and recording, or in any information storage or retrieval system, without permission in writing from the publishers.

Trademark notice: Product or corporate names may be trademarks or registered trademarks, and are used only for identification and explanation without intent to infringe.

Library of Congress Cataloging-in-Publication Data
Names: Lutkewitte, Claire, author.
Title: Writing in a technological world / Claire Lutkewitte.
Description: London ; New York : Routledge, 2020. | Includes bibliographical references and index.
Identifiers: LCCN 2019033593 (print) | LCCN 2019033594 (ebook) | ISBN 9781138580978 (hardback) | ISBN 9781138580985 (paperback) | ISBN 9780429507014 (ebook)
Subjects: LCSH: Online authorship. | Social media—Authorship. | Literature and technology.
Classification: LCC PN171.O55 L88 2020 (print) | LCC PN171.O55 (ebook) | DDC 808.02—dc23
LC record available at https://lccn.loc.gov/2019033593
LC ebook record available at https://lccn.loc.gov/2019033594

ISBN: 978-1-138-58097-8 (hbk)
ISBN: 978-1-138-58098-5 (pbk)
ISBN: 978-0-429-50701-4 (ebk)

Typeset in Myriad Pro
by Apex CoVantage, LLC

Visit the eResources: www.routledge.com/9781138580985

Contents

Acknowledgments xi
Preface. xiii

Part 1	Technology Is Multimodal 1
Chapter 1	Introduction. 3
	Writing and Technologies: Your Past, Present, and Future. 4
	Signs and Symbols 6
	Writing Is Technology. 7
	What Is a Technology? 11
	Final Thoughts 17
Chapter 2	Writing Is Multimodal 21
	Thinking Rhetorically 22
	Writing Is Multimodal. 24
	Modes Work Together 28
	Writing for Multiple Audiences 35
	Final Thoughts 36
Chapter 3	Non-Digital and Digital Technology. 39
	Purposeful Writing. 40
	Non-Digital Texts 42
	Digital Texts Distributed Non-Digitally. 46
	2D and 3D Texts 49
	What Things Are Made of Matters 51
	Final Thoughts 54
Reading:	*Can We Define "Technology"?* 57
	by David E. Nye
	Reading Questions 67
Part 2	Technology Is Active. 69
Chapter 4	Plan, Research, and Cite 71
	Writing in Action 72
	Suggestions for Planning Your Writing 74

Suggestions for Researching Your Writing	81
Suggestions for Citing Your Writing	86
Final Thoughts	93

Chapter 5 Design 95

Making Observations on Designs	96
Reading Path	97
Principles for Designing With Technologies	100
Principle 1: Color	100
Principle 2: Size	105
Principle 3: Organizing With Proximity	106
Principle 4: Alignment	107
Principle 5: Repetition and Moving Through a Text	108
Principle 6: Typography	109
Principle 7: Emphasis	110
Principle 8: Point of View	111
Principle 9: Creativity and Imagination	112
Principle 10: Make Everything Work, but Don't Go Overboard	113
Final Thoughts	114

Chapter 6 Draft, Test, Revise, and Edit 117

Another Look Back at History	118
Drafting Your Text	118
Testing Out Your Drafts	120
Revising Your Text	122
Editing Your Text	127
Editing a Text Based on Words	129
Editing a Text Based on Visuals	132
Editing a Text Based on Sounds	133
Editing a Text Based on Videos	134
Final Thoughts	135

Reading: *Handwriting Is History* 137
by Anne Trubek
Reading Questions 144

Part 3 Technology Is Narrative 145

Chapter 7 The Stories We Write 147

What Technologies Tell Us	148
Stories Matter to Our Communities, Our Culture, and Our Heritage	151
The Many Ways We Write Stories	153

	Online Storytelling	155
	You Write Stories, Too	156
	One Version of a Story	158
	Protecting Stories	159
	Final Thoughts	160
Chapter 8	**Information at Our Fingertips**	**163**
	A Story for the Ages	164
	When We Seek Information	168
	Expand Your Search	173
	Narrow Your Search	177
	Research Your Sources for Credibility and Bias	179
	Organizing Information for Your Own Use	183
	Sharing Information With Others	184
	Using Multiple Modes Can Help Express Information Differently	186
	Final Thoughts	188
Reading:	***The Disappearance of Technology:***	
	Toward an Ecological Model of Literacy	**191**
	by Bertram C. Bruce and Maureen P. Hogan	
	Reading Questions	207
Part 4	**Technology Is Embedded**	**209**
Chapter 9	**Technology Is a System**	**211**
	What You See and Don't See	211
	Translating From One System to Another	214
	Your Role in a System	215
	Language in a System	217
	Can You Trust Systems?	222
	Search Engines	224
	Data, Data, Data	225
	Searching Data	228
	Using Data to Make Writing Better	229
	Too Many Systems at Work at One Time	229
	Hacking the System	230
	Final Thoughts	231
Chapter 10	**Technology as Situated**	**233**
	Reading the Technological World	234
	Gaming in the Technological World	236

		Writing Impacts Places and Spaces 239
		Places and Spaces Impact Writing 240
		Stakeholders and Infrastructures 241
		Connected Online Spaces 243
		Tracking Time, Place, and Space 244
		You Are One Writer in a World of Many 246
		Final Thoughts 249

Chapter 11 **Writing Messages** **253**
Messages Can Help Save Lives 253
Choosing the Right Text and Technology for Your Message 256
Email Messages 258
Suggestions for Writing Emails 261
Emails Serve Lots of Purposes 263
Why Email Is Not Always the Best Way to Communicate 266
Text Messages 267
Think about Accessible Messages 268
Final Thoughts 270

Reading: *Predictive Algorithms and Personalization Services on Social Network Sites: Implications for Users and Society* 273
by Robert Bodle
Reading Questions 288

Part 5   Technology Is Connected 289

Chapter 12 **Writing for Social Media** **291**
A Story of Two People 291
Locally and Globally 293
Writing for Social Media 297
Social Media Impacts More Than Just People 301
Social Media Is a Business 302
Steps to Help With Privacy 304
Final Thoughts 306

Chapter 13 **Writing for Websites** **309**
The World Is Online 310
Computer Programming (the Backend) 311
Suggestions for What You See (the Frontend) 316
The Consequences of Design 321
Making a Website Usable and Accessible 322
Final Thoughts 325

Chapter 14	Writing for Mobile Devices	327
	Mobile Technology to the Rescue	327
	What Is a Mobile Technology?	328
	Comparing the Past With the Present	329
	Smartphones and Good Consequences	331
	Smartphones and Bad Consequences	331
	Writing With a Smartphone	333
	Suggestions for Designing Apps	334
	The Backend: To Template or Not	341
	Final Thoughts	342

Reading: *Thank You for Letting Me Share* 345
by Michelle R. Gould
Reading Questions 353

Part 6 Technology Is Embodied 355

Chapter 15	Feel, Hear, and Speak	357
	Embodied Actions	358
	Textures in a Technological World	361
	Sound in a Technological World	363
	Analyzing Sound: Music and Emotions	365
	Suggestions for Creating Podcasts	368
	Creating Sound: Public Speaking	373
	Final Thoughts	375

Chapter 16	Picture, Preform, and Present	377
	Images in a Technological World	377
	Suggestions for Writing Still Images	379
	Suggestions for Creating Moving Images	386
	Suggestions for Creating Live Images	388
	Final Thoughts	393

Reading: *The Voice of Lived Experience:*
Mobile Video Narratives in the Courtroom 395
by Mary Angela Bock and David Alan Schneider
Reading Questions 412

Index 413

Acknowledgments

I would first like to thank Nova Southwestern University and my colleagues for their continued support. Without their help, a project such as this textbook would not have been possible. I'd also like to thank my students, past and present, for teaching me more about writing than I had ever imagined. Finally, thank you to all those at Taylor & Francis, and Routledge especially, who helped make this project a success.

Preface

Dear Readers,

I am excited that you will be reading this book. My hope is that you will come to realize that all writing is technological and that in order to be a successful communicator, you must be willing to think critically about what it means to write in a technological world. To help you with your writing, this book centers on one question: How do we write in a technological world?

The answer to this question reveals that technology and therefore writing are: (1) multimodal, (2) active, (3) narrative, (4) embedded, (5) connected, and (6) embodied. These six characteristics make up the framework for this book, which is based on the work of a number of scholars, such as Joddy Murray's work on the image, multimodal, and affect, David E. Nye's work on technology (which you will find in the readings section of this book), and the work of writing scholar Christina Haas, who has written extensively on technology.

In writing this textbook, I relied on a number of technologies myself; too many to count, really. I wrote this textbook over a period of months, in different locations: on a plane, at my desk, on a computer, on my phone, through email, in a notebook, and so on. It is safe to say that technologies played a key role in the development of the pages you will soon be reading. Then again, technologies play a key role in all writing people do. To that end, this book aims to help you develop a hyperawareness of the ways in which writing is a technology as well as the fact that writing often relies on other technologies. Technologies are not autonomous or devoid of human influence. People can use technologies to do good things and bad things. My hope is that this book will help you do good things.

What you will find in this book are rhetorical strategies and suggestions, not necessarily hard rules that you must follow unquestioningly. Calling what you will find on the pages suggestions was a deliberate decision on my part. I believe writing, and thus the use of technology, should be rhetorical. Each time writers write, they are tasked with important rhetorical decisions about what should be written, how it should be written, where it should be written, and for whom it should be written. Not every writing situation will require the same rules. Besides that, using "rules" runs the risk of normalizing things, and in a diverse, global society there is no such thing as normal. In every writing situation, for instance, you will find an exception to a "rule," thus rendering that rule not so much something that must be absolutely followed each and every time you write, but making it more of a suggestion that might or might not be helpful depending on the situation.

What I am saying here is that this book shows you what others have done, what you could possibly do, or what you possibly don't have to do depending on what writing situation you are in. What you do in your writing and with your writing is entirely up to you.

Thus, this book is a starting point, not an ending. In fact, I believe this book will provide you the motivation to engage in thinking, discussing, and writing that extends well beyond the pages you will find here. My hope is that this book will encourage you to explore your world and how you and others use technologies on a daily basis. I also hope that you will question and investigate deeply what it is you do when you write. What technologies do you use? Why? Where? Who invented them? Where do they come from? What do they do? How do they change you? The people around you? The world? I hope that you will not be passive consumers of technologies. That instead, you approach writing projects and every writing act with critical eyes, with an attention to the rhetorical decisions you make and those your audience makes when you communicate to them. To help you investigate, you will find a number of questions to consider in each chapter, questions designed to highlight the many ways in which people use technologies in our world in order to communicate.

As the writer of this textbook, I had to make important decisions about breadth and depth of the information contained in these pages. While I wish I could have devoted more time to every topic featured here, it simply was not possible. As mentioned before, I used a variety of technologies to write this book, technologies that limited me in what I could and could not do. For example, I wanted so badly to include actual textures within these pages that readers could feel with their bodies, but it was not possible given that many readers will be reading this book as an ebook.

Finally, as the writer of this textbook, I am aware that my choice in subject matter should be considered just that, a choice, one of many I could have made in writing about technology in this world. My hope is that you will be critical of my choices, that you will think deeply about what I say about writing and technologies. That you will consider what is not on the following pages. That you will consider what is left out and what possibilities are still out there.

—Claire Lutkewitte, PhD

PART 1

Technology Is Multimodal

Writing and technology play a role in most everything we do. If you were to stop reading this textbook for a moment and look around at your surroundings, most likely you would find evidence of writing and technology. Take, for instance, the clothes you are wearing. At several points in the making of those clothes, writing and technologies were used by a number of people. Designers created sketches, which in turn were translated into purchase orders for materials and instructions for sewing. Company employees made plans based on these instructions to hire more sewers and to revise job duties. Machines and sewers worked together to produce the new clothing. Merchandise descriptions on websites were updated. Marketing campaigns were formed. Customer orders were created, and so on and so on.

While writing is itself a technology, when we write, we do so rhetorically and with a number of other technologies, both digital and non-digital. When you write an essay, for instance, you may decide rhetorically that the best way to do so is to rely on an alphabet, on paper, on a computer, on a flash drive, and/or on a software program given your audience and your purpose. All the while you do so, you are also relying on a number of different modes of communication, from thinking spatially to thinking visually. Therefore, in Part 1, you will learn about the various ways that writing, technology, rhetoric, and modes come together when we communicate.

Key Questions _____

1. What is technology?
2. Why is writing multimodal?
3. Why is writing rhetorical?
4. What is the difference between digital and non-digital technology?

Technology Is Multimodal

Key Terms

Chapter 1
1. semiotics
2. signs
3. symbols
4. language
5. grammar
6. morphology
7. syntax
8. technology
9. rhetoric
10. ideology

Chapter 2
1. genre
2. conventions
3. modes
4. medium
5. multimodal
6. affordances

Chapter 3
1. digital text
2. non-digital text
3. dimension
4. prototype
5. materials
6. texture

CHAPTER 1

Introduction

Contents

Writing and Technologies: Your Past, Present, and Future.............................. 4
Signs and Symbols 6
Writing Is Technology.. 7
What Is a Technology? 11
Final Thoughts 17

IMAGE 1.1 antoniodiaz / Shutterstock

Writing and Technologies: Your Past, Present, and Future

Meet Jose Medina, a senior at North University. Jose is majoring in biology and minoring in chemistry. When he graduates, he plans to attend medical school to become a pediatric surgeon. During his senior year, Jose spends a lot of time studying. Not only does he use textbooks and notebooks, but he also uses his computer, his iPhone, and his iPad to research medical practices, take notes on key concepts, study images of the body, and watch videos of surgeries. Jose knows that in the future when he becomes a surgeon, he will be writing with and for several technologies. For example, he might have to write digital patient reports for a central database that nurses, other doctors, the patient, and insurance companies will need to access and utilize to make important decisions about his patients' health. He might also develop an interactive digital text for a mobile device that represents the latest breakthrough in his medical research, will help other doctors treat patients, and will be used at medical schools around the world to prepare future doctors.

Like Jose, Katrina Carlson is a senior at North University. She is a marketing major and art minor with hopes of working for a publishing firm in London. She also utilizes technology throughout her day to accomplish several writing tasks. In fact, for her capstone project, she is developing marketing materials for a nonprofit organization to send to senior citizens about the free educational events in their area. One of those materials is a brochure. To create her brochure, Katrina uses a sketch book to draw and plan the brochure, a software design program to bring her sketches to life, a class blog to generate feedback on her project from her peers, and a sharing platform that will help her distribute the brochure in print as well as in digital form.

Think About Your Present

Whether or not your major is biology, like Jose's, or marketing, like Katrina's, you most likely use technologies to write on a regular basis, too, and not just for academic purposes. Think for a moment about all the different texts you write now for your friends, your family, your job, and your community. Think about the different reasons why you write these and the different reasons why you use technology to do so. Perhaps you use a smartphone to text with friends and family to check in and say hi, to communicate information, to coordinate get-togethers, to answer questions. Perhaps you use a computer and Instagram to share images of what you are doing. In comparing your reasons for writing and your reasons for using technologies to do so with those of your fellow classmates' reasons, you might find that your classmates have similar or different experiences. Now, imagine what it would be like without those specific technologies you use to write on a regular basis. How different would your life be?

Think About Your Past

Chances are that while growing up you used a variety of different technologies to communicate. Think back to the time you learned to write. What technologies did you use? How did you use these? Where did you use them? How are these technologies different from the technologies you use today to write? As you grew up, the technologies you used evolved over time. As a result, you've had to learn to use newer technologies; otherwise, you might have been less successful in communicating effectively.

Think About Your Future

Most likely you will use writing and technologies in college and beyond to accomplish a variety of work. After all, can you imagine a career that doesn't require writing or technologies? Probably not. In addition to using writing and technologies in your career, you will also likely use them for civil and social purposes in your day-to-day life. For instance, as a community member, you might be tasked with planning an upcoming event in your neighborhood. To make sure the event is a success, you will need to make sure information about the event gets communicated in a variety of ways to a variety of people. You might need to use social media to collaborate and coordinate the event with other neighbors and city officials. You might need to create flyers and posters to advertise the event to ensure people attend. And you might need to create a budget to keep track of the event's expenses. Doing all of these things most likely will require writing and technologies.

There will be other times in your life, too, when you will need to write and to use technologies to do so. In fact, your life or the lives of your loved ones may even depend on using writing and technologies to communicate in emergency situations. In many areas of the United States, for example, when speaking on the phone is not an option (or even could be dangerous in a situation), you can text 911 to reach emergency call centers to let them know you are in trouble. Likewise, you may need writing and technologies to find help and advice for important life issues and/or to cope with challenges and tragedies. Worldwide, those who battle diseases and addictions such as cancer and alcoholism, and those who survive natural disasters such as earthquakes and hurricanes, find solace in online support groups, which, in order to work effectively, demand the use of writing and technology. While there are a thousand more examples of how writing and technology intersect and can be useful in life, the point is clear: **Your future will involve writing, and it will involve technology.**

To help you develop the skills and know-how to write with and for technologies, let us start by thinking more deeply about what it means to write in a technological world. You probably have taken a writing class or two. In so doing, you probably learned that writing isn't just about putting letters and words together to make correctly punctuated sentences. Writing, in fact, is much more than correct grammar.

Signs and Symbols

bird

 Gallinago_media / Shutterstock

The two images you see above have many differences and similarities that can help us think more critically about what it means to write. The word *bird* on the left is an image itself much like the image on the right is. If we break down the word *bird*, we would see that it is made up of letters *b, i, r,* and *d* which are images too, images made up of lines—some straight, some short, some long, and some curved. If we break down the image on the right, we would see that it too is made up of lines—some straight, some short, some long, and some curved.

In terms of differences, we can see that the image on the left and the image on the right along with their shapes are different. Their lines have different lengths and curvatures. Some are shorter and others are longer. The images also occupy different amounts of space on the page. Some lines are thicker than others. The one on the right has more black space than the one on the left. There is also a different amount of white space between their different elements.

Despite their differences, the ways in which we create these two images are very similar. If we were to use a pen and paper to create both of these, we might use similar movements of the hands to create them, lifting our pen from time to time as well as pressing our pen from time to time.

So, which one of these two images can we call writing?

Before answering such a question, it may be necessary to distinguish between two important terms: signs and symbols and the study of them. Semiotics is the study of signs and symbols and their uses. Perhaps you learned a long time ago from the people around you that both images above represent a bird. Perhaps you learned that the one on the right is an "image" and the one on the left is a "word." However, words are images, too. After all, you do use your eyes to read the bird on the left just as you use your eyes to read the bird on the right. Likewise, when you read these two, you develop a mental image of a bird in your mind.

Signs can be thought of as just markers for things that have no meaning. Symbols, on the other hand, are signs that we ascribe meaning to based on what we learn from our environments. Rhetoric scholar Joddy Murray's work on multimodal composition and images provides one useful understanding of signs and symbols. Drawing from Susanne Langer's research on symbolism, Murray writes that symbols are our perceptions and interpretations of signs (24).

The physical word "bird" written on paper (or in this textbook, in this case) is a sign. It becomes a symbol only when we interpret and ascribe meaning to it. Of course, the meaning that we ascribe to it is dependent on our experiences in the world at particular times and in particular environments. It could change with time. If you were to write the word "bird" on paper today while studying in your room for this class, you would understand that sign to mean something. In that very act of ascribing meaning to that word, that sign becomes a symbol. Perhaps your meaning of the word "bird" is one that reminds you of the golden finch that lives in the oak tree on your campus. Twenty years from now, after you've had many different experiences, when you write "bird" again on a piece of paper, you may have a different understanding, and you may ascribe a different meaning to it. Perhaps, then, the bird will remind you of the robin that visits your backyard every morning.

The answer, then, to the question posed above is that both birds (the one on the left and the one on the right) are writing. When we put three lines together to form a B, one straight, two curved, we know that B represents the second letter of the alphabet and has a distinct sound. We know this because we were taught this by the people in our society. Three lines arranged in a different matter, like this, -/-, for instance, isn't the same symbol as a B that we have memorized and ascribed meaning to. Organizing symbols in a certain way through the use of letters, words, phrases, sentences, and space helps us to communicate messages to one another using a language. Writing is a human invention and action, and is itself a technology involving a system of symbols. Such symbols could be represented through language, but that doesn't always have to happen as meaning can be derived using a variety of modes.

Writing Is Technology

While in the previous section of the book and in the pages to come, writing and technologies are spoken about in separate terms—as in the phrase writing *and* technologies—you should not think of writing as something other than technology. **Writing is a technology**. However, because there are many other kinds of technologies besides writing, you will see that the word *writing* and the word *technologies* are often separated in this book. Doing so offers you some necessary clarification and a way to understand the key ideas in each chapter.

Today, our writing may appear more complex than the writing of ancient times. But, let's consider this: when writing was first developed in ancient civilizations, it was a system of markings for commercial purposes, purposes that enabled people to live. People used markings to record the amount of goods they wanted to sell. By making marks on clay surfaces, they were able to keep track of those goods. Since this first use, however, writing has evolved to include many more signs and symbols, creating new grammars, morphologies, and syntaxes that help develop languages. Writing scholar Christina Haas explains that "writing is language made material," and that "writing is made material through the use of technologies" (3). Put a different way, Walter J. Ong, renowned historian and philosopher, contends that writing is more than a "simple scratch on a rock or a notch on a stick"; that is, it derives from orality and is a "coded system of visible marks" that "a writer could determine, in effect without limit, the exact words and sequence of words that a reader would generate from a given text" (34).

Check It Out YouTube: For a more thorough account of how writing began, search YouTube for "The Evolution of Writing (8000 BC to 2017)" posted by the Honorable Caligula.

A *language*, therefore, is a system of things (which could include structured words) by which we communicate within our cultures. Later in this book, you will be asked to think more critically about systems, but for now, let's think of a system as an organized method or set of principles or rules that guide us in using or doing something. In this case, we are thinking about the rules that guide us in communicating. In the English language, we use letters, which are symbols that represent a sound in speech. Together, all the letters make up an alphabet, and when arranged in certain orders, they create words. We then organize these words based on the system of rules our society has set forth for communicating. Yet, not all languages use letters. Some languages, like Mandarin, use other signs that have come to be symbols for their words and ideas. Other languages, like body languages, use gestures, while others, like braille, use raised dots.

Think for a Moment

How much of your life is governed by the technology that is language? The college or university you attend, for instance, has rules, laws that are created in, among other things, language. The language that administration, departments, and your teachers use all govern what you can and cannot do on your campus. Your syllabi, your notes, your school's policies and procedures, all are created in language. It is through language that you learn and communicate with your classmates, your teachers, your dean, and your advisors.

What You Should Know About Grammar

In the past, certain thoughts may have come to mind when you heard the term *grammar*. You may have thought of it in terms of writing correctly, for instance, making sure you have chosen the right words or punctuating sentences in the right places. You would be right in those thoughts to a degree, though thinking of grammar as just writing correctly would be shortsighted.

Grammar is an encompassing term that we can use to describe the rules that govern a language. Every language has a grammar. After all, without an understanding of how a language works (in other words, what rules should be followed), it would be hard for us to understand each other when we speak.

In addition, we have to rely on grammar, which uses morphology and syntax, in order for us to make sense of what we are reading. Morphology refers to how we form words using morphemes. A morpheme is not quite a word, but rather is the smallest meaningful unit of a language. Let's look at some examples: there are three morphemes (*black, smith, -s*) in the word *blacksmiths*. These morphemes are the smallest units that make up the word. It is important to know that we use morphology to put these morphemes or units together to create the word *blacksmiths*.

To determine how to use such a word like blacksmiths in a sentence depends of course on the rest of the sentence. That's where syntax can help. Syntax is the study of sentences and their structure. In other words, syntax has to do with how we construct and arrange phrases, clauses, and sentences. A sentence like the following makes sense in the order in which it appears:

> *In the 1800s, blacksmiths were crucial to the development and survival of settlements in the American west.*

It would not make sense if we were to rearrange the order, perhaps like this:

> *blacksmiths were crucial to in the 1800s and survival of American west of settlements in the*

Grammar doesn't belong to spoken or written language. Each mode of communication has its own grammar. The visual mode, used in film for instance, has a grammar, its own language with guiding principles/rules for creating. According to the New London Group, who you will read about in the next chapter, grammar is "a specialized language that describes patterns of representation" (78).

Bottom Line: Grammars are the rules that govern a language, while morphology and syntax are parts of grammar and refer to how we form words and then arrange those words into sentences.

Over time, humans have used language and writing to do much more than trade goods; they have used these to record history, to share knowledge, to build communities, to create laws that govern societies, to save lives in emergencies, and to spread cultural and family traditions from one society and generation to the next. Nevertheless, while language and writing have done a lot to advance our way of life, when used for the bad, they can also do a lot to hinder our way of life. Yes, there are plenty of examples of good uses of language and writing, many in the pages of this book, but there are some examples that speak to the ills that technology, writing included, can bestow on us. With the increase in popularity of instant messaging and social media, for example, many societies have witnessed the negative impact that cyberbullying can have on people. One could argue that bullying has been a part of humanity since the beginning of time. One could also argue that such bullying has involved writing and technology over the span of human history—feuding kings sent threatening letters to one another, propagandists wrote false newspaper stories about others they opposed. All these actions were done with the hope of slandering the recipients and tarnishing their reputations. But one could not argue that people did this online until computers, the internet, instant messaging, social media, email, and so forth were invented. As language and writing have evolved alongside of technology, people have found ways to write for good and for bad purposes.

Did You Know? Alphabets

The world has many alphabets, each with its own history. Today, the Greek alphabet is one of the world's most widely used alphabets. You may know the Greek alphabet from your science classes or you may know it because you are in a fraternity or sorority represented by Greek letters. The word *alphabet* has Greek origins. It's a combination of the first two Greek letters "alpha" and "beta." Like writing, the alphabet is a technology, one that is a set of letters used to represent sounds that helps us write language.

The first uses of the Greek alphabet date back to the 8th century BC. In ancient times, the Greeks borrowed and adapted Phoenician letters to include both consonants and vowels to create the Greek alphabet. The Phoenician alphabet was solely made up of consonants and was derived from Egyptian hieroglyphs. One of the differences between hieroglyphs and the Phoenician alphabet is the fact that the Phoenician alphabet was based on sounds while the hieroglyphs were visual representations of objects. When the Greeks adapted the Phoenician letters, they thought it necessary to include letters for vowels.

Like the Greek alphabet, many alphabets borrowed from the Phoenicians. Another widely used alphabet, the modern English alphabet, for instance, is derived from the Roman alphabet, which was derived from the Greek alphabet, which was derived from the Phoenician alphabet. Over time, alphabets have changed as a result of cultural, political, economic, and technological influences. What has constituted the design of each individual letter (and the way it looks) has changed, too, from people rotating, extending, flipping, removing, and shortening lines and curves in order to adapt to their writing needs.

What Is a Technology?

So, now that we have a better understanding of writing, what then does it mean to write in a technological world? To answer this question, we should first define what we mean by technology. The word technology is derived from the ancient Greek techné (also written as *tekhnē*) and *logia*. Combined, the word was *tekhnologia* and meant a systematic treatment. The ancient Greeks thought of techné as an art or craft that involved action (the making and doing of something). In fact, the Greek philosopher and mathematician Aristotle wrote that techné was the producing or making of something. He saw techné as humankind's way of representing what is in nature. With the passage of time, the word *tekhnologia* transformed as many words do, taking on new meanings. In the 17th century, the word technology referred to "a systematic study of one of the arts" (Nye 11). By the 19th century, however, the English word *technology* (drawing much influence from German engineers) meant "the sum total of systems of machines and techniques that underlie civilization" (Nye 13). In other words, technology referred to a greater sense of how machines and techniques impacted societies. At the end of Part 1, you will have a chance to read more about the history of technology in David E. Nye's "Can We Define Technology?" and think further about how we define technology.

Today, when we think of technology, we often think of something new, digital, and/or electronic, like a computer. But, not all technologies are new, digital, electronic, and/or computers. Take for example chisels. In ancient Egypt, chisels were made of copper or bronze and were used to create hieroglyphs. Today, sculptors use chisels in much the same way the ancient Egyptians did, carving ideas into stone and other surfaces. Though many of us are not sculptors, we do rely daily on a variety of non-digital and non-electronic technologies. A construction worker, for instance, might need to rely on a pencil when on a job site to write notes about measurements on a board in order to make the right cut. A nurse who visits patients in their homes might need to rely on a pen to take notes and write patient reports on a clipboard. A community activist may need to rely on a marker to make a poster for a protest rally.

Activity: Writing Technologies

Writing technologies are technologies that help us write. In a group, create a list of all the writing technologies you can think of that college students use. Next to each writing technology, describe (1) what actions students perform with them, and (2) what knowledge they need when using them. Then, share your list with the class and discuss the following:

1. Why do college students use the technologies on your list as opposed to other writing technologies? For example, why wouldn't a college student write with a crayon?

2. Who or what decides which writing technologies are most appropriate for a college classroom?
3. What would it be like if you did not have these writing technologies? What difficulties would you encounter?
4. As a college student, how did you learn how to use the technologies on your list?

In the rest of the chapter, you will find a brief overview of the main themes that define technology that will be explored in the remaining chapters of the book. Defining technology, as you will soon see, involves thinking critically and rhetorically about how technologies are created, how they operate, and how they are used by people who are situated in a variety of environments.

Part 1: Technology Is Multimodal

While writing necessitates rhetorical thinking and story building (more on this later), writing is also about design. You may have heard the term multimodal in previous writing classes, and you may have explored the various modes (linguistic, visual, aural—to name a few) that we use on a regular basis to communicate. Throughout this book, especially in Chapter 2, you will explore how writing is multimodal and how writers design different types of texts using multiple modes, relying on technologies to do so. You will see plenty of examples of different types of texts, each involving more than just words on a page, and you will see plenty of examples of how we use multiple modes to create and read different kinds of texts. For instance, you will see how writers design texts using words, spacing, alignment, images, sound, and so forth. Indeed, in this book, design principles will play an important role in thinking critically about how texts come to be and what they do for audiences.

Part 2: Technology Is Active

Tied closely with the previous part about multimodality is the idea that technologies require action. Technologies do something, and that something is instigated by our bodies. Therefore, a technology is not a technology until it is used, that is, until it is acted upon. The technology of writing is active in this sense. During the act of writing, we perform; we move our bodies to communicate to an audience who always must act in order to understand. Without action, we cannot write, and therefore, writing does not exist, and therefore, an audience has no need to act.

At the same time, not all things that move are technologies. There must be a purpose for our actions. To understand what makes a technology a technology, we can use a bit more rhetorical thinking. A leaf, for example, would not be considered a technology if it is just hanging from a tree branch and blowing in the wind. That's because technologies are defined by their uses and by when they are used, not just what they are made of. A chisel and a pencil have no meaning, no value on their own, just lying on a shelf or in a drawer somewhere. They become technologies only when used or applied by someone to do something in a particular moment and place in time. They are not technologies until someone picks them up and begins chiseling or writing for a particular purpose in a particular place.

When someone uses the chisel or the pencil, they must rely on skills and abilities (actions, in other words) that help them to accomplish a goal or to solve a problem. It is these actions that define technologies because it is these actions that point to their usefulness. We could say a leaf could become a technology only when someone uses the leaf to accomplish a goal or to solve a problem. Specifically, someone uses it to perform an action for a particular purpose. If a person was stranded on an island and needed some way to collect rain water to drink, they may pick a leaf from a tree branch, fold it, and use it as a cup to collect water. In that regard, the leaf would become a technology because a particular person used it to solve a problem in a particular place and at a particular moment in time.

Part 3: Technology Is Narrative

Narrative, as an adjective, describes the process of storytelling. As you will read in Part 1, David E. Nye reminds us that to understand technology is to understand a story. While writing is a technology, and a powerful one at that, it is one we must use rhetorically in order to be effective in our communication. But to do so, we must understand what story we are telling. You may recall from previous writing classes that rhetoric, as defined by Aristotle, means finding all the available means of persuasion in a given situation (Kennedy 37). Today, rhetoric generally means being able to communicate effectively. Effective communicators are those who pay attention to their rhetorical situations. They think critically about what must be communicated and how best to communicate it in a particular moment in time and in a particular environment. Such thinking allows us to organize our ideas, our words, our sentences, our paragraphs, our designs, our images, our sounds, and so forth in a way that is most helpful to us and our audiences. When communicating, we pay attention to the who, what, where, when, why, and how of communicating. In other words, when we communicate rhetorically, we make appropriate decisions about:

- *whom* we are communicating with
- *what* we are communicating
- *where* we are communicating
- *when* we are communicating
- *why* we are communicating
- *how* we are communicating

In answering these questions, we are in essence narrating or creating a particular story. We are thinking about actors performing actions in a particular setting at a particular time for a particular audience.

Part 4: Technology Is Embedded

So far, this book has presented several examples of technologies that are systems (alphabet, language) and tools (chisels, pencils, notebooks). But there are other types of technologies. Around the world, different societies rely on different technologies to accomplish a variety of tasks, including using technologies to communicate ideas. To write in a technological world means to think carefully about the situation you are in, what you want to accomplish with your communication, and how best to do so. That means you must think about which technologies are most appropriate for the task at hand, given your audience and given your resources and abilities. But you must also think about the context, where you are writing and at what time you are writing. Writing scholar Christina Haas contends that "technology is a place where culture and cognition meet—technologies are cultural artifacts imbued with history, as well as tools used by individuals for their own motives and purposes" (229).

Undeniably, technologies are embedded in societies, societies that determine which technologies are appropriate for particular tasks in particular moments. Filling out tax forms with a red crayon is not appropriate according to our society. Filling out tax forms electronically using a technology like a computer is, however. Therefore, when we think about writing in a technological world, we must think about which technologies are most appropriate to complete the tasks we are wishing to complete at a particular place and moment in time.

In truth, technologies are situated. In order for the user to act, that is, to use the technology, the user must understand *where* they are using the technology and *when* they are using the technology, and how those two acts are shaped not only by *purpose*, *time*, *space*, and *place*, but by a society's understanding and defining of these things.

Yet, there is more to thinking rhetorically about context. In thinking about context, we have to think about the cultural, political, institutional, ethical, and economic influences that shape technologies and our uses of them. These are ultimately tied to ideology (a system of ideas that form our ways of knowing and communicating). Most likely you know that when you go to a movie at a theater, you are not supposed to use your smartphone to video-record what is on the screen. Not only is it illegal, but such an action might be looked upon as rude and disruptive by other moviegoers. Our culture has deemed recording someone else's work as stealing, calling it piracy and unfair. Politicians determined that such piracy could have a negative financial impact on the movie's creators. Those who steal movies are prosecuted as a result. As someone who believes in being respectful of others, you most likely wouldn't record the movie with your smartphone.

Finally, when we think about technology as embedded in our society, we have to think about it being embedded at a particular moment in time, and when we make decisions about using technology based on time, we have to determine how long this technology will take to use, whether or not it is the right time to use it, and whether or not it is outdated given our audience and purpose.

Part 5: Technology Is Connected

Because technologies are embedded, they are connected to people, places, and things in our world. To see technologies working in isolation would be a mistake, as seeing them as connected allows us to see how technologies shape our writing and how our writing shapes technologies. Think about your smartphone. It is certainly connected to a lot of people (your friends, family, and coworkers). But, it is also connected to other technologies (other phones, computer systems, the internet), as well as institutions (governments, schools, businesses). A government, for instance, regulates commerce. A smartphone is a good that can be bought and sold on a market as long as such a transaction follows the government's laws. Schools advertise by sending potential students text messages and Snapchats. Businesses connect via your smartphone to gather data on users, to sell products to users, and to collect payments from users.

While these examples of connections are just a few of the millions that exist, knowing the connections and identifying how they work or don't work can give us a more comprehensive understanding of our writing situations. When we can see such connections, we are better positioned to make smart rhetorical decisions as to which technologies we should use to write and how and when to write, and to whom we should write.

Finally, with connectivity comes the power to engage with millions quickly. Such power lends itself to our abilities to influence markets, educate people, and share information in ways technology didn't allow for hundreds of years ago. Our connections thus shape our world's history, its politics, its cultures, and its social practices.

Part 6: Technology Is Embodied

So far, we can see that technology doesn't happen in a bubble, that it is connected in many ways to other people, places, and technologies. And, by now, it should be clear that technologies don't operate on their own. Our bodies have to move in order for technologies to move and thus work.

Therefore, in the final part of the book, you will not only consider how our bodies make technologies work and how technologies can help our bodies to write, read, and understand, but you will discover how technologies can pose challenges to or hinder our bodies in our abilities to write, read, and understand with them. That's because technologies shape our bodies just as much as our bodies shape technologies. The motions that our bodies undertake when writing, reading, and understanding shape our brains in many different ways, forming the basis for how we understand and communicate with others. Technology is truly a bodily experience, one in which our bodies shape technologies and are also shaped by technologies.

In another sense, technologies also embody ideas, representing reflections of human beliefs. Societies and the people in them ascribe meanings to technologies, and those meanings shape what we can and cannot do with our bodies as we operate those technologies. To be successful writers, to make smart rhetorical decisions, we have to be aware of the ideas that technologies embody.

Activity: Daily Technology Use

Technologies can be defined in terms of actions and the stories they tell when they are acted upon: who uses them, what they are used for, where they are used, when they are used, why they are used, and how they are used.

Think about all the things you did today from the moment you woke up to this moment right now. How much of your day included the use of technologies? Keep a log of all the technologies you use in one day. Then, write a few reflective paragraphs that explain your uses of these technologies. To help you write these paragraphs, think rhetorically. Here are some questions to consider:

a. How many technologies did you use?
b. Why did you choose these technologies over others?
c. How did you use these technologies, and for what purposes?
d. What knowledge and skills did you need in order to use them?
e. When did you use these technologies?
f. Where were you when you used these technologies?
g. Could you live without the technologies you use on a daily basis? Why or why not?

Putting It All Together

A text is a technology and the sum of the actions taken to create it. Sometimes, we have a tendency to think of a text as a product, a finite, stable thing that can be assessed and graded by what is left on the page, the screen, the file that we have turned in, published, and shared. But in thinking this way, we allow ourselves only to know part of the story of a text. To more fully understand a text, we must think about the actions a writer took to create it. What were the circumstances that prompted the ideas for the text in the first place? What were the decisions and the physical moves that a writer took? What was talked about? Who listened? What was drafted? What was revised? What was cut? What was added? What technologies were used? When? Where? How? These questions point to the need to think not only about actions, but also how those actions are tied or connected to a person, a place, and a time.

As mentioned a moment ago, just as our bodily actions in writing shape technologies, over time, technologies also shape our bodily actions. When humans began using chisels to carve stone, they created markings to represent ideas. Over time, as situations in society demanded more intricate markings, humans made better chisels in order to make such markings. Those better chisels, however, in turn allowed humans to create even more intricate markings, ones users did not originally imagine they could make. The new technology, the new chisel, had presented users with the opportunity to discover new uses and new markings and develop new techniques that involve new bodily actions.

For a different, more modern example, we could use Twitter. When Twitter's founders first imagined its purpose, they imagined it as a social networking and microblogging platform for hosting short comments and status updates. At first, users did use Twitter to post status updates, making sure to shape their thoughts and writing in ways that fit the allowable 140 characters. Over time, users began using Twitter for purposes other than to post status updates, purposes that continued to shape the way writers write. Writers saw how such a platform could enable social change, could be used for political purposes, could spread information during natural disasters, and much more. As a result of these new uses, Twitter then made some changes, creating a more user-friendly app and redoing their website based on user feedback and the millions of tweets happening each day. In 2017, Twitter changed its character limits. Now users can tweet using 280 characters as opposed to 140, allowing people to think and write in different ways. People don't have to be as concise in their thoughts and writing as before.

Final Thoughts

Now that you have begun defining technology and contemplating what it means to write, you start to see what it means to write in a technological world. Across the globe, millions of people use technologies, especially for writing, in order to communicate daily. Throughout the rest of the book, you will consider many different contexts in which we write and how we use different technologies to do so for a variety of purposes and a variety of audiences. In each chapter, you will discover suggestions for writing effectively while critically thinking about and using technologies rhetorically. To help you get a handle on writing in a technological world, you will also read stories and examples of writing from professionals who rely on writing and technologies to be successful in their careers. Finally, each chapter in this book will challenge you to discuss the many impacts technologies have on communication and the many impacts writing has on the technologies of our world.

Additional Discussion Questions

1. Throughout history, writing technologies have made an impact on societies. For example, Gutenberg's improvement on moveable type made the printing process much easier and economical in Western Europe. Chose a technology from the past and discuss its impact on writing and on the world.
2. Think back to your past. Growing up, what were the technologies that helped you learn to write? Discuss how your writing has evolved because of technologies. Give examples.

3. Think about the writing technologies your great-grandparents used when they were growing up. Discuss how they are similar to and different from the writing technologies you used when growing up.
4. Discuss which writing technologies would be best for the following scenarios. In your discussion, talk about the advantages and disadvantages of using such technologies. Thinking rhetorically. Think about where and when you will be using such technologies and how such technologies can help you communicate your messages effectively.

Scenario 1: During your senior year, you enroll in a botany class. One day, your professor takes you on a field trip to the botanical gardens. There you are to learn about different plant species which you will have a test on later in the semester. Because you want to do well on the test, you decide you will need to keep track of the different plant species you observe at the gardens. How will you do so? What rhetorical decisions will you make in deciding what is best?

Scenario 2: On the news, you learn that your local government is considering closing your favorite park in your area. Because you love that park and spend so much time there, you decide to tell the government not to close it. How would you go about telling your local officials what this park means to you and your fellow citizens?

Additional Activities

1. Weekly Log: Every day, you rely on a variety of technologies to write, whether in class, on the job, or at home. Over the course of one week, make a log of all the technologies you use to compose ideas and messages. Then, next to each technology on your list, write a description that explains how and why you used each technology. Bring your list to class and compare it to your classmates' lists. Do they have similar technologies on their lists? Do they use the technologies in ways that are similar to the ways you use them? Or, do they use the technologies differently? Why do you suppose you use them in similar and different ways?
2. Digital and Non-Digital Texts: Collect a variety of texts, both digital and non-digital. Discuss what writers did to create each of these texts. What writing technologies did the writers use? How did they use them? Why didn't they use other writing technologies?
3. When Not to Use Tech: Make a list of places where using certain technologies is frowned upon by your culture. Come up with examples and discuss why they would be frowned upon.
4. One Technology Leads to Another: Come up with examples of behaviors with technologies that have led to the development of other technologies. For

example, because internet technologies make available millions of texts online, it has become too easy to copy and paste someone else's work online into our own texts. As a result, companies like Turnitin have developed a program to help stop students from plagiarizing.

Additional Assignments

1. A Story About Learning: Write a narrative in which you tell a story about a time when you learned to use a new writing technology. How did you learn to use it? What challenges did you face? Why did you learn it?
2. A Writing Technology and Its Impact: Compose a project that describes the impact a writing technology has had on shaping writing and our society.
3. New Writing Technology: Compose a presentation for your classmates that introduces them to a new writing technology. In your presentation, first explain the characteristics that make your writing technology a writing technology to begin with. Second, demonstrate how it works and why it is useful. Finally, imagine the writing technology's future and its impact on writing.
4. How Tech Comes to Be: Choose a technology and write a report about how you think it came to be. Was the technology created out of necessity? Out of curiosity? From our ability to improve on previous technologies? Using that same technology, discuss what makes it a technology. That is, discuss how it is used, when it is used, where it is used, who uses it, and for what purposes. Using that same technology, discuss what changes it has undergone over time and what caused those changes. In what ways can you imagine this technology evolving over time?
5. How Language Evolves: Create a project in which you research the origin and evolution of a language or a letter from a particular alphabet. Share with your classmates.

Works Cited

Aristotle. *On Rhetoric: A Theory of Civic Discourse*. 2nd ed., Translated by George A. Kennedy, Oxford University Press, 2007.
Haas, Christina. *Writing Technology: Studies on the Materiality of Literacy*. Lawrence Erlbaum Associates, 1996.
Murray, Joddy. *Non-Discursive Rhetoric: Image and Affect in Multimodal Composition*. State University of New York, 2009.
Nye, David. *Technology Matters: Questions to Live With*. MIT Press, 2006.
Ong, Walter J. "Writing Is a Technology That Restructures Thought." *The Written Word: Literacy in Transition*, edited by Gerd Baumann, Oxford University Press, 1986, pp. 23–50.

CHAPTER 2

Writing Is Multimodal

Contents

Thinking Rhetorically 22
Writing Is Multimodal... 24
Modes Work Together 28
Writing for Multiple Audiences.. 35
Final Thoughts 36

IMAGE 2.1 Viktor Gladkov / Shutterstock

Thinking Rhetorically

As a boy, Mike Butler loved to take apart things. First, a radio. Then a bike. Then, much to his father's dismay, a lawn mower. Mike was curious to know just how things worked, and he figured by taking things apart and putting them back together, he could learn some valuable insights. Growing up, his love of learning how things worked never waned and led him to a double major in engineering and computer science. As an undergrad, he learned all sorts of things from his engineering classes like the mechanics of motion, machine systems, and physics. But what Mike didn't anticipate as an undergrad was just how much writing he would do on the job once he graduated.

Now as an engineer and the supply chain manager for a manufacturing company, Mike not only takes apart and fixes things, like machines the size of football fields, he also must communicate locally, nationally, and internationally with others on a daily basis. He writes emails, reports, manuals, presentations, instructions, organizational updates, and reviews as well as purchase orders and inventory lists. As he does so, he must rely on his rhetorical writing skills, knowledge of design principles, and technological know-how.

Mike is not alone in his writing endeavors. Millions of workers across the globe in a variety of career fields also write daily. To do so effectively, they must rely on a variety of writing technologies. Recent research proves that written communication skills are at the top of employers' wish lists. In fact, more than four out of five employers in the 2019 Job Outlook Survey, conducted by the National Association of Colleges and Employers in the United States, indicated that their most sought-after attribute on a candidate's resume was strong written communication skills.

Below, you will find an organizational update, just one example of the kind of writing Mike does as an engineer and supply chain manager. As you read through his organizational update, an update he sent via email to his employees, make note of Mike's rhetorical decisions. For instance, Mike made sure to consider his audience (his fellow employees) while writing this document, as evidenced by his language choices in communicating information about a recent hire. As you can see, from the start, Mike's words, syntax, and grammar all help to achieve a professional tone and style (how you say what you are saying). As an example, he begins with "I am pleased to announce Tim Smith has joined A&C Supply Chain team reporting to Mike Butler." Of all the words Mike could have chosen, these seem like the most appropriate given his audience, his purpose, and his context for writing. Putting these words first means letting his audience know right away what this document is about. Also evidenced is Mike's awareness of his audience's time. In his update, he gets straight to the point, uses uniform paragraphs, and a structure that is well organized, all of which Mike hoped would help readers move seamlessly through the document.

Mike's language choices are not the only indications that he thought carefully about his audience. The design of the organizational update was also deliberate. As you will learn in the interview with Mike later in this chapter, he used a company template to create the document. The template contains recognizable features (headings, fonts, paragraphing, wording, and so forth) that his fellow employees have seen before at other times on the job. Such features help his colleagues read and understand the document. Knowing the type

---

A&C Industries

"Excellence with Integrity"

Organizational Update
August 24, 2017

I am pleased to announce Tim Smith has joined the A&C Supply Chain team reporting to Mike Butler. Tim comes to A&C with experience in production planning and logistics scheduling for multiple high volume production lines.

As part of the A&C production planning team, Tim will start providing additional support in scheduling for the metals plant. Tim will work closely with Bill Johnson to further analyze customer demands and provide input to how we improve our production planning processes. Tim's interactions with supply chain and production will also help serve our customer focused objectives.

Tim has a Bachelor's Degree in Sociology, a Minor in Military Science, and a Master's of Science in Transportation and Logistics Management from the American Military University. Tim has also served as an Army Quartermaster for Army Supply Chain Management.

Among other career highlights, Tim has previously worked as an Operations Planner to schedule products and personnel on multiple production lines. He also coordinated production scheduling and transportation for multiple high volume canning plants, including the one right across the street from A&C. Tim's experience in the US Army as a Logistics Platoon Leader in charge of parachute production has helped prepare him to be an excellent written and verbal communicator and an exceptionally organized leader with focus on every detail.

Please join me in welcoming Tim to our Supply Chain planning team.

Mike Butler
Supply Chain Manager
A&C Industries

METAL STAMPING • TOOL & DIE • PLASTIC MOLDING

A&C Industries
Phone: 555-555-5555   Fax: 555-555-5555

IMAGE 2.2 Writing Example: Organizational Update

of text (also known as genre) he was supposed to write, Mike made sure to include all the common or expected features (also known as conventions) of that genre. In other words, because Mike knew he needed to write an organizational update (the genre of text), he made sure that he included the necessary headings, paragraphs, white space, organizational cues, alignment, signature, keywords, and so forth. At the same time, he also had to pay attention to his medium (a digital text), the modes that enable him to create such a text, and the technologies to write (computer, language, writing) and distribute it (email).

Audience played a key role in the decisions Mike made indeed. Because Mike's company is an international one, he works with a translating service company to translate the update to be shared with his clients and employees abroad. Once again, he must think rhetorically about his audiences and the cultures they reside in, making sure he follows appropriate conventions.

Writing Is Multimodal

As mentioned briefly in Chapter 1, writing is multimodal, and if we examine the organizational update, we can see why. All writing involves multiple modes (whether or not you are actively aware of them). In fact, "there is no such thing as a monomodal text" (Ball and Charlton 43). To write is to make meaning and "all meaning-making is multimodal" (The New London Group 81). To be a better writer and thinker, it makes sense, then, to develop an awareness of how modes work together to create meaning. Writing scholars have been studying modes of communication for centuries. A look back in time shows us that ancient Greek and Roman philosophers and educators were highly aware of speaking in public forums and how different sounds carried different meanings. Their written texts allude to the various modes people relied on to communicate, too.

Thinking of writing as just letters and words on paper or screen would be a very narrow way to think of writing, not to mention limiting to our understanding of what makes communication work effectively. When our brains process information, we rely on multiple modes. That's because multiple modes supply our brains with different kinds of information that we then put together in order to make sense of what we are experiencing. In other words, we combine what we know about each mode to make sense of communication. If we look back in time, we can see that writing has always been multimodal. Take, for example, Egyptian hieroglyphs, of which there are thousands. Such writing included modes such as the visual, the spatial, and the textual as writers of the hieroglyphs wrote on many surfaces such as papyrus, clay, metal, stone, and leather to communicate different things. Fast forward to today, and we see that writers use multiple modes as well. In Mike's organizational update, he uses written text in the English language, organized into sentences and paragraphs. Mike paid close attention to the visualness of the text, placing a header and footer at the top and bottom of the page, and using blank space effectively to help separate information into a visually coherent text. He also thought carefully about how his text would be received by his audience and how they would feel when reading it. He wanted his audience to feel excited and encouraged by the recent hire, and so he chose his words wisely in order to evoke such feelings.

If you are not familiar with the word *multimodal*, you may be familiar with the word *multimedia*. But, be careful; multimodal is not the same as multimedia. Multimedia is a term used to describe multiple media. *Media* is the plural form of the word *medium*. A **medium** is a go-between, a text that provides the space for our message, a space between the communicator and the communicatee. Specifically, the medium is part of the message as well as how the message gets delivered. A medium could rely on multiple modes. A book, for example, is a medium. In it, you will see several different modes at work. You may see the linguistic mode, the spatial mode, the visual mode, and so forth. Whether you realize it or not, when you write, you are doing so using multiple modes. When you type on a computer, for instance, in a program such as Microsoft Word, you utilize such modes as the spatial mode (using space to separate letters and words), the visual mode (using colored font), the linguistic mode (using letters), and so forth.

In addition, when you encounter texts, you need to rely on multiple modes in order to understand how such modes work together to create meaning. This means that while modes can appear in texts, modes can also be actions that we undertake when communicating. When you write about your high school graduation, for example, you might visualize the ceremony in your mind, recall feelings that you had, and then use not just words to communicate it to others, but also these same images and feelings. To understand multimodality is to think not only about the texts themselves, but also the actions it takes to create and understand them.

Over the years, writing scholars have attempted to classify and name the different modes of communication and their characteristics, but it has been a difficult task given the dynamic nature of them. For instance, according to The New London Group, a group of academics who met in New London, New Hampshire, in 1994 to develop new literacy pedagogy to account for the multiple ways in which students learn, **multimodal** "represents the patterns of interconnection among the other modes" (78). This group identified five modes: linguistic, visual, audio, gestural, and spatial (78). Yet, this group's treatise on how to define multimodal is just one of many attempts to define what multimodal means. Their classification is certainly useful for us for many reasons, but at the same time, it doesn't account for or make clear how other modes of communication (such as the temporal mode or the tactile mode) might help us to make meaning. That is, there are other modes than the five identified by The New London Group. Indeed, we use a variety of modes for different reasons in a variety of different texts. Over the course of this book, you will see lots of modes at play besides just five.

Check It Out YouTube: If you want to know a little more about The New London Group's take on the five modes and how learning them helps students in their academic, social, and civic lives, search YouTube for Larissa Babak's "A Pedagogy of Multiliteracies: Designing Social Futures."

Consider These Words of Caution

For the purposes of this book, you will be asked to consider the following modes as they relate to writing and technology. The chart in Box 2.1 presents an expanded interpretation of The New London Group's work on modes and provides more possibilities for them (83). While these modes appear in separate columns and have distinct examples, please note that modes themselves are multimodal, meaning they cannot work on their own. They are always in operation with at least one other mode. Evoking the linguistic mode when writing the word *bird* would require you to think visually about the shape of the letters *b, i, r, d*, and spatially about the space between the letters in the word. You would have to think about *how* you should arrange them and *where* you should arrange them. If you don't think about these things, you wouldn't be able to communicate effectively.

Box 2.1 Modes

Visual	Linguistic	Temporal	Spatial	Aural	Olfactory
Examples: images, color	Examples: letters, words	Examples: changes in time, a pause, speed up, slow down	Examples: arrangement of elements to one another, blank space	Examples: sounds, music, utterances	Examples: flowery, rotten
Gestural	**Tactile**	**Connected**	**Mobile**	**Emotional**	**Gustatory**
Examples: facial expressions, body positions	Examples: felt sense, rough, smooth, rigid	Examples: hyperlinks, tagging people in social media, texting chain, copied on an email	Examples: when objects move, direction, forward, backward	Examples: feelings of happiness, sadness, excitement	Examples: sweet, sour

Modes Are Multimodal

If you think of modes as multimodal, therefore, the chart in Box 2.1 featuring a list of modes and some examples of them could be misleading. The chart is not meant to suggest that a mode is distinct or is itself singular in nature belonging to just one section on this chart. Strictly speaking, you should not think of a mode as being monomodal, of being of just one mode.

The term "multimodal," therefore, is a bit redundant given that writing is always multimodal. The reason for its use in this book is to draw attention to the fact that writing is multimodal and to help you develop an awareness of what you are doing when you write.

The chart isn't all encompassing, either, as meaning could be communicated in other ways. The chart could just as easily have been conceived of in a different representation, perhaps some sort of giant Venn diagram, or perhaps one big box with all modes in it or a layered image to show how the modes work with one another. However, perhaps, there is no way of visualizing or representing them here given the medium of this book and its limitations.

Instead, the chart is meant to help us use a technology such as language to talk about modes and to see modes in action. In fact, actions play key roles in our understanding of modes. The modes listed represent some of what we do as we are creating texts and what we do when we are trying to make sense of them. If one were to pick a particular mode—say, gestural, for instance—to communicate cradling a baby carefully to someone who had never done so, one would also, in picking such a mode, be always picking other modes. To communicate with gestures the cradling of a baby, one would need to use the temporal mode (how fast of a swing), the spatial mode (how wide and where to place the arms), and the emotional mode (a soothing, calm face). To understand these gestures, one would need to rely on modes as well, such as the visual mode. As such, in the experience of the gestures, there are multiple modes at play, and it would be hard to distinguish each alone.

So, herein lies the problem: it is impossible to use one mode (like the linguistic, for instance) to describe another, because modes in and of themselves are multimodal. So, while the modes in the sections of the chart in Box 2.1 appear to be separate (due to the limitations of this printed text), they in fact rely on one another. Instead of seeing these modes as individual, it would be best to see these as working together in particular contexts.

One More Thing

Consequentially, modes are not stable. They are always evolving. Their past, present, and future are shaped by a number of factors, such as cultures, economics, politics, technologies, and histories, and these in turn shape the way we think and use modes. Take, for example, technologies' influences on our uses of the spatial mode. Before computers, people used typewriters to write documents. Such a technology demanded that we write in certain ways. For instance, using two spaces after a period and before the next sentence made sense because each typed letter on a typewriter occupied the same amount of space (a typed letter "w" took up the same space as a typed "I"), and using two spaces between sentences helped with readability, helped us to distinguish where one sentence ended and another began. Nowadays, thanks to computers, typed letters do not occupy the same amount of space, and therefore the two spaces are not as necessary.

Because modes are influenced by a number of factors, as a writer, you should think carefully about who or what dictates how, when, and where we use modes and how modes change over time because of cultures, economics, politics, technologies, and histories. Question how modes came to be, how they evolved, and how they are shaped, by asking yourself:

- Why are some modes privileged over others?
- Why have modes evolved over time?
- Why are some modes no longer appropriate in certain contexts?
- Who is responsible for deciding what modes are appropriate? Who is not?

Modes Work Together

Imagine what we would miss out on if we only conceptualized ideas in words alone. Without emotions, without sounds, without movements. Would this even be possible? Would this be limiting to our understanding of the world? The goal of writing is to make meaning and to have an audience understand it. For these to happen, we need modes.

Let's take a closer look at modes to better understand how modes work together. In Chapter 1, you were introduced to grammar and syntax. Those are important to the reading of a sentence and certainly come into play when working in the linguistic and spatial modes. To demonstrate, read the following:

> The PARK.allHisstrengthwhitfieldusingRoger,out baseball hit teh,of

This probably doesn't make much sense to you. Instead, based on our knowledge of grammar and syntax, we know that the following makes much more sense:

> Using all his strength, Roger Whitfield hit the baseball out of the park.

That's because the words have been arranged in the order that makes the most sense according to a particular culture, and that culture uses syntactical and grammatical rules to help us read and understand the words in that order. At the same time, we also need other modes besides the linguistic (and everything we know about that mode) to make sense of this sentence. We need, for instance, to use the spatial mode. In the second sentence, you can see spaces between the words. Those spaces are important because they help us recognize where a word starts and ends. We could take out those spaces, but doing so makes reading harder. Try to read the sentence now without the spaces:

> UsingallhisstrengthRogerWhitfieldhitthebaseballoutofthepark.

Not easy, is it? The spatial mode also helps us organize our sentences on a page in a sequential order. In Western cultures, like in the United States, people read left to right on a straight line and then down the page. That's not possible without the use of the spatial mode. Try reading the following:

Box 2.2

                     of the   Using

                                    out   park

all   the

                            Roger   his

Again, it's tough to read because the words are not organized on the page in a way that we are accustomed to when working with the English language in the context of a college course.

Let's look at this sentence again within a particular context. To make extra money as a college student, Matt Gray puts on a baseball boot camp every summer for local Little Leaguers. To recruit players, Matt created the flyer below using Microsoft Word and then handed it out to parents whose children attended grade schools in his area. In this text, there are even more modes at play and more modes that we need to rely on when understanding this text.

To begin with, in order to understand that you are looking at is a flyer, you have to know some things about flyers such as the genre conventions and the modes flyers rely on. In this case, Matt used a number of modes, including the linguistic, spatial, gestural, and visual modes. The sentence we've been studying so far is just one part of this flyer. Read within the genre of the flyer, the sentence now carries greater meaning. That's because the several modes Matt used work together in the flyer to create greater meaning. The sentence now seems to say to readers that if a child attends Matt's boot camp, that child might be as successful as Roger, and good things will come as a result.

Understand Medium and Genre

To determine which modes we should use, we first have to think rhetorically about our communication situation. We need to figure out what *genre* (type of text or form of writing) we should use, and what medium will carry this genre. A technology can certainly be a medium. For Mike, the engineer and supply chain manager you met earlier in this chapter, choosing an organizational update as his genre made sense given that he wanted to tell his employees about a new hire. Given his genre, choosing two media (Microsoft Word and email) to deliver this update made sense as well.

BASEBALL BOOT CAMP

Children ages 11-13, all skill levels welcome!

When: June 23-July 30
Time: 9:00 am-noon
Where: Broadview Park
Cost: $125/player

Hi, I'm Matt Gray. I currently play second base for North University. This summer, I'm hosting my third annual baseball boot camp for Little Leaguers in Detroit. I have a lot of baseball experience and would love to share it with your son or daughter so they can do their very best. Don't just take my word for it. Check out Roger Whitfield who attended last summer's camp.

Skills Development

Sportsmanship

Batting Clinics

Game Strategies

Strengthening Exercises

MATT GRAY

4565 N. E. First Street
Detroit, Michigan 48001

555-555-9087

mattgray@gmail.com

On May 9th, Roger Whitfield's Little League team was down 2-1 in the bottom of the ninth inning. With one player on third base and two outs, Roger stepped up to the plate. When the first pitch came careening over the plate, he knew what to do. Using all his strength, Roger Whitfield hit the baseball out of the park. The rest, as they say, was history. His team went on to win its division in the Little League World Series.

Writing Example: Flyer. RBFried / iStock; baiajaku / iStock.

Genres have unique features that readers expect to see when reading the texts within those genres. In other words, there are conventional characteristics that all texts in a particular genre are likely to have. The genre of an organizational update has several conventional characteristics, including a heading, a salutation, body paragraphs that are left aligned on the page, professional language, and a greeting. When readers read the document, they know that they are reading an organizational update because they have read updates before and have grown accustomed to the features of such a document. For writers, paying attention to the conventional characteristics of the genre they are working in can help them be successful in communicating their ideas.

Box 2.3 Genre and Examples

Genre	Tweet	Thank you note	Action film
Conventions	Limit of 280 characters, hashtags, emojis, text speak, abbreviations, informal language	Greeting, closing, the words *thank you*, friendly tone, brief	Hero, antagonist, journey to defeat evil, problem solved, climax and resolution, plot, setting, dialogue
Modes	Linguistic, spatial, visual, emotional	Linguistic, spatial, visual, emotional, gestural, temporal	Visual, aural, spatial, gestural, temporal, mobile, linguistic, emotional
Technologies and media	Smartphone, computer, Twitter	Pen, card	Camera, editing software, computer, Movie theater screen, TV, iPad, smart phone

Genres Are Influenced by People and Their Technologies

As new technologies evolve, we create new media and new genres. As a result, media and genres are not static things that we can easily define. When creating his organizational update, Mike used a template to create his document. A technology such as Microsoft Word enabled him to do so. Microsoft Word's ability to create, save, and reuse templates has been a convenient way for Mike to write updates for his company for several years now. But, that wasn't always so. Before computers and before the ability to save templates in Microsoft Word, updates had to be typed on a typewriter or written by hand, and as a result, they looked a bit differently from Mike's update. The font styles were different. The spacing was different. Creating updates via a typewriter or handwriting was time consuming, too, especially if the document needed to be revised. The typed or handwritten update back then was not emailed to all employees, either. Most likely it would have been copied on a copy machine and put in the mailboxes of employees. Or, it could have been posted to a board in a meeting room. In some ways, someone's idea of an update and the conventions of its genre back then are different from someone's idea of an update and the conventions of its genre today.

Activity: Investigate Modes Working Together

In a group, investigate how modes work together and how they are created using technologies. To do so, gather several texts in a particular genre and consider (1) this genre's conventions (or unique features) (2) how those conventions are created by technologies, and (3) how those conventions are also created using different modes. In your discussion, consider the following questions:

a. What conventions do you see in the texts?
b. How do modes aid in creating the texts and therefore the conventions of the genre?
c. How do technologies aid in creating the texts and therefore the conventions of the genre?
d. Who might be excluded from such a genre and why?

Further your investigation by discussing your group's findings with the rest of your classmates. As you discuss, compare your findings and explain why you believe your society has created such a genre with those particular conventions.

Technologies play a significant role in the creation of a text as they dictate what we can and cannot do. The technology we use to communicate has its own set of unique affordances (or capabilities). In other words, certain technologies allow us to more easily employ certain modes over others. As a writer, you will need to think about the affordances and the limitations of the technologies you use. For instance, Microsoft Word let Mike create an organizational update using a template, but it wouldn't let him take a picture of the new employee. If Mike wanted to include a picture, he would have used a different technology, such as a camera. That's because Microsoft Word doesn't have the ability to capture a picture. One of its affordances, however, would let Mike embed a picture (that he previously saved on his computer) into the document using the "Insert Picture" function.

Genres Change Over Time Because of People's Social and Political Beliefs

The magazine genre provides one way of seeing how a genre has evolved over time. In comparing magazine covers from today with those from a hundred years ago, you'd most likely see quite a few differences. Today, covers of magazines are likely to feature people, such as celebrities and models, dressed in clothes that reflect today's hottest trends, trends that might have been too risqué and socially unacceptable a hundred years ago. The magazine cover of a hundred years ago likely featured people dressed more conservatively by today's standards.

Genres Can Exclude

Because genres are shaped by the political and the social, they can sometimes exclude groups of people. Who gets to decide, after all, what conventions make up a genre? Who doesn't get to decide? Who decides that magazine covers should have celebrities and models dressed in trendy clothes? As you work on your own writing and you consider genre expectations, do so with caution. Think about who writes and uses the genre, and who doesn't or who can't.

As a future employee, you may be tasked with writing documents like the one Mike wrote for his company that use a variety of modes. To be successful, you will need to think rhetorically. You will need to think about your audience and their needs, your purpose for writing, and your abilities as a writer. Whether or not you use a template like Mike did, in order to effectively communicate information to your fellow employees and to ensure you have included all the necessary conventions of your genre, you will also need to think about the context in which you are writing. Because he works for a company and was tasked with writing for that company, Mike had to think carefully about where he was writing and how his writing would reflect his company's professionalism. Writing poorly would have reflected negatively on his company and put his company at risk of losing employees and business. In the interview shown below, Mike describes the importance of writing and how he wrote the organizational update for his company, an international company that, in today's economy, has to maintain good professional standing through public-facing writing. As you will learn, he considered his context in relationship to his rhetorical situation, choosing his modes and genre carefully.

INTERVIEW
MIKE BUTLER, ENGINEER AND SUPPLY CHAIN MANAGER

Q: What writing advice would you give a student who wants to join your field?
A: Ensure you are sending the message you intend and in the right tone. Whether you are writing an internal email or a letter to a customer, your words can make or break a profitable business relationship and company morale. One of the most important things to keep in mind is how your audience will receive your message. Put yourself in the recipient's shoes. Choose your words wisely. Always proofread your writing for spelling and grammar errors, too.

Q: What technologies do you use on a regular basis to communicate your ideas?
A: I use a wide range: bulletin boards, network TVs, phone calls, WebEx, text messages, and email. Sending a clear and concise message becomes extremely important as you reach upper management. At that level, you can expect upwards of 250 emails every day.

Q: What kinds of texts do you write?
A: I write all sorts of different texts. For example, I write organizational announcements such as the update I shared with you which include personnel changes, strategic business changes, policy changes, messages relating to areas in need of improvement, messages relating to good business news to improve morale, and several different types of messages to customers.

Q: How do you communicate with customers and employees outside of your country?
A: Communication takes place via phone calls, text messages, and emails. So, writing plays an important role in my line of work when I have to communicate with others working in another country. In doing so, I really have to think about my audience and the cultures they live and work in. I definitely make sure to tailor my writing so that it is appropriate to them.

Q: How did you write the organizational update? Did you have a model? What writing technologies did you rely on?
A: Most companies use Microsoft Word and have their own template with company logos already loaded. That's what we have at my company. Using templates ensures my message looks and feels professional and that I remember to include all the necessary parts. I also think that using a template lets my readers get to my points sooner. When they see the document, they quickly recognize what they are reading since they have seen that kind of document before and know what to expect.

Q: How did you distribute the update? And to whom?
A: Most companies use email distribution lists. The organizational update I sent was a message to the entire company. The message was sent to our "Everyone" email distribution list and was also posted on our company TVs which are located in the lunch rooms for all to see.

Mike regularly thinks about the different audiences he writes to so as to represent his company in a professional manner. Most likely in your future career, you too will write a variety of texts. To prepare for the types of writing you will do, it would be a good idea to investigate your future career and the writing that is involved. How does that writing use and shape genre conventions? One strategy is to speak with people who are already working in your career field. Another would be to look at the writing this field produces and the audiences they write to. Yet, another would be to learn more about the technologies the people in the field use in order to write different texts. You will find an assignment below that can help you in discovering and preparing for the kinds of writing you may do in your future career.

Assignment: Technologies and Your Career

Developing and sharpening your writing and technological skills will be crucial to you as you pursue your career. For this presentation assignment, you will investigate the impact that technology has on your future career field, particularly as it relates to writing. In doing so, you should research and collect the kinds of writing people in that field do on a daily basis. You should also interview (and, if appropriate, shadow and observe) professionals in this field in order to do the following:

1. Describe the kinds of writing professionals do in this field. What modes do they use? If they use the linguistic mode, for instance, what language do these professionals use? If they use the visual mode, how do they do so? If they use the gestural mode, how do they do so? And so on.
2. Investigate how professionals in this field write with and/or for technologies. What rhetorical decisions do they make when doing this writing? What influences what gets written, by whom, to whom, and with what?
3. Define how particular technologies have affected the writing in this field over time.
4. Determine what writing skills someone would need in order to write for this field in the future.
5. Create a presentation for your class that shares what you learned about your future career.

Writing for Multiple Audiences

One strategy for writing for different global audiences is to think about what these audiences have in common and to use these commonalities to build texts that can be read and utilized by many audiences. Technologies can certainly help us do so by helping us learn more about our audiences and what they have in common. We can do research online, for instance, and quickly find out about our different audiences. We can research the similarities between cultures and between languages by looking at the different online texts that each produces. We can find out what modes are appropriate for each of our audiences and see if they share common uses of them, highlighting and utilizing these commonalities then when we write texts for such audiences.

However, while recognizing similarities is important, we also have to acknowledge differences. Working with a translating service company can only get Mike Butler so far. That's why Mike relies on his rhetorical skills to think carefully about all his audiences, including those abroad that he writes to on a regular basis. When Mike writes to his customers in other countries, he likes to learn about them first, paying close attention to their specific needs. If he already knows someone in or from a particular country, he will contact that person and ask for their help in revising and editing a document intended for an audience abroad so as to make sure his writing is appropriate. He wants to make sure that he chooses his words carefully and that literal translations carry the same meanings in his native language as they do in other languages. For instance, his company often does business in Mexico. Over the years, Mike has relied on the help of a number of colleagues in Mexico when writing different documents for the employees that work there. Besides learning about customary greetings in Spanish, Mike learned how to address his writing properly, taking into account the differences between the English and Spanish languages, customs, and histories.

Final Thoughts

As we do this research and as we think about how we will write for different audiences, it is important that we always remember that different modes, genres, and technologies work differently in different cultures. So, while we might find commonalities between our audiences, we must not completely ignore their differences. Not all cultures have the same perceptions of concepts and ideas. Nor do they have the same experiences with modes and technologies. For example, the concept of privacy differs from one culture to the next. In one culture, people might be more open to directly sharing personal information freely through connected digital texts, while in others, people might not want to share such information in public spaces. So, it is important, then, to think about how different cultures might perceive your communications and value these differences. As you move on to the rest of the book, think rhetorically about how writing operates in different cultures and make smart decisions to ensure your texts are accessible and appropriate for them.

Additional Discussion Questions

1. Why is writing multimodal, and why are modes multimodal?
2. Who or what decides who can and cannot use a particular mode of writing?
3. In a group, choose a career field everyone is familiar with and discuss the writing people in that field do. Then discuss the following:
    a. How do they write in this field?
    b. What technologies do they use to write?
    c. What texts do they write?
    d. What skills do they need to write these?
    e. What career fields rely on non-digital and non-electronic technologies?
    f. Do these fields have a disadvantage to those that do rely on digital and electronic technologies? Why or why not?

Additional Activities

1. A Career Field's Texts: In a group, chose one career field and gather texts that people in that field produce. Together, analyze these documents and share your

findings with your class. Pay particular attention to what technologies were used to create the documents. Compare the types of writing different career fields do.
2. International Careers: Develop a list of strategies people who work in international careers can use when writing a variety of texts to a variety of audiences.

Additional Assignments

1. Create an Online Resource: After the Technologies and Your Career assignment, that is, after you investigate how a career field utilizes technologies to write and after you present your findings to the class, create an online resource that discusses your findings in an interesting and coherent manner to help those who wish to pursue a career in that field. As you do, think rhetorically about your resource and the technologies you will use to create it.
2. History of Uses: Research the history and evolution of one of the following: The use of black font, the use of indenting, the use of paragraphing, the use of headers.

   What roles do modes and technologies play in such use?
3. Cultural Uses: Investigate how another culture uses modes in their texts. How are these uses different from uses in your culture? To begin with, you could use one genre of text and then investigate and compare that genre's use of modes in your culture with how that genre uses modes in another culture.

Works Cited

Ball, Cheryl, and Colin Charlton. "All Writing Is Multimodal." *Naming What We Know: Threshold Concepts of Writing Studies*, edited by Linda Adler-Kassner and Elizabeth Wardle, Utah State University Press, 2015, pp. 42–43.

National Association of Colleges and Employers. "Employers Want to See These Attributes on Students' Resumes." *Naceweb*, 12 February 2018, www.naceweb.org/talent-acquisition/candidate-selection/employers-want-to-see-these-attributes-on-students-resumes/. Accessed 23 February 2019.

The New London Group. "A Pedagogy of Multiliteracies: Designing Social Futures." *Harvard Educational Review*, vol. 66, no. 1, 1996, pp. 60–92.

CHAPTER 3

Non-Digital and Digital Technology

Contents

Purposeful Writing 40
Non-Digital Texts 42
Digital Texts Distributed Non-Digitally 46
2D and 3D Texts 49
What Things Are Made of Matters 51
Final Thoughts 54

IMAGE 3.1 Magdevski / Thinkstock

Purposeful Writing

At a community fair, Nikki Gomez wanted to educate fairgoers about a local park that was in need of help. During a recent storm, the park had suffered damage (trees fell, trails flooded, a creek washed away its banks, and habitats were destroyed), but there were not enough volunteers or enough donations to help restore it. As an environmental studies major, Nikki loved spending time outdoors in nature and felt she had the right knowledge to try to convince her fellow community members to make a difference. Therefore, at the fair, Nikki set up a table and used a variety of texts to generate support for the park's restoration.

Long before the storm, Nikki had gone to the park and had photographed the trees, trails, creek, and habitats as part of an assignment for her biology course. After the storm, she returned to the park and took more photos. For the fair, then, Nikki created a poster board using recycled cardboard in which she attached the photos. That way fair goers could make a comparison between what the park looked like before the storm and what it looked like afterward. This appeal to pathos, she hoped, would motivate fairgoers into helping the cleanup efforts.

In addition to the before and after photos, Nikki created a map on the poster board using different-colored markers to represent the different kinds of support the park needed. She chose her colors purposively, choosing earthy, natural tones. Green represented trees that needed to be removed from trails and turned into mulch or used to build habitats for animals in the park. Brown represented the trails that needed new boardwalks. And, blue represented the different areas of the creek that needed volunteers to clean up.

To complement the poster and map, Nikki also developed handmade pledge cards on recycled paper that she passed out to as many people at the fair as possible. The pledge cards included the name of the park and its address as well as a list of upcoming volunteer days. The card also included the different tasks that were featured on the map (removing trees, building boardwalks and habitats, and cleaning up the creek). Each person who had a pledge card could pledge to complete as many of the tasks they wanted to at one of the upcoming volunteer days at the park.

Finally, to drive home the severity of the situation, Nikki went so far as to set up a trash bin of debris she had collected in the park. On the same day she had taken photos of the damage, she had decided to start the cleanup process on one of the trails where the floodwater had receded. Instead of throwing the debris away, she separated it and put it in recycling bins and brought one of them (the one with plastics seen in Image 3.2) to the fair so that fairgoers could collect what was left behind in the storm and what didn't belong on a trail, in a creek, and as a part of animals' habitats. After the fair, she planned on taking the bins to a recycling center.

IMAGE 3.2 narapornm / Thinkstock

All of the texts, from the poster to the trash bin, enabled Nikki to get the word out that one of her favorite parks needed help. In Chapter 2, you learned that writing is multimodal, but that doesn't necessarily mean that multimodal texts must be digital. And, as stated in Chapter 1, not all technologies are digital. There are plenty of ways in which we can communicate without relying on digital tools and digital distribution. Nikki created a cardboard poster using markers to draw a map to show that the damage in the park was widespread. She handcrafted pledge cards using recycled paper. She even collected and displayed trash to communicate her message.

While digital technologies can sometimes make creating multimodal texts easier and more convenient, there are certainly other non-digital technologies we can use that, in some cases, might be more appropriate to our writing situations. Nikki could have relied on a digital technology like a computer to create texts for the fair, but they may have had a different impact on fairgoers. Sometimes, computer-generated materials appear computer-generated, that is, less organic and less natural. In some cases, that is perfectly fine. But for Nikki, such an effect might have worked against her cause. Nikki's subject matter was a park, a natural space where nature and wildlife should thrive. In using natural resources (like recycled paper) and other technologies like colored markers, Nikki was hoping for a more natural and organic effect. Given her purpose to save the park, she wanted her texts to have a more natural and organic appearance, something a computer wouldn't quite help her achieve when passing out materials to fairgoers. Likewise, a computer wouldn't have helped her display her trash bin of debris. She could have taken a picture of the recycling bin to the fair, but actually having the recycling bin had a much more powerful effect.

In Chapter 1, you read that writing is rhetorical. Choosing which technology to use means you have to think carefully about the rhetorical situation you are in. Nikki certainly thought carefully about her situation. She thought about her subject matter (park), she thought about her purpose for communicating to a particular audience (community members), she thought about where (fair) and when (just after the storm) she would be displaying and distributing her texts, and she thought about what those texts would say about the park (it needs help). Taking her situation into consideration, she then chose her technologies and texts accordingly, and in the end, her decisions paid off. A few weeks later, volunteers gathered to rebuild the park during one of the volunteer days.

Non-Digital Texts

Long before the invention of computers, people around the world created, distributed, and read non-digital texts. In ancient Chinese cultures (around 1200 BC), for instance, people used a script called *jiǎgǔwén*, or oracle bone script. It is the earliest known form of Chinese writing. And, it was nothing like the digital texts we have today. At that time, people wrote the script on animal bones and turtle shells for the purpose of forecasting the future. A writer would inscribe a question (usually about weather or hunting) on the bone or shell, then heat it up over fire so that the bone or shell would crack. Upon reading the cracks, people would ascribe meaning to them in hopes of discovering divine answers to their questions.

Methods for writing and the technology used to do so have evolved since then. To record their writing, for example, ancient Roman cultures preferred what is called a codex, a book made from stacking pages of papyrus, parchment, and other materials and then binding them with a cover (sometimes made of wood). Codices resembled something like that of our modern-day books and replaced the use of scrolls, providing people an easier way to store and transport writing. The codex was used for a variety of purposes, too, from recording law to recording literature. The poet Virgil's *Vergilius Augusteus*, a manuscript written around the 4th century that contains the *Georgics* and the *Aeneid*, is an example of a codex.

Non-digital doesn't mean non-technological. In fact, there are lots of technologies that help us to create non-digital texts. Nikki's use of colored markers to create a map on her recycled poster board demonstrates this. Today, even as computers dominate our daily lives, we still rely on non-digital texts in a variety of ways. As another example, take the March for Our Lives rally in Washington, D.C., on March 24, 2018. Thousands of people used handwritten poster boards to voice their concerns and call the government into action to improve gun control laws.

Did You Know? Paper Cutting

As was discussed in Chapter 2, writing takes on many forms. Paper cutting, or *jianzhi*, is an ancient tradition important to many cultures such as those found in China and is another example of non-digital communication. It is hard to say exactly when this tradition began (some say it was around the 6th century), but today, it is still practiced by many worldwide. People cut paper—using scissors or a knife—to create many different intricate designs that represent different meanings. For this tradition, people then hang the paper cuttings on doors, windows, walls, and other places in their homes. While paper cutting is often done for festivals, the designs represent people's wishes for a good future, for good fortune, and for good health. In China, many people use red paper as it is associated with happiness. Paper that is cut into the shapes of animals and flowers often tell the traditional stories of the people.

To see some examples, check out the work of Qiao Xiaoguang at the permanent exhibit *City Windows* at the Chicago O'Hare International Airport. If you cannot visit there, check out pictures of the exhibit online.

Understand the Differences

A **digital text** is a text which is processed electronically using a finite or limited set of values (basically numbers). On the other hand, a **non-digital text**, also known as an analog text, is one that is processed using an infinite set of values (or numbers) that represent physical measurements. The differences between a digital and a non-digital text can help you think more historically and critically about the impacts that technologies have on society and how, when, and where we write. And, they can help you develop an awareness of what makes digital and non-digital texts unique so that you can take full advantage of each of their affordances as you write.

Check It Out YouTube: For more on the differences between digital and analog, search YouTube for Techquickie's "Analog vs. Digital as Fast as Possible."

Think about using sounds and moving images in your writing. Today, all you need is a smartphone camera to capture a video. In fact, you may have several videos on your smartphone right now. Think about how easy it is to make a video using such a smartphone. All you have to do is open your camera app, push a few buttons (like the record button), and voilà—you have a video. Storing such videos is easy, too. You can do so right on your smartphone. Indeed, digital space allows for more storage compared to the physical space home moviemakers needed 30 years ago to store videos. Even if you don't have enough space on your phone, there are other digital spaces to store your videos, like on social media, YouTube, and in your email. After uploading your videos to sites like these, you can erase them from your phone with a push of a button.

Technology Is Multimodal

Before digital texts, sounds and moving images were recorded using a number of analog technologies, like a tape recorder or camcorder. Because analog texts are representations of real measurements and there are an infinite set of values to make these representations, recording and storing sounds and moving images were not as convenient; you may have needed more materials to record, store, and use them. Take, as another example, a VHS (video home system) cassette. To create a video, the cassette would have to be placed into a camera so that the tape within the cassette could record pictures. Then, to watch the VHS, you would have to take the cassette out of the camera and put into a VCR that is connected to a TV. To store the cassette, you would need to have a place (a box or a shelf) where you could put it until you watched it again. If you had hundreds on VHS cassettes, the physical space needed to store them would be so much greater than the storage needed for the videos on your smartphone.

homydesign / Shutterstock

This example of a VHS cassette, a non-digital text, is one of many that can help us to think more carefully about how digital technologies have impacted not only the way we create, but also the way we move from texts to texts. Writing, searching for, and revising such texts in digital spaces have presented us with new ways and systems for developing, thinking, organizing, storing, and connecting ideas. Storing and locating a VHS cassette are much different processes than storing and locating a video on your smartphone.

As another example of how digital and non-digital technologies are different, we can think about how we find information today. Before digital texts, finding information about a city, like Jakarta for instance, may have involved the following: going to the library, searching the card catalog for an index containing information about Jakarta, and then locating a book about the city on the shelf using the Dewey Decimal System, a classification system designed around subjects. Next, you'd have to rent the book and bring it home. At home, you would have to use the book's index and then thumb through the pages until you found what you were looking for. If you wanted to take notes, you would have to do so on a separate paper or make photocopies of the book's pages.

Today, that process for finding information is rare. If you have access to the internet and digital texts, you can locate information about a foreign city relatively quickly and in a variety of formats, from books to videos to websites. And, there are technologies that let you digitally take notes on these. Even the way in which you search and find information about Jakarta using digital technologies is much different from using the Dewey Decimal System. You can use a number of search terms in a number of databases to locate information rather than use a card catalog. Today, if you find a book about Jakarta by a particular author, you can find out what other books the author writes by clicking a few links on a site like Amazon or Google Books. If you wanted to know more about Jakarta's landmarks or architecture or history, you can use several different search engines to find out that information, all while making connections between such information. You can save this information too in a number of ways, "favoriting" a site in your browser, or downloading the site as a PDF file so that you can write notes on it. You can even come back to this information a year from now because unlike a library book, you don't have to return it. Moreover, if you wanted to learn more about the city's food, in seconds, you could do a Google search and find information. Before the internet, you would have had to locate several books and manually search through those until you found information about the city's food.

You can also search information using different modes. Let's say you were interested in taking a trip to Jakarta to study its architecture. Your friend emails you a photograph of a building in Jakarta that features a colonial style you want to see in person. Your friend isn't sure of the name of the building, so you save the photo to your computer and upload it to Google's image search function until you find similar photos. You click on one of those photos and it takes you to a site like TripAdvisor where you learn the name of the building. Using Google Maps, you then locate it within the city near other colonial-style buildings. You make plans to visit, and once there, you are able to use your smartphone to locate additional information about those buildings as you are looking at them.

The connections you make through a series of digital technologies help you to understand things, like a place such as Jakarta, in a much different way from what you may have done 30 years ago. Later in this book, you are going to read more about the power of making connections. Here, it is important to note that being an effective writer in a world of digital technologies means paying close attention to connections people make between information and technologies, thinking critically about how people make such connections through writing, finding ways to help people make such connections more efficiently, and making sure that we organize and distribute information in the most effective ways given our uses of technologies.

Yet, it is also about remembering how we got to where we are today. Ignoring history limits our understanding of what factors have influenced our uses of non-digital and digital texts. Just because we don't use a VHS cassette as often as we did before doesn't mean that we should forget this past. This past reveals a history of technology that is shaped by a number of people, from the people who built the technology, to the people who sell it, to the people who govern it, and the people who use it. This history also points out the need to be sensitive to just how diverse people's experiences are with technology.

Discussion Questions: Comparing Digital and Non-Digital Technologies

With your classmates, compare digital and non-digital writing technologies and in doing so, consider their histories. As you make these comparisons, answer the following questions:

a. What are the similarities between them?
b. What are the differences between them?
c. Why do (or did) people use them?
d. What are their histories? By histories, think about who created them and for what purposes. Think about who governs their uses, who regulates them, who sells them, and so forth.
e. What do these histories say about how technologies evolve over time?
f. What would be the differences in experiences between someone who grew up learning to write with non-digital technologies and someone who grew up learning to write with digital technologies?

Digital Texts Distributed Non-Digitally

In 1517, fed up with Catholicism's use of indulgences, a German professor of moral theology, Martin Luther, wrote a letter containing *Ninety-Five Theses* to Albert of Brandenburg, the Archbishop of Mainz, condemning what he considered corrupt practices. His writing of the *Theses* (also known as *Disputatio pro declaratione virtutis indulgentiarum*) played a pivotal role in the Reformation, shaping religious, political, and cultural practices worldwide. Over time, his *Theses*, originally written in Latin, spread across Germany and Europe and then worldwide as they were reprinted and circulated in many languages, thanks in part to the technologies of that time. Guttenberg's developments in movable type and the printing press just prior to that time helped spread Luther's words. However, before Guttenberg's improvements to movable type and the printing press made the printing process easier and faster in Europe, printing and distributing texts were painstakingly slow processes. Scribes, for example, had to handwrite books to make copies of them. That took years. Martin Luther's letter would not have reached as many people as quickly had scribes been the only ones making copies of it.

Today, there are lots of technologies that make creating and distributing texts easier and faster than in Luther's time. We can use digital technologies, for example, to create hundreds, thousands, even millions of printed texts in a short amount of time. But, just because you may use a technology to create a digital text doesn't mean the text has to be digitally distributed, though digital technologies have made the process of distributing easier and faster. Each day, millions of texts that we create digitally are distributed non-digitally through the mail, on the shelves of kiosks, on the bulletin boards at schools, in our neighborhoods, and at businesses.

Assignment: Creating and Distributing Digital Texts Non-Digitally

Learning how to create and when and where to distribute texts is a great way to improve the effectiveness of your writing. The middle of a church service probably isn't the best place or time to pass out a flyer about an upcoming battle of the bands event at your favorite venue.

For this assignment, create a flyer, a sign, or a brochure for an upcoming event on your campus. Print out copies and take them to a place where you would find people who may be interested in the event. Pass out or post your text. As you do this, consider the following:

THINK CAREFULLY ABOUT THE ACTUAL PLACE WHERE PEOPLE WILL ENCOUNTER YOUR TEXT

How will people encounter your text in this place? Where in this place will they encounter it? Will you post it to a wall? Will you put a sign in the grass next to a sidewalk? Where is the most traffic? Will people see it? If you post your text, for example, to a bulletin board where there are lots of other texts, how will your text stand out and catch the attention of passersby?

THINK CAREFULLY ABOUT THE PEOPLE IN THE PLACE WHERE YOU WILL DISTRIBUTE

Your goal, after all, is to get people to come to the event, so thinking about the people you hope to attract is a first step in accomplishing this goal. What will they be doing? Will they be on their way to work, drinking coffee, on their phone? How will you get their attention with your text?

THINK CAREFULLY ABOUT TESTING YOUR IDEAS

You might consider doing a pilot test of your text by going to the actual place where you plan to distribute and conducting some observations about where in this place you would distribute, how best to do so, and to whom. You might find, for example, that the green-colored flyer you had planned to post to a bulletin board won't work anymore because there are lots of other green flyers already, and if you were to post yours, it would blend in and go unnoticed. Or you might find that the sign you made is shaped too small for the place you want to put it. Or you might find that people are in a hurry and won't like it if you stop them to give them a brochure. So, think carefully about how you will distribute your text in the place you intend to.

Often, we rely on a combination of printed texts and digitally distributed texts at the same time. Here are some examples of printed and digital texts in action. To get the message out to their residents about an evacuation plan during a hurricane, officials from the City of Lighthouse Point, Florida, placed a flyer on every resident's door within their jurisdiction. The flyer contained important information about how, when, and where to evacuate for the storm. The text was created using a computer program. Then, it was printed on bright pink paper and distributed door-to-door. In addition to the flyers, the City of Lighthouse Point produced a number of other texts, including publishing and mailing a newsletter, to communicate with their residents about staying safe during a hurricane. As well, to really drive home the point of safety, they also communicated online through their website, making sure to include additional information about what to do during a hurricane. The combination of all these texts ensured they would reach as many citizens as possible.

Activity: Analyze Your Mail

Every day, people around the world receive mail, from letters to advertisements to bills to magazines to flyers. Some of this mail is handwritten, while some of it is produced digitally and then printed in order to be mailed. Gather the mail you receive in one week's time and analyze it, paying close attention to how it was created. Here are some questions to consider as you write up this analysis:

a. Were the texts created non-digitally or digitally?
b. What technologies do you suspect were used in the creation of the mail?
c. What rhetorical decisions did the writers of your mail make?
d. What modes did the writers of your mail use?
e. Why do you receive mail?

f. How different do you think this mail is compared to the mail that was distributed 100 years ago?
g. Will technologies change the future of your mail? If so, what impact will technologies have on the mail system in the future?

Share your findings with your classmates.

2D and 3D Texts

To promote their team and to generate support, a local hockey team gave away purple hats at one of their games. The team's logo, a polar bear holding a hockey stick, was featured on the front panel along with the team's name. The purple hat itself is a text that can be read. The color purple, the logo, and the team name indicate to all those who read the hat that it represents the hockey team and that the person wearing the hat is a supporter.

To create the hat, a team of people worked together using a variety of technologies, such as a specialized manufacturing computer (see Image 3.4). On a computer screen, the hat and its design are represented as two-dimensional (2D). However, once the hat becomes reality—that is, it is sewed—the hat is no longer a 2D text; it is now three-dimensional (3D).

IMAGE 3.4 mputsylo / iStock

Digital texts, the kind you see on a computer screen, are flat, two-dimensional texts. That's because screens can work only in two dimensions (the horizontal and vertical dimensions), though it is possible to make a 2D text appear on a computer screen or a movie screen to have three dimensions with the help of technological effects. But, 3D really only occurs in our physical world, our reality, so to speak.

Three dimensions means there is another dimension (the depth dimension) which can occur only off of a screen in our physical world. A *dimension* is a measurable extension of some kind, such as length, width, breadth, depth, or height. A line, for instance, has only one dimension. That's because it has only one measurement. If we were to place a dot on the line, we would need only one measurement to locate where on the line the dot was placed. We would not need any other coordinates or measurements because the dot is on a line and a line is one-dimensional. If we were to place the dot on top of a surface such as a plane, we would need two coordinates or measurements (length and width) to locate it because a surface, like a plane, has two dimensions. Where the two measurements intersect is where we will find the dot. Finally, if we were to place the dot inside a box, we would need three coordinates or measurements (length, width, and depth) to locate the dot. Where all three measurements intersect is where we will find the dot.

So, why does knowing the difference between 2D and 3D matter to writing? When creating an effective text, whether digital or non-digital, you must think rhetorically about where and how you will distribute your text. In doing so, you have to think about the technologies you are using and the type of text you are creating. That means you have to think carefully about what your technologies and your text are and are not capable of doing. As mentioned in Chapter 2, a text can be a medium, a go-between between a writer and an audience. While a medium is part of the message, it also holds the message. Every medium has affordances or capabilities, just like technologies do. If you choose to create a text such as a purple hat, you have to be aware that if you create your hat on a computer, you are doing so digitally and are therefore limited in what you can do. However, when printed, your hat would become a 3D non-digital text. Your digital text, in other words, must go from 2D to 3D, and what sometimes looks good in 2D does not look good in 3D. Non-digital 3D texts have different angles, contours, and shapes that you would have to account for when working digitally.

In designing your hat, you would need to make important decisions about where on the hat you should place the logo. You would need to consider measurements such as height and length, but also the round contoured surface of the hat's front panel. When the hat is placed on the head, you would need to account for the fact that the logo may move or stretch. You would need to make sure that the team's name is visible and readable. Again, what might look good on a computer screen might not look good on someone's head once worn. So, how do you account for this? In Box 3.1, you will find some suggestions when creating 2D and 3D texts that are important to successful writing.

Box 3.1 Suggestions for Working With 2D and 3D Texts

1. **Prototype It:** a prototype is a model or example of something. Designers often make prototypes in order to test their ideas to ensure they work. When creating a text, it would be a good idea to test out your text's features. For example, when creating a hat, you might want to make several prototypes to make sure that when the hat is worn, the logo and the team's name appear readable and represent the team in a good way. You would also need to make sure the colors you are using still work once they go from your screen to reality.
2. **Test It:** Even when you are not creating a 3D text such as a hat, it is always a good idea to print a test copy of your text. If you were to design a flyer for your community, it would be a good idea to print a colored copy to see what it looks like in printed 3D form before you print thousands of copies. Oftentimes, printers can distort images and colors. You would also need to test it out on location to make sure your text will still work for that location. It is one thing to create a flyer on your computer and another thing to print it and place it in a particular location.
3. **What, When, and Where:** Knowing when and where people will use your text could help you make important decisions about the material of your text (in other words, the *what* of your text). If you are making a hat, for instance, there are lots of different materials and shapes you could use. So, it makes sense that you should consider when and where people would wear it. If your intention is to have people where the hat year round, you wouldn't want a material that is too heavy for hot climates or too thin for cool ones. If you think people would wear it outdoors, making sure your hat has a good, strong bill would be a good idea to shade the sun from people's eyes. If your intention is to create a sock hat to be worn in colder climates, a thicker, softer material might be best.

What Things Are Made of Matters

Think Carefully About the Materials of Writing

When writing, you use all sorts of technologies that are made up of or rely on a variety of substances, in other words, materials. Likewise, while using these technologies, you create texts made up of a variety of materials that matter in a number of ways to the texts themselves but also to the people and places they are meant for. For starters, the materials you use come from some place and from some resources that were created, collected, and/or shaped by someone.

Ask anyone in the clothing industry, and they will tell you that they write a lot. They write designs, product descriptions, purchase orders, website content, business proposals, and letters to politicians, and most importantly, they write apparel. They also do so using a variety of materials. Fabrics, buttons, zippers, glitter, and stitching, just to name a few, all carry meanings that are shaped by our politics, economics, and social beliefs. For more on the reasons why materials matter, see the box below.

> **Did You Know? How Materials Are Chosen by Apparel Companies and Consumers**
>
> There are a number of considerations designers, and thus apparel companies, and their consumers have to make when creating, selling, and buying new products, including decisions based on politics, economics, and social beliefs. The following list provides examples of what influences such decisions:
>
> **Politics:** laws, regulations, tariffs, and so forth all determine what materials can and cannot be used in apparel. In the United States, for instance, laws mandate that apparel companies must provide a label for each article of clothing produced in order to indicate to consumers what materials that clothing is made of. Such labels allow companies and the government to keep track of inventory as well.
>
> **Economics:** governments, apparel companies, and consumers all make financial decisions that shape what materials are used in the apparel industry. For instance, if a material is too expensive, not many companies or consumers would be able to afford it.
>
> **Social beliefs:** our culture decides what is and isn't socially acceptable in terms of what materials are used in apparel. These beliefs could be influenced by race, ethnicity, gender, and religion. If customers feel a company's materials are made in less than favorable conditions and that workers who produce these materials under such conditions should be treated more fairly, they may not purchase clothing from such a company until those practices change.

Think Carefully About Textures

When you think about materials, you also have to think about the textures those materials are made of and what meanings they communicate. Texture refers to the way things (like a surface) appear or feel. When it comes to textures, working with and reading non-digital texts allow us different understandings from working with and reading digital texts, in part because of their materials and our bodily experiences of them. Reading about a sweater's particular texture on a clothing store's website is not the same as feeling that same texture in person for a number of reasons, one being the physical actions we take to encounter such a text. When we feel a texture with our fingers, our bodies receive information differently from when we read about a texture with our eyes.

Textures themselves carry meaning, too, and so we have to be careful about how we create texts using materials with different textures. Choosing your textures depends on your audience and your purpose for writing, but also on economics and feasibility. Perhaps, you live in a culture where certain meanings have been ascribed to specific textures. Hard surfaces may come across as uncomfortable, soft surfaces may come across as weak, or smooth surfaces may come across as professional. In certain Asian cultures, such as those found in India, people use embroidery to create different textures. Using gota, the weaving of ribbons and the application of them onto fabric, can create different textures on garments to be worn for special occasions. Those who live in those cultures recognize those textures and ascribe meaning to them.

Activity: Reading and Experiencing Materials

Collect a variety of texts and technologies for your class. Bring them to school and display them on a table in the center of the classroom. Walk around the table and observe what you see. Don't touch the objects just yet. In a discussion, describe what you see.

a. What materials are they made of, and why?
b. What do these materials communicate?
c. What textures do you see?

Next, feel the texts and technologies. Think about how they are constructed. In another discussion, consider the following questions, keeping in mind how your body learns to read such texts and learns to use such technologies by using your senses:

a. How do you read the texts and technologies with your body?
b. What textures do you feel, and what do they say about the text and technologies?
c. How did you learn to ascribe meaning to different textures?
d. Would these texts and technologies be more or less effective had they been constructed with different materials and textures?

Next, consider the materials of these texts and technologies in terms of their impacts on the economy, politics, the environment, and our social and cultural beliefs.

a. What impact do the texts and technologies' materials have on the economy, and what impact does the economy have on these materials?
b. What impact do the texts and technologies' materials have on politics, and what impact does politics have on these materials?
c. What impact do the texts and technologies' materials have on our environment, and what impact does the environment have on these materials?
d. What impact do the texts and technologies' materials have on social and cultural beliefs, and what impact do our social and cultural beliefs have on these materials?

Then, Choose the Right Materials and Textures

Choosing the right materials and textures (and thus choosing the right technologies) for your own writing project is an important decision, and looking further at the clothing industry can certainly demonstrate why. Outdoor clothing companies like Patagonia, Cotopaxi, and Columbia use recycled materials so that they can ensure they are doing their best to help the environment. Companies such as these go to great lengths to ensure the materials they use and the products they produce are done so in ethical, fair, and sustainable working conditions. They are aware of their impacts on their communities and how their choices in materials affect people and places. Their want to be sustainable and environmentally conscious companies has made them successful.

Writers, too, can choose their materials and textures according to their own political, economic, and social beliefs as well as those of their audience members. When Nikki created her poster board for the community fair, she didn't just go to the store to buy it. Instead, she thought carefully about using a recycled poster board; not just because she wanted a specific aesthetic, but she also wanted to reduce her impact on resources and on the environment. Her materials send a clear message to her audience: she is serious about helping the environment.

Take a moment now to reflect on your writing experiences and think about the materials you have used to write. Have you ever thought about where the writing technologies you use on a regular basis come from? Have you ever thought about who built your computer? Your pen? Your pencil? Your notebook? What materials are they made of, and where did they come from? What are their costs, financially and labor wise? If you haven't thought about these questions before, you might consider doing so. In addition, you might consider the histories of the materials and their impacts on societies. Perhaps you will find that some materials are more sustainable than others but also more important to your audience. If you think about your audience and their beliefs, you might be able to use materials that they would support and care about.

Final Thoughts

No matter if you are creating digital or non-digital texts, you have quite a few rhetorical decisions to make about how those texts will come to be and what materials and textures they will be made of. When you carefully consider these, you are in a better position to understand texts and technologies as being multimodal as well as situated in a particular place among a particular audience. When examining materials and their textures, you are able to see how your writing impacts and is impacted by audiences in a particular society that is influenced by politics, economics, and social beliefs. Later in this book, you will further consider such impacts and influences. For now, remember that your writing does not and cannot exist in isolation, devoid of any connections to people and the places they come from.

Additional Discussion Questions

1. At a community gathering that highlights various organizations, clubs, and groups in your community, you are tasked with informing participants about an upcoming farmer's market. Because you will need to make sure the turnout for the farmer's market is a good one, you will need to make sure that your communication is effective. Discuss what kind of texts you could create and distribute at the community gathering to inform people of the upcoming farmer's market. Think about whether you would create digital or non-digital texts. Why would your choice in texts be the best option given the situation?
2. You will be attending a rally at the state capital to raise awareness about childhood hunger. Your hope is that the governor will take action to support efforts that work to rid your state of childhood hunger. Discuss what texts you could bring to the rally to raise awareness. Why would your choice of texts be the best option given the situation?
3. As an intern working for your local government, you are tasked with creating a text that lets residents know about the recycling resources in their area. The government wants to encourage its residents to recycle more. Discuss what text you could create to let them know of the recycling resources in your area. Why would your choice of text be the best option given the situation?

Additional Activities

1. History of a Material: Investigate the history of a material and its textures in a particular culture (think about the gota example you read earlier in this chapter). Who ascribes meaning to this material and its textures in the culture? How are the material and textures made and used? What impact does it have on social issues? What impact does it have on environmental issues? Gather examples and share your findings with your classmates.
2. Observing Texts: Bring along a means to record observations and find a seat in a busy public place. Write down the different texts you see. Perhaps, you see a ball cap, a T-shirt, or a flyer. As you write down different texts, think about how those texts were created. What did writers do to create them? Think about the people who are wearing, using, reading, and passing by such texts? What impact do such texts have on these people? Do people even notice them? Summarize your observations in a report to your class.

Additional Assignments

1. Create 3D Texts: Partner with a local store, organization, restaurant, or club and help them design promotional 3D texts (such as a T-shirt, water bottle, or bag) for

an upcoming meeting, get-together, or event. Present your final texts to the class and with your community partners.
2. Industry Materials and Textures: Investigate how materials and textures are purchased and used in an industry of your choosing and create a presentation for your class that explains your findings. In your investigation, you should speak with those who are involved in the industry to find out the purpose for using particular materials and textures and the decisions they make when working with them.

Can We Define "Technology"?

David E. Nye

This reading is the first chapter in David E. Nye's book, *Technology Matters: Questions to Live With*, published by The MIT Press in 2006. The MIT Press has granted permission to reprint this chapter.

One way to define "technology" is in terms of evolution. An animal may briefly use a natural object, such as a branch or a stone, for a purpose, but it was long thought that only human beings intentionally made objects, such as a rake or a hammer, for certain functions. Benjamin Franklin and many others thought that tool use separated humans from all other creatures. Recent fieldwork complicates the picture. Jane Goodall watched a chimpanzee in its own habitat. It found a twig of a certain size, peeled off its bark, looked for a termite hill, thrust in the peeled twig, pulled it out covered with termites, and ate them. This chimpanzee not only made a tool, it did so with forethought. In 2004, scientists announced discovery of the bones of a previously unknown species in an Indonesian cave. Standing only three feet high, this dwarf species lived and used tools as recently as 12,000 years ago.[1] Yet if Franklin's idea needs modification, it seems that only intelligent apes and human species are toolmakers, while the vast majority of animals are not. Birds construct nests. Beavers cut down trees and build dams. Ants and bees build complex communities that include a division of labor and food storage. But only a few species have made tools. Notable is a hand axe widely used by *Homo erectus* 1.6 million years ago.

Homo sapiens have used tools for at least 400,000 years, and seem to have done so from their first emergence. Technologies are not foreign to "human nature" but inseparable from it. Our ancestors evolved an opposition between thumb and fingers that made it easier to grasp and control objects than it is for other species. Indeed, prehensile hands may even have evolved simultaneously with the enlarging human cortex. Learning to use tools was a crucial step in the species' development, both because it increased adaptability and because it led to a more complex social life. Using tools, the relatively weak *Homo sapiens* were able to capture and domesticate animals, create and control fire, fashion artifacts, build shelters, and kill large animals. Deadly tools also facilitated murder and warfare. Tools emerged with the higher apes, and one might argue that humanity fashioned itself with tools.[2]

The central purpose of technologies has not been to provide necessities, such as food and shelter, for humans had achieved these goals very early in their existence. Rather, technologies have been used for social evolution. "Technology," José Ortega y Gasset argued, "is the production of superfluities—today as in the Paleolithic age. That is why animals are atechnical; they are content with the simple act of living."[3] Humans, in contrast, continually redefine their necessities to include more. Necessity is often not the mother of invention. In many cases, it surely has been just the opposite, and invention has been the mother of necessity. When humans possess a tool, they excel at finding new uses for it. The tool often exists before the problem to be solved. Latent in every tool are unforeseen transformations.

Defining technology as inseparable from human evolution suggests that tools and machines are far more than objects whose meaning is revealed simply by their purposes. As the great stone circle at Stonehenge reminds us, they are part of systems of meaning, and they express larger sequences of actions and ideas. Ultimately, the meaning of a tool is inseparable from the stories that surround it. Consider the similarity between what is involved in creating and using a tool and the sequence of a narrative. Even the chimpanzee picking up and peeling a twig to "fish" for termites requires the mental projection of a sequence, including an initial desire, several actions, and successful feeding. The sequence becomes more complex when more tools are involved, or when the same tool is used in several ways. Composing a narrative and using a tool are not identical processes, but they have affinities. Each requires the imagination of altered circumstances, and in each case beings must see themselves to be living in time. Making a tool immediately implies a succession of events in which one exercises some control over outcomes. Either to tell a story or to make a tool is to adopt an imaginary position outside immediate sensory experience. In each case, one imagines how present circumstances might be made different.

When faced with an inadvertently locked automobile with the keys inside, for example, one has a problem with several possible solutions—in effect, a story with several potential endings. One could call a locksmith, or one could use a rock to break one of the car's windows. Neither is as elegant a solution as passing a twisted coat hanger through a slightly open window and lifting the door handle from the inside. To improvise with tools or to tell stories requires the ability to imagine not just one outcome but several. To link technology and narrative does not yoke two disparate subjects; rather, it recalls an ancient relationship.

Tools are older than written language (perhaps, as the chimpanzee's "fishing stick" suggests, even older than spoken language) and cannot merely be considered passive objects, or "signifieds." Tools are known through the body at least as much as they are understood through the mind. The proper use of kitchen utensils and other tools is handed down primarily through direct observation and imitation of others using them. Technologies are not just objects but also the skills needed to use them. Daily life is saturated with tacit knowledge of tools and machines. Coat hangers, water wheels, and baseball bats are solid and tangible, and we know them through physical experiences of texture, pressure, sight, smell, and sound during use more than through verbal description. The slightly bent form of an American axe handle, when grasped, becomes an extension of the arms. To know such a tool it is not enough merely to look at it: one must sense its balance, swing it, and feel its blade sink into a log. Anyone who has used an axe retains a sense of its heft, the arc of its swing, and its sound. As with a baseball bat or an axe, every tool is known through the body. We develop a feel for it. In contrast, when one is only *looking* at an axe, it becomes a text that can be analyzed and placed in a cultural context. It can be a basis for verifiable statements about its size, shape, and uses, including its incorporation into literature and art. Based on such observations, one can construct a chronology of when it was invented, manufactured, and marketed, and of how people incorporated it into a particular time and place. But "reading" the axe yields a different kind of knowledge than using it.

Telling stories and using tools are hardly identical, but there are similarities. Each involves the organization of sequences, either in words or in mental images. For another investigation it might be crucial to establish whether tools or narratives came first, but for my argument it matters only that they emerged many millennia ago. I do not propose to develop a grand theory of how human consciousness evolved in relation to tools. But the larger temporal framework is a necessary reminder that tools existed long before written texts and that tools have always embodied latent narratives. My definition of technology does not depend on fixing precisely when humans began to use tools, although it is pertinent that they did so thousands of years before anyone developed tools for writing. Cultures always emerge before texts. Long before the advent of writing, every culture had a system of artifacts that evolved together with spoken language. Objects do not define words, or vice-versa; both are needed to construct a cultural world. Only quite late in human development did anyone develop an alphabet, a stylus to mark clay tablets, or a quill adapted for writing on paper. Storytelling was oral for most of human history.

A tool always implies at least one small story. There is a situation; something needs doing. Someone obtains or invents a tool in order to do it—a twisted coat hanger, for example. And afterwards, when the car door is opened, there is a new situation. Admittedly, this is not much of a narrative, taken in the abstract, but to conceive of a tool is to think in time and to imagine change. The existence of a tool also immediately implies that a cultural group has reached a point where it can remember past actions and reproduce them in memory. Tools require the ability to recollect what one has done and to see actions as a sequence in time. To explain what a tool is and how to use it seems to demand narrative. Which came first? This may be a misleading question. It seems more likely that storytelling and toolmaking evolved symbiotically, analogous to the way that oral performances are inseparable from gestures and mimicry.

Technology Is Multimodal

It is easy to imagine human beings as pre-literate, but it is difficult to imagine them as pre-technological. Most Native American peoples, for example, did not write, but they did develop a wide range of tools, including snowshoes, traps, tents, drums, hatchets, bows, pottery, ovens, bricks, canals, and irrigation systems. All social groups use tools to provide music, shelter, protection, and food, and these devices are inseparable from verbal, visual, and kinetic systems of meaning. Each society both invents tools and selects devices from other cultures to establish its particular technological repertoire of devices.

In Herman Melville's *Moby Dick*, Queequeg, a South Sea harpooner visiting Nantucket, was offered a wheelbarrow to move his belongings from an inn to the dock. But he did not understand how it worked, and so, after putting all his gear into the wheelbarrow he lifted it onto his shoulders. Most travelers have done something that looked equally silly to the natives, for we are all unfamiliar with some local technologies. This is another way of saying that we do not know the many routines and small narratives that underlie everyday life in other societies.

As the evolutionary perspective shows, technology is not something new; it is more ancient than the stone circles at Stonehenge. Great stone blocks, the largest weighing up to 50 tons, rise out of the Salisbury Plain, put precisely into place in roughly 2000 B.C. The stones were not quarried nearby, but transported 20 miles from Marlborough Down. The builders contrived to situate them in a pattern of alignment that still registers the summer solstice and some astronomical events. The builders acquired many technologies before they could construct such a site. Most obviously, they learned to cut, hoist, and transport the stones, which required ropes, levers, rollers, wedges, hammers, and much more. Just as impressive, they observed the heavens, somehow recorded their observations, and designed a monument that embodied their knowledge. They did not leave written records, but Stonehenge stands as an impressive text from their culture, one that we are still learning to read. Transporting and placing the massive stones can only be considered a technological feat. Yet every arrowhead and potshard makes a similar point: that human beings mastered technologies thousands of years ago. Stonehenge suggests the truth of Walter Benjamin's observation that "technology is not the mastery of nature but of the relations between nature and man."[4]

Technologies have been part of human society from as far back as archaeology can take us into the past, but "technology" is not an old word in English. The ancient Greeks had the word "techne," which had to do with skill in the arts. Plato and Plotinus laid out a hierarchy of knowledge that stretched in an ascending scale from the crafts to the sciences, moving from the physical to the intellectual. The technical arts could at best occupy a middle position in this scheme. Aristotle had a "more neutral, simpler and far less value-laden concept of the productive arts."[5] He discussed "techne" in the *Nicomachean Ethics*[6] (book 6, chapters 3 and 4). Using architecture as his example, he defined art as "a rational faculty exercised in making something . . . a productive quality exercised in combination with true reason." "The business of every art," he asserted, "is to bring something into existence." A product of art, in contrast to a product of nature, "has its efficient cause in the maker and not in itself."[7] Such a definition includes such actions as making pottery, building a bridge, and carving a statue. Just as important, Aristotle related the crafts to the sciences, notably through mathematics. In Greek thought as a whole, however, work with the hands was decidedly inferior to philosophical speculation, and "techne" was a more restricted term than the capacious modern term "technology." Perhaps because the term was more focused, classical thinkers realized, Leo Strauss wrote, "that one cannot be distrustful of political or social change without being distrustful of technological change."[8] As Strauss concluded, they "demanded the strict moral-political supervision of inventions; the good and wise city will determine which inventions are to be made use of and which are to be suppressed."[9]

The Romans valued what we now call technology more highly than the Greeks. In *De Natura Deorum* Cicero praised the human ability to transform the environment and create a "second nature." Other Roman poets praised the construction of roads and the pleasures of a well-built villa. Statius devoted an entire poem to praising technological progress, and Pliny authored prose works with a similar theme.[10] Saint Augustine synthesized Plato and Aristotle with Cicero's appreciation of skilled labor: ". . . there have been discovered and perfected, by the natural genius of man, innumerable arts and skills which minister not only to the necessities of life but also to human enjoyment. And even in those arts where the purposes may seem superfluous, perilous and pernicious, there is exercised an acuteness of intelligence of so high an order that it reveals how richly endowed our human nature is."[11] In contrast, Thomas Aquinas characterized the mechanical arts as merely servile.[12] Some medieval thinkers, notably Albertus Magnus, appreciated iron smelting, the construction of drainage ditches, and the new plowing techniques that minimized erosion. A few drew upon Arabic thought, which presented the crafts as practical science and applied mathematics. Roger Bacon, in his *Communia Mathematica*, imagined flying machines, self-propelled vehicles, submarines, and other conquests of nature. Bacon put so much emphasis on the practical advantages of experiment and construction of useful objects that he "came close to reversing the usual hierarchy of the speculative and useful in medieval thought."[13]

The full expression of a modern attitude toward technology appeared only centuries later, during the Renaissance, notably in Francis Bacon's *New Atlantis* (1627). Bacon imagined a perfect society whose king was advised by scientists and engineers organized into research groups at an institution called Saloman's House. They could predict the weather, and they had invented refrigeration, submarines, flying machines, loudspeakers, and dazzling medical procedures. Their domination of nature, which had no sinister side effects, satisfied material needs, abolished poverty, and eliminated injustice. This vision helped to inspire others to found the Royal Society.[14] Established in London in 1662, this society institutionalized the belief that science and invention were the engines of progress. The Royal Society proved to be a permanent body, in contrast to earlier, temporary groups that could also be seen as originators of modern research, such as those gathered in Tycho Brahe's astronomical observatory on an island near Copenhagen, or Emperor Rudolf's group of technicians and scientists in Prague.

Today, a large bookstore typically devotes a section to the history of science but scatters books on technological history through many departments, including sociology, cultural studies, women's studies, history, media, anthropology, transportation, and do-it-yourself. The fundamental misconception remains that practical discoveries emerge from pure science and that technology is merely a working out or an application of scientific principles. In fact, for most of human history technology came first; theory came along later and tried to make sense of practical results. A metallurgist at MIT, Cyril Stanley Smith, who helped design the first atomic bombs at Los Alamos, declared: "Technology is more closely related to art than to science—not only materially, because art must somehow involve the selection and manipulation of matter, but conceptually as well, because the technologist, like the artist, must work with unanalyzable complexities."[15] Smith did not mean that these complexities are forever unanalyzable; he meant that at the moment of making something a technologist works within constraints of time, knowledge, funding, and the materials available. It is striking that he advances this argument when discussing the construction of the first atomic bomb, which might seem to be the perfect example of an object whose possibility was deduced from pure science alone. However, Smith is correct to emphasize that the actual design of a bomb required far more than abstract thinking, particularly an ability to work with tools and materials. In fact, one sociologist of science has concluded that, although we cannot turn back the clock and "unlearn" the science that lies behind nuclear weapons, it is conceivable that we will manage to lose or forget the practical skills needed to make them.[16]

As Smith further pointed out, technology's connection to science is generally misunderstood: "Nearly everyone believes, falsely, that technology is applied science. It is becoming so, and rapidly, but through most of history science has arisen from problems posed for intellectual solution by the technician's more intimate experience of the behavior of matter and mechanisms."[17] Often the use of tools and machines has preceded a scientific explanation for how they work or why they fail. Thomas Newcomen, who made the first practical steam engines in Britain, worked as an artist in Aristotle's sense of the term "techne." He conceivably might have heard that a French scientist, Denis Papin, was studying steam and vacuum pumps. However, Newcomen had little formal education and could not have read Papin's account of his experiments, published in Latin (1690) or in French (1695), though he conceivably could have seen a short summary published in English (1697). He never saw Papin's small laboratory apparatus—and even had he seen it, it would not have been a model for his much larger engine. Newcomen's steam engine emerged from the trial and error of practical experiments. Papin's scientific publications were less a basis for inventing a workable steam engine than a theoretical explanation for how a steam engine worked. However, further improvements in the steam engine did call for more scientific knowledge on the part of James Watt and later inventors. Likewise, Thomas Edison built his electrical system without the help of mathematical equations to explain the behavior of electricity. Later, Charles Steinmetz and others developed the theoretical knowledge that was necessary to explain the system mathematically and refine it, but this was after Edison's laboratory group had invented and marketed all the components of the electrical system, including generators, bulbs, sockets, and a wiring system. Science has played a similar role in the refinement of many technologies, including the windmill, the water wheel, the locomotive, the automobile, and the airplane.[18] The Wright Brothers were well-read and gifted bicycle mechanics, and they tested their designs in a wind tunnel of their own invention, but they were not scientists.[19]

If one bears these examples in mind, the emergence of the term "technology" into English from modern Latin in the seventeenth century makes considerable sense. At first, the term was almost exclusively employed to describe a systematic study of one of the arts. A book might be called a "technology" of glassmaking, for example. By the early eighteenth century, a characteristic definition was "a description of the arts, especially the mechanical." The word was seldom used in the United States before 1829, when Jacob Bigelow, a Harvard University professor, published a book titled *Elements of Technology*.[20] As late as the 1840s, almost the only American use of the word was in reference to Bigelow's book.[21] In 1859, the year before he was elected president, Abraham Lincoln gave several versions of a lecture on discoveries and inventions without once using the word.[22] Before 1855, even *Scientific American* scarcely used "technology," which only gradually came into circulation. Instead, people spoke of "the mechanic arts" or the "useful arts" or "invention" or "science" in contexts where they would use "technology" today. A search of prominent American periodicals shows that between 1860 and 1870 "technology" appeared only 149 times, while "invention" occurred 24,957 times. During the nineteenth century the term became embedded in the names of prominent educational institutions such as the Massachusetts Institute of Technology, but it had not yet become common in the discussion of industrialization.[23] "At the time of the Industrial Revolution, and through most of the nineteenth century," Leo Marx writes, "the word *technology* primarily referred to a kind of book; except for a few lexical pioneers, it was not until the turn of [the twentieth] century that sophisticated writers like Thorstein Veblen began to use the word to mean the mechanic arts collectively. But that sense of the word did not gain wide currency until after World War I."[24]

This broader definition owed much to German, which had two terms: "teknologie" and the broader "technik." In the early twentieth century, "technik" was translated into English as "technics."[25] From roughly 1775 until the 1840s, "teknologie" referred to systems of classification for the practical arts, but it was gradually abandoned. During the later nineteenth century, German engineers made "technik" central to their professional self-definition, elaborating a discourse that related the term to philosophy, economics, and high culture. "Technik" meant the totality of tools, machines, systems and processes used in the practical arts and engineering.[26] Both Werner Sombart and Max Weber used the term extensively, influencing Thorstein Veblen and others writing in English. As late as 1934, Lewis Mumford's landmark work *Technics and Civilization* echoed this German usage. However, Mumford also used the term "technology" not in the narrow Germanic sense but in reference to the sum total of systems of machines and techniques that underlie a civilization. In subsequent decades the term "technics" died out in English usage and its capacious meanings were poured into "technology."[27]

Mumford had these larger meanings and the German tradition in mind when he argued that three fundamentally different social and economic systems had succeeded one another in an evolutionary pattern. Each had its own "technological complex." He called these "eotechnic" (before c. 1750), "paleotechnic" (1750–1890), and "neotechnic" (1890 on). Mumford conceived these as overlapping and interpenetrating phases in history, so that their dates were approximate and varied from one nation to another. Each phase relied on a distinctive set of machines, processes, and materials. "Speaking in terms of power and characteristic materials," Mumford wrote, "the eotechnic phase is a water-and-wood complex, the paleotechnic phase is a coal-and-iron complex, and the neotechnic phase is an electricity-and-alloy complex."[28] Although historians no longer use either Mumford's terms or his chronology, the sense that history can be conceived as a sequence of technical systems has become common. Along with this sense of a larger sequence came the realization that machines cannot be understood in isolation. As Mumford put it: "The machine cannot be divorced from its larger social pattern; for it is this pattern that gives it meaning and purpose."[29]

One important part of this pattern that Mumford missed, however, was how thoroughly "technology" was shaped by gender. For example, legal records from the thirteenth and fourteenth centuries show that in rural England women were entirely responsible for producing ale, the most common drink of the peasantry. Men took control of alemaking only when it was commercialized.[30] Similarly, some scholars argue that in the early medieval era European women worked in many trades, but that in early modern times women were gradually displaced by men.[31] Ruth Oldenziel has persuasively extended such arguments into the twentieth century, showing that Western society only relatively recently defined the word "technology" as masculine. Between 1820 and 1910, as the word acquired its present meaning, it acquired male connotations. Before then, "the useful arts" included weaving, pottery making, sewing, and any other activity that transformed matter for human use. The increasing adoption of the word "technology," therefore, is not simply a measure of the rise of industrialization. It also measures the marginalization of women.[32] In the United States, women were excluded from technical education at the new university-level institutes, such as the Rensselaer Polytechnic Institute (established in 1824) and the Massachusetts Institute of Technology (founded in 1861). Nevertheless, because one could become an engineer on the basis of job experience, there were several thousand female engineers in the United States during the nineteenth century. Likewise, despite many obstacles, there were female inventors. The women's buildings of the great world's fairs in Philadelphia (1876), Chicago (1893), Buffalo (1901), and St. Louis (1904) highlighted women's inventions and their contributions to the useful arts. Furthermore, even though women had been almost entirely excluded from formal engineering education, many worked as technical assistants in laboratories, hospitals, and factories. Engineering was culturally defined as purely masculine, pushing women to the margins or to subordinate positions. Only in recent years have scholars begun to see technology in gendered terms, however, and this realization is not yet widely shared.

Indeed, the meaning of "technology" remained unstable in the second half of the twentieth century, when it evolved into an annoyingly vague abstraction. In a single author's writing, the term could serve as both cause and effect, or as both object and process. The word's meaning was further complicated in the 1990s, when newspapers, stock traders, and bookstores made "technology" a synonym for computers, telephones, and ancillary devices. "Technology" remains an unusually slippery term. It became a part of everyday English little more than 100 years ago. For several hundred years before then, it meant a technical description. Then it gradually became a more abstract term that referred to all the skills, machines, and systems one might study at a technical university. By the middle of the twentieth century, technology had emerged as a comprehensive term for complex systems of machines and techniques.

Indeed, some thinkers began to argue that these systems had a life and a purpose of their own, and no sooner was "technology" in general use than some began to argue for "technological determinism." A single scene in Stanley Kubrick's film *2001* captures the essence of this idea. A primitive ancestor of modern man picks up a bone, uses it as a weapon, then throws it into the air, where it spins, rises, and metamorphoses into a space station. The implications of this scene were obvious: a direct line of inevitable technological development led from the first tools to the conquest of the stars. Should we accept such determinism?

Notes

1. "Ancient hobbit-sized human species discovered," Associated Press, October 27, 2004.
2. I will not try to make this argument, but some scholars contend that the brain developed in interaction with tool use and therefore should be considered a human technology. See e.g. Beniger (1986, p. 9).
3. José Ortega y Gasset, "Man the Technician," in Ortega y Gasset 1941, p. 100.
4. Benjamin (1986, p. 93).
5. Whitney (1990, pp. 50–51).
6. Aristotle, *Nicomachean Ethics*, book 6, chapters 3 and 4.
7. *The Ethics of Aristotle* (Penguin Classics, 1953), p. 175.
8. Strauss (1959, p. 298).
9. Ibid.
10. Pavlovskis (1973, pp. 20 and 33), passim.
11. Cited on p. 52 of Whitney (1990).

12. Whitney (1990, pp. 139–140).
13. Ibid., pp. 143–145.
14. Sibley (1973, p. 264). See also Wallace (2003, pp. 11–21).
15. Cyril Stanley Smith, cited on p. 331 of Rhodes (1999).
16. MacKenzie (1998).
17. Smith, cited on p. 331 of Rhodes (1999).
18. Don Ihde, "The historical-ontological priority of technology over science," in Ihde 1983.
19. On the Wright Brothers, see Tobin (2003).
20. Bigelow (1840).
21. This statement is based on a survey of 100,000 nineteenth-century journal articles in Cornell University's electronic archive "Making of America" (available at http://moa.cit.cornell.edu/moa/index.html). Before 1840 there are only 34 uses of the term, all but three either in writings by Bigelow or in references to them. Two referred to curricula in German universities, and the last was an eccentric usage in a legal context that seems unrelated to machines.
22. Abraham Lincoln, "Second Lecture on Discoveries and Inventions," in *Collected Works of Abraham Lincoln*, volume 3, ed. R. Brasler (Rutgers University Press, 1953–55), pp. 357–358.
23. Oldenziel (2003).
24. Marx (1997).
25. Schatzberg, "Technik Comes to America."
26. Ibid.
27. Ibid.
28. Mumford (1934, p. 110).
29. Ibid., p. 100.
30. Bennett (1996).
31. Herlihy (1990, pp. 75–97).
32. Oldenziel (1999).

Bibliography

Beniger, James R. 1986. *The Control Revolution: Technological and Economic Origins of the Information Society*. Harvard University Press.

Benjamin, Walter. 1986. *Reflections: Essays, Aphorisms, Autobiographical Writings*, ed. P. Demetz. Shocken.

Bennett, Judith M. 1996. *Ale, Beer and the Brewster in England: Women's Work in a Changing World, 1300–1600*. Oxford University Press.

Bigelow, Jacob. 1840. *The Useful Arts*. Thomas Webb.

Herlihy, David. 1990. *Opera Muliebria: Women and Work in Medieval Europe*. Temple University Press.

Ihde, Don. 1983. *Existential Technics*. State University of New York Press.

MacKenzie, Donald. 1998. *Knowing Machines*. MIT Press.
Marx, Leo. 1997. "Technology: The Emergence of a Hazardous Concept." *Social Research* 64, no. 3: 965–988.
Mumford, Lewis. 1934. *Technics and Civilization*. Harcourt, Brace.
Oldenziel, Ruth. 1999. *Making Technology Masculine: Men, Women and Modern Machines in America*. University of Amsterdam Press.
Oldenziel, Ruth. 2003. "The Genealogy of Technology: Race, Gender, and Class." Presented at annual meeting of Society for the History of Technology, Atlanta.
Pavlovskis, Zoya. 1973. *Man in an Artificial Landscape: The Marvels of Civilization in Imperial Roman Literature*. Leiden: Mnemosyne, Biblioteca Batava.
Rhodes, Richard, ed. 1999. *Visions of Technology*. Simon and Schuster.
Sibley, Mulford Q. 1973. "Utopian Thought and Technology." *American Journal of Political Science* 37, no. 2: 255–281.
Strauss, Leo. 1959. *Thoughts on Machiavelli*. Free Press.
Tobin, James. 2003. *To Conquer the Air: The Wright Brothers and the Great Race for Flight*. Free Press.
Wallace, Anthony F. C. 2003. *The Social Context of Invention*. University of Nebraska Press.
Whitney, Elspeth. 1990. *Paradise Restored: The Mechanical Arts from Antiquity through the Thirteenth Century*. American Philosophical Society.

Reading Questions for "Can We Define 'Technology'?" by David E. Nye

1. Why is composing a narrative and using a tool similar?
2. Why is it hard to define technology?
3. What does "developing a feel for a technology" mean?
4. How is the word "technology" used in modern times compared to how it was used 150 years ago?

PART 2
Technology Is Active

As you have learned, technology is not technology without human actions. Indeed, when we write, we engage in numerous actions. Our bodies and our minds move, and thus we learn. To act with a technology, then, is to learn a new experience, one we imprint in our brains and recall the next time we act in similar experiences. When it comes to writing, there are so many actions we can perform, from moving a pencil, to moving a mouse, to moving our mouths. But, in order to be successful in using our writing to effectively engage our audiences, we have to make smart choices about our own actions so as to initiate the actions of our audiences to engage in our writing. Throughout this book, you will learn strategies for making smart decisions, that is, for performing smart actions. This second part of the book will add to these, and in particular, provide practical advice on writing processes that demand writers act in researching, drafting, testing, revising, and editing. You will think carefully about how such actions influence others into acting on their own and how such acts change our world.

Key Questions _____

1. What actions do we take when writing?
2. How do these actions shape writing?
3. How does writing shape our actions?
4. What roles do technologies play in shaping our actions?

Key Terms

Chapter 4

1. recursive
2. exigency
3. macro level
4. micro level
5. pilot test
6. copyright
7. WIPO
8. copyleft
9. GNU Project
10. fair use
11. public domain
12. attribution
13. annotation

Chapter 5

1. design
2. reading path
3. clean design
4. design principles
5. complimentary colors
6. analogous colors
7. monochromatic colors
8. contrast
9. saturation
10. RGB
11. CMYK
12. proximity
13. alignment
14. repetition
15. typography
16. fonts
17. emphasis
18. negative space

Chapter 6

1. draft
2. test
3. revise
4. edit
5. flex text
6. natural language processing

CHAPTER 4

Plan, Research, and Cite

Contents

Writing in Action 72
Suggestions for Planning Your Writing 74
Suggestions for Researching Your Writing 81
Suggestions for Citing Your Writing 86
Final Thoughts 93

IMAGE 4.1 Indypendenz / Shutterstock

Writing in Action

This chapter will outline suggestions you can use for approaching a writing situation while thinking about the impact that technologies have on your actions and the impact your actions have on technologies. To demonstrate how such suggestions operate, we will look at an example of writing and how that writing came to be. The example is that of a memo written by Tammy Franks, a volunteer for a community soccer league who wanted to request funding for her organization, the Ballwin Women's League (BWL). The memo was sent to the treasurer of a larger state organization (the Florida Adult Soccer Foundation) that helps smaller organizations in many ways, including providing funding for soccer programs. In her memo below, Tammy explains BWL's need for additional funding.

The suggestions center on what we have been doing throughout this book, that is, thinking rhetorically about a writing situation. As you have learned, when you think

---

To: Nick Bello, Florida Adult Soccer Foundation, Treasurer
Copy: Jennifer Sheridan
From: Tammy Franks, BWL Lead Coordinator
Subject: Request for Funds from the Florida Adult Soccer Foundation

My name is Tammy Franks. I have been a member of the Ballwin Women's League (BWL) for the past five years and its lead coordinator for the past two years. The BWL has been in existence for over fifteen years. It is one of many adult athletic programs in the community of Ballwin, but the only program exclusively for women. As you are aware, recreational programs, such as soccer, provide people with health and wellness opportunities that can in turn make communities better. The BWL is one such recreational program that has had consistent turnout over the years with many of the same players returning year after year.

As such, since I have taken over as the lead coordinator, the league has reached capacity for both our spring and fall league sessions. Each session can only support 120 players who are divided onto eight teams. As a result, many women who want to play have had to be placed on a waiting list. Because costs for fields, referees, uniforms, and so forth are high, it is difficult for the league to support the addition of extra players and thus extra teams without raising the cost of registration, which is already high.

Ballwin is one of Florida's wealthiest areas and as a result, there is a misconception that all people who live in this area are wealthy. The players who play in the BWL, however, come from middle to lower income households and most live paycheck to paycheck.

Writing Example: Memo Funding Request

For instance, many of our players are elementary school teachers who have families of their own to support. Many of our players are also college students struggling to pay tuition. Paying close to $200 (the current cost of fall and spring registrations combined) to play in the fall and spring leagues is a lot of money to these players.

Therefore, I am seeking funds from the Florida Adult Soccer Foundation to offset some of the costs associated with the fall and spring leagues. With the help of additional funding from Florida Adult Soccer Foundation, the BWL will be able to lower its costs for registration and will be able to include more players in the fall and spring leagues with the formation of two additional teams.

If we were to include two additional teams, here are the estimated costs for future fall and spring sessions:

Field Permit Costs	$2800
Referees	$2500
Insurance fees	$5250
Jerseys	$1200
Equipment	$220
Estimated Total	$11,970

To ensure that BWL can get enough players for the additional two teams for the fall and spring sessions, I would like to lower registration costs to around $50 instead of the current cost of $100 per session. While BWL does have a waiting list, I get inquiries from interested players all the time who can't afford to sign up in the first place. If the cost for registration was lower, then they would most likely be able to sign up and enjoy the same health and wellness opportunities as the other women in their area do. This would also give BWL an even better chance of maintaining the 10 teams per session in the future.

Because your organization helps adult soccer leagues, I am asking for $6,000 from the Florida Adult Soccer Foundation for the upcoming fall session. The $6,000 will make it possible for BWL to lower its fee for registration to $50. If BWL charges $50 for registration and is able to register 150 players for the fall, BWL would collect a total of $7500. With this money and the additional $6,000, BWL would cover its costs for field permits, referees, jerseys, and equipment. The leftover money would then be used for the spring league to offset costs again, making sure registration costs remain low.

Thank you for your time and consideration. I will be visiting your office in two weeks during the upcoming Adult Soccer Conference and would like to discuss this request with you then. In the meantime, should you have any questions, I can be reached at BWL@gma.com or by phone at 314-555-5555.

IMAGE 4.2 (Continued)

rhetorically, you put yourself in a better position to succeed in effectively communicating your ideas to your intended audience. As you know, a writer has to make important decisions about *what* to write and *how* to write it. By using the suggestions outlined in this chapter, you can develop strategies for making such decisions as you plan and draft your ideas, and then test them out to ensure they have the potential to work with your intended audience. As you read Tammy's request for funding and how she planned and drafted the request, you will see that she made important rhetorical decisions along the way that helped her create her final draft.

Suggestions for Planning Your Writing

While in this chapter, planning appears as a first step in writing, planning actually takes place throughout the writing process. That's because planning is recursive, meaning that over time, as writers and ideas change, so do plans. As you work through a writing project, return time and again to your original plans and make necessary adjustments to account for such changes. Always remember that while this book provides you with suggestions for writing, the order in which you utilize them is up to you. Though it would probably not be a good idea to wait until the last moment to begin a major writing project without planning it out.

As mentioned previously, different writers have different ways of approaching a writing situation, that includes the planning of it. Planning a major writing project can be a lot of work. When you are on the job, you may find yourself in a position where you will be the one to lead a team that is responsible for completing a major writing project. At times like those, and even times when you are working on your own, you will certainly need to consider how technologies can help you accomplish your goals in the planning stage, a stage that will most likely include brainstorming, researching, and testing ideas. In this chapter you will consider the rhetorical decisions needed to perform these actions with a variety of technologies. In addition, to help you think critically, you will also find key questions to consider as you work through your ideas.

Before you read on, however, as a first step, you may want to conduct a personal technology assessment to find out what you are capable of and what you will need to do in order to work with various technologies. Table 4.1 represents one such assessment.

Suggestion 1: Brainstorm Your Ideas With Different Technologies

Not all writing has to begin with a concrete idea. Sometimes, we can begin sketching or writing without a clear direction, just to get our thoughts out of our minds and into a text. At other times, we may have a good idea but the details need to be worked out. To avoid getting hung up on writer's block, it might be best to start with what you know first by jotting down, drawing out, outlining a bit, or talking out loud about what you already

TABLE 4.1 Personal Technology Assessment

List of technologies I have access to:	My skill level with this technology is:	Who or what can help me with this technology:	What I need this technology for:	Will audiences will be able to access texts created by this technology?

know about your subject matter. In planning your text, writers brainstorm or envision what kind of text they will write in many ways.

While not everyone approaches writing a text in the same manner, everyone should think rhetorically during brainstorming so that they can begin to formulate an idea that will align with their audiences' expectations and the purpose for writing (more on this in a moment). In other words, in brainstorming, you are essentially developing the *what* and *how* of the project, and that *what* can be tied to your audience and purpose. Through the act of brainstorming, we can test out ideas to see if they are rhetorically sound, figuring out if such ideas are worth pursuing or better left for another writing situation in the future. The *how* can be tied to the technologies, the genre, the media, and the modes you will use.

To brainstorm, we may pick up a pencil and pad of paper and use both to draw out ideas, visually representing concepts. We may turn to apps on our phones to map out ideas, connecting different concepts with one another digitally. We may journal in a text editor in order to outline our ideas, organizing them in particular ways. As Tammy was developing ideas for writing her request, she relied on a number of technologies to help her brainstorm. A fan of lists, Tammy decided that she needed to make a list of all the points she wanted to include in her request. Early on, she opened up a Google document and made three lists. She first came up with a list of BWL's expenses and then came up with a list of reasons why BWL needed the funding to manage those expenses. That list included talking about the women in the league and how recreational programs benefit people's health and wellness. Finally, she came up with a third list of writing techniques she would need to use while writing the request. For instance, she made a note to look at examples of previous requests for funding to ensure she paid attention to what was expected in this genre of text.

So, technologies allow us to brainstorm in many ways by giving us tools to think about ideas in different forms, from visualizations to outlines to word maps. As you work on your own projects, you might try different ways of brainstorming (see the Activity on the next page) in order to generate more ideas and connections between ideas.

Check It Out YouTube: If you are interested in learning more about using an online tool to help you brainstorm, check out bubbl.us, an online platform that enables you to create mind maps. To find out how this platform works, search YouTube for "How to Do Mind Mapping and Brainstorming Ideas Online" posted by Best Video Tutorials and Help from HowTech.

Another way to brainstorm is to use technologies to connect with others to test out your ideas and get feedback on them. Whether you informally speak with others or conduct a formal interview, speaking with others can help you generate additional ideas for your text. Newer technologies especially allow for brainstorming together from afar. Research supports that this way of brainstorming is effective, even more so than in-person brainstorming. According to the *Harvard Business Review*, virtually brainstorming with others produces "more high quality ideas" and

> a higher average of creative ideas per person, as well as resulting in higher levels of satisfaction with the ideas. As shown in meta-analyses, virtual brainstorming enhances creative performance—versus in-person brainstorming sessions—by almost 50% of a standard deviation. This means that almost 70% of participants can be expected to perform worse in traditional than virtual brainstorming sessions.
>
> (Chamorro-Premuzic)

One of the reasons why virtual brainstorming may be better is that it allows for people to remain anonymous and to feel free to speak their minds. If you want honest opinions on your ideas, this might be an option for you when brainstorming. In the future, you may be part of a team that needs to develop ideas for projects at work. Your team may be located in different offices around the world. To brainstorm ideas, you may need to rely on different technologies that make it possible to brainstorm together virtually. Prepare for such experiences and learn how virtual brainstorming can work for you while you are in college. The more practice you have in doing so, the better you will be able to get feedback.

Tammy had quite a few people helping her with her request, including the BWL board of directors. After creating her lists in a Google document, she shared this document with the board who offered their feedback virtually, adding ideas of their own into the document and providing comments in the margins over a period of time. Tammy was able to use this feedback to shape her draft and brainstorm even more. As you think about getting feedback like Tammy did, it would be a good idea to keep in mind the following questions:

- How does technology shape the way I brainstorm?
- What technologies best help me brainstorm?
- What technologies can I use to brainstorm with others?

Activity: Different Ways of Brainstorming, Different Ways of Thinking

A whole host of free technologies can help you brainstorm ideas, from phone apps to online sites. Perhaps, if you do not wish to brainstorm online, you could rely on non-digital technologies such as a bullet journal. Try out a number of technologies as you brainstorm ideas for a writing project and think about how each of these technologies enables different kinds of brainstorming actions and ways of thinking. For example, if you were to use a bullet journal to outline ideas for a project, how would this experience compare to an experience using a brainstorming app? Such an app may enable you to think through your ideas by visually mapping them out using notes and images and sharing them with others. Write a reflection on your experiences and share it with your classmates.

Suggestion 2: Determine Your Purpose and How Technologies Can Help

Brainstorming her lists helped Tammy to think deeply about her purpose for writing her request in the first place. She saw her request as an opportunity to make a difference in the lives of the women in her community. Thinking through her purpose enabled Tammy to plan out the important points she wanted to make in her writing. Your purpose for your writing is always tied to *exigency*, the need for your writing, and it should be thought through in terms of the technologies you will use to accomplish this need.

As you begin writing a text, think about the following questions in regard to determining your purpose for writing and how technologies can help:

- Why are you writing?
- What do you hope to accomplish with your writing and how will technologies help?
- What do you want your audience to do as a result of using or reading your text?

- What is needed (such as what technologies are needed) because of this writing?
- Why does the situation demand I write this text and in the ways I have planned?

Suggestion 3: Understand Your Audience

Because Tammy was only slightly familiar with her audience, the Florida Adult Soccer Foundation, she was able to use technologies to determine what arguments would persuade this audience in granting her request for funding. By conducting preliminary research online, she found that her audience was a proponent of health and wellness. In fact, after some research on the foundation, she found that two of its core values were health and wellness. Tammy made sure to use these exact words in her request as they would be familiar and valued by her audience.

Not only should you understand your audience, but you should be mindful of the needs of your audience once you have learned more about them. International audiences demand different needs from those of local and national audiences. In Chapter 2, you learned about engineer and supply chain manager Mike Butler. When Mike writes for his company, which does business internationally, he thinks about his local audience, that is, his fellow employees at the plant where he works. He thinks about their history, their relationships, and their knowledge of the subject matter. When he writes a text that will be read by a global audience, such as his employees and customers in other countries, Mike must think about those audiences' specific needs. He must think about cultural traditions and the languages that they speak. He must think about what is and is not professionally and technologically acceptable in their countries. Is email acceptable? Is a letter acceptable? Is a video message acceptable?

Suggestion 4: Explore New Technologies

As you think about the technologies to which you have access, think carefully about what kind of text is appropriate for your audience and purpose. As you know, Tammy relied on a number of technologies throughout the writing of her request, in brainstorming, researching, designing, drafting, citing, and delivering her text. For her final draft, she used Microsoft Word and thought carefully about how the modes in this document conveyed meaning to her audience.

During your planning, think about how you can utilize technology throughout your project. It may mean that you need a computer for some parts, and it may mean you need some other type of technology for other parts. Figure out which technology will allow you to do what you want to do, while at the same time provide you with possibilities you might not have thought of before. In other words, take some time to explore different technologies and their affordances, ones you have never tried before. If you are writing a podcast, try out different recording programs. If you are writing a video, try out different editing programs. In exploring, you may find one that gives you an opportunity to visualize your text in ways you hadn't previously imagined.

Suggestion 5: Plan Which Technologies You'll Use for Initial Research

A lot of writing projects begin with research questions. As you plan your project, think carefully about the questions you are asking and how you will use technologies to find them. Not all technologies will help you find the answers you are seeking. Later in this book, you will learn how technologies can shape your search engine queries. For now, develop a research plan that includes technologies that will help you in your searches for information. As you do, keep in mind the following questions:

- Will you need to rely on your computer and the internet to conduct research? If so, what are their limitations?
- Will you need to rely on technology to create a survey and/or interview to find out information? If so, what are their limitations?
- Will you need to rely on a mobile device to make observations on location? If so, what are its limitations?
- What can you do to minimize the limitations of technology and use technology to conduct research in a way that is most helpful to you?

Did You Know? Survey Builders

Later in this book, you will learn that not all search engines are created equal. That is, when you search multiple search engines, you most likely will get different results. The same can be said about survey building software. They are not created equal, and if you were to use different software to conduct the same research, you most likely will garner different results. When creating your own survey to conduct research, think carefully about which technologies you are using and what results they will lead you to. SurveyMonkey is a popular free online survey builder. It can help you build a survey in a matter of minutes with the use of its templates. However, there are limitations to using such a site. For example, you are limited to only the templates the site offers, templates that were not designed specifically with your research project in mind but rather ones designed for the masses. Therefore, when developing a survey, think carefully about what you are hoping to find. Think about the questions you want to ask your participants. Then, determine whether or not survey technology and templates are right for you. In addition, you need to determine the limitations of using a free online survey site builder instead of designing your own. There are plenty of other ways in which you can build your survey and administer it without using an online survey builder that utilizes templates. Take some time to explore all your options and weigh the benefits and limitations of each.

Suggestion 6: Plan Which Technologies Will Help You Design

As you plan your text, you may find that the technologies you used to plan it might not be best for designing it. Tammy planned in Google Docs but wrote her text in Microsoft Word. Later in this book, you will read a story about Meghan Pearson, a graphic artist who created and published a wildlife calendar. To create such a calendar, she first sketched out some ideas on paper. But, because her final draft would need to be digital (so that she could send it to a professional printer), Meghan had to rely on several Adobe computer software programs to design the final draft. As you think about the technologies you will use to design your text, think about how those technologies can effectively make your idea a reality. Not all design programs are easy to use, so you will need to know your abilities in using them or your willingness to learn them as you go along. As you consider designing your texts, also consider answering the following:

- What will your text look like, and how will your chosen technology help you create it?
- Will you compose it with words, images, sounds, or other modes?
- If it is a printed or digital text, will you need to think about margins, headings, layout, organization, etc.?
- Will you need to think about whether or not your design will hold up when viewed on multiple devices?
- Will your design be suitable for online viewing?
- Will your audience find your text appropriate and professional given the technologies you use to create it?

Suggestion 7: Plan Which Technologies Will Deliver Your Text

Tammy delivered her funding request as an attachment via email to the board of directors at the Florida Adult Soccer Foundation. Meghan Pearson first delivered her digital files of her calendar via email to the professional printer, and then hand-delivered or mailed her printed copies to her customers. Mike Butler delivered his new-hire announcement by emailing it as an attachment to every employee at his company, including the board of directors. Just like Tammy, Meghan, and Mike had to make sure that their texts could be successfully delivered, you too will need to think about how you will get your finished text to your intended audience. To get you started in exploring your options for delivery, try asking yourself:

- How will I share this text?
- Where will I share this text?
- When will I share this text?
- What technologies are needed to share this text?

Suggestion 8: Troubleshoot Your Problems

Throughout your writing project, you may find that you will need help with your technologies. Perhaps you will want to use a technology, but you don't know how. Or, perhaps, your technology stops working correctly in the middle of your project. Either way, you will need to troubleshoot the situation; that is, you will need to find a solution to the problems you face. Today, there are a number of online ways in which you can find help in troubleshooting, from searching online manuals to help forums to YouTube how-to videos. Having more than one approach to solve a technological problem will better provide you with several solutions, however. Having a support system in place in addition to utilizing online help can make you a more successful writer. Think about where and to whom you go to for help when you have a technological problem. Do you go to your school's computer help desk? Do you call a tech specialist? Do you ask a friend? Do you ask a family member?

Suggestion 9: Gather Examples

As you plan what and how you will write, it would be a good idea to collect examples of writing in the intended genre you plan to write in, paying close attention to the genre conventions on both the macro level and the micro level. Looking at the macro level elements can be thought of as seeing the big picture: how does such a text operate in our society? What shapes such a genre? What can and cannot be included in the genre, and who decides that? Looking at the micro level elements of a genre can be thought of as seeing the smaller picture: what kinds of words/sentences/grammars/images/sounds/etc. does this genre employ, and for what reasons? How are texts formatted? What style is used? What language is used?

As Tammy was planning her request, she looked at other similar types of texts she found online. She looked at previous requests sent to the Florida Adult Soccer Foundation by other soccer organizations in the state that were successful in obtaining funds. She also looked at proposals and grants, as such documents are often written with the intention of garnering support, such as resources and funding. From her examination of similar texts, Tammy was able to think about what to include in her own text and how and where to include it.

Suggestions for Researching Your Writing

After you have a good plan in place and have done preliminary research, it might be a good time to dig deeper, whether that be using primary, secondary, or tertiary research, whether that be using qualitative or quantitative research, or whether that be using a combination of all of these. In Tammy's case, she had to research the Florida Adult Soccer Foundation to find out more information about the organization, what their procedures were for submitting a request for funding, and what the organization valued. In order to include a budget in her request, she also had to research the expenses of BWL by speaking with BWL's treasurer and looking at past expenses, receipts, and budgets. She did this research using a number of technologies: email, smartphone, computer, Google, and websites. Like Tammy, you will probably use multiple technologies. So, to help you research, consider the following suggestions:

Suggestion 1: Question What You'll Need

When conducting research, you will need to think about how technologies can help you, and how they can hinder you, in finding the information you need. Using a search engine can be convenient due to its ability to provide instantaneous results. But, if those results contain thousands of online texts that you must search in order to find what you are looking for, such a technology might actually prevent you from finding the right information. When researching, you should start your research by assessing what information you actually need and to ask yourself these key questions to better gauge what technologies will help you find what you are looking for:

- What information do I need?
- Why do I need this information?
- What are the best ways to obtain this information?
- What are the least effective ways?
- What technologies can I use to obtain this information?
- What technologies will make it difficult to obtain this information?
- What will I do with this information once I have obtained it?

Suggestion 2: Go Beyond Online Sources When Gathering Information

At times, you might need to find information by using online library databases in order to locate journal articles or by using websites in order to find out more information about organizations, as was the case for Tammy. However, not everything should and can be found online. Learning other means for gathering information is important for successful writing. Box 4.1, on conducting a survey, an interview, or a focus group, provides a few more information-gathering techniques and can help you think more carefully about how you find the necessary information you need to be successful in your research.

Box 4.1 Conducting a Survey, an Interview, or a Focus Group

CHOOSE YOUR QUESTIONS

Asking the right questions during a survey, an interview, or a focus group is imperative to good research. But writing good questions is no easy task. For starters, questions can take on many forms, from fill-in-the-blank questions to yes-or-no questions to ranking and scale questions. The way in which you ask a question, the form the question takes, will garner a particular response and thus particular data. Your hope is that this data will help you with your research, so make sure to test out your questions before you conduct your survey, interview, or focus group.

To begin with, use your overarching research questions to help you create questions for your survey, interview, or focus group, because the answers to those questions should help you answer your overarching research questions. Put differently, your overarching research questions should help you determine which questions to ask in your survey, interview, or focus group, and those questions in turn will garner answers to help you answer your overarching research questions. For example, if you were Tammy and had a chance to interview a board member from the Florida Adult Soccer Foundation, and one of your overarching research question was, "How can I secure funding for the BWL?" you might ask during the interview, "What procedure does the Florida Adult Soccer Foundation use to evaluate requests for funding?" The response would then help you write your own request in a way that is in line with how the organization evaluates.

Questions to Ask in the Question Building Phase

- What are my overarching research questions?
- How can I use those overarching research questions to write questions for a survey, interview, or focus group?
- Do my questions ask more than one thing at a time? (Using a question that asks two things at once can be confusing to participants.)
- Will my audience understand the words I am using in the questions? (Using unfamiliar words may garner responses that are invalid.)
- Will my audience know the answer to my questions? (If your audience can't answer a question, you have wasted your time and your audience's time in asking it.)
- Do I already know the answer to my questions? (If you can answer a question, use a different one that you can't answer instead.)
- What order of questions will I use? (Choose an order of questions that will make most sense to your audience.)
- How many questions will I use? (Think about your audience's time in choosing how many questions to ask. Choosing too many may garner bad results if people get tired of answering.)

CHOOSE YOUR TECHNOLOGIES

In conducting a survey, an interview, or focus group, no doubt you will need to rely on technologies, but determining which ones can be challenging. For a first step, you might begin by figuring out which technologies you have access to and what their advantages and disadvantages are. For example, a number of free survey technologies are available online, as mentioned earlier. They provide templates for building and distributing surveys quickly. However, such free resources and the templates they provide may limit you in what you can do with your survey. Always weigh the advantages and the disadvantages of a technology before you invest time and energy into using it.

Questions to Ask in the Technology Phase

- What do you wish to accomplish with the survey, interview, or focus group, and how will technologies help you accomplish this?
- What technologies do you have access to?
- What technologies will allow you to ask the questions you need to ask?
- What are the advantages and disadvantages of using a technology?

TEST THEM OUT

Not only should you test out your questions to ensure they are not confusing or will garner the necessary answers for your research, you should also test out your technology prior to conducting a survey, interview, or focus group. Whether that be a survey technology, a voice-recording device, or a video-recording device, conduct a pilot test (a practice or mock survey, interview, or focus group usually with a smaller population) to make sure you know how to use it, your audience will be comfortable with it, and it will help you record data in a way that is useful and effective to you. In addition, test out how you will securely store the recorded data when the survey, interview, or focus group is over.

Questions to Ask in the Testing Phase

- How did the technology work during the pilot?
- What did my audience have trouble with?
- How did the technology prevent me in gathering the data I needed to gather?
- Will I need a password-protected technology to store it, and if so, how will this work?

ADMINISTER THE SURVEY, INTERVIEW, OR FOCUS GROUP

As you conduct your survey, your interview, or focus group, make sure to monitor the technologies you are using so as to ensure they are working properly throughout the duration. Troubleshoot and adjust accordingly if problems arise during these activities. For instance, if you are conducting an interview, make sure that you have a backup plan if your voice recorder suddenly stops working in the middle of your interview.

ANALYZE THE DATA

There are a number of tools and resources that can enable the representation and analyses of data, from compiling it to organizing it to coding it. As you think about how you will search and analyze your data, think about the advantages and disadvantages of using particular technologies to do so, as some will have different capabilities than others that may or may not provide insight into your data. For instance, using one data analysis software may enable you to search for keywords within your data while using another data analysis software may enable you to build maps of how keywords are connected to one another within the data.

Questions to Ask in the Analysis Phase

- What technologies will help me analyze the data collected?
- How will they help me organize and analyze the data collected?
- What are the advantages and disadvantages of using such technologies to analyze the data collected?

Still, conducting surveys, interviews, or focus groups are not the only ways in which you can research your subject matter offline. You might, for instance, need to conduct a different type of study, like a case study in which you study a small group of people on location. The reading *The Voice of Lived Experience: Mobile Video Narratives in the Courtroom* by Mary Angela Bock and David Allen Schneider, included at the end of Part 6, provides a good example of a case study.

Indeed, there are quite a number of ways in which to find information about a subject matter. While throughout this book you will discover several ways in which using the internet can lead you to important information, you should consider all that you need to know for your project and consider doing more than just googling it. Gathering information can be a long, tedious process in which you will rely on a number of technologies and methods to do so. If you are patient and work to make sure you are gathering information in the best ways possible for your project, then more likely you will be successful.

Suggestion 3: Ask for Help

Your school's library most likely has librarians who are eager to help you with your research, including helping you identify important sources and databases and showing you how to use them effectively. You might consider making an appointment with a librarian early on in your research project to ensure you have ample time to learn from the librarian and ample time to apply what you learn in your research. More likely than not, the librarians will be able to help you determine what kinds of information you will need and how best to find it.

Your instructors, your teaching assistants, your writing center tutors, and your fellow classmates are also good resources to turn to when researching. Too often, students do not take the time to ask for help from these people and end up learning less than if they would have asked. If you are not sure how to find and gather research for your project, ask those around you. Ask them to show you how to do so. Even if you don't necessarily have questions about researching, it doesn't hurt to have people around you with whom you can discuss your research. If you are willing to share your research, you might find that your fellow classmates are willing to share theirs, too, and in doing so, you might learn something you didn't know before.

Suggestions for Citing Your Writing

Later in this book, you will learn more about how to search and gather information. In the remainder of this chapter, however, you will learn about choosing the right kind of information and how to go about citing it or not citing it.

During the 2016 U.S. presidential election, there was a lot of speculation about fake news stories. People claimed that technologies like social media made it easier for fake news stories to be circulated and retold a hundred times over. The truth is that fake news stories have been around for as long as people have been communicating. A look back through history provides evidence of this. As you research and start writing your text, you will need to be careful about vetting your sources of information to make sure that what you are relying on is credible and trustworthy. After all, if your audience sees that you are citing a fake news story, your own credibility as an author will be lost.

But determining whether or not a source is credible is easier said than done. There are some steps, however, we can take to help us to make such a determination. Check out these suggestions that follow.

IMAGE 4.3 RichVintage / iStock

Suggestion 1: Think Critically

When it comes to sources of information, know the right questions to ask yourself. In communication classes, journalists are taught to ask the *who, what, where, when, why,* and *how* questions when covering a news story. The same questions can be helpful in determining whether a source is credible or not. The chart in Table 4.2 lists several of these questions that you can and should use when working with sources. However, do remember that whether or not a source is credible will also depend on what project you are working on, who your audience is, and what purposes you are writing for. The chart is not a foolproof formula for determining quality resources. As technology evolves, so too do ways to create fake news. Rather, the questions are meant to act as a starting point for your investigation and to help you think critically about the sources you are using.

The answers to the *who, what, where, when, why,* and *how* questions are not always easy to find. To begin with, some technologies have made it more difficult for us to find them. But, we must try nonetheless. While some technology companies, like social media companies, are doing their best at shutting down fake stories, we also have a responsibility in the matter. We should not actively partake in spreading fake news stories, because doing so could have devastating consequences. If we have a hard time answering these questions about a particular source, we might be better off turning to a different source instead.

In answering such questions, we likewise need to be on the lookout for sources that look very much like reliable sources but, upon further examination, are not. Just because a website URL ends in .gov or .org doesn't mean it is reliable, either. And just because a website looks professional and has an "about" page doesn't mean it is reliable as well. There is no magic formula or heuristic for deciphering whether or not you are looking at fake news. Tactics used to create fake news have evolved to mimic our evolving technologies. In fact, producers of fake news have become so sophisticated with their tactics that it is sometimes hard for us to decipher their fake news stories without spending a great amount of effort to do so. Think of Table 4.2 as less of a checklist and more of an investigative process that happens over time and in many different places and spaces. Talk with others, consult other resources, and always look beyond the source itself for answers. While it may take quite a bit of time to do these things, they will be worth it if it means your writing will ultimately be successful as a result.

In addition, when thinking critically about a source, be aware of your own ideologies, your own positions, your own preferences, and where you encounter information on a day-to-day basis. Who you are and where you get your information matters. While your own beliefs and ideologies may make you less likely to think critically of sources you agree with, the technologies you use also shape your ability to think critically and to question whether a story is true or not. For example, in a recent study on social media and trust, researchers found that "females, individuals who are twenty or younger, and more frequent social media users, and also those who use Instagram and LinkedIn" are

TABLE 4.2 Questions Table: Who, What, Where, When, Why, and How

	Purpose for Questions:	Examples of Questions:
Who?	To learn more about an author's (or authors') background, credentials, biases, affiliations, etc.	Who wrote this source of information? Who supports, cites, or relies on this source? Who are the people associated with this source? Who else is writing about this information? Who else corroborates this information?
What?	To learn more about what this source consists of and how it will be of value to you. If you can determine the purpose of the source, you can also think more critically about the author's (or authors') motivations.	What are the claims of this source? What can you do with this source? What influences or biases had a hand in shaping this source? What else has been written on this information, and is it comparable to the source you want to use? What kind of language was used in the writing of this source? What are the purposes of the source? What sources and research did the source use or consult? What technologies did the author(s) use to create their text?
Where?	To learn more about how this source will work in your project but also to determine more about where this source comes from.	Where will I use this source? Where did I find this source? Where is it cited? Where is it circulated?
When?	To learn more about the relevancy of the source.	When will I use it? When was it written? When was the publisher established? When did others cite it?
Why?	To learn more about the motives behind the source, and why you should use the source, too.	Why was it written? Why do I want to use this source? Why would this be a credible source? Why would this not be a credible source? Why would my audience appreciate (or not appreciate) this source?
How?	To learn more about how your audience may interpret your use of this source.	How will my audience view this source? How do I feel about this source? How was this source written? How was this source distributed? How are others using it?

more likely to trust social media and are less likely to be skeptical of it (Warner-Søderholm et al. 310). If you happen to be a 20-year-old female and use social media frequently, for instance, research shows you may be more likely to trust social media posts and less likely to question their validity. But, even if you're not a 20-year-old female who uses social media frequently, you need to consider your own dispositions, your own habits, and your own biases when it comes to believing information and the places where you find this information.

Activity: Research Tool Box

Research technological tools that can help you determine whether or not a source is reliable and develop a toolbox (or list of tools) you can use to help you in your research projects. For example, in the search engine Google Scholar, you can use the "cited by" tool to help you see who has cited a source. By examining those who cited a source, you can determine whether or not such a source has been accepted by the people in our society who have been deemed experts. Use the *who*, *what*, *where*, *when*, *why*, and *how* questions in Table 4.2 to help you determine which research tools can best help you answer these questions. Your toolbox (or list of tools) could also include strategies and notes to yourself for finding the answers to these questions, such as using different search terms to find out more about the authors of sources.

Suggestion 2: Understand Copyright and Fair Use

Instead of creating their own images, often when students are creating a project that includes images, their first inclination is to use images they find through googling or through searching their social media feeds. After all, it is fairly easy to copy and paste images from Google or social media thanks in part to computer technologies. Doing such actions can lead to trouble, especially because using someone else's work, like images, without their permission is in violation of their rights as creators of that work.

So, there are two steps you must remember when using someone else's work: (1) you must determine whether or not the work has copyright or copyleft protections or falls under fair use, and (2) you must determine if you need to obtain permission to use the work from the people who created it. Just because you saw it online doesn't mean you have the right to use it.

Copyright gives creators (authors, painters, sculptors, photographers, musicians, and so forth) protection for their creations (what is referred to as intellectual property), meaning that no one can use their work without permission, and to do so would result in being penalized by governing bodies. In the United States, copyright law states that the owner of the work has several rights, including the ability to reproduce that work, make derivatives of that work, and distribute or perform that work in public spaces.

While every country decides to what extent their copyright laws will protect their citizens' intellectual property, there is no one universal copyright law that protects every creator on the planet in the same way. Nevertheless, there are international institutions that work with intellectual property rights on a global scale. For example, the World Intellectual Property Organization (WIPO), established in 1967 and part of the United Nations, works to ensure effective strategies for people working across borders by bringing together its members to work on issues related to intellectual property. As of the writing of this textbook, 191 countries belonged to WIPO.

Under copyright, copyleft (also known as a reciprocal license) is a practice whereby creators of works give up not all, but some of their rights as the creators, enabling other people to freely use their works as long as they do so under the same terms as the originals. In other words, if you use someone else's work bound by a copyleft license for a remix project, for instance, you would not be able to change any of the original restrictions. The original restrictions would continue on and apply to your use, adaption, or modification of the work you are using from someone else. While copyleft can apply to different kinds of work, it is often used in software development. For a more comprehensive look at copyleft, you might consider learning about the GNU Project, a project that started in the 1980s to develop completely free software. This project went on to create a copyleft GNU General Public License that is still used today.

Give Credit to Those Who Deserve It

When using someone else's work for your own purposes, you may need to get permission from them first, and then determine how best to give them credit, that is, to acknowledge that they are the creator or creators of that work. This depends, however, on a number of factors, mainly how you determine:

- what work of others you will use and how you will use it
- how much of the work of others you will use
- where the work is published
- where or how you will share your own work that includes the work of others

In the United States, the fair use doctrine states that you may use brief excerpts of copyrighted work for educational purposes or for criticism (such as parody or commentary), news reporting, scholarship, and research. If you are using work from a source for educational purposes that will not result in any profits, then your use of the work may be considered fair use. In that case, you would not need to seek permissions to use such work as long as you are reasonable in the amount you are using and the purposes for which you are using it.

If you plan to share your work that includes the work of others in it beyond an educational setting (such as the classroom), or if you plan to use a lot of the work of others, you would need to get permission from the creators of those works (or copyright holders). This would mean that you would have to contact them, explain your reason for using their work, and request their permission.

No matter in what country the source was created, you need to keep in mind that the creator has property rights. Because laws in every country change on a regular basis, you should always do your research before deciding whether or not to use someone else's work.

There are alternatives, however, if you feel you can't afford to pay for such permissions (because sometimes there are fees involved) or you don't have the time to track down the creator or copyright holder. The internet is a good place (though not the only place) to find works that you can use free of charge, are in the public domain (works not protected by copyright), or have minimal permissions requirements. You may have heard of Creative Commons, a site devoted to educating the public about using others' work and helping creators ensure their work is used fairly. Such an organization allows you to use their online site to search for work you can use as long as you adhere to the work's licenses, which are outlined on the Creative Commons site.

However, there are certainly other sites online that provide all sorts of usable content and media, some of which are free and in the public domain, while some must be accompanied with an attribution, such as:

> Wikimedia Commons
> Morguefile
> Internet Archive
> Pexels
> Prelinger Archives

The online resources we have available at our fingertips can often make understanding property rights more complicated. Social media, for instance, makes it easy for us to share and spread information, images, videos, and so forth quickly. However, such content belongs to someone and that someone has rights. For more on using other people's social media work, check out Michelle R. Gould's reading later in this book.

Bottom line: It is your role and responsibility to find out if your sources should be given credit and whether or not you need to seek permissions to use and share the work of others.

Suggestion 3: Determine How You Will Present and Cite Your Sources

In your previous writing classes, you may have learned about citation styles such as MLA and APA. When figuring out how you will give credit to the sources you use, you should think about to whom you are writing and what kind of text you are creating. It's not always necessary or appropriate to use MLA or APA. In fact, there are a lot of other citation styles that people can use, like Chicago or IEEE, to name a few. Also, when obtaining permission to use the work of others, the creators of the work might stipulate just exactly how you need to give credit (what is known as attribution) when they give you permission.

If the creator doesn't stipulate, the first step, then, is to figure out where your work will be shared and/or published. If, for example, you are creating a text that will be published in a journal or magazine, you would need to find out what that journal or magazine's submission guidelines are. Most likely, in those guidelines, the journal or magazine editors will stipulate what kind of citation style is acceptable. If they say to use APA, then you would need to follow the APA guidelines when citing your sources within your text.

There are plenty of resources online that can help you with citing in different citation styles. The Purdue OWL, for example, has examples of MLA and APA citations. There are also software programs and free online resources, like citation generators, that can help you create your citations too. But, note that not all resources are up-to-speed on the latest guidelines and that MLA and APA, as well as the other styles, regularly update their guidelines. Always make sure that the technologies you are using to create your citations are up-to-date.

If you are publishing or sharing your work where no specific citation style is recommended or expected, then it is up to you to organize and create your own ways of giving credit to the work you are using from others. As you create your own, your main goal should be to think rhetorically. Your audience will need to know what work you are citing and should be able to find more information about this work based on the citation information you provide. Remember to keep your citations organized and consistent to help your readers understand what sources you are using and citing from.

Suggestion 4: Keep Track and Annotate as You Go Along

The act of annotation can help you make sense of the sources you are using. In annotating, you are able to make notes about your sources as you are working with them. While doing so helps prevent you from forgetting what they are about and from forgetting to give credit to their creators, it also helps you to avoid plagiarizing, that is, passing others' work off to your audience as if it were your own. Technologies such as hypothes.is (available online) have made online annotation possible. Online annotation involves people (individually or collaboratively) annotating online texts such as websites and digital documents.

When creating a project that requires lots of research and lots of annotating, you may find yourself in need of a system to help you keep track of the sources you will rely on. Just as there are free online citation generators, there are also tools and resources that can help you keep track of the sources you are working with. Zotero, for instance, is a free software program (available online) that works like a personal research assistant in that it can help you keep track of your sources, organize them, retrieve them, and even cite them. Test out several different tools like Zotero to find the ones that work best for you and your projects.

Final Thoughts

There are a lot of technologies to consider when planning and researching your writing projects. As you consider which ones will work best for you, think carefully about the actions you must take with each and the consequences that such actions have on your ability to communicate. Not all technologies that you encounter in researching will be helpful, as you will discover with a bit of practice. Finally, consider making ethical choices at every step of the writing process, especially as you research. Misrepresenting research or using other people's work without their permission may render your ethos unreliable, not to mention unethical. As a writer, those are the last things you want your audience to believe about you, as it would make your efforts in reaching this audience worthless.

Additional Discussion Questions

1. Why should you test different brainstorming technologies when working on a writing project?
2. Do you think technology, people, or both are responsible for spreading fake news? Explain your answer.
3. Why must you cite sources?

Additional Activities

1. Intellectual Property Rights: Find out more about intellectual property rights on a global scale by researching organizations like the WIPO and what they do. Are these rights effective? How do countries protect the rights of creators using WIPO? What technologies help or hinder the protection of intellectual property in your country? Write a reflection on your findings and share with your classmates.
2. Question Your Sources: Using Table 4.2 from earlier in this chapter, examine five different sources for a writing project and determine whether or not these sources are credible and reliable. As you do, try annotating them using an annotation technology so that you are equipped to best synthesize and integrate your sources into your project.

Additional Assignments

1. Technologies and Research: Critically examine several technologies that claim to make the research process easier. Assess their effectiveness and their impact on copyright holders and on the research process itself. Present your findings to the class.

2. Survey Creation: Build a survey using two different technologies in order to compare how technologies can shape a research instrument such as a survey. Determine and reflect on the impact that each technology has on the actions of the researchers and the potential survey participants. Test out your survey using these technologies in two small pilot tests. Report your findings.
3. Fake News: Working with a group of classmates, investigate a fake news story online and discuss how such a fake news story came to be and how people can prevent such a story like it from spreading. Present your findings to the class.

Works Cited

Chamorro-Premuzic, Tomas. "Why Brainstorming Works Better Online." *Harvard Business Review*, 2 April 2015, https://hbr.org/2015/04/why-brainstorming-works-better-online. Accessed 1 July 2018.

Warner-Søderholm, Gillian et al. "Who Trusts Social Media?" *Computers in Human Behavior*, vol. 81, 2018, pp. 303–315.

CHAPTER 5

Design

Contents

Making Observations on Designs	96
Reading Path	97
Principles for Designing With Technologies	100
Principle 1: Color	100
Principle 2: Size	105
Principle 3: Organizing With Proximity	106
Principle 4: Alignment	107
Principle 5: Repetition and Moving Through a Text	108
Principle 6: Typography	109
Principle 7: Emphasis	110
Principle 8: Point of View	111
Principle 9: Creativity and Imagination	112
Principle 10: Make Everything Work, but Don't Go Overboard	113
Final Thoughts	114

IMAGE 5.1 Inspring / Shutterstock

Making Observations on Designs

For the purposes of this book, to design means to imagine something new, to set out with a plan for creating and making function a concept, an idea, or a thing, that will in some way influence an audience. As writing scholar Joddy Murray contends, "design is just another word for composition," meaning it "is the act of putting together with intent, and that is exactly what students must do no matter if they are writing the most traditional type of academic essay, or if they are creating a poster for a local event" (174). While in this chapter, you will think more about a variety of ways in which you can approach designing texts, remember that this entire textbook is really about designing all kinds of texts. Developing an awareness of how you plan, shape, and create a text so that you will influence your intended audience is ultimately approaching the act of designing rhetorically. Thinking rhetorically, in other words, means thinking about design.

Take a few minutes right now and look around you. Really pay attention to the objects, the people, the noises, the things you see, feel, and hear. What things do you see? What do they look like? What do they feel like? What do they smell like? Taste like? What people do you see? What are they wearing? What are they doing? What noises do you hear? Where are these noises coming from? How do they sound?

Save for the natural things in this moment, most everything you encounter was designed by someone, from the clothes you are wearing, to this book you are reading, to the room you are reading in, assuming you are inside. Before today, have you given much thought to how these things are designed? Most likely the things you are seeing, feeling, and hearing started with someone's idea. Perhaps someone wanted to solve a problem, improve upon an existing concept, or make someone's life easier. Along the way, someone had to make rhetorical decisions and put materials purposively together to create the very things you are looking at, touching, and listening to.

Most likely, at some point in your life, you have designed things, too, whether or not you called what you were doing at the time *design*. Have you written a paper? Have you created a bibliography for a research project? Have you written a text message? Have you jotted down a note? If you answered yes to any of these questions, then you have designed. That's because in creating texts you are designing texts, whether those are essays, brochures, text messages, or sound recordings. If you haven't given much thought to the concept of designing texts, you should start now. Good writers are writers who think carefully about how they design texts.

But what is design? Design can mean a lot of different things to different people. Design to a computer engineer may mean to use code to create a functioning online game. Design to an architect may mean to draw blueprints for a house that a builder can then use to build it. Design to a CEO of a toy company may mean to develop sketches and a prototype of a new toy that all kids will want. To an author, it may mean to draft and write a text that an audience will read and understand.

Before you learn about design strategies in this chapter, keep in mind that these strategies are not an all-inclusive list. In fact, there are probably enough design strategies that writers can use to fill lots of books. But, the strategies you see here in this chapter offer a good starting point if you are new to thinking about design, as they will help you develop a critical eye for designing texts and provide you with a bit of guidance as you use technologies to do so.

Reading Path

As a writer, you may start to think about a text's design by thinking about your audience and your purpose for communicating to that audience. In doing so, you might think about what you want your audience to know, how will they know this, and when will they know this. In other words, consider how your audience might read and interact with your text and in what order they will do so. This is known as the reading path. Read the example A and example B posters (Images 5.2 and 5.3), paying attention to how you moved through each of these texts:

IMAGE 5.2 Example A: Motivational Poster. julymilks / Shutterstock

Example B: Brainstorming Poster. Rawpixel.com / Shutterstock

Now that you finished reading each of these texts, answer the following questions:

- How did you read these texts?
- Where did you start reading each of them?
- What elements or features on the page helped you decide where to start and where to end?
- In what order did you read the elements on the page?
- What previous knowledge of reading did you use to help you read these texts?

If you began reading example A with the word "Always," you are not alone. Many people in Western societies would likely begin there, too, reading this word first, followed by the words "believe" and "in." That's because in such societies people have been taught to read such texts from left to right and in a downward path. The way in which this poster is designed also contributes to the reading path. The main mountain (and the smaller ones, too) are shaped in a way that make them appear to point to the words above them, as if to say to readers the words are what you should read first. They are important. The words themselves are large, too, centered above the mountains, taking up a prominent place within the text, drawing our eyes to them.

Example B is a much different text from that of example A, and that's because unlike example A, example B is more of a nonsequential, nonlinear text. In example B, what did you read first? What did you read second? Third? Fourth? What path did you use as you moved through this text? Maybe you began in the middle, with the lightbulb or the word

Brainstorm. Maybe you went to the image of the brain next, and then onto the image of the trash can. Maybe you had an entirely different path.

A Reading Path Is Created by Both the Designer and the Audience

In linear, sequential texts, the designer creates a text with elements that work together to form a path much like the one you see in example A. The audience's brain and eyes work together to recognize a path (perhaps it's the path the designer intended, perhaps it is one they created themselves based on previous reading experiences). In example A, it makes the most sense to start with "Always" instead of the word "in." When creating a text that expresses ideas meant to be understood in a particular order, a reading path should play a role in your design. In thinking about designing your text and thus designing a reading path, you should think about what you want your audience to read and know first, second, third, and so on. Order does matter in such cases.

Other times, order doesn't matter as much, as demonstrated by example B. In example B, it is mostly up to the reader to decide where to start and end. The starting point, the direction of the readers' eyes, and the ending point don't have much of an effect on the understanding of the reader like it would in example A. The way in which example B is designed (a circular pattern with elements that are similar in size and similar in how they are positioned on the page) allows readers to choose the order in which they wish to read it.

In thinking about your reading path for a text you are creating, there are some key considerations you should make. For example, you might want to make a good first impression as well as leave a good lasting impression. In this case, you would need to determine if your audience needs to know one thing before they can understand another, and you would need to think carefully about the order in which you present all the information. In so doing, you would need to think about how to guide readers through your text.

If the order in which readers read your text doesn't matter to their understanding of your text, or if you would rather have your readers find their own paths, you would need to create a text like that in example B, making sure of where and how your elements on the page enable readers to choose their own paths.

Help Your Audiences Read by Using a Clean Design

Designer and blogger Daniel Higginbotham writes that a clean design is a design that diminishes the amount of time and effort a reader needs in order to find the information they are looking for. In other words, "a clean design is one that supports visual thinking so people can meet their informational needs with a minimum of conscious effort." This is particularly evident in example A. In this example, you are able to read without any unnecessary distractions. Every element on the page was designed purposefully to help you move through the text smoothly in a particular direction, and every element on the page helps you understand the writer's intended message.

Principles for Designing With Technologies

To think more about reading paths and about designing readable and usable texts, ones that feature a clean design, is to think about what successful texts do. This can be referred to as principles, and writers who write in a variety of genres and with a variety of technologies may rely on these principles to guide them in their design decisions. Such principles may transfer from one genre to another or may reside only within a particular genre. However, you should not think of these principles as hard rules that you always have to adhere to (more on this in a bit), but rather, you should think of them as suggestions you might want to consider when creating texts of your own.

As you know, when we look at a text that we feel is successful and compare it to other successful texts, we can identify the common characteristics of these texts and the principles that they abide by. While genre conventions refer to the unique features of texts within a particular genre, design principles can refer to the common successful characteristics that texts in a variety of genres utilize. For instance, conventions of the website genre may include the use of hyperlinks. Other genres of texts, like printed brochures and printed books, would not contain hyperlinks as such a convention is most commonly used in the website genre. However, we might see that each of these genres (websites, brochures, books) do feature similar conventions (such as bold headings, paragraphs, images) and we may see that each of these genres employ similar design principles such as the way they use color contrast and spacing appropriately with such headings, paragraphs, and images.

While not all genres use the same design principles, just like not all genres have the same conventions, it is up to the writer to decide what design principles are most appropriate by thinking rhetorically about their writing situation. Worldwide, there are a number of design principles in a variety of industries. What follows are just ten such principles (along with suggestions for using them). Use these as a starting point rather than an ending point when designing your texts. When you've got a handle on these, you might want to research others and learn to use them, too.

Principle 1: Color

Thousands of years ago, people developed technologies that enabled them to use color to communicate. Ancient civilizations used stone and shell tools to mix ochres (pigments) to form colors for rock painting. During those times, there was no written language that contained an alphabet. People depicted stories using colors and symbols, representing

| Example A | Example B |

IMAGE 5.4 Example A and Example B

thoughts and feelings. Today, color is just as powerful in communicating ideas as it was in ancient times.

Think about the color red, for instance. In Western societies, this color is often associated with things you should not do, with blood, with danger, and even with death. In the iconic poster for the 1975 movie *Jaws*, the word *Jaws* is written in red above a giant shark. The red adds to the meaning of the poster, that is, to warn everyone there is danger lurking in the water. When designing a text, you have to choose your colors carefully and according to your purpose and audience. Look at the bumper stickers contained in Image 5.4.

If you lived by the motto: *Live life on the beach!* would you want a bumper sticker on your car expressing that motto in black and red? If you live in a culture where black and red are associated with bad things (like danger, blood, and death), then most likely not. Most likely you would want to use bright, cheery colors; perhaps yellow and blue, colors that remind you of the sun and water. When you choose colors for your text, think rhetorically about your purpose for writing to a specific audience and how colors can help you do that. In addition to thinking about your purpose and your audience, there are a few other suggestions to keep in mind when working with colors. Use colors to help convey meaning, to make important elements stand out, and to help stress the order in which you want your reader to read your text.

Suggestion 1: Know How to Work With Colors

Know how to create a color scheme or palette and what colors complement one another and which ones don't. If you understand primary, secondary, and tertiary colors and their relationships, you will have a better understanding of what colors to use when designing texts for certain purposes. For example, use **complementary colors** to accentuate elements in your text. Use **analogous colors** to provide a cohesiveness to your text and use **monochromatic colors** for harmony.

In Image 5.5 you will find a color wheel depicting primary, secondary, and tertiary colors. When creating a color scheme, purposively choose two to three colors for your design based on this wheel, rather than randomly choosing a whole bunch of colors, especially if you are new to designing. It might also help to keep in mind the types of colors you will use in order to achieve a certain effect. To this end, use the color chart in addition to the wheel when choosing your colors.

TABLE 5.1

Types of Colors	What They Consist Of	What They Are Used For
Analogous	Colors that are next to one another on the color wheel	Developing serene and pleasing-to-the-eye designs
Complementary	Colors that are opposite one another on the wheel	Creating contrast and therefore interest in your designs
Monochromatic	One color hue/base and variations of shades or tints of this hue/base	Adding simplicity and harmony to your designs
Warm	Colors (like red, yellow, and orange) that are bold and vivid, and give the feeling of warmth	Making text, objects, etc., stand out, come forward, or advance, giving the impression that they are closer
Cool	Colors (like blue, green, and purple) that are calm and soothing, and give the feeling of coolness	Making text, objects, etc., recede, giving the impression that they are further away

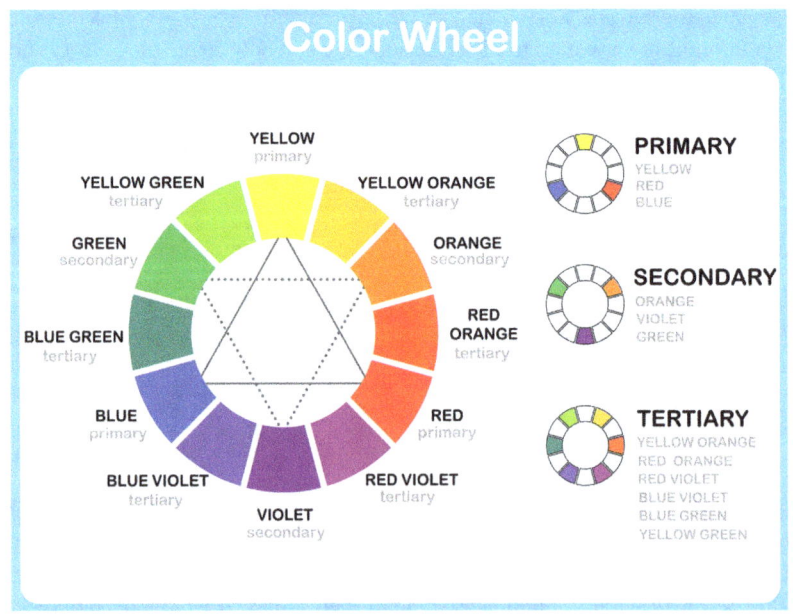

aekikuis / Shutterstock

Suggestion 2: Know How to Work With Contrast

Typically, when designing, you should use contrast to help make your texts readable. Contrast means that you can clearly distinguish colors from one another. When you read navy and white next to one another, or even when one is written on top of the other, you can clearly see two different colors. That's because they stand out from one another, as one is a dark color and the other is a light color. When designing, a good contrast in color can help readers read your text. You can do this by making sure there is a high enough contrast between the background and the foreground elements. As seen in the image of the subway system (Image 5.6), the subway lines and the wording are in dark colors. We can easily read these colors because they appear on a light-colored background. If the background was a darker color, say green, some of the elements, such as the words, would be harder to read. Another consideration to make when working with contrast is to think about color saturation (how heavy the color is). Too much saturation in all your colors could make your design overwhelming and unpleasant to look at.

Suggestion 3: Use Colors to Organize

Another way to use colors effectively is to use them to organize information. In the photo taken of the subway system map (Image 5.6), you can see that colors are used to organize the different subway lines, making it easier for people to distinguish the different lines and find what they are looking for quickly.

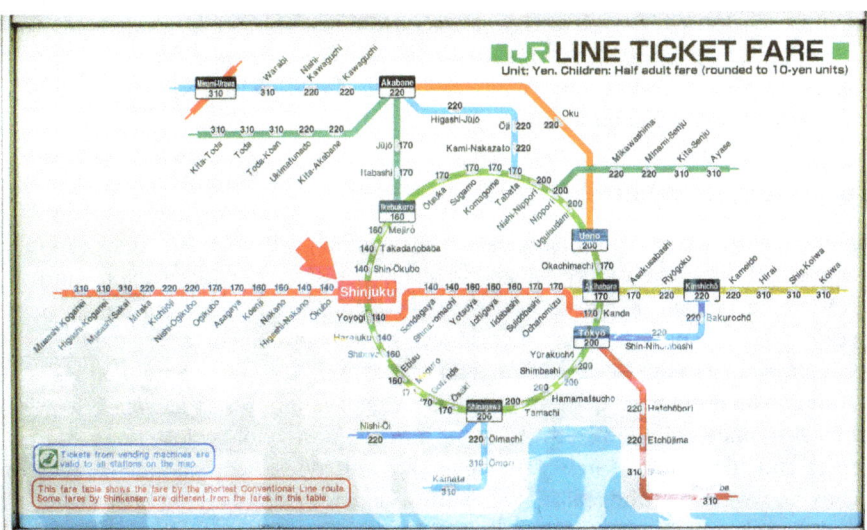

IMAGE 5.6 Subway Map. Pichit Tongma / Shutterstock

Suggestion 4: Know the Difference Between RGB and CMYK

When working with different technologies, such as when using art software programs on your computer, you might not be paying much attention to the type of colors you are using, but you should. Understand that not all digital color is created equal. For starters, there are two options you can use, RGB and CMYK, and the difference between them has to do with adding and subtracting. RGB refers to red, green, and blue and is an additive color model. Adding red, green, and blue light together creates white. RGB is used for digital texts that appear on screens. CMYK, on the other hand, is a subtractive color model that stands for cyan, magenta, yellow, and key (black). When these colors are combined, they subtract light, meaning they produce a darker color. CMYK is used for printed images.

To determine what color you should use in your design, think rhetorically. Digital and printed colors don't look the same. As noted throughout this book, a picture on your computer screen could look differently when printed on paper. That's because of RGB and CMYK colors. When creating digital texts that are meant to be distributed and displayed on screens (such as a website), it is best to use RGB. Conversely, when you are producing a printed text (such as a postcard or flyer), it would be best to use CMYK, especially since most printers use CMYK to print documents. So, when working with colors, choose yours wisely by thinking about how your text will be distributed, whether that will be digitally or in print.

Check It Out YouTube: If you are interested in learning more about using colors to create websites, check out this tutorial on how to define RGB colors using the hexadecimal system. Search YouTube for Richard Homa's "RGB-HexColors-Explained." While this video talks about colors in terms of designing websites, it is also helpful in understanding how colors work in digital platforms.

Suggestion 5: Where Matters

Another consideration you should make when working with color is to think carefully about where your text will be read and to test it in this place or space beforehand. For example, say you are creating a flyer for an upcoming event on your campus. Because your campus has strict rules as to where flyers can be hung, you determine it is best to stick to the authorized bulletin boards around campus. Since you are promoting an event and you want people to attend, your hope is that your flyer will catch everyone's attention on the boards. So, you choose bright colors, make 20 copies, and head out in search of the bulletin boards. When you find the first bulletin board, however, you soon realize that the flyers already posted on the board have the same colors as your flyer. How will your flyer stand out if yours is the same color as the rest?

Before you decide on colors, go to the place you will post it and find out what colors are already being used there. Then, determine how your colors will contrast with the background and how your colors will stand out. Consider what time of day people will see your text, too. If it will be dark, make sure people will see it.

Suggestion 6: Know Your Audience

While colors are important to many designers, be aware that you may exclude those audience members who have difficulty reading colors. If you must use color, keep in mind that different cultures read colors differently. Make sure you do your research if you are creating a text for an international audience much different from your own culture. To do so, examine the texts of other cultures and see how they use colors in a variety of texts. For example, flags of countries often use colors to symbolize important meanings, events, and values. The Nigerian flag contains two vertical green bands and one white vertical band between them. The color green represents the country's natural and agricultural wealth, while the white band represents peace. In other countries, these two colors, green and white, have very different connotations. In some Latin American cultures and Asian cultures, these colors represent death.

Discussion Questions: Colors

1. What implications do your choices in color have in furthering stereotypes within a culture? For instance, in Western cultures, pink is often associated with females, while blue is often associated with males.
2. Why should you pay close attention to where colors are on the color wheel?
3. Why is it important to consider your audience when choosing colors?

Principle 2: Size

Contrast isn't just for choosing colors, but it can also relate to the juxtaposition in sizes of elements in a design. The contrasts in big and small elements in your design can help readers determine what to read first, second, and third. In other words, contrasts can help establish a reading path much like the largest mountain in the poster at the beginning of this chapter did. In addition, contrasts in sizes can help create emphasis in your design. Bigger elements might mean that they are more important than smaller elements.

Size can also help with readability. If you are creating a text like a flyer or sign, you have to make sure that the elements are big enough to read from the place where passersby will see it. If you were creating a billboard, you would need to think about a car on a highway and how passersby would have only a few seconds to read your billboard. If you have ever been driving on the road and saw a sign that was too small to read, that is a result of poor rhetorical thinking. The designer didn't take into consideration size in relationship to where people would read it.

Finally, when it comes to size, think about the sizes of your files for your digital designs. They should not be too big to transfer or store. If you need to deliver a text via an email, flash drive, or drop box, you will need to make sure such delivery will be possible given the size of your design.

Principle 3: Organizing With Proximity

When you organize elements on your page close to one another, you tell your audience that there is a connection between these elements, that they are related in some way. The farther apart your elements are, the less connection they have. When you put elements that are unrelated to one another in close *proximity* (which means nearness in space, time, order, and relation), you may confuse your audience and distract them. It is best to put like information together so as not to confuse your audience and waste their time. Don't make your audience work hard to understand the relationships between your elements.

Did You Know? Gestalt Principles

Learning more about Gestalt principles can help you make effective design decisions. These principles were developed by German psychologists in the early 1900s and refer to how we perceive and organize information, whether through visualizations or through sounds or other modes. One such principle, the proximity principle, states that objects that are placed near one another are perceived as being in groups because of the spatial or temporal distances between objects.

•••• •• ••••

When we look at the above dots, we see three groups. That's because some of the dots are in closer proximity to one another than others due to spatial distancing. There is more space between the fourth and fifth dots, for example, than there is space between the first, second, third, and fourth dots. The first four dots, equally spaced from one another, then are perceived as being a group, while the fifth and sixth dots are perceived as being a different group.

This principle of proximity can also apply to sounds because of temporal distances. If we hear 15 seconds of silence, followed by one loud screech, one second of silence, another identical loud screech, one second of silence, another identical loud screech, and then 15 seconds of silence, we might group the three identical loud screeches together since the temporal distance between them is equal.

Principle 4: Alignment

If you want to achieve a clean design for your text, think carefully about how alignment of your text elements can help you in this endeavor. There are a number of ways you can align words. For instance, you could use the same center alignment as this paragraph does. But, different alignments have different effects. Because this paragraph utilizes center alignment, the edges on both sides of the paragraph are jagged. That is, the first words on each line of this paragraph do not line up, neither do the last words of each line. Such an alignment is difficult to read when there is a lot of text.

This paragraph, however, uses left alignment. Each of the first words on each line actually line up with one another, creating a clean, straight edge. In other words, you could draw a line from the left edge of the "T" in the word "This" at the beginning of this paragraph downward to the left edge of the "u" in the word "up" and the "t" in "the" and so on, and it would be a straight line. Indeed, *alignment* means a forming or arrangement of elements in a line or within agreement. In the previous paragraph, if you were to draw a line from the left edge of the "I" in the word "If" down to the "o" in "of" and the "w" in "words" and so on, it would be a jagged edge. Because there is a clean, straight edge in this paragraph, it is much easier to read.

Often, you will see that books produced for Western cultures use left alignment as we are accustomed to reading left to right. When a different alignment is used in such cultures, such as center alignment, the reader is required to do more work. Typically, center alignment should be used for short texts such as titles and headings, while an alignment with at least one straight edge should be used for longer text.

Though the above examples focus on the alignment of words, other elements in your text can be aligned in different ways, too. You should think rhetorically about the alignment of images and colors and how those are located in your text. Determine if you want to create smooth reading paths or jagged ones. Placement of elements should not be arbitrary as you learned in Principle 3 when thinking about proximity. Proximity and alignment are related in that they can provide a smooth reading path, help you organize your elements, and bring cohesion to your text.

Many design software programs have tools to help you ensure you can properly align the elements in your text. Use tools such as grid lines and rulers to see how all elements in your text (whether words or images or shapes) are in line with one another.

Activity: Alignment

1. Gather a wide range of texts and examine them based on their alignments. What do you notice about how words and images are aligned? Do they also create smooth reading paths, or do they create jagged ones? Write up your observations based on how well the alignments you see aid in your appreciation and understanding of the texts. Then, share them with the class.
2. Next, try designing your own text by paying close attention to the alignment of your elements within it. Technologies that can help you in designing, especially when thinking about alignment, include the following: grids, rulers, boxes, frames, and templates. Using a ruler, for instance, can help you see whether or not your elements are aligned. Print out your text, if possible, and use a ruler to figure out whether or not each of the elements on your pages are aligned in a way that will help readers understand your text.

Principle 5: Repetition and Moving Through a Text

Organization, proximity, and alignment can certainly help create cohesion, but they are not the only ways to do so. Repetition refers to establishing patterns using the same or similar elements again and again within a design. Repetition of elements in a text, such as placing menu links and headings in the same location on all pages of a website, can help your audience navigate a text smoothly. In such an example, repetition can help readers orient themselves quickly each time they land on a new page because they recognize a pattern and expect it to be carried out throughout the design. Having repetition can help readers find what they are looking for quickly. Without repetition there is no pattern. Imagine if you found a website in which all of its pages had a different design. Each page you visited within the website would require a bit of time to get your bearings and orient yourself in how to move through it. Repetition from one page to the next could reduce the amount of time it takes for you to get to the page you want to see.

Repetition happens not just in linear texts, but in nonlinear texts, too. In nonlinear texts, repetition can help provide cohesion. In the brainstorm poster at the beginning of the chapter, the writer uses several repetitions. The use of hands arranged in a circle is one example, while the use of arrows and coffee mugs are other examples. All three of these represent the use of repeated circular forms and contours, making for a cohesive design.

Practice recognizing how designs use repetition. Gather designs that you feel are successful, and make note of how each uses repetition. They could use repetition of colors, of shapes, of placements of elements, of wording, of images, and so on. Use what you find in your own designs.

Principle 6: Typography

Typography (and more specifically, typeface) refers to the visualness (style, arrangement, and appearance) of a set of characters (letters, numbers, and punctuation) and how that set looks on the screen or printed text. While all the characters within a set have a similar look, one type of typeface is different from another. Fonts provide the necessary information that technologies (such as computers) use to create the dimensions of the typeface. Those dimensions could include how thick the characters are, what shape they take, how they are spaced, and how tall and wide they are. John Brownlee, a writer for Co.Design, a blog devoted to the relationships between business and design, provides a useful way of distinguishing between font and typeface by saying, "A font is what you use, a typeface is what you see." Much goes into creating typefaces, and as you will discover by working with different writing technologies, there are hundreds of typefaces available. Good designers pay close attention to how each character is shaped and how each works and looks with other characters.

Take a moment and think about the texts you have designed in the past that contained typefaces. When you chose a typeface for such texts, did you think about how the arms and legs of letters looked? Did you consider their strokes or their uses of serifs? Did you pay attention to the way a typeface shaped its loops, its open and closed counters, its terminals? Did you think about how your audience would interpret these? Because you are not a typographer, you probably didn't even see these things or think about them.

Knowing more about typefaces, however, can help us make important design decisions when creating texts. Though using the default font style on your computer might seem like a good idea and might save you a bit of time, you should choose your font styles carefully for several reasons. First, font styles have their own personalities.

In Image 5.7, example C uses the font style of Old English Text MT, a serif font that looks like an old formal font you might see in a historic book, not on a bumper sticker about the beach. Example D uses another font style, the sans serif font style of Haettenschweiler. This font, too, isn't a good font as the letters are so close together that it may make reading the bumper sticker difficult. Neither font really provides a sense of how fun the beach is, and neither has a personality that would work for the purpose of the bumper sticker.

                Example C   Example D

Example C and Example D

Did You Know? Working With Characters

The processes of kerning, tracking, and leading are used to adjust the space around and between characters such as letters and numbers. Computer technologies can do these processes for you automatically, but you can and should do this yourself when you need to achieve a certain look. *Kerning* is used to adjust the space between two characters. It has to do with the perceived equal amount of space we see when we look at characters such as letters or numbers. *Tracking* adjusts the space between groups of characters, and *leading* adjusts the space between lines of characters.

If you want to practice your design skills when it comes to kerning, check out KERNTYPE, an online kerning game at http://type.method.ac/.

In the meantime, here is a trick you can use to change the kerning in a computer program such as Microsoft Word: Place your cursor between two letters in a word, and then press Ctrl+D to open the Font dialog box. In the dialog box, look for the advanced options and for the box on kerning for fonts. From there, you can adjust the spacing between your letters.

Principle 7: Emphasis

Emphasis can help in a number of ways to get your message across, from making something on a text stand out to repeating key elements. The purpose of emphasis is to make sure your reader pays attention. However, just because we have technologies that have the capabilities to produce emphasis in our texts, and can make it easy for us to add in elements in our texts that provide emphasis, that doesn't mean we should. When creating your texts, you should think about how your text looks or sounds, from the photographs to the words to the noises you use. The way something looks and the way things sound carry meaning. For instance, WHEN YOU USE ALL CAPS TO WRITE WORDS, YOUR AUDIENCE WILL THINK YOU

ARE SHOUTING AT THEM. DOING THIS A LOT WITHIN A TEXT MIGHT ANNOY YOUR AUDIENCE, AND THE EFFECT THAT YOU INTENDED TO HAVE WOULD BE LOST. So, unless you have something that you really need to shout, think twice about using all caps for emphasis.

The same can be said about using exclamation points!!!! Exclamation points work best with short, exclamatory expressions like "Help!" or "Good Job!" Part of why this is so is because with short expressions, the reader can see and therefore anticipate and read the exclamation in the way the writer intended and in the right tone of voice. When the exclamation point is put at the end of a rather long sentence, the reader doesn't know to read the sentence with the right tone of voice! Notice how awkward that exclamation point was? It comes at the end of a very long sentence in which you didn't anticipate it. Therefore, you weren't able to put the right emphasis on it from the moment you began to read the sentence.

Principle 8: Point of View

Prior to this point, I (the author of this textbook) have used "I" only once. That was in the Preface. By now, I believe you are probably accustomed to the second-person point of view I have been using throughout this book. My decisions to not use "I" and its forms of "me," "my," and "mine" are deliberate. I felt that inserting myself as the author of this book, that is, making myself more visible to you by using first-person point of view, would take away from some of the points I wanted to make in this book. I wanted this book to be about you, the reader, and therefore, I used second-person point of view, using "you" a lot in this book to draw attention to the fact that you, as a reader of this book, do have power.

My decision to do so was influenced by the cultures of academia and publishing. I took into consideration other textbooks on the market and whether or not they use first person. I also took into consideration whether or not first person would be distracting and make me seem like an authoritative, all-knowing expert. I preferred the "you" and "we" (in the general sense people use "we" to refer to humankind) over the use of "I" mainly because a classroom should revolve around students—that's you, my readers. Too many references to "I," I believed, would make it seem like I'm the authority on this subject matter, and I didn't want to run the risk of readers not making up their own minds. I prefer to think of students as those who can have agency in making decisions.

My decision to use second-person point of view was intentional and one I thought carefully about. I recommend that you think carefully, too, about point of view and what each kind of point of view might mean to your audiences and the purpose of your project. Point of view, by the way, isn't just meant for texts that rely on words. Videos, for instance, can be created in a particular point of view, too. A point of view most certainly influences the way a story is told and how it is perceived.

Principle 9: Creativity and Imagination

History is abundant with stories of risk takers and adventurers who, when told to turn back by their peers, fearlessly pushed on for the sake of testing humankind's abilities and furthering our knowledge of the world. What started as a dream for Orville and Wilbur Wright became a reality when, in 1903, they ignored popular engineering theories and turned a new technology into a flying machine by flying their plane for the first time. Their knack for experimenting, their willingness to take on risky trial-and-error methods, and their sense of adventure are inspiring. Technology, both the building of it and using of it, certainly requires assembling, remixing, testing, revising, and editing, but it also relies on imagination, innovation, risk taking, and creativity. Writing needs imagination, especially because it is imagination that helps us to see the future and see possibilities for things. In other words, what things might be. You learned about several design principles in this chapter, but those are not enough to be successful in writing.

Principles imply there is a norm, a standard way of doing something. But, who decides what these are in the first place? What is the norm? This book doesn't contend that the principles and suggestions that appear on its pages are the only ways of writing, just that these are some things, some examples of what a lot of writers in a particular culture at a particular time in history have done. You don't have to do these yourself if your purpose in creating doesn't call for them. Indeed, you should think carefully about all your decisions in writing. There will be times when you will need to go against the principles and suggestions on these pages.

Know the Rules Before You Break the Rules

As you read this chapter and this book, you may have recalled a time or two when you noticed that a designer or writer you read didn't follow such principles or suggestions. Yet, the text they produced was still effective. Yes, it is true. There are credible instances when not following a rule can be a good idea. For example, in nonlinear texts, you might encounter more abstract elements that cannot subscribe to the principles in these pages.

Bottom Line

Think rhetorically, but also think about purposeful creativity. Conventions of texts are often based on using principles of design, but they can sometimes be boring, just like templates can be generic, and clip art can be overused. Sometimes, when we want our texts to stand out, using principles can render our texts less than unique.

Discussion Questions: Breaking the Rules

Discuss examples of texts that seem to go against the principles and suggestions outlined in this book. Why do these texts go against them? What were their authors' intentions in breaking the rules? Are the texts successful in getting their messages across as a result of breaking rules?

Principle 10: Make Everything Work, but Don't Go Overboard

Along the lines of being creative, you should also think about how to make the whole of your text work, and to consider purposes for all aspects of your work without going too far. Striking a balance in your work is key to making your work effective for you and your audiences. Let's look at a specific example to understand why this is so. In 1994, when creating the now famous logo for FedEx, Lindon Leader had lots of design choices to consider, from color to contrast, to size, to alignment, to space, to proximity.

The logo (shown in Image 5.8) is a simple one indeed, using only two colors upon a white background. If Leader had added in any more elements to this logo, they would have taken away from the effectiveness of its simplicity; that is, the logo would not have been as powerful as it is in its current state. In its simplicity, you can see that Leader thought carefully about its design. First and foremost, he thought creatively about using **negative space** (the space devoid of elements and color—what we would call white space in this design). You can see the space between the "E" and "x" is not an ordinary space. It is a space that creates a forward-pointing arrow. To create such space, he had to think about such things as typeface and kerning in ways that hadn't been done before.

Just remember that the more elements you add in—that is, the more bells and whistles you include—the more complicated your designs can become, which may in turn render them less effective. So, think carefully about adding in things to your design without having a specific and important reason for doing so.

IMAGE 5.8 FedEx Logo. Tanuha2001 / Shutterstock

Final Thoughts

Designing great texts takes time, and you may need some practice in it before you improve your skills. But, if you are patient, if you do practice, and if you do think rhetorically about the principles outlined in this chapter, more likely you will be successful in communicating your ideas in a variety of texts. Remember that every element of your design should be there for a reason, and that reason should be evident to your audience. In other words, it should serve a clear purpose for being a part of your design. As you move on to the rest of the book, you will find even more strategies for designing a variety of texts that can work with the strategies you learned in this chapter.

Additional Discussion Questions

1. Why must you think carefully about color choices when designing texts?
2. In the mostly black-and-white film *Schindler's List*, director Steven Spielberg uses color in a very purposeful way to convey meaning. In one instance, a little blonde girl appears in a red coat on screen amid the Nazis' occupation of Poland. The site of her on screen is a turning point in the film for the main character. What other film examples can you think of that use color in a purposeful way? Why do you think the director used color in this way?
3. The FedEx logo is an example of a successful design. Other logos utilize successful design as well. Discuss specific logos you are familiar with, and why these logos are successful based on what you read in this chapter.

Additional Activities

1. Product Packaging: Analyze a product's packaging for the principles of design outlined in this chapter, from uses of proximity to uses of color. Explain how and why those principles were used in the packaging.
2. Colors: In a group, determine what colors you would use (and why) to create the following:

    a. A baby shower invitation
    b. A brochure for a nature park
    c. A wedding greeting card
    d. A jersey for the mighty penguin's hockey team

    Discuss what led you to choose the colors that you did.

3. Typefaces: Collect texts with a variety of typefaces. Determine if their personalities are appropriate for the texts. Present your findings to the class.

Additional Assignments

1. Flyer: The Department of Arts and Performances wants to create a flyer to advertise upcoming performances. Using the principles of this chapter, help them rework the following information about the upcoming events by creating a flyer that is both readable and effective. Think specifically about a place on your campus where you would distribute the flyer.

The Department of Arts and Performances Presents
Upcoming Events

An Evening with John Silas

Date: Saturday, February 24, 2020 Time: 8:00 p.m. Venue: Davis Performing Arts Center

Multitalented John Silas has performed with artists around the world. His contemporary style both captivates and inspires audiences whether he performs solo or with large orchestras. His 11 Grammy Awards place him among the best in musical history.

An Evening with Max S. Waters

Date: Saturday, March 11, 2020 Time: 7:30 p.m. Venue: Davis Performing Arts Center

Waters blends bold and creative sounds in his live performances. Drawing on his African heritage, he brings music to life, telling stories that make for memorable audience experiences. His award-winning tour is not to be missed.

An Evening with The Bennett Group

Date: Saturday, April 18, 2020 Time: 2:00 p.m. & 7:00 p.m. Venue: Davis Performing Arts Center

The Bennett Group has been performing for over 20 years together, presenting tributes to famous musicians worldwide. The ensemble includes famous musicians Kate Dillion, guitarist and singer, Mitchel Hamilton, drummer, and Scott Sanders, pianist. Their tribute to Todd Wilcox is heartwarming and authentic and will leave audiences speechless.

2. Colors in Other Cultures: Research how other cultures use colors to communicate different meanings. Present your findings to the class in a presentation. Make sure to provide examples.
3. Advertise an Event: Create several different types of texts to advertise an upcoming event in your community. You could create a flyer, a radio announcement, and a video commercial. In a reflection, discuss the decisions you made in creating each and how you thought and applied the principles and suggestions in this chapter.

Works Cited

Brownlee, John. "What's the Difference Between a Font and a Typeface?" *Fast Company*, 6 May 2014, www.fastcodesign.com/3028971/whats-the-difference-between-a-font-and-a-typeface.

Higginbotham, Daniel. "Clean Up Your Mess: A Guide to Visual Design for Everyone." 2011, www.visualmess.com/.

Murray, Joddy. *Non-Discursive Rhetoric: Image and Affect in Multimodal Composition*. State University of New York, 2009.

CHAPTER 6

Draft, Test, Revise, and Edit

Contents

Another Look Back at History	118
Drafting Your Text	118
Testing Out Your Drafts	120
Revising Your Text	122
Editing Your Text	127
Editing a Text Based on Words	129
Editing a Text Based on Visuals	132
Editing a Text Based on Sounds	133
Editing a Text Based on Videos	134
Final Thoughts	135

IMAGE 6.1 Pencil Sketch of God and Adam's Hands from the Sistine Chapel Ceiling. aleisha / Shutterstock

117

Another Look Back at History

Art historians of Michelangelo often point out that the famous renaissance artist drew out many of his works before completing them, whether they were a sculpture or painting. While the sketches were called cartoons at that time and were often drawn with chalk, they reflect his genius, and his ability to work on his craft in order to perfect it. One of his most famous works of art, *The Creation of Adam* on the ceiling of the Sistine Chapel, began in part as drawings of the human figure, including that of a torso thought to be Adam's.

Throughout history, people (not just famous artists) have used a number of technologies to produce drawings and sketches as a way to draft out texts. In drafting, people can capture ideas, develop plans, and work out problems. In fact, drafting can especially be a valuable skill to writers. However, drawing and sketching are but a few ways in which writers draft. Therefore, in this chapter, in addition to drawing and sketching, you will consider many other ways in which writers can draft, giving you an opportunity to determine which is best for you and to show you that drafting provides you with a means to test out ideas and work on revising and editing.

Drafting Your Text

Once you have a good understanding of what you will design, it might be a good time to start drafting and building your text. To draft means to plan, sketch, or outline your ideas for your writing. Drafting can help you think temporally and spatially about the content of your text. Later in this book, you will read an interview with Meghan Pearson, a graphic design artist, and how she created her nature calendar. In her interview, she talks about using various drafts and mockups to create the final version of her calendar. She did these by hand using paper and also digitally on her computer in order to make sure that when printed, the final calendar would be a professional text. Using outlines, mockups, sketches, and other forms of drafting, however, will depend on personal preference, what your goal is for writing, and the kind of text you are writing. In Table 6.1, you will find a number of different ways to draft and the technologies that can help you do these.

TABLE 6.1 Different Types of Drafting

Different Types of Drafting	What This Is:	Might Work Best For:	Try These Technologies:
Alphabetic draft	A draft whose main mode of communication is through words	Writing longer textual texts, such as an essay, a proposal, a chapter, a book	Notebooks, paper, word processing software, or a text editor such as Microsoft Word, Writebox, or Google Docs

Prototyping	A kind of rapid application development, or an early sample or model	Programming language, developing an application, or creating a website	Programming software or internet resources like Mockplus or Justinmind
Boxing	Using drawings of boxes or frames to map out layout and design elements such as images	For aligning elements and for creating a website, app, or other texts that have multiple elements to organize	Paper cutouts of boxes that allow the testing of different arrangements, or programming software that allows for the laying out and layering of boxes or frames
Sketching	A quick drawing of an idea	Visual elements of a text	Sketch book, drawing software such as GIMP, Photoshop, or Paint
Mockup	A rough model of a text either in digital or physical form	3D texts, such as product labels, calendars, promotional materials	Sketch book, software programs, or internet resources like Mockplus or Justinmind
Storyboard	Scene-by-scene drawings using frames in a particular order	Comics, stories, videos, presentations, and photo essays	Sketch book, sticky notes, software programs such as Storyboard That
Demo	A rough audio draft	Audio texts	Smartphone recording app, sound recording computer software such as Audacity

Be aware that the actions that you use to draft using a variety of technologies will shape your writing in different ways. Drafting in a notebook is different from drafting on a computer. That's because the physical actions you take are different with a notebook and with a computer, and those differences allow you to learn and grow in different ways. As you work on various writing projects, you should try out the different types of drafting options outlined in Table 6.1, making note of what actions you take with each and what advantages and disadvantages come with those actions. In the end, you should choose those that can best help you achieve your goals in writing.

Testing Out Your Drafts

After you have a draft, whether that be a mockup or storyboard, share your work with others to get feedback on it. In other words, test out your ideas to prove they will work. At this point, it might be a good time to even conduct a focus group. If you can, show your work to your actual audience, whether that be your instructor and your fellow classmates, or some other group of people beyond your classroom's walls to whom you are writing. That way you can get feedback from the very people who will be receiving the text once you are finished writing it. If you cannot get feedback from your audience (as was the case with Tammy's writing in a previous chapter), find other people who can give you honest feedback on your draft or will have some knowledge on what you are writing about. Tammy had the BWL board of directors read her drafts but also reached out to another person at an organization who had previously been granted funds from the Florida Adult Soccer Foundation. Since that person had written a request a year earlier, he was able to provide detailed feedback to Tammy that proved helpful when writing and revising her request.

Having another set of eyes on your writing can help you determine usability, readability, and functionality as well as what you still need to include and what you need to leave out in the final draft. They can also help you spot mistakes that you didn't spot on your own. In addition, sharing your work also gives you a chance to discuss your work out loud. Discussing your work out loud may lead to ideas you never thought about before. Today, thanks to technologies such as instant messenger, FaceTime, Google Docs, wiki sites, and email, you can get feedback on your work in a number of online ways, either synchronously (happens immediately in real time) or asynchronously (doesn't happen immediately, but happens over a period of time).

Online writing groups, for example, can be helpful since they are made up of people who are interested in writing. The people who participate not only share their own work, but they also provide feedback to the other members of the group. Such groups can provide both synchronous and asynchronous feedback. If you can, find a group that has interest in the genre you are writing in and then weigh the advantages and disadvantages of both synchronous and asynchronous feedback to decide which is best for you. Synchronous feedback might be helpful when you have easy-to-answer questions about your draft. Asynchronous feedback might be best when you want your peers to be thoughtful in their feedback and spend more time responding to it. In other words, giving them enough time to think about your draft and then respond thoroughly might mean that you should consider this type of feedback.

Check It Out YouTube: If you want to know more about the differences between synchronous and asynchronous communication, check out "Synchronous vs. Asynchronous Communication" posted on YouTube by L Saylor. This video highlights the advantages and disadvantages of each.

In addition to what you just read about testing your drafts, the following suggestions can help you think more critically about securing feedback on your drafts as well as how you can test them in ways that will help you later revise those drafts.

Suggestion 1: Ask Questions

Regardless of whom you share your draft with, develop a list of questions about your draft that you would like your peers to answer as they read and test your draft. For example, you may find asking your peers these key questions to be very helpful when you revise and edit your work:

- What do you find interesting, useful, and helpful about my project?
- What are the strongest parts of my project, and why?
- What worked?
- What can I expand on?
- What are the weakest parts of my project, and why?
- Where do I need more information, examples, design elements, or details?
- Where does my design get in the way of your understanding?
- What doesn't work?
- What was difficult?

Suggestion 2: Observe Your Audience Reading, Listening, and Interacting

In observing your audience as they use your text for the first time, your goal is to find out how your audience is interpreting and using it and whether or not these match your intentions. One of the best strategies for improving a text that is primarily based on written words is to have someone read that text out loud to you and listen to how your writing sounds. As they do, take notes and think carefully about how your reader is reading your text. If your text is based primarily on sounds or moving images, immediately after they finished listening and/or watching, have your audience explain what they heard and/or saw during their experience. If your text involves audience interaction, such as a website or app, watch as they interact and navigate the text, making notes on where things went smoothly, where things were confusing, and/or where things were time consuming. If you can't do these in person, find a technology that can help you, such as FaceTime or Skype.

Suggestion 3: Take Things Apart and Put Them Back Together

Another strategy for improving your text has to do with taking it apart and putting it back together again. Computer technologies allow us to cut and paste sections of a text in a matter of seconds. As you take apart your text, question the different parts and how they are assembled together. That is, question your decisions to write your draft the way you did. If, for example, you break your text down rhetorically, you might ask about your language and design choices and whether or not they are appropriate for your audience, your purpose, and your context for writing. As you put your text back together again, think carefully about your order of information, what reading paths your audience will take, and if anything should be left out or added. You could take apart your drafts several times and then test out different ways to put it back together again to see if there are other possibilities for your text.

Check It Out YouTube: If you are working in the Windows operating system, one tool that can help you take apart your text and rearrange it is the Snipping Tool. Such a tool lets you cut out portions of your screen and save them as images. To help you understand how such a tool works, watch the YouTube video "How to Use Snipping Tool (Beginners Guide)" posted by TechGumbo. For Mac users, you can use Grab, a built-in tool that is included in most Mac computers. It works in similar ways to the Snipping Tool.

Suggestion 4: Use Your Audience's Feedback

All successful writers revise their work by listening to their audience's feedback. While you don't have to attend to every concern your audience has about your draft as some of it might not be helpful, it would be a good idea to at least consider it. You could do this by creating a separate document that keeps track of all your audience's concerns. Next to each concern, you could write a note or two in response to how you will handle each concern. If your reader suggests that you add more details, you could make a note that indicates what you will specifically do to add (or not add) more details. Keeping track of these concerns can help you think through your writing and the decisions you make when creating a text.

Activity: Observe Your Draft

In a group, take turns reading, watching, and listening to each other as everyone shares and interacts with each other's drafts. As your peers read, watch, and listen to your draft, take observational notes that capture these experiences. Then, write a reflection on how you will use these notes (or not use them) to revise your draft.

Revising Your Text

As a cartographer, Juan Ramirez's job is to develop maps to help people locate and navigate places on Earth. Juan knows all too well that making maps is not an easy job. That's because maps evolve over time due to a number of reasons: the discovery of new places, the changing of landscapes, and the building of roads. In addition, Juan's evolving rhetorical choices as well as evolving technologies impact what his maps will look like, how they will be shaped, accessed, and distributed to those in his society.

Though a map is a text, all texts, like a map, tell readers where to go and what to see. And like a map, texts evolve over time for a number of reasons: when new ideas are discovered, when new ways of thinking need to be accounted for, when contexts change, and when technologies change. People change over time, too, and therefore knowledge, ideas, and cultural meanings change as well. Often texts have different versions to suit different people and different ideas. Have you ever read a book that had multiple editions? In its evolution, a text gets reworked and rewritten to account for changing rhetorical circumstances.

To help you create and revise your own texts, you might consider different ways of looking at those texts. Technologies can help you do this, but they can also serve as metaphors for texts and for the reworking of them. Google Maps, one technology that can serve as a metaphor, can help you think about the different ways in which to examine your writing and to think more carefully about the differences and connections between revising and editing your work. Think about Google Maps' capabilities of zooming out and zooming in on a location. (If you are not familiar, take a moment to open Google Maps and try zooming in and zooming out on a location.)

Let's say you were interested in applying for graduate schools. You do some research about the best graduate programs in the world and narrow your choice down to one. Because it is located in a town you never heard of, you turn to Google Maps to find the school's location. To get a sense of its location, you first enter in the town and zoom out to see in which country, continent, and hemisphere that town is located. When you zoom out on the Google Map, you see the location from a vast perspective. You see that the town is located in the United States, in the state of Alabama. By zooming out, you get a sense of where the school is located within the state but also where the location is compared to other states in the country. Zooming out further, you can also see the location compared to other countries, to other continents, and even to another hemisphere. Zooming out allows you a better understanding of the school's global location. Given your knowledge of the world and its geography, you can make a reasonable guess as to what kind of landscape and terrain you might expect there, what the climate might be, whether or not it is summer or winter at the moment.

But, zooming out on the Google Map gives you only some information about the location. To decide whether or not moving to that town to attend school is a good idea, you may need more information about where the school is located. If you decide to go visit the school, zooming out on the map would only partially help you plan your trip. If you were to take public transportation, for instance, you would need more details about the school's location. You would need to know the street address, locate the buildings on campus, and so forth.

To get more details, you zoom in on the town and then further still on the school, seeing that the school's building is rather large in comparison to other buildings on the four-lane street on which it is located. By zooming in to street level, you see that the school is near a bus station. Looking on this small zoomed-in scale, you develop an understanding of the school's place on the street by noticing specific details about it. If you were to visit the school, you note that in walking down the street after exiting the bus station, the school would be on your left. In fact, it would be the second building on the street and it would have two entrances, one in the front and one in the back. While these details are rather small in comparison to the nature of a location on a global scale, they are important nonetheless because this information enables you to have a better, more coherent understanding of the location. When you combine this information with the information you learned by zooming out, you are in a better position to decide whether or not moving to that town and getting to the school would be a good idea for you. Both zooming in and zooming out help provide you information about the school's location.

The act of zooming out and zooming in can also help us think carefully about revising and editing our texts. If we think of our texts as maps, as mentioned earlier, we can think about how our readers will interact with them, how we might help them to navigate, and also how we might revise and edit our texts. In a sense, when we revise, we zoom out and look at our text as a whole, considering our text on a global scale. We think about its place in our world, making sure we know our audiences, our contexts, and our purposes in the process. We think about how our whole text appears, and if it looks like other texts in the genre. We think about how the different elements fit on a page or screen or some other medium. We think about the relationships between the elements, how far they are to one another, if they are in the right order, and if they belong with the other elements. We think about the elements in relationship to how our readers will read through the entire text.

On the other hand, when we edit a text, we are essentially zooming in and looking at the smaller details. Like when we zoomed in to street level, in editing, we zoom in to sentence level, picture level, sound level, and so forth, paying close attention to syntax and grammar, word choice, transitions, colors, pauses, and silences.

Because texts are always evolving, the line between revising and editing isn't always a definitive one. Just like on Google Maps, it might be hard to discern at what point you are no longer zooming out and instead zooming in, and vice versa. While in this chapter, you will learn specific strategies for revising your texts, and while sometimes it may be better to tackle global concerns within your text first, there will be times in writing when you will need to go back and forth between zooming out and zooming in on your text. Therefore, even though later in this chapter you will learn specific editing strategies, you should think about revising and editing strategies as working together to achieve your goals.

Remember that drafts are versions of a text as they evolve over time. Below, are two drafts of Jeweliana Register's infographic project. While you will read more about Jeweliana and another one of her projects later in the book, know that she is a student in a writing course like you. For an assignment in her class, Jeweliana was tasked with creating an infographic to visually represent information about a technology. Jeweliana decided to create an infographic for students who were new to Adobe Photoshop. Images 6.2 and 6.3 represent two of the drafts Jeweliana created for this project.

When you compare the two drafts, you can see that Jeweliana made some substantial changes to revise the infographic from draft 1 to draft 2. Because her purpose was to

IMAGE 6.2 Draft 1   IMAGE 6.3 Draft 2

briefly introduce beginners to Adobe Photoshop, Jeweliana didn't want her infographic to be too text-heavy but rather a simple reference. Draft 2 moves in that direction since it no longer features the section called "The Tools and Their Uses," which is text heavy because of its long list of tools. That section was nixed based on feedback she received from her peers and her professor. If you think about her decision to remove this section, you can see that rhetorically, she is thinking about not only her purpose, but the genre of an infographic as well as her audience.

Jeweliana also changed the section on gaining access, moving it up on the infographic and adding in an additional way to access Adobe Photoshop. A decision like this one is based on rhetorical thinking as well. Jeweliana thought about her audience and what would be most helpful to them as she revised her draft. Jeweliana's two drafts represent a few ways in which a writer might revise by zooming out. Besides thinking about how Jeweliana revised her drafts, here are some more helpful suggestions for your consideration as you revise your own work:

Suggestion 1: Revise First (Most of the Time)

Here's why it might be best to revise first before you begin to edit: say you are just starting to write a draft like an infographic. Worrying about whether or not you have a comma in a sentence at this point isn't as important as thinking about the idea of the sentence in relationship to the point of the entire infographic. If you went through your infographic to make sure you had included commas correctly, and then afterward, you realize that you have to cut two sections from your infographic entirely since they don't make sense to the main point of the infographic, you would have wasted your time making sure you had commas in those sections.

Suggestion 2: Revise and Edit Together

Here's when it might be best to revise and edit together. Say that you are under a time crunch and your deadline is looming. You might consider revising and editing your work at the same time in order to meet that deadline. However, there are other reasons to revise and edit together. If you wait until the last moment to edit your sentences in an essay, for instance, you might find that when you do so, your sentences take on completely new meanings. In order to make judgments concerning your entire essay, your sentences have to make some sense to begin with. If they don't, how can you say that your essay has a clear focus or has developed ideas? You may find you need to make bigger changes in addition to smaller ones at the same time.

Suggestion 3: Use Different Techniques

There are a number of ways and a number of technologies that can help you revise your work. Not all writers will find the same techniques and technologies helpful for all their writing projects. Some writers use digital Post-it notes to make notes about revising;

some writers like to print out text, cut it down into parts, rearrange the parts, and then put them back together with glue; while some writers like to use different color fonts for different areas of a draft to see how it visually comes together. No matter which technique and which technology you use, think rhetorically about them. Not all technologies are created equal, as has been mentioned throughout this book, and not all uses of these technologies are helpful to all writers. You might consider what the advantages and disadvantages are, let's say, between using a printed copy of your text to revise as opposed to a digital copy, or vice versa. Using different technologies (a pen and paper, a computer, a word processing program, a mouse, and so forth) require different cognitive tasks, and each has limitations that could lead you to different results in your revising. So, try different technologies and compare your results to know what is best for your project.

Suggestion 4: Learn How to Draft

If you receive feedback from your peers and they suggest a particular revision, don't ignore this revision if you think it would be too hard. In other words, don't give up on a challenging revision. Learn how to do the revision. A number of helpful tutorials are available online for free that can walk you through virtually anything. If, say, you were working on a video and someone suggests that you use a sound effect, learn how to use it. If the sound effect would make a big difference to your video, don't ignore it because you don't know how to use the technology to do so.

Suggestion 5: Revise for Different Audiences and Contexts

You may find yourself in a position where you will develop content about something that will need to be revised for different audiences and different contexts. Marketers and communication directors often build what is called a *flex text*, a text that contains content that can be revised for different audiences and contexts. A flex text maintains the core points but can be adapted to present them differently for different situations. For example, a flex text could have core points that could be used in an app and on a website. An app and a website are two different texts with similar and not-so-similar features. Using the core points in a flex text, you could build your app and your website around them so as to adhere to the conventions of each genre of text while still having consistent points. Even if you are not a marketer or communication director, you might find that you must revise a text for different audiences and contexts, perhaps in a remix assignment that your instructor assigns. If that is the case, think rhetorically again about your new purpose, your new audience, and your new context and use the flex text accordingly.

Editing Your Text

Once you have a handle on revisions, you might move next into editing your work, making sure it is ready for distribution. At this point, you have worked out any major concerns you had for your text, and you are shifting your focus to smaller issues. In other words, you are fine-tuning your text, ensuring it is acceptable for your audience. Editing goes beyond using the technologies we sometimes take for granted like spell checker and autocorrect. Editing involves selecting, correcting, condensing, last-minute fact checking, modifying, lighting, darkening, shortening, and lengthening with the goal to produce the final polished draft. Editing should not be mistaken for proofreading (looking for spelling and punctuation errors and typos), though proofreading is a part of the editing process.

As technologies have evolved over time, our processes of editing a text have, too. Before computers made moving and changing our writing as easy as pushing a few keys on a keyboard and clicking a mouse, editing included such tasks as handwriting new drafts using an eraser or whiteout, retyping it on a typewriter, redrawing it, and rerecording it. Today, there are a number of ways in which we can edit, from textual editing, to visual editing, to sound editing, to video editing.

Editing can sometimes be thought of as a negative process. You may have spent a lot of time on your draft and the thought of having to change any of it could be daunting. But, rest assured, editing can be a good and positive experience. It is the last step you have to take to ensure your work is of great quality. By the time you do your last edits, you will have a great project, worthy of your audience's attention.

With that being said, there is no one magic formula you can use each time you edit. However, there are a few strategies you can think about that might work for the texts you are creating using a variety of technologies. Whether you are editing a text based on words, sound, visuals, or video, you might consider (when appropriate) the strategies outlined in Table 6.2 as you edit:

TABLE 6.2 Strategies for Editing

Clarity	When your words, images, sounds, movements, spatial cues, transitions, etc., are clear and easy to understand.
Coherence	When your words, images, sounds, movements, spatial cues, transitions, etc., help your audience understand your text as a logical whole, that there are no unconnected ideas.
Unity	When your words, images, sounds, movements, spatial cues, transitions, etc., focus on main ideas to form strong units within your text, i.e., a paragraph with one main focus, a scene with one main focus, and an image with one clear focal point.
Flow	When you use elements that act as transitions and signposts to help your audience move smoothly through your text.
Consistency	When you use words, images, sounds, movements, spatial cues, transitions, etc., in the same or similar ways throughout a text in order to create a unified text whereby patterns help audiences move through the text smoothly.

While there are certainly more, these five criteria can serve as a starting point for thinking critically about editing your work. As an example of how these can apply to different kinds of texts, let's look at the last one: consistency. A consistent repetition of color, size, alignment, and placement of images within a text such as a flyer can help you unify all aspects of your design. As another example, websites contain a number of visual elements. Making sure you consistently place the same elements (such as links, images, headings, and colors) on all your website's pages can help readers move through your website smoothly and quickly. That's because consistency can help you establish a pattern that readers will recognize and use to read your text. And, they will be able to anticipate how to navigate each new page within your website when they visit. The more differences, the less consistency, and the more time it will take your audience to understand what they are looking at.

Editing a Text Based on Words

When working with texts that rely heavily on words, there are some additional strategies you might consider. Today, there are a number of tools that can help you analyze your writing in order to edit it. Free online editing tools, for example, can help you analyze your writing style, identify such things as repetition, word choice, sentence structure, and pointing out areas where you may need to improve your writing. Using natural language processing (this happens when a computer understands human language), such tools can also help you locate writing errors. For instance, After the Deadline is a free open-sourced software you can download from its website, editMinion and Hemmingway App are free web-based editing tools you can use online, while Grammarly is an extension tool editor you can add to your browser. All of these can analyze your writing. As an example, the first two paragraphs of this chapter were copied and pasted into the Grammarly tool. Grammarly then analyzed the text, and its findings appear in Table 6.3.

TABLE 6.3 Grammarly Findings

Performance			
The text scores better than 84% of all text checked by Grammarly where comparable goals were set.			
Word Count			
Characters	1,200	Reading time	50 sec
Words	210	Speaking time	1 min 36 sec
Sentences	8		
Readability			
Word length	4.6	Average	
Sentence length	26.3	Above Average	

Grammarly gives you the option to download a longer report that includes a list of writing issues as well as the percentages of unique and rare words you use in your text. If you were trying to strengthen your writing, you could use such analysis to determine your weaknesses and what actions you could take in order to make it stronger. Other tools, such as concordance tools like AntCon and WordSmith, go a bit further in their analyses, letting you see word frequencies, patterns in your writing, connections between words, and the location of the words used.

Discussion Questions: Editing Tools
1. Do you think editing tools can make writers better at writing? If so, why? If not, why not?
2. Why should you use editing tools?
3. Why shouldn't you use editing tools?
4. What implications do such editing tools have on the kinds of writing that are valued by our society?

If you don't have access to such tools, there are some things you can do on your own to ensure that you have a clear, coherent, and unified text. Try the following suggestions when it is appropriate given your audience and purpose for writing.

Suggestion 1: Let It Go

A phrase like this is apropos for writing concisely in Western cultures that prefer communication to be direct. Let go of all your unnecessary words, sentences, and paragraphs if they contribute nothing to your text. Paying attention to your efficiency in words can help your readers move through your texts quickly and effectively. Time is not on a writer's side. Readers don't want to waste time reading unnecessary words in order to figure out what exactly you mean. They want to get to the point as soon as possible. That said, being concise doesn't necessarily mean all your sentences have to be short sentences. Varying the length of your sentences makes your writing interesting to read. So, you will need to have long sentences sometimes as long as they utilize words efficiently. Think of concision as a means of making sure that each of your words matter to a sentence's point no matter the length of it.

Suggestion 2: To Be or Not to Be? That Is the Question

In writing, it is not to be (at least not often). Look closely at your verb usage. When writing concisely, rethink your unnecessary uses of "be" verbs (am, is, are, were, was, be, being, been) and determine if you can get your point across without using them. This may mean that you must rework sentences in order to use stronger verbs instead. Most often you can accomplish this task if you use active voice rather than passive voice. With active voice, the subject of the sentence performs the action (e.g. Tahir kicked the ball). In passive voice, the subject receives or gets acted upon (e.g. The ball was kicked by Tahir). Passive voice sentences tend to "be" longer and contain unnecessary words like "be" verbs. Perform a word search in your document to highlight your uses of "be" verbs. See if you can then replace some of these with stronger verbs so that you rely less on "be" verbs in your writing.

Suggestion 3: Here a Comma, There a Comma, Everywhere a Comma

Bad writers tend to put either too many commas in their writing or not enough without really thinking about the purpose of a comma. Knowing where commas go and why should be a priority when editing (and especially when proofreading). A court battle can demonstrate why this is so. In 2017, a group of dairy drivers in the state of Maine filed a lawsuit for overtime pay that stated their company owed them money for particular work they had done. The court reviewing the case sided with the dairy drivers because of the lack of an Oxford comma in the wording of the law. An Oxford comma is a comma used before the words "and" or "or" in a list of three or more items in a sentence. The law lists the work that does not merit overtime pay in this way: "The canning, processing, preserving, freezing, drying, marketing, storing, packing for shipment or distribution of: 1) Agricultural produce; 2) Meat and fish products; and 3) Perishable foods" (qtd. in Willingham). What was at issue here was the lack of an Oxford comma after the word "shipment." Because of a lack of a comma there, the sentence is ambiguous. The law could mean the "packing for shipment or distribution" does not merit pay. But, that doesn't mean drivers shouldn't get paid for distribution itself. Since it was ambiguous, the court sided with the drivers.

Bottom line: learn how to use a comma so your writing isn't rendered ambiguous and hard to read. A number of free online writing resources can help you learn how to use a comma, such as the Purdue OWL.

Activity: Editing Log

Over the course of a semester, keep track of your editing habits by making a list of the changes you make to your drafts. Also, keep track of the technologies you use to make such changes. For example, you might use Track Changes in Microsoft Word or the information you gather from Grammarly reports. At the end of the semester, go through all your saved files, drafts, lists, and notes to find any patterns in your editing process. Write a reflection on your findings, and as you write, think about your answers to the following questions:

1. What kinds of edits did you make, and did you find yourself making the same kinds of edits over and over again?
2. If so, what does this mean? If not, what does this mean?

3. Do you think your use of certain technologies influenced the ways in which you edited your texts? If so, why and how? If not, why not?
4. Moving forward, how will you use the data of your editing habits to write and edit in the future?

Editing a Text Based on Visuals

In Chapter 16, you will learn about composing images, such as photographs. That chapter can certainly serve as a reference point when editing your images. In that chapter, you will consider such things as focal points. When working with texts that rely heavily on visuals, however, there are some additional strategies you might consider. Just as in editing texts based on words, there are a number of tools that can help you edit images, from Photoshop to GIMP to phone apps. There are also a number of free online videos that can make learning how to use these tools easy. As you work with these tools, think about how you can ensure your visuals are clear, coherent, and unified. Consider the following suggestions.

Suggestion 1: Quality Matters

You should make sure when using visuals that they are clear rather than blurry. This is easier said than done because sometimes what looks good on a computer screen doesn't look so good when printed. In editing, you may need to resize your images, making them larger or smaller, or you may need to use a certain type of image. In doing so, the quality of the image, and therefore its clarity, could be compromised each time you make changes. Use tools that maintain the quality of the image so that it appears clear to your audience, whether on a screen or on a printed text. A rule of thumb is to make sure your resolution is 300 dpi for images that will be printed.

Suggestion 2: Think Direction

Tools such as Photoshop and GIMP give you the ability to flip and rotate images as well as move them from one area to another on a text. When you create your visuals, think about whether or not you want to guide your audience to move through those visuals in a certain way, or if you would rather have your audience make their own path. Look for elements within your visuals that will help or hinder your audience from moving smoothly through your visuals. Add in elements that will help with direction and remove those that don't.

Suggestion 3: Think Distance

Spatial distances should be considered when editing. Too much or too little space between elements can also render a visual confusing or misleading. Remember in Chapter 5, you learned about proximity and how things that are close together are seen as relating to one another. Determine whether or not your use of space creates appropriate relationships between elements. You should not mislead your audience into thinking there is a relationship between elements when there shouldn't be. A good use of space can provide balance in your visuals, especially when you use equal amounts of it. Too much negative space might mean your text looks unfinished, but not enough negative space may make it appear too crowded.

Editing a Text Based on Sounds

While in Chapter 15 you will learn about creating sounds in different ways, there are some additional things to consider when using editing programs (like Audacity) to edit your sound files.

Suggestion 1: Quality Matters

When student Ty Daily created a podcast about his fellow students and their music preferences, he interviewed one of his university's DJs at the radio station on campus. When Ty listened to his recording of the interview afterward, he noticed a few background noises that made hearing what the DJ had to say difficult. In fact, he couldn't clearly hear the DJ talk about his music preferences, important points for Ty's podcast. During the editing stage, Ty was able to edit out the background sounds and increase the sound of the DJ's words so that listeners would be able to hear him. As you edit sounds, listen carefully to the quality of those sounds, making sure that your listeners will be able to hear them clearly.

Suggestion 2: Think Distance

Temporal distances should also be considered when editing. Too much time or too little time between elements can render a sound recording confusing or misleading. As mentioned in the previous section on editing based on visuals, remember Chapter 5 when you think about distance. In that chapter, you learned about proximity and how things that are close together are seen or heard as relating to one another. Determine whether or not your use of time creates appropriate relationships between sounds or not. You should not mislead your audience into thinking there is a relationship between sounds when there shouldn't be. A good use of time can provide balance in your recordings, especially when you use equal amounts of it appropriately. Too much silence might mean your text sounds unfinished or lacking, but not enough silence may provide too much information at once.

Suggestion 3: Be Careful With Special Effects

When you want to add special emphasis, make an impact, or create a certain mood within your sound recording, using special effects during the editing process can help. Special effects can include such things as shortening or lengthening sounds, adding in noises, music, reverberation, echoes, and so forth. However, you should consider the consequences of adding in special effects by testing them out and getting feedback on them. When Al-ex Huck, a singer/songwriter you will read about later, added in reverberation into a song he was working on, a peer advised against it, saying that most radio songs don't utilize such an effect. Al-ex admitted that he had just added in the reverberation without really having a good reason for doing so. Ultimately, he took his peer's advice and removed it as he was editing the final cut.

Editing a Text Based on Videos

Video editing can be a time-consuming process. However, the more practice you get in it, the better you will become in making successful videos that reach your intended audiences. Throughout this book, you will consider several strategies for creating and editing videos. For now, here are three suggestions that you can add to your to-do list when editing videos:

Suggestion 1: Think Purposefully

When Josh Arnold created a video project about his community's nature park, he thought shooting his video at the nature park would be a good idea. However, in one scene where he captures a serene landscape—one featuring ducks swimming on a pristine lake—a man on a lawn mower comes into view in the background towards the end of the shot. Because Josh wanted the scene to be one of serenity, he determined that he would need to trim or shorten the length of the scene in order to cut out the last part, which included the man on the lawn mower. During the editing phase of a video, you may find that you have to do more than just trim like Josh did. You may need to cut out scenes altogether if they work against your purpose for creating the video in the first place.

Suggestion 2: Utilize Transitions

Using transitions like fade-ins and fade-outs, or the lack thereof, can help you achieve certain effects in a video. During the editing phase, you can put your creativity to work, finding unique ways to help your audience move from one scene to the next. Just don't go overboard. You should think purposively in deciding which transitions to use and how to use them given your audience and your purposes for creating your video in the first place. You might, for example, think about how consistency and repetition can help you use transitions in a way that will help viewers anticipate what will come next or will help ease them into a new scene or section of the video.

Suggestion 3: Think About Your Audience

Along the lines of thinking about your audience in terms of transitioning between scenes in your video, you should also work to make your video accessible to as many people in your audience as possible. Consider adding in titles, headings, and closed captioning as well as providing a transcript to your audience members. When you do this, you will need to make sure that your editing techniques aid and not take away from the clarity of information your video presents and that your editing techniques ensure access to as many in your audience as possible.

Final Thoughts

No matter what you do to edit, you should think about whether or not your editing is done in an ethical way. Purposely editing your work in order to mislead your audience, especially into believing something that is not true, could prove dangerous. Editing is a necessary step in the writing process. It helps your audiences make sense of what you have to say, but manipulating others through your editing work is unethical. While the suggestions in this chapter can serve as a starting point, they shouldn't be seen as an ending point. Seek out other means for editing your work to expand and practice your skills.

Additional Discussion Questions

1. When and why should you seek feedback from others on your writing?
2. How can technology help or hinder your ability to revise and edit your writing?
3. Should we rely on natural language processing to help us edit? Why or why not?
4. Imagine the future of writing. In what ways do you think technology will shape our ability to write, revise, and edit texts 100 years from now?

Additional Activities

1. Writing Tools: Investigate a number of writing tools that can help analyze your writing. Test them out, compare your findings from each tool, and present your findings to the class.
2. Revising and Editing: Compare the processes for revising and editing a print text with that of the processes for revising and editing a video. How are they different, and how are they similar? Write a reflection and share it with the class.

Additional Assignments

1. Interview a Writer: Interview a writer to find out about his or her techniques for revising and editing. Consider the processes and technologies they use to revise and edit. Present your findings to the class in a presentation.
2. Flex Text: You are tasked with creating a website, an app, and a brochure to help educate the public about a local business. Develop content for a flex text you can use for these texts using your knowledge of a local business. Then, write a reflection that talks about your decisions for including what you did in your flex text.

Works Cited

Willingham, A. J. "An Oxford Comma Changed This Court Case Completely." *CNN*, 16 March 2017, www.cnn.com/2017/03/15/health/oxford-comma-maine-court-case-trnd/index.html. Accessed 11 July 2018.

Handwriting Is History

Writing words by hand is a technology that's just too slow for our times, and our minds.

Anne Trubek

This article was first published by *Pacific Standard* on their website on December 17, 2009. *Pacific Standard* has granted permission to reprint this article in this book.

At 11 p.m. on Dec. 27, I checked my inbox out of habit. I had 581 new e-mails. All had been sent between 8 and 11 p.m. The days between Christmas and New Year's are not usually a busy time for e-mailing. What was going on?

It turns out that the home page for MSN.com had linked to a short article I had published a year earlier. In the article, I argue that we should stop teaching cursive in primary schools and provide some background on the history of handwriting to back up my claims.

The comments on my piece were hostile, insulting and vehemently opposed to my argument. The onslaught continued for a few more days: Some 2,000 comments were submitted, and editors took down about 700 of the worst. If you check this article online today, you will find more than 1,300 comments. For some reason, people are very invested in handwriting.

If we define writing as a system of marks to record information (and discount petroglyphs, say), handwriting has been around for just 6,000 of humanity's some 200,000 years. Its effects have been enormous, of course: It alters the brain, changes with civilizations, cultures and factions, and plays a role in religious and political battles. Throughout the even smaller slice of time that is American history, handwriting has reflected national aspirations. The comments posted on my article about handwriting were teeming with moralism. ("I'm sorry, but when I see messy handwriting it tells me something about the person; maybe carelessness? Impatience? . . . Penmanship is everything. . . . Good penmanship shows the world we are civilized.") One might consider handwriting as a technology—a way to make letters—and conclude that the way of making them is of little moment. But handwriting is bound up with a host of associations and connotations that propel it beyond simply a fine-motor skill. We connect it to personal identity (handwriting signals something unique about each of us), intelligence (good handwriting reflects good thinking) and virtue (a civilized culture requires handwriting).

Technology Is Active

Most of us know, but often forget, that handwriting is not natural. We are not born to do it. There is no genetic basis for writing. Writing is not like seeing or talking, which are innate. Writing must be taught.

About 6,000 years ago, the Sumerians created the first schools, called tablet houses, to teach writing. They trained children in Sumerian cuneiform by having them copy the symbols on one half of a soft clay tablet onto the other half, using a stylus. When children did this—and when the Sumerians invented a system of representation, a way to make one thing symbolize another—their brains changed. In *Proust and the Squid: The Story and Science of the Reading Brain*, Maryanne Wolf explains the neurological developments writing wrought: "The brain became a beehive of activity. A network of processes went to work: The visual and visual association areas responded to visual patterns (or representations); frontal, temporal, and parietal areas provided information about the smallest sounds in words . . . ; and finally areas in the temporal and parietal lobes processed meaning, function and connections."

The Sumerians did not have an alphabet—nor did the Egyptians, who may have gotten to writing earlier. Which alphabet came first is debated; many consider it to be the Greek version, a system based upon Phoenician. Alphabets created even more neural pathways, allowing us to think in new ways (neither better nor worse than non-alphabetic systems, like Chinese, yet different nonetheless).

When we think of handwriting, we often assume a script, a regularized way to make letters, to which all writers adhere in order to aid communication. A famous early script is Roman square capital, which looks exactly as you imagine it: monumental u's in the shape of our modern v's and no spacing between words. It was written with a stylus and chiseled onto the sides of buildings.

Proclaiming the virtuousness of one way of forming a "j" over others is a trope that occurs throughout handwriting's history. For instance, early Christians jettisoned Roman scripts they deemed decadent and pagan. In their scriptoria, monks developed Uncial to replace Roman scripts. An internecine battle ensued when Irish monks developed a variation on Uncial that traditionalists deemed an upstart, quasi-heretical script.

Puritans in England and America also developed a script to distance themselves from the seeming Catholicism of the elaborate scripts popular in the 18th century. They adopted the plainer copperplate, or round hand. The Declaration of Independence is written in copperplate.

In the American colonies, a "good hand" became a sign of class and intelligence as well as moral righteousness. Benjamin Franklin was a proponent of proper handwriting, and when he founded the Academy of Philadelphia (which became the University of Pennsylvania), those seeking entrance were required to "write a legible hand." But very few Americans were eligible to enter Franklin's academy. First, to do so, you had to be male. Second, you had to have been taught to write; many women and non-wealthy men were taught to read, but not write. Only wealthy men and businessmen learned to write. Even when public schooling began, writing was not always included in the curriculum, so many colonists could read but not write. It was not until the beginning of the 19th century—a scant 200 years ago—that schooling became universal. Then, handwriting was finally taught to American schoolchildren.

For many, the prospect of handwriting dying out would signal the end of individualism and the entree to some robotic techno-future. (As one comment on my article put it, "What's next, putting programming chips in our brains?") But when we worry about losing our individuality, we are likely misremembering our schooling, which included rote, rigid lessons in handwriting. We have long been taught the "right" way to form letters. The history of American penmanship is dominated by two true believers, Platt Rogers Spencer and A.N. Palmer, whose fiercely moral and economic attachments to their scripts nicely sum up much of what we consider essential to American identity.

Spencer, "the father of American handwriting," was a fanatic who was obsessed with script even as a child. He made it big when he established a chain of business schools—the slogan was "Education For Real Life"—to teach his script, Spencerian, which he based on natural forms: leaves, trees, etc. Spencerian was the standard script taught from the 1860s to the 1920s. This transcendentalist move toward a script that better followed the human body's movements is belied by his insistence on rigor and standardization. He advised his students to practice six to 12 hours a day. Mastering his script would, Spencer believed, make someone refined, genteel, upstanding.

Later in the 19th century, Palmer invented a script that would better suit the industrial age. The Palmer Method stresses a "plain and rapid style." He rejected the slightly fey Spencerian for a muscular, rugged script better suited to a commercial culture. By 1912, Palmer was a household word, and a million copies of his (printed) writing manuals had sold. Educators taught his method, and millions of Americans were "Palmerized."

The Palmer Method was gradually supplanted when educators decided to teach children manuscript (or printing) first, and cursive later, to get them started writing younger. Handwriting enthusiasts consider the end of the Palmer Method to be the end of good handwriting in America.

It took the printing press to create a notion of handwriting as a sign of self. For monks, whose illuminated manuscripts we now venerate as beautiful works of art (as they most certainly are), script was not self-expressive but formulaic, and rightly so. When the printing press was invented, the monks were worried about this new capricious technology, which was too liable to foibles and the idiosyncratic mark of the man helming the press. A hand-copied manuscript was for them then the authoritative, exact, regularized text. In his treatise, "In Praise of Copying," the 15th-century monk Trithemius argued that "printed books will never be the equivalent of handwritten codices, especially since printed books are often deficient in spelling and appearance."

Handwriting slowly became a form of self-expression when it ceased to be the primary mode of written communication. When a new writing technology develops, we tend to romanticize the older one. The supplanted technology is vaunted as more authentic because it is no longer ubiquitous or official. Thus for monks, print was capricious and script reliable. So too today: Conventional wisdom holds that computers are devoid of emotion and personality, and handwriting is the province of intimacy, originality and authenticity.

This transition, and the associations we make with old and new technologies, played out while millions of Americans were being Palmerized in school, and the Palmer Method is inextricably linked to a new writing technology that was starting to compete with handwriting: the typewriter.

In post-Civil War America, the Remington Arms Company needed a new product to boost sales (rifles were moving more slowly). The company unveiled the first typewriter in 1874. It was heavy and loud and looked like a big metal sewing machine, as it was set on a table with a treadle at the bottom. The machine was cumbersome, the noise it made cacophonous. Worse, you had to write blind: the keys hit the underside of the paper. It did not sell. Businesses wouldn't accept documents written on it because they were not penned. Remington sold only a few of that first model, but Mark Twain bought one. In his autobiography, he claimed to be the "first person in the world to apply the type-machine to literature" when he submitted a typed manuscript of *The Adventures of Tom Sawyer* to his publisher.

Twain hated blind typing, though, and he gave his Remington away to his friend William Dean Howells, the eminent Atlantic editor and novelist. Howells returned it, uninterested, six months later. But as with personal computers and cell phones, early adopters of a good technology will eventually persuade the rest of us we need it, too. In the 1890s, the typewriter gained a carriage return, and the new models allowed you to see the page while typing. By 1905, it was a curiosity *not* to own a typewriter.

That first Remington introduced the QWERTY keyboard, which separates common letter pairs to prevent bars from sticking when struck sequentially. Although others have developed more efficient, user-friendly and ergonomic keyboards, none has caught on. We seem stubbornly wed to QWERTY, as our thirst for the new new thing accompanies a stubborn grip on the familiar.

When Kitty Burns Florey's *Script and Scribble: The Rise and Fall Of Handwriting*, a nostalgic look at handwriting's history and call to revive it in schools, came out early in 2009, the reviews tended to follow a pattern: The reviewer begins by admitting he or she never handwrites anymore, but thinks that is a shame. He or she goes on to laud Florey's book and ends by promising to do more handwriting in the future. Michael Dirda writes, "After reading *Script and Scribble*, I feel like digging out my beat-up calligraphy manuals. . . . Of course, I also need to clean out the dried ink from my italic pen. But before you know it, even Ludovico Arrighi—the great Renaissance master of italic—will be envying my p's and q's." Florey wrote her own version of this genre in an article on the writing of her book. She tells how she always writes on the computer, never longhand: "My last eight books are children of Microsoft Word, and virtually everything I write, from a long book to a short e-mail, is done on the computer." While researching the book, she learned how to do italic script, and became enamored of it. She ends her piece by advising all of us to do more handwriting: "I suggest you set aside half an hour, grab a piece of paper and a pen, and, in your best script (be it Italic, Palmer, or a cleaned-up version of your usual scrawl), write a poem, start a diary, send a note to a friend, or . . . compose a love letter."

I doubt whether the critics or Florey have followed up on their pledges to handwrite more. Nevertheless, people seem to think that school kids should be spending more time honing their mastery of the capital G. A 2007 U.S. Department of Education study found that 90 percent of teachers spend 10 minutes a day on handwriting. Zaner-Bloser, the most popular handwriting curriculum used today, deems that too little and is encouraging schools to up that amount to at least 15 minutes a day.

But typing in school has a democratizing effect, as did the typewriter. It levels the look of prose to allow expression of ideas, not the rendering of letters, to take center stage. Florey is aware of this but does not take the time to unpack the assumptions contained in her reason why we should continue to teach handwriting: "Children are judged by their handwriting; if they produce indecipherable chicken-scratching, a teacher will not be sympathetic." Florey mentions that when she was asked to judge handwritten applications for writing positions, she was "drawn to those with legible handwriting and prejudiced against the scrawlers."

Does having good handwriting signal intelligence? No, not any more than it reveals one's religiosity. But many teachers make this correlation: It is called the "handwriting effect." Steve Graham, a professor at Vanderbilt University who studies handwriting acquisition, says that "teachers form judgments, positive or negative, about the literary merit of text based on its overall legibility." Graham's studies show that "[w]hen teachers rate multiple versions of the same paper differing only in terms of legibility, they assign higher grades to neatly written versions of the paper than the same versions with poorer penmanship." This is particularly problematic for boys, whose fine-motor skills develop later than do girls. Yet all children are taught at the same time—usually printing in first grade and cursive in third. If you don't have cursive down by the end of third grade, you may never become proficient at it.

While we once judged handwriting as religiously tinted, now secular, we transpose our prejudices to intelligence. The new SAT Writing Exam, instituted in 2006, requires test takers to write their essays in No. 2 pencil. Not only will those with messy handwriting be graded lower than ones written more legibly, but those who write in cursive—15 percent of test takers in 2006—received higher scores than those who printed.

As of 2002, public schools had one computer for every four students, and since then, the number has risen. Despite talk of the digital divide, most high school students, even in low-income schools, are required to type and print out their essays, and they are able to find the means to do so. So assuming access, a standard font and printer paper, typing levels the playing field. Is this egalitarianism not a key value that, like the alphabet, goes all the way back to the Greeks?

When my son was in second grade, he had to stay in for recess almost every day because he could not properly form his letters. I was called in for "interventions," warned that he would fail the Ohio Proficiency Tests if scanners could not read his test answers. (No Child Left Behind leaves teachers with less time to teach handwriting and fewer means to teach it, yet more tests students must take to prove they have mastered it.) For Simon, homework was always stressful. He would stare at a blank page for an hour. Then he would write one word and then stop; write a few letters and then stop. Soon, he began to fear taking up a pencil at all, and we had nightly battles over his language arts worksheets. Then he began to worry about not having anything to say, not knowing how to say it, or he would come up with ideas that he would not write down because they would take too long and thus write nothing. Perennially being told his handwriting was bad transmuted in his mind into proof that he was a bad writer—a poor student incapable of expressing ideas. He simply hated the physical process of writing. And since handwriting dominated his education in grades 1, 2 and 3, he hated school, too.

I transferred him to a private school where he was allowed to dictate his writing assignments. For his fourth-grade assignments, I sat at the computer, my laptop on the dining room table, as he paced the dining room, wildly gesticulating, sometimes stopping to put his hand on his chin in thought, but mainly speaking without stopping. I am a fast typist, but I could not keep up; I had to break his train of words. He spoke aloud in full clauses and paragraphs. What would have taken him about three or four hours (I am not exaggerating) by hand took him about four minutes by mouth.

The moral of this story is not that typing is superior to handwriting, that parents should have to transcribe the stories of their offspring or that private schools are superior to public ones. The moral of the story is that what we want from writing—what Simon wants and what the Sumerians wanted—is cognitive automaticity, the ability to think as fast as possible, freed as much as can be from the strictures of whichever technology we must use to record our thoughts. As Wolf writes: "A system that can become streamlined through specialization and automaticity has more time to think. This is the miraculous gift of the reading brain." This is what Palmer wanted for his students—speed. This is what the typewriter promised Twain. This is what typing does for millions. It allows us to go faster, not because we want everything faster in our hyped-up age, but for the opposite reason: We want more time to think.

This is how Simon describes why he hates to handwrite: "I have it all in my memory bank, and then I stop, and my memory bank gets wiped out."

Whatever we use to write, there will be a shortfall between conception and execution, between the ideas in our heads and the words we produce. We often insert nostalgia into this gap. Today, writing a novel with a BIC pen and a legal pad is considered as sweetly funny as William Dean Howells composing his first short story in a compositor's stick, upside down and backwards (his father was a printer) or Gay Talese's habit of writing on shirt boards (those cardboard panels they put in your shirts at the dry cleaners). Toni Morrison, Jim Harrison, John Updike and others write (or, unfortunately, have written) by hand.

We also make up stories to romanticize the mundane. The Sumerians used writing for accounting—they developed tokens to count sheep. But the Sumerians made up a better story for the invention of writing: "A messenger from the lord of Kulab arrived at a distant kingdom, too exhausted to deliver an important oral message. So as not to be frustrated by mortal failings, the lord of Kulab had also 'patted some clay and set down the words as on a tablet . . . and verily it was so.'" (As Wolf points out, this tale "sidestep[s] the awkward matter of who was able to read the lord of Kulab's words.")

Handwriting does have a presence that can be absent in typed prose, I admit. I have a binder of notes my grandmother wrote shortly before she died. She scrawled her life story in thick black felt-tip on the backs of envelopes. I have been slowly typing up her notes to preserve them for the family, and as I squint to make out words, I sense the felt experience of her hand on paper. And I will admit that when I find a smooth expanse of sand or a bark-less tree trunk, I long to scratch my name in them.

I have no desire to lose the art of handwriting, to lose the knowledge retained in archives or to take pencils away from those who seek to wield them: Matthew McKinnon, a freelance writer, re-taught himself cursive at the age of 30 because he had forgotten it, found it useful for his work and wanted to "shake the cobwebs" out of the area of his brain it activates. Kitty Burns Florey is starting a "slow writing" movement, mimicking the slow food movement, to revive the art of handwriting. Each year, the Spencer Society holds a weeklong "saga" where you can learn to master Spencerian script. Handwriting has always been both a way to express thoughts and an art, and preserving the artistic aspects, be it through calligraphy or mastering comic book lettering, is worthy. In schools, we might transition to teaching handwriting as we do other arts, specifically as a fine-motor skill and encourage calligraphers as we should letter press printers or stained glass window makers. These arts have a life beyond nostalgia.

When people hear I am writing about the possible end of handwriting, many come up with examples of things we will always need handwriting for: endorsing checks (no longer needed at an ATM), grocery lists (smartphones have note-taking functions), signatures (not even needed to file taxes anymore). These will not be what we would lose. We may, however, forsake some neurological memory. I imagine some pathways in our brains will atrophy. Then again, I imagine my brain is developing new cognitive pathways each time I hit control C or double click Firefox. That I can touch-type, my fingers magically dancing on my keyboard, free of any conscious effort (much as you are looking at letters and making meaning in your head right now as you read), amazes me. Touch-typing is a glorious example of cognitive automaticity, the speed of execution keeping pace with the speed of cognition.

Do not worry. It will take a long time for handwriting to die, for us to have the interview with the "last handwriter" as we do today with the last living speakers of some languages. By 1600 B.C., all Sumerian speakers had died, but the writing system that replaced Sumerian, Akkadian, kept aspects of Sumerian alive. It would take another 1,000 years—until 600 B.C.—for Sumerian writing to disappear completely. Even the revolutionary Greeks took a long time to change habits. After they created the Greek alphabet, they spent 400 years doing nothing with it, preferring their extant oral culture. Handwriting is not going anywhere soon. But it is going.

Reading Questions for "Handwriting Is History" by Anne Trubek

1. What stories can we learn from the history of handwriting as presented in this reading?
2. Why did handwriting become a form of self-expression?
3. What is the handwriting effect, and how does typing level the playing field?
4. What is cognitive automaticity and how is it related to writing?
5. Do you think handwriting will ever become history? Why or why not?

PART 3

Technology Is Narrative

Narrative, as an adjective, means relating to the process of storytelling. In noun form, a narrative refers to the actions we take when telling a story. That is, it refers to the choices about what and how we communicate when communicating our version of a story.

People write narratives and thus versions of stories all the time. In fact, no matter what kind of writing you do, you are, in a sense, telling a version of a story to an audience. If a friend were to write a text message to you, such as "Hey, how's it going? Want 2 hang out l8tr?" you would understand such writing by piecing together a version of a story based on the information you gather and the information you must seek: right now, your friend just took a moment from her present situation to find out how you are doing. She also wants to know what you have in store for later in the day and whether or not that could include her. So, you start to think about your day, what plans you have, and whether or not you can see those plans including your friend. In so doing, you are creating a version of a story, one that has actors and actions, a beginning, middle, and end.

Technologies also tell stories. They tell the stories of people and how people solve problems. To use a technology is to solve a problem, and to solve a problem, one must think of the problem as a story and how that story can work out. In Part 3, then, you will think carefully about the relationships between writing, story, information, and technology so as to better position yourself to make the best rhetorical decisions possible when communicating your ideas.

Key Questions _____

1. What stories do we tell with technology?
2. What stories do technologies tell about us?
3. What do we learn from these stories?
4. How do technologies shape, share, and organize information?

Technology Is Narrative

Key Terms

Chapter 7

1. storytelling
2. story
3. assonance
4. computer forensics
5. viral

Chapter 8

1. internet
2. web
3. World Wide Web Consortium (W3C)
4. World Wide Web Foundation
5. personalized web
6. confirmation bias
7. wiki
8. crowdsourcing
9. organization

CHAPTER 7

The Stories We Write

Contents

What Technologies Tell Us 148
Stories Matter to Our Communities, Our Culture, and Our Heritage 151
The Many Ways We Write Stories 153
Online Storytelling 155
You Write Stories, Too 156
One Version of a Story 158
Protecting Stories 159
Final Thoughts 160

IMAGE 7.1 Ancient Egyptian calendar engraved on the stonewall of the Temple of Karnak, Luxor, Egypt. Sompol / Shutterstock

What Technologies Tell Us

By studying the calendar systems of ancient Egypt, Egyptologists are able to piece together stories of ancient civilizations. Uses of a lunar calendar (which is based on the phases of the moon) tell of a civilization that was reliant on agriculture. To ensure enough crops at harvest time, people needed to know when the Nile would flood, and that prediction was best made by learning and recording the lunar cycle. Another calendar in ancient times that was used for administrative purposes, the civil calendar, tells yet another story, a story of a people who worshiped many gods and participated in festival celebrations.

Today's societies are not much different from those of years past in terms of wanting and needing to tell and understand the passage of time. Today, we also utilize various calendars to remind us of and to record historical, cultural, political, financial, religious, educational, and weather events. There's the Hebrew calendar, the Gregorian calendar, the Chinese calendar, the Julian calendar, the Islamic calendar, and the Indian calendar, just to name a few of the more than 40 in use today. It is true that physically our calendars may be a bit different in some ways from those of ancient civilizations. Ancient Egyptian societies carved symbols into stone, like Image 7.1 demonstrates, while today, many societies rely on printed and digital calendars. Yet, some of the same principles that ancient civilizations used to create their calendars are similar to that which we use today. Many of the world's calendars are based on our study of the solar system and can be classified as lunar, solar, or lunisolar calendars.

Technologies, Like That of a Calendar, Tell the Stories of Their Creators and Users as Well as the Very Places They Inhabit

In fact, you could say that the history of a people is the story of its technologies. Even the way a technology was constructed can tell us a lot about a civilization. The calendars of ancient Egypt and their construction tell us about Egyptians' abilities to do calculations; show us what tools they might have used at that time to create the calendars on stone surfaces, what the geography was like; and how the landscape changed with different seasons of the year, as well as shed light on our understanding of the concept of time itself.

Today, we too have calendars that tell stories about our world, from showcasing our world's historic landmarks each month to capturing our world's sense of humor in cartoons each day. Meghan Pearson, graphic designer, artist, photographer, and owner of Yellow Pear Designs, has lots of experience designing texts, including calendars. Recently, she created a calendar that features wildlife in the United States. One look at Images 7.2 and 7.3 shows that her calendar looks a lot different compared to the calendars of ancient Egypt. Nonetheless, it still tells a story. In fact, 500 years from now, if someone were to find a copy of this calendar, they would be able to learn about the wildlife in the United States at this moment in time through the story that Meghan tells with her calendar.

As an environmentalist and wildlife enthusiast, Meghan hoped to show the beauty of wildlife and, in doing so, made some important design decisions, choosing certain colors, fonts, and photographs to best represent her story. Five hundred years from now, historians will see that her calendar tells the story of what Meghan's culture valued in terms of designing, presenting, and communicating information, what fonts were used, how they were used, and so on. It too will tell the story of how her community measures time by days and months.

IMAGE 7.2   Example page from Meghan's calendar

IMAGE 7.3   Another example from Meghan's calendar

INTERVIEW
MEGHAN PEARSON, GRAPHIC DESIGNER, ARTIST, PHOTOGRAPHER, OWNER OF YELLOW PEAR DESIGNS

Meghan creates a wide variety of texts for her clients including illustrations, logos, marketing materials, email blasts, brochures, and product and packaging artwork. In an interview, she explains what she does to create such texts.

Q: What technologies do you use on a regular basis?
A: In terms of low-budget technologies, I use pencils and paper to do sketches and get my ideas down. Then, when I am ready, I use Adobe Photoshop to edit photos and do digital paintings. I also use Adobe Illustrator and InDesign for page layouts and vector illustrations.

Q: How do you print your texts or deliver them to your clients once you are finished designing?
A: For small-scale projects, like brochures, rack cards, business cards, posters, and other marketing materials, I work with a local printer who prints my designs. For larger projects, such as those that deal with product design, I work with a studio in Miami, Florida, to print things like the boxes and point-of-purchase containers. Sometimes, I work with companies in Asia who manufacture things like bottles that my clients then use for their products.

Q: What advice would you give someone who wants to be a graphic designer?
A: Really mastering the software makes such a difference. It is not so important when working with a team per se, but it does change a lot, so having a basic understanding of software can help you tremendously. I have found a lot of success in being well versed in different styles. Some people have a specific look and make it work for them. But, having a specific look results in a specific clientele and sometimes work can be hard to get. If you can branch out into different styles, it is easier to get work. So, being open to different styles can make a difference. You also need to be open-minded and a people person so that you can work with all kinds of clients. You also need to enjoy what you are doing so that when it comes time to be creative, you don't have to force yourself.

Q: Why did you create your calendar?
A: This was more of a selfish project for me. I have really taken an affinity to photography, particularly nature photography. I kept taking photographs that I wanted to share with others. So, I thought about the different materials I could use to do this and to also tell people about the animals and places that I captured in the photographs. My hope is to get people interested in conservation efforts and to enjoy the beauty of nature through the calendar.

Q: How did you create your calendar?
A: I choose a clean layout and a font that was similar to my own handwriting to match the logo for my company which is on the front of the calendar so that I could carry out that design element throughout the calendar. I tried to pick photographs for months that were reminiscent of the weather during those months, that would have animals moving around those months, that had particular colors that set the mood and tone for

those months. In selecting my photographs, I looked at which ones would give me a nice variety, which ones would work well together.

Q: What technologies did you use to create your calendar?
A: I used Adobe Lightroom to edit the photographs. It is a digital darkroom for photograph development. So, you can edit them, lighten them, darken them, crop them, reduce noise, and smooth out details. Then, I exported them to use in Adobe InDesign, so I could make a multipage document.

Activity: Investigate Your Own Calendar

Write a reflection in which you consider the following:

a. What kind of calendar do you keep?
b. What modes does it utilize?
c. Why do you keep a calendar?

Investigate what story your calendar tells about you.

a. If someone who didn't know you examined your calendar, would they be able to piece together a story about you? If so, what would this story be? If not, why not?
b. Imagine that 500 years from now, a copy of your calendar is discovered by an archeologist. What would the archeologist learn about you, the people of your time, the technologies you might have used, and the places where you come from?

Share your findings and reflection with your classmates.

Stories Matter to Our Communities, Our Culture, and Our Heritage

Stories are just as old as humankind. We have been writing stories for centuries for a number of important reasons: to teach, to preserve history, to entertain, to share news, to improve civil life, to raise awareness, to heal, to maintain traditions, and to persuade. The ways in which humankind has written stories have been in large part influenced by technologies, and stories have taken on many forms, from books to baskets to jewelry to papyrus to calendars. Many of the surviving texts of ancient civilizations have been passed down from generation to generation or have been discovered by archeologists and archived as artifacts in museums around the globe so that historians, scholars, and virtually everyone can study and learn from them.

Technology Is Narrative

As you read in "Can We Define Technology?" in Part 1 of this book, when talking about technology, David E. Nye says that we cannot separate the stories that surround a technology from the actual technology itself. They are inseparable. Likewise, he writes, "Composing a narrative and using a tool are not identical processes, but they have affinities" (3). They both require action, that is, someone doing something.

Storytelling has played a crucial role in developing and preserving cultures throughout history. For example, the official book of Guatemala, *Popol Vuh* (translated as "the book of events"), an ancient text created by the Mayan people K'iche' of the 16th century, tells of Mesoamerican traditions and beliefs. The K'iche' created it to tell their stories, such as the story of the K'iche' people, a story of how the gods created humans and earth. The text has, throughout the years, been influential in religious and spiritual ceremonies but also has played a vital role in the fight to preserve indigenous culture and the land of the K'iche' people. While this is just one example, it shows why stories are important to us and our heritages. If you examine the culture you live in now, chances are you will see that it has a long history of writing stories in many ways.

On a basic level, a story is an account of an event, one that involves actors performing actions. Beyond this level, stories take on many forms, which is why historians and scholars of storytelling agree that stories are multimodal. A look back through history provides plenty of examples as to why. In China, during the Tang dynasty (618–907 CE), some folktales were told by story-singing, or what is known as Shuochang. A practice that combines singing and narration using a vernacular style of wording called Bianwen, Shuochang incorporates music and drawings to enhance what is story-sung.

Throughout more recent times, scholars in the field of writing who study modes of communication, like Glynda A. Hull and Mark Evan Nelson, have contended that in creating stories, people use multiple modes that demonstrate powerful meaning-making processes. In their study of an urban California neighborhood's center for digital storytelling, the scholars found that the use of multiple modes enabled participants to tell personal experiences in ways that authentically represent their cultures and lifestyles. Studying the work of one participant, Randy, the researchers concluded that his "Lyfe-N-Rhyme," a story that combined poetry, rap, and autobiography, revealed how modes work together to create meanings in powerful ways. Drawing on his own life as well as the lives of historical black figures, Randy's story represents the struggles many in a neighborhood like his face.

Hull and Nelson's findings are not surprising given the long history of multimodal composing in many cultures around the world and how those practices have evolved from one generation to the next. Writing scholars Gail E. Hawisher and Cynthia L. Selfe, along with many other writing scholars, argue that multimodal composition allows composers to use a "rich set of linguistic resources" and practices that traverse national, cultural, and linguistic borders, which are fully drawn upon through multimodal practices (66). The stories of your own culture most likely utilize those multimodal practices that are important to your culture, and those may (or may not) be similar to those found in other cultures.

Did You Know? Culture and Technologies

Many cultures use technology to write and pass down their stories from one generation to the next. Quilts, for instance, tell stories of Amish heritage. In an auto-ethnographic study investigating the multimodal practices of heritage literacy, in other words, "lifelong, cross-generational learning and meaning making" (575), scholar Suzanne Kesler Ramsey says that quilts "use multiple media and modes such as texture, movement, pattern, and color to make meaning" (583). Amish women are not the only ones who use quilts to tell stories, though. Artist, songwriter, poet, and sculptor Faith Ringgold uses paint, fabric, and storytelling to create works of art that are exhibited in museums around the world. At the Spencer Museum of Art in Lawrence, Kansas, she exhibited her *Flag Story Quilt*, a work inspired by stories of her great-great-grandmother, Betsy Bingham, and her great-grandmother, Susie Shannon, both slaves who sewed quilts for plantation owners. *Flag Story Quilt* weaves together a U.S. flag, tie-dyed fabric, and written text. According to the museum,

> The handwriting narrates the wrenching story of a quadriplegic Vietnam War veteran wrongly accused of the rape and murder of a white woman. The work plays on the political and textile characteristics of the flag and the tensions between the traditional quilt medium and contemporary violence and racism.
> (Spencer Museum of Art)

Creating such a quilt, then, enables Faith to draw on history to tell a story.

The Many Ways We Write Stories

Take a moment and think about your daily life. How many stories do you encounter on a daily basis? How many of those rely on technologies to convey meaning? Most likely, the people and technologies around you write stories in a number of ways. So, to get a better understanding of the many ways in which people and technologies write stories, let's take a look at some more examples that demonstrate the rhetorical thinking needed to be successful in storytelling.

Phoebe Robinson and Jessica Williams, also known as 2 Dope Queens, a black female comedy duo, tell stories through podcasting and live comedy shows. Based in New York City, both women see their work in storytelling as empowering marginalized voices and regularly invite female comedians, comedians of color, and LGBT comedians to be guests on their podcasts, and provide those comedians with a space where they can talk freely about topics such as race, politics, and sex. In an interview on *CBS This Morning*, the duo talked about how telling authentic and truthful stories enables their audiences to relate to their experiences (Kegu). Due to the success of their podcast and live shows and the impacts they made on people, in 2018, HBO aired a four-part special series featuring the comedy duo. The series consisted of taping live stage shows hosted by the duo and like their podcasts, featured a host of diverse guests. The stage for the shows was a rooftop setting situated in New York, and Robinson and Williams opened the show by telling stories about moving to New York. For their stories to work, the two comedians needed to think rhetorically. In their case, that meant developing a good sense of timing, cadence, and suspense in order to deliver punchlines. The duo was successful because they combined a multitude of modes to reach their audiences.

In a similar fashion, singers and songwriters tell stories too by developing necessary rhetorical skills and applying them when writing with technologies. Grammy winning Christian hip-hop artist Lacrae uses music to tell the stories of his life from overcoming drug and alcohol abuse to turning his life over to his faith in God. He raps in "Just Like You" on his album *Rehab*, for example, about his life growing up without his father, about having to look up to his uncles instead, and about having a son of his own. To understand his story, you are encouraged to go online and read the lyrics. Those are available online at genius.com, which also provides annotations of these lyrics. Think about Lacrae's choices of modes, about his language uses, about the nature of the song genre, and about how such a song represents a member of a particular society.

Check It Out YouTube: Listen and watch Lacrae perform his song on YouTube (posted by Reach Records). When sung, the words flow, keeping with the beats of the instruments. When the words work together with the music, the listener experiences meaning in a number of multimodal sensations felt throughout the body.

Blending poetic language, Lacrae uses words and syllables with rhythms and beats to tell his story through the technology that is music. If you were to analyze the lyrics, looking closely at his uses of language, lines, and verses, you would see he has used different styles of rhymes, such as assonance. Assonance happens when words don't have the same ending but share a vowel sound. For example, using words such as *bright*, *like*, and *diamond*, all use the same "i" sound in the song "Diamonds" by Rihanna. As a result, the words sound like they rhyme.

Discussion Questions: Stories

1. What stories do your communities write/tell, and how do they write/tell them?
2. What technologies do they rely on to write/tell these stories?
3. What are the purposes for writing/telling such stories?
4. How do the stories we write/tell in our communities and the stories that technologies write/tell in these communities impact people in other communities?

As mentioned earlier, the ways in which stories are told and shared have evolved over time, especially since ancient Egyptian times. Meghan used a variety of digital technologies—a camera, a computer, and Adobe, for instance—to create her photos and thus her calendar, while 2 Dope Queens told their stories via episodes as part of an HBO TV series, and Lacrae told his through music videos and MP3 files sold online through stores like iTunes. Texts like these and the technologies used to create them didn't exist during Ancient Egyptian times, and as a result, there are clearly some differences in the ways such texts came to be.

Online Storytelling

Today, many of our texts are digital and are shared online. The internet has indeed provided a place for virtually anyone to write their stories. Since 2003, for instance, StoryCorps, a nonprofit organization devoted to preserving and sharing the stories of people, relies on their online platform (along with other technologies) to do so. Through sound recordings, videos, animations, and languages, the organization features stories about people from all walks of life and backgrounds. Because stories can be shared online, virtually anyone can read and learn from them, which can leave lasting impacts on people.

> ### Discussion Questions: Online Storytelling
>
> 1. How and where are stories told online?
> 2. Who (and who doesn't) get to tell them? Why?
> 3. What are the impacts that online storytelling has on our world?
> 4. In what ways do technologies help or hinder the telling of stories online?
> 5. Is it possible to prevent technologies from telling stories?

The digital stories that do exist online have led to innovative techniques in a variety of fields. For instance, computer forensics, the study and practice of legally collecting and analyzing data from computers and social media, has been crucial in preventing and solving crime. Criminal investigators use technologies to understand the story of a crime and its aftermath by piecing together bits of digital data. As such, criminal investigators use a variety of sophisticated technologies to track down criminals, from scanning tweets in order to pinpoint the location of those criminals, to reading Facebook posts and profiles in order to understand the identities of those who break the law.

The tragic events that unfolded in 2013 during the Boston Marathon can serve as an example of how investigators are able to use a series of technologies to piece together the stories of an event itself and the suspects who committed the crime. Immediately after the bombing, crime scene analysts converged on the streets of Boston to read the situation, collect evidence, and do their best to assess what happened. At the same time, hundreds of law enforcement members and investigators began using computers to scroll through video surveillance, social media, and news footage in order to examine photos of people in the area, to learn information about when and where the bombing took place, and to enlist the public's help to identify the suspects and find them through social media. In fact, investigators had to sort through 120,000 still photos and nearly 13,000 video clips over and over again, reading faces and body language, until they were able to isolate images of the suspects and get a better understanding of the story (Kiger).

You Write Stories, Too

gerasimov_foto_174 / Shutterstock

No matter what career field you pursue, chances are you will write stories, some your own and some not. Marketers create stories about products that companies can sell. Scientists create graphs and charts to tell the story of their research. Restaurant owners tell their stories via their menus. Nonprofit leaders tell the stories of those in need through their websites. The technologies we use today, like those in the examples in this chapter, are not used just by the professionals in your future career field. You tell stories too, even right now as a student, and your stories are most likely digital.

To demonstrate, try doing the following:

First, get your computer and think about the story it tells about you. You could start with the type of computer you have. Not all computers are designed the same. What does the design of your computer say about you? Is it small? Large? Covered in stickers? Covered in dust? Covered in scratches? Is it a laptop? A desktop? Is it a Mac? A PC? Is it new? Is it old? Was it expensive? Or, budget friendly?

Second, think about what enabled you to obtain the computer. Why do you have that computer instead of another? Did you earn money to purchase it? Was it a gift? Is it a rental from the library? Why do you even have the computer to begin with?

Third, turn your computer on. What do you see? What does the screen tell you about yourself? Did you customize the screen? Did you save an image for your background? Do you have files? What are these? Why are they there? How are they arranged? What stories do they tell about you?

Fourth, open up a browser and look at your search history. What story does this search history say about you? What websites did you visit? Which ones did you save or favorite? If you type your name into the browser and click "search," what stories appear as a result? Are they stories others have written about you, or did you write them yourself? Who can see these? Why? Can you erase them?

Finally, check your social media feeds. Do your Instagram pics tell of a neatly curated life? Do they tell stories about your family? Your friends? Your social habits? Your job? Your religion? Your political beliefs?

By answering these questions, you must realize by now that with just one technology such as a computer, the stories you write and the ones written about you are the result of a number of factors.

Activity: Your Stories

Write a reflection in which you investigate the stories that one of your personal technologies writes about you over time. You can choose, for example, to examine an electronic or digital technology such as your phone, your computer, your iPod, and your social media. Or, you could choose a non-digital one, perhaps your favorite notebook, pen, or journal.

In this reflection, talk about what stories you (and others, if applicable) tell about yourself with this technology. Consider why this technology (with the help of you and possibly others) writes these stories about you in the ways it does. In other words, how do you create and engage your stories with this technology? If possible, how do other people create and engage your stories with this technology? Finally, talk about how this technology shapes the ways in which you write stories about yourself and other people over time.

Share your reflection with the class.

One Version of a Story

As you think about your own personal stories, think about the other stories you encounter on a daily basis and how those get told. Stories are told from the perspective of the teller who is embedded in a society. The teller picks and chooses what parts of a story get told given the teller's situation. The audience then can choose whether to approve or disapprove of the story told from this perspective. This is particularly evident in news stories. The ways in which reporters have told and presented news stories have evolved over time. Several factors can account for such changes, including the use of new technologies. Today, TV news programs use technologies in a variety of ways to film, edit, and present what is happening in this world, and they do so during a specific duration of time. For example, they may tell lots and lots of short stories within a half hour-to-hour TV news show. In fact, according to the PEW Research Center, the median length of a story is 41 seconds. While reporters interview people, research what happened, and speak with officials concerning an event (tasks that take a long time to accomplish), what ultimately gets included in those 41 seconds is the decision of the reporter and the other decision makers at the news program. Out of all the facts, the news program has to weigh what will best fit in 41 seconds, provide a story of interest, contain the best camera shots, generate the most interest and revenue, and so forth. Thus, those 41 seconds can provide only one version of a story.

The same can be said of online news. While online news stories take on many forms from Facebook posts to online magazine articles, and while they may contain audio, video, or paragraphs, they present only one version of a story, and that version has been crafted by a storyteller for a particular online publication.

Because we encounter stories through a multitude of technologies, we have to actively recognize that those stories have other versions. Likewise, not all technologies enable all people to tell their sides of a story. For instance, there are many people who are silenced as a result of not having access to particular technologies. Without access, they cannot write their stories. There are also political agendas that limit some voices from telling their stories, too. When you encounter a story, whether online, on TV, or in a book, how often do you think about the fact that what you are reading is just one version of a story? Do you ask yourself, who wrote this version, and what were their motives for doing so? While you will learn more about this later on in this book, as you write and read stories, you might want to consider what implications there are when you do not seek out other versions of a story and how those implications could limit your understanding of the world.

Activity: The Many Versions of an Event

In a group, pick one event that occurred in your community. Then, find out what stories different technologies tell about this one event. For instance, you could look at an online newspaper, a social media post, a TV program, and so forth, and find out how and what they say about this one event. As you do, ask yourself these questions:

a. How do these technologies help you investigate the event?
b. How do these technologies hinder your ability to investigate the event?
c. What stories does each of these technologies tell about the event?
d. What are the similarities between the stories?
e. What are the differences between the stories?
f. Finally, what might happen to someone's understanding of the event if they encounter only one story about it?

Create a report on your findings to share with your class.

Protecting Stories

Currently, digital technologies like social media give people a place to share their stories. They can do so with friends and family and with the public, if they so choose to. But, such technologies also enable people to share other people's stories, whether or not those other people want them to. The evolution of the smartphone is one reason why this can happen. Being able to easily use a smartphone on the move and on location, people are able to record events the second they happen and upload those records through social media immediately. Facebook Live, for instance, lets people even share video of an event as it is happening.

In 2014, when a photo of 16-year-old Alex Lee went viral, the teenager's life changed forever. A shopper at the Target in Texas where Alex worked snapped a photo of him bagging groceries on the job and uploaded it to the internet via Tumblr. A week later, a teenage girl in Britain found it on Tumblr and tweeted it with the caption "YOOOOOOOOOO." Soon the image went *viral* (in other words, it was shared over and over again), and teenage girls began showing up at the Target in Texas to snap more pictures of Alex.

After that, someone went on to create a meme with the photo, and Alex was soon referred to as "Alex from Target." He became so popular on Twitter that his followers went from 144 to 730,000 (Bilton). According to reports, 2.3 million people were following him on Instagram, and he was more popular than Justin Bieber in Google searches (Bilton). While the attention led him to appearances on TV, not all the attention was wanted or good. There were times when Alex was afraid to go out in public, especially after online posts made fun of his looks, made up stories about him being fired from Target, and even threatened his family. People even went so far as to find out private information about his family, like Social Security numbers, and shared those online. Alex's life changed dramatically because people told stories about him and shared them online with millions of other people.

Final Thoughts

Writing with all sorts of technologies, especially those that share stories with the public, has its consequences, both good and bad. In the case of Alex, the consequences were not so good. As a writer, you have to consider which technologies to write with but also who your writing will impact. Will it impact yourself, others, or both? If you fear that your writing will tell stories about yourself that you don't want shared with millions of people, perhaps you should consider whether or not writing your stories and making them public to begin with is a good idea.

Not all is lost if you ever find yourself in a position like Alex's where people tell stories about you without your wanting them to. You can talk with experts and officials about how to stop others from telling stories about you and find out ways in which you can remove the stories that already do exist. You can encourage others not to participate in helping stories go viral when they shouldn't. Finally, you can stand up for yourself and take legal actions if the stories about you pose a danger to your safety.

Additional Discussion Questions

1. What are the consequences of telling stories using technologies that share them with the public?
2. How can you protect your stories?
3. Is it fair what happened to Alex from Target? Why or why not?

Additional Activities

1. Museum Stories: Visit a local museum and examine the artifacts you see there for the stories they tell. Think rhetorically and write a reflection in which you answer the following questions about at least three artifacts:
    a. What stories do you see, hear, and encounter with these artifacts?
    b. What technologies did people use to write and create these artifacts and thus their stories?
    c. Why do you suppose people who created each artifact did so?
    d. What do the artifacts' stories say about what their creators' cultures valued or did not value?

e. What impact do you think creating these artifacts had on the history of its creators' people and the places where they lived?

  Share your findings with your fellow classmates.

2. Calendars of the World: Calendars are created using a number of technologies in a number of media and materials. Gather as many calendars as you can and analyze them.

   a. What do the materials, media, and technologies say about the people who created them?
   b. What stories are written on the pages (if they contain pages) of these calendars?

   Share your findings with your fellow classmates.

Additional Assignments

1. Design Your Calendar: Design your own calendar that tells a story. In doing so, you will need to make important rhetorical decisions about the technology you will use and the audience you will create the calendar for.
2. Online Story: Use a program like Twine to create a story for an online audience. Consider how such a program helps or limits you in your writing.
3. Remix Assignment: Think back to a time when you created a story. Tell this story in different ways, perhaps as a website, app, photostory, magazine, podcast, video, presentation, map, or infographic. Compare your rhetorical choices as you tell your stories in different ways. Showcase the different ways you tell your story to the rest of your class.

Works Cited

Bilton, Nick. "Alex from Target: The Other Side of Fame." *The New York Times*, 12 November 2014, www.nytimes.com/2014/11/13/style/alex-from-target-the-other-side-of-fame.html. Accessed 6 February 2018.

Hawisher, Gail E., and Cynthia L. Selfe, with Gorjana Kisa and Shafinaz Ahmed. "Globalism and Multimodality in a Digitized World." *Pedagogy*, vol. 10, no. 1, 2010, pp. 55–68.

Hull, Glynda A., and Mark Evan Nelson. "Locating the Semiotic Power of Multimodality." *Written Communication*, vol. 22, no. 2, 2005, pp. 224–261.

Kegu, Jessica. "'2 Dope Queens' on Their HBO Special Series, the Day They Met and What Makes a 'Zaddy.'" *CBSNews*, 31 January 2018, www.cbsnews.com/news/2-dope-queens-jessica-williams-phoebe-robinson-podcast-hbo-show/. Accessed 1 February 2018.

Kiger, Patrick. "How They Identified the Bombers." *National Geographic*, 1 April 2014, http://channel.nationalgeographic.com/inside-the-hunt-for-the-boston-bombers/articles/how-they-identified-the-bombers/. Accessed 29 January 2018.

Pew Research Center: Journalism & Media Staff. "Video Length." *Pew Research Center Journalism & Media*, 16 July 2012, www.journalism.org/2012/07/16/video-length/#_ftn1. Accessed 3 February 2018.

Spencer Museum of Art. "Faith Ringgold." *Spencer Museum of Art—The University of Kansas*, 2016, http://collection.spencerart.ku.edu/eMuseumPlus?service=ExternalInterface&module=collection&objectId=17289&viewType=detailView. Accessed 1 February 2018.

CHAPTER 8

Information at Our Fingertips

Contents

A Story for the Ages	164
When We Seek Information	168
Expand Your Search	173
Narrow Your Search	177
Research Your Sources for Credibility and Bias	179
Organizing Information for Your Own Use	183
Sharing Information With Others	184
Using Multiple Modes Can Help Express Information Differently	186
Final Thoughts	188

IMAGE 8.1 nikolaich / Shutterstock

A Story for the Ages

The origin of today's modern marathon race is attributed to the story of Pheidippides, an Athenian day runner, or *hemerodromos*, who traveled great distances to deliver information. In 490 BC, many legends state that Pheidippides ran 25 miles from the battlefields in Marathon to Athens, carrying with him some important information for the magistrates. The Athenians had been victorious over the Persians in battle and it was his job to share the news. Pheidippides's job was an important one indeed. Relatively speaking, at that time, information was shared slowly compared to how fast information is shared today. There were no phones or computers or social media back then, so Pheidippides could not call, email, or tweet the Athenian victory. If someone wanted to share information in 490 BC, they had to do so by foot, by boat, by horseback, or by word of mouth, which required a lot of time.

It would be hard to imagine what it must have been like in Pheidippides's time, that if you wanted to share information with someone living in the next town over, you would have to walk (if you had several days to spare), run (if you were healthy and fit enough like Pheidippides), or ride (if you were wealthy enough to own a horse or boat). Today, we are lucky enough to have technologies that make gathering, writing, sharing, and protecting information quickly and more convenient than years past. Some would say writing and sharing is almost instantaneous now that we have connected computers. But, with such ease comes the challenges we must face. Sharing information quickly isn't always a good thing. For instance, resources and people sometimes are exploited when we do, information isn't always properly vetted or researched in a short amount of time, and we can overshare information as with people we didn't intend to, potentially letting the whole world know our business.

Medieval letter with a pentagram red wax seal. Moussa81/ Thinkstock

Building on what you learned about stories in the previous chapter, here you will think about the relationships between information, writing, and technologies, again looking at both the past and present and comparing history to today's world. As the story of Pheidippides demonstrates, we didn't always have the modern writing technologies we have today. In fact, if you look back through history, you can see that it took thousands of years to get to the point where we are now. Over the years, people have tried lots of means for writing and sharing their messages with others. Some used animals such as courier pigeons and ponies. Some developed technologies like using quill and ink, chisel and stone, pigments and papyrus. Some even devised new languages and machines (think Morse code and the telegraph) and new symbols to keep that information safe and secure (think an emblem seal during the Middle Ages as a sign of authentication).

If we look back through time, we can see instances when technologies have impacted the ways in which societies and people have gathered, written, shared, and protected information. In many Western societies, much credit has gone to Johannes Gutenberg for helping the spread of information with the printing press processes he developed in the mid-1400s. At that time, Gutenberg was a skilled craftsman who used his knowledge of metals to experiment with lead, tin, and antimony alloys. Those alloys proved particularly useful for creating a kind of type conducive for quality printing. Using a template, Gutenberg molded a type case of almost 300 letter boxes that proved more robust than previous methods. With those letters, he was able to more quickly produce texts. The faster texts were made, the more texts could be made, and as a result, texts became more affordable, allowing more people to obtain them.

The Development of Technology Is an Evolution Rather Than a Revolution

While Gutenberg's work did make an impact on the world, just how big of an impact is up for debate. The story of Gutenberg and the printing press, like many stories of technology, is a complex and complicated one, one that is related more to an evolution than a revolution. Long before Gutenberg's time, people in other countries such as China and Korea had been experimenting with movable type. Working in China in 1040 AD, Bi Seng developed a process for using porcelain to create movable type for printing books. Later, in Korea, Buddhist monk Baegun wrote *Jikji* (translated, it means "Anthology of Great Buddhist Priests' Zen Teachings"). Printed in 1377 by his student priests in the Heungdeok Temple, *Jikji* is said to be the world's oldest book printed using metal movable type. Thus, it could have been possible for Western traders and missionaries, who traveled to East Asia, to bring back to Europe information about movable type, which eventually led to improvements in printing, including the use of movable type by Gutenberg.

It might be best to say that Gutenberg's methods for printing proved valuable and helped facilitate printing activities in Europe. Those who followed Gutenberg's lead no doubt improved upon his work, too, and that led to improvements in societies in a number of

Gutenberg at Work. Everett Historical / Shutterstock

ways. Such efforts made learning to read, for instance, more widespread simply because it gave people greater access to things to read. Before this time, reading was done by the few who had access to texts. Likewise, because more people were reading, more people were knowledgeable, which challenged the status quo. No longer were elitist authorities the ones with all the knowledge. Gutenberg's work and that of others who followed also changed the nature of texts, their structure, organization, and content. It became more common to see books in vernacular languages (as opposed to Latin, as was common prior to his work) printed on uniformed pages with page numbers on them.

Assignment: Gutenberg's Impact

Critiquing the work *The Printing Press as an Agent of Change* by Elizabeth Eisenstein, writing scholar Christina Haas warns that we have to be careful in the ways in which we talk about technology and its impacts. She warns against calling technology *revolutionary*, saying that such a word "implies a clean break from the past, the beginning of a new history" (214). She explains that "(a) the development of literacy technologies is slow, uneven, and seldom unitary" and "(b) new technologies are dependent in complex ways on other technical and cultural systems" (214). Writing scholar Denis Baron has a similar viewpoint in that he sees technologies of past, present, and future, not as revolutionary but as steps in a long line of technologies. In other words, technologies evolve over time.

Research Gutenberg's printing press processes and their impacts on writing. Create a project in which you answer the following questions:

a. Do you believe that his work was revolutionary or just one step in a long line of technologies? That is, do you think his work was entirely new, or that it was built upon the history of other technologies?

b. In what ways did his work have a positive impact on writing?
c. In what ways did his work have a negative impact on writing?
d. Is his work related to other technologies used before his time? If so, how? If not, why not?

With the invention and improvements to printing processes came effects both good and bad. More affordable texts meant that more people had access to them, so the rich and powerful were no longer the only ones reading. That led to a spread of information, which was a good thing. More people could make more informed decisions in their lives as a result.

However, with the circulation of more printed texts, those who stood to make a profit off of those texts needed ways to protect their investments. Thus, authors and publishers pressured authorities into creating protections like copyright laws to prevent other people from making money off their work. As a result of such protections, information could be owned. That is, information now had a price.

In addition, because more and more texts were printed, more and more people began to rely and put more authority on the printed word (some historians would say to the determent of other forms of communication). In schools, children were instructed on writing and reading the printed word as opposed to other modes. Essays became a means for instructors to assess students' learning abilities. Mastering the writing of an essay became a benchmark, changing the way students learned about all sorts of subjects and also standardizing language. Rules for language privileged some uses over others, and with so much concentration on the printed word, other modes of communication were ignored, put on the backburner, and, worse, yet considered not good enough. Literacy became synonymous with reading and writing the printed word. For students who came from cultures that relied heavily on a rich set of modes to communicate on a day-to-day basis (which included more than just the printed word), such a focus on the printed word proved difficult as they had to ignore their way of learning for fear of being deemed uneducated or uncivilized. Some could even argue that such reliance on the printed word in schools has led to a number of limitations in human development as a result.

Fortunately, over the past few decades, the tables have turned, so to speak, due to the evolution and use of newer writing technologies. Today, classrooms invite students to compose and engage with texts that don't necessarily rely on the printed word. You may have had classes yourself where your professor encouraged you to create a project where you used moving images and sound, for instance. Such texts provide people opportunities for different kinds of learning, different from the kinds of learning that people 100 years ago engaged in. One hundred years ago, people were not creating social media posts, short videos, or podcasts in their writing classes. They were not writing such texts, learning with such texts, or sharing such texts.

Did You Know? Copyright

With the increase in texts being produced and the improvements in the printing process, people felt it necessary to protect their work and their profits. Such beliefs led to copyrighting texts, making sure that no one else could reproduce the same text for a profit. In fact, copyright ensured that the information in one book was indeed the only place in which that information could be found. The author and publishers thus owned the rights to that information. Today, while we still have copyrights in place to protect authors and publishers, new technologies, such as those involving networked computers, have challenged the notion that information belongs in one place or that it can be owned and sold. Think about all the information there is in this world about fitness. Information about fitness is not just in one book that is owned by an author or a publisher. Information about fitness is on the internet, in journals, in magazines, in videos, in podcasts, and so forth. All of these texts can inform people about fitness in many different ways and can be read and accessed at the same time in different locations by different people. In many cases, people don't have to pay for information by buying a book about fitness if they don't want to. They can find information about fitness in a plethora of free sources instead.

When We Seek Information

Every Monday morning, Jamal Baker, co-owner of an international company, sits in a boardroom in a London office. Seated next to him are many of the company's executives. On the far wall is a large screen. On one half of the screen are presentation slides. On the other half, there is a live video feed of his partner's office in Shanghai. As his partner in Shanghai works through his presentation slides, detailing the week's agenda, everyone, including Jamal, takes notes on their iPads, making sure that they prepare themselves for the work ahead. When his partner proposes to open up two new stores in Shanghai's Pudong district, Jamal quickly turns to the internet to find out more about the location. According to Wikipedia, he learns in a matter of seconds that Pudong is the most populous district in Shanghai, is home to the Shanghai Stock Exchange, and is located east of the Huangpu River. Jamal writes these down and when the meeting is over, he decides he's going to need more information on Pudong before making a decision. He reaches out to his network of colleagues and business partners as well as a consulting firm. Within a few days, Jamal has a much better understanding of Pudong and whether or not his company should move forward with opening new stores there.

A meeting like the one Jamal and his associates conduct each week could not happen without the use of several technologies such as computers. Moreover, Jamal couldn't have found information about Pudong as quickly as some other means without the help of technologies like the internet and the World Wide Web. Today, when we need to get in contact with someone, share information, or when, like Jamal, we need information quickly, we often turn first to our computers, the internet, and the World Wide Web. The internet is a large network of computers that communicate with one another and use a variety of different languages (also called protocols). The web is just one part of the internet and relies on one language (HTTP) that enables people to access webpages through various browsers. Later in this book, you will learn more about computer languages. In the meantime, let's consider how the web got started.

In the late 1980s and early 1990s, the web was developed by Sir Tim Berners-Lee, a British scientist who worked for the European Council for Nuclear Research (CERN). Berners-Lee invented the web so that scientists around the world could share their research. But, once the concept was tested and the value realized, CERN made the web public to all rather than patent it and profit from it themselves.

Activity: The First Webpage

Do you believe Berners-Lee could have imagined all the possibilities for the web when he created it? The first webpage address ever published to the web explains what the web is and does.

Check it out here: http://info.cern.ch/hypertext/WWW/TheProject.html.

Then, examine this webpage and discuss with your classmates how the web has changed since it expanded to include other webpages and how different those webpages look today compared to this very first webpage. In a sense, you are researching and discussing how webpages have evolved since this very first webpage. If you compare this first webpage, for instance, to your school's webpages, what are the differences?

Berners-Lee's story is an important one as it points to the political, economic, social, and ethical issues that one must consider when thinking carefully about how information is written and shared using technology. Knowing the potential power of such technology, Berners-Lee recognized his responsibility in making sure that everyone had a fair chance to use it. In 1994, he founded the World Wide Web Consortium (W3C), an international organization that develops and maintains standards for web growth. In 2009, he also founded the World Wide Web Foundation, an organization that seeks digital equality for all. By researching and working with governments, this foundation advocates for fair policies that will ensure the web is for all.

Activity: Information for All

According to the World Wide Web Foundation's website, Sir Tim Berners-Lee and the early web community developed important ideas that can help us think about the impact the web and other technologies have on the world in terms of how information is written and shared. These ideas are guidelines for creating sources of information (like the web) that remain accessible to all. As you read the World Wide Web Foundation's ideas below, think about how such ideas can ensure that the web remains open to all:

- Decentralisation: No permission is needed from a central authority to post anything on the web, there is no central controlling node, and so no single point of failure ... and no "kill switch"! This also implies freedom from indiscriminate censorship and surveillance.
- Non-discrimination: If I pay to connect to the internet with a certain quality of service, and you pay to connect with that or a greater quality of service, then we can both communicate at the same level. This principle of equity is also known as Net Neutrality.
- Bottom-up design: Instead of code being written and controlled by a small group of experts, it was developed in full view of everyone, encouraging maximum participation and experimentation.
- Universality: For anyone to be able to publish anything on the web, all the computers involved have to speak the same languages to each other, no matter what different hardware people are using; where they live; or what cultural and political beliefs they have. In this way, the web breaks down silos while still allowing diversity to flourish.
- Consensus: For universal standards to work, everyone had to agree to use them. Tim and others achieved this consensus by giving everyone a say in creating the standards, through a transparent, participatory process at W3C. (World Wide Web Foundation)

As a class, discuss:

a. What impact does each of these ideas have on the web?
b. Who or what enables or prevents these ideas from being enacted?
c. How do these guidelines help ensure everyone has access to information online?
d. Can you think of any examples of people, policies, or practices that might not fall in line with these ideas?

As with the evolution of the printing press (a technology that evolved out of other technologies), the evolution of the web (another technology that evolved out of other technologies) has had major impacts on the creation, sharing, and finding of information.

Take a moment now and reflect on how important the web is in your life. Think about how you help write the web by creating, sharing, and finding information.

Check It Out YouTube: For more on the power of the internet and how technology has changed the world, search YouTube for World Science Festival's "Internet Everywhere: The Future of History's Most Disruptive Technology."

Today there are over 1.5 billion websites currently on the web, and while fewer than 200 million websites are active, it is astonishing how fast the web has grown given that the web is less than 40 years old. However, given the sheer number of existing websites and the fact that each contains information in some form or another, finding and sorting through information has become a daunting task, especially since anyone who has access to the internet can create and change that information in a matter of seconds. So, with nearly 200 million active websites, writers have to ask themselves: how do we find good information? How do we know we can trust it? What is fake and what isn't? What can we do to keep track of all the information once we do find it, and then how do we organize it in a way that is helpful to us and to others?

We can find information in a number of ways, from using a free search engine like Google, to using a school library's paid subscriptions to databases, to using a social media site's news feed; all of these are accessible on the web. In the next couple of chapters, you will be reading more about how search engines, databases, and social media sites operate. For now, it is best to start with a few general strategies for finding information.

Forty years ago, when computers and the internet were not in wide use, researching information sometimes required a lot of time. Let's say that 40 years ago, you were interested in learning more about animals that live in the Sahara Desert. Finding information about such animals 40 years ago may have required the following steps: going to the library, searching the card index for a book on the Sahara Desert, locating that book on the shelf, turning to the book's index to locate the keyword "animals," determining where in the book that keyword was used, and then going to those pages and reading about the animals.

Activity: No Computer Information

Take a week or weekend break from your use of computers and smartphones (unless you need it for schoolwork). Pay attention to where you find answers to questions you might have during this week or weekend. Keep a journal and answer the following questions:

a. How different is your life and your way of thinking without computers and smartphones? Where did you go to find answers to the questions you had?
b. What information did you need that you couldn't find without the use of a computer or smartphone?

c. How do you feel without these technologies and their ability to provide information at your fingertips?
d. In what ways do these technologies shape the way you know the world? What are the impacts of these ways?

Today, if you wanted to know what animals live in the Sahara Desert, chances are, in a matter of seconds, you could get a general idea just by googling it. In a matter of seconds, you could also find out what animals live in the Mojave Desert and the Gobi Desert, too—or anywhere else, for that matter. That's in part because technologies like Google changed and, in some cases, simplified our search processes. In this instance, the simplification of the search process saved you time, enabling you to find more information about more animals and places. In this instance, such technology proved valuable.

However, what this example doesn't demonstrate is that in some cases, such a technology could pose a challenge to finding the *right* information for your needs. Now let's say that you are a student who wants to write a biology project in which you argue that animals in the Sahara Desert are in danger of habitat loss due to climate change. In this case, you would need to do more than just google animals. Google might be a good place to start so that you could get a general idea of the subject matter, but you would need to find reliable information from reliable sources, such as experts who study climate change and animals in the Sahara Desert. That's not to say that googling may not provide reliable sources. You just might find reputable and reliable sources by googling.

Nevertheless, experts that make a living conducting scientific studies on habitat loss, animals, and so forth most likely publish their findings in texts other than free websites findable by Google. Rather, they publish in journals or books. That's because they want their work peer reviewed and validated by other experts. A lot of scientific research is often published in scientific journals that are owned by publishers who make money by selling those journals. Such publishers don't necessarily publish their journals openly to the internet, giving anyone who googles access to the articles published in those journals. Instead, publishers charge money for people to use their journals, or their journals are found in subscription databases that libraries subscribe to and pay for.

Even though it is convenient, Google, therefore, may not be the best place to turn to for the right information. We might need to take more time, roll up our sleeves, and use other technologies. While elsewhere, this textbook talks more about where information comes from and about citing credible sources, the following sections in this chapter can help you get started in thinking about how technologies can help or hinder our ability to search and gather the information we use to write with.

Expand Your Search

A Dutch proverb says, "Slowly but surely the bird builds its nest." Such a proverb is a good way to think about when searching for information, especially when using search engine technologies like Google. While Google can provide you with search results in about the same time it takes you to blink, the results might not be the best results and might not contain the best information. In Jamal's case, he was able to find out about Pudong because Google provided him with the Wikipedia page almost instantly. In fact, it was the first site listed on the results page.

But, if Jamal used only Wikipedia to make important decisions for his international company, Jamal might not have a company to run for very long, especially because Wikipedia is a basic online encyclopedia, hardly a place where in-depth discussions about the profitability of opening a business in a particular location take place. Likewise, if you were doing a report on how the animals in the Sahara Desert are in danger of habitat loss due to climate change, you would be limiting your understanding and your ability to make a good argument, if you only took a look at the first five search results in Google. Most likely, those first five results won't provide you with enough (not to mention far-reaching) information from the best in the field of climate studies, scientists who research animals, and those who measure changes to habitats in the Sahara Desert.

It would be in Jamal's best interest and that of his company's to dig a little deeper, spend more time, and think about other possible resources online and elsewhere to learn more about whether or not Pudong would be a good place to open more stores. It would also be in your best interest to cast a wider net and explore more than the first five search results in Google in order to write your biology project about animals in the Sahara Desert and the impacts of climate change on their habitats.

All Questions Are Important Enough for Us to Think Critically About the Technologies We Use to Find Their Answers

Jamal's case seems like a no-brainer. If you were in charge of a large company, you would probably also want to spend more time looking at the information in search results as well as seek out other sources of information such as your colleagues, experts in Pudong, and consultants. Yet, we are not all co-owners of a business like Jamal. We probably turn to the internet for a number of questions that seem so unimportant compared to Jamal's questions about Pudong that we don't give much thought to whether or not there are better sources of information. But, our seemingly unimportant questions like "What animals live in the Sahara Desert?" should not be looked at as being unimportant at all. In fact, if you want to be smarter in your ability to find information and to actually know good answers to your questions, it might be best to think of all your questions as important enough to warrant spending more time thinking critically about where information comes from and how to find it.

Let's say that you don't spend the time thinking critically about the search results you get when you google the question, "What animals live in the Sahara Desert?" Let's say you look only at Google's first result. That happens to be a page on the website Themysteriousworld called "Top 10 Amazingly Adaptive Sahara Desert Animals." Let's say you read through this list and decide that since you now know of ten animals that live in the desert, you can stop looking for information.

But, here's why that wouldn't be a good idea. Not going beyond one source of information means you have only a very narrow and limited understanding of the animals that live in the Sahara Desert. Way more animals live in the Sahara Desert than the ten listed on Themysteriousworld's website, after all. And, there are probably much better sources to read about those animals than Themysteriousworld's website, even though that website is listed first in your search results. Being first doesn't mean it's the best. Imagine if you went through your whole life operating in this manner, looking only at the first few search results in Google for all your inquiries. Think of how many things in your life you would have only a very narrow and limited understanding of.

People often use Google, and search engines like it, because it is so fast and convenient. While other means of finding information, say looking through your library's databases, may take more time, they should not be counted out. As a writer and seeker of information, you have to weigh the costs of fast and convenient sources with those that aren't. You may find that you are missing out in knowing the world in different and important ways.

Discussion Questions: Fast and Convenient Sources of Information

Think about your use of fast and convenient sources of information, like search engines such as Google. Then answer the following:

1. What are the consequences (both good and bad) when you rely heavily on such quickness and convenience?
2. Whose information do you find? What information gets left out in search results?
3. What happens when everyone relies on one large search engine like Google that seemingly controls the flow of information for everyone?

There are other reasons why you might want to expand your search, too. For example, if you rely on social media for information, you might run into similar challenges that could limit your understanding. By expanding your search for information, you can help to mitigate things like filter bubbles, echo chambers, and confirmation bias, things that lead to a highly personalized web. According to scholar Robert Bodle, "personalization is when online content conforms to the prior actions of the user in an algorithmically generated feedback loop" (130). In other words, your actions online now could lead to technologies (like Google) personalizing your future experiences, such as personalizing your search results based on what their algorithm thinks you would be interested in given what it knows about your searching history.

People searching for the same thing in the same online spaces might not get the same results due to a personalized web. Social media is particularly in the business of personalizing online experiences. When you interact with your social media platform, that social media platform gathers information about you: your likes and dislikes, your patterns of uses, what you click on, and so forth. It then uses that information the next time you interact to provide you with personalized content, filtering out content it believes you would filter out on your own. Some search engines do this, too; that is, they return search results to you based not on rankings related to your search terms, but based on their knowledge of you from the previous searches you made. These search engines might use their knowledge of your location, interests, search history, and more to return search results to you that they think you will appreciate.

Personalized content could be a good thing in that it makes your job easier and faster to find content that you like; however, as Bodle writes, it can also be harmful. That's because, Bodle argues, the personalized web makes it harder for people to make informed decisions when they are not exposed to a wide range of views (137–139). As mentioned earlier, we need to be careful where our information comes from. If you rely on social media for information, you should remember that people tend to be friends with like-minded people and that social media can filter out other people's opposing viewpoints based on your usage history. It would be in your best interest to seek out all perspectives on an issue such as protecting animals in the Sahara Desert in order to mitigate confirmation bias and be able to make well-informed decisions that make the best impact.

Confirmation bias happens when you (1) seek out information that you know will confirm your point of view, and (2) discount looking at points of view that would disagree with you. Say you woke up this morning and believed that today was going to be a sunny day. You were sure of it. To prove this, you head outside and search the sky. You discount all the darkening clouds that are rolling in, and you ignore the sound of thunder and the powerful breeze on your face, until you find what you are looking for. In the distance, you see one ray of sun peeking through a dark cloud. That one ray of sun makes you feel good about your belief. Indeed, all you needed was proof, and that one ray of sun provided that for you. You take a picture of the ray and post it to your friend circle on social media with the tag: It's going to be a sunny day. Your friends take one look at the picture and agree. They echo your tag by posting it within your network and within a matter of minutes everyone in your circle has made a comment about how sunny the day will be.

But, that ray of sun and that picture tell only one story about today's weather possibilities, the one from your point of view. And, it doesn't seem like a well-researched and informative one at that. By focusing just on that one ray of sun, you ignored the dark clouds rolling in, the sound of thunder, and the powerful breeze on your face. Those bits of information would have made you question, if not contradict, your belief that today would be sunny. Because you wanted to avoid uncertainty and avoid feeling uncomfortable in being wrong, you didn't pay attention to the rest of the sky. You didn't even entertain the idea that rain could be a possibility. And when your friends agreed with you, you felt even more confident that you were right and that anyone who disagreed would be wrong.

Confirmation bias prevents us from objectively looking at the world around us and making informed judgments. Had you looked at the whole sky, had you paid attention to the dark clouds, the thunder, the breeze—the things you didn't want to see, the things that were different from your point of view—you might have considered keeping an umbrella handy today.

It is hard not to favor information or place greater value to it when that information confirms what we want to believe. Who likes to be wrong, after all? If you want to believe it will be sunny today, seeking out evidence to confirm this will be true seems like a natural first step. But, while it might be your first step, you can't stop there. You have to make a conscious effort to take additional steps to pay attention to and seek out information that is different from your point of view. And, to do so, you need to expand your searches to spaces where you might not regularly look.

Expanding and diversifying your search is easier said than done, especially when technologies make it difficult to do so. Nonetheless, we must try. You might start by depersonalizing your online spaces so that you can search without feeling like you are stuck in a bubble. Delete your search histories. Expand your preferences. Use popular search engines without their tracking your every move. For example, Google gives you the option to open an incognito window in Chrome. While the window still makes you visible to the websites you visit and your internet service provider, it won't save your browsing history, cookies, or the information you enter into any forms. If you find that you want more privacy, find alternative search engines. In fact, there are a number of search engines that don't track your history, such as DuckDuckGo or Swisscows.

You can also make an effort to find out what others outside of your social and political circles are reading and talking about. While the example described here is about a sunny sky, you can apply the example to your online searches, most likely ones that seek to find important answers to important questions.

Discussion Questions: Language and Search Engines

1. What sources and technologies do you turn to regularly for information?
2. What language do you use to perform a search?

3. What language do you look for in the search results?
4. Do you look for language that would agree or disagree with what you believe?
5. In what ways do languages change as a result of technologies like search engines?
6. What languages are privileged in search engines? Why do you believe this is so?

Think carefully about the news sources where you get your information. Did you know that "just under half (45%) of U.S. adults use Facebook for news," and that "half of Facebook's news users get news from that social media site alone, with just one-in-five relying on three or more sites for news"? (Grieco). Perhaps one strategy you could use in expanding your search is to think about proving yourself wrong before you try to prove yourself right. If you want information related to, say, a political candidate you like, chances are you will find online sources such as social media that paint that person in a good light without so much as looking at those that don't. Spend time actually reading sources that might prove your candidate might not be the best person for the position. Try not to ignore what the sources are saying, and instead, really take the time to think about what those sources are saying. You might find in the end that you ultimately can make a stronger case for your own candidate.

Activity: Search Engines

A number of private companies host their own search engines and make them available to you, like **Yippy** and **Qwant**. But, like all search engines you use, you should always use them with caution. Find out who owns them, how they work, and what they do with your information. If don't want your search history recorded or your searches tracked, you might try the search engines **DuckDuckGo** or **Swisscows**. If you want a search engine devoted to social media, you might try **Social Searcher**.

Working with other students in your class, develop a list of questions that you can search in a number of online places like Google, DuckDuckGo, Swisscows, social media, your library's online databases, and so forth. Compare your results with each of these. What differences do you see in your findings? Do you have a better understanding of your questions' answers as a result of looking at multiple sources of information? Why or why not?

Narrow Your Search

It may seem counterproductive, but while you expand your search, you should also at the same time try to narrow it using a number of tools. Part of the reason why we may have the urge to look only at the first few results we garner from a search engine query is because of the shear plethora of information there exists online. Too much information can be overwhelming, and our time on this planet is precious. Who wants to waste time clicking through pages upon pages upon pages of search results? Instead, we might think of narrowing our search as a way of making smarter searches to begin with so that we get quality results.

Confucius, an ancient Chinese teacher and philosopher, once said that "The man who moves a mountain begins by carrying away small stones." If you have a writing project about how the animals in the Sahara Desert are in danger of habitat loss due to climate change, you may feel as if you have a mountain to climb while sorting through all the information you will find on animals in the Sahara Desert. To tackle this mountain, you could start by breaking this mountain down into pieces and doing smaller searches of those pieces. You could start by searching for specific animals in the Sahara Desert. You could then search for specific desert climates. You could then search what specifically causes those climates to change. Breaking the search into smaller ones could help you keep your sanity and not strain your patience when looking at results.

Still, it might be even better to consider instead making the mountain itself smaller at the onset of your search. In other words, narrow your inquiry. Starting with broad, general ideas will lead you to find broad, general information. Instead, you might be better off if you have specific ideas to search for. You might start by using just one animal in a particular region of the Sahara Desert that is susceptible to a specific type of habitat loss.

> Broad search: How does habitat loss affect animals in the Sahara Desert?
> Narrower search: How does desertification affect the habitats of dama gazelles in Sudan?

Using a narrower search may provide you with more specific results that can help you make a better, more specific argument, not to mention help you gain a deeper understanding of a situation like a specific habitat loss. Likewise, making a narrower search can make the results more manageable because there would be less of them. In other words, the more narrow the search, the less information you will have to sort through.

Check It Out YouTube: For more on using tools in a search engine like Google to narrow your search results, check out the YouTube videos, "How to Get Better Search Results/Be a Google Pro/Study Tips," posted by Socratica; and "Beginner's Guide to Google Search Basics and Tips and Tricks," posted by Technology for Teachers and Students.

Activity: Specific Ways of Searching

When we conduct a search, we do so by using specific languages. Computer technologies like search engines and databases are designed to read language and interpret it in the hopes of retrieving the search results you wanted. Knowing how to use different keywords and search functions can help you find specific information. For example, using quotation marks around words in Google means that you are looking for an exact phrase. The search engine reads the quotes and will make sure that the results do indeed contain that exact phrase.

For this activity, create a narrow search question, like the one about dama gazelles, and try using different search techniques such as the following to find information that can help answer your question. Then write a reflection on your experiences.

1. Use quotation marks around words. Quotations mean that you are looking for those exact words.
2. Use a "-" mark before a word. This mark means you want the results to exclude that particular word. If you notice that in your search results you are getting unrelated or unwanted search results, using a - mark plus whatever keywords show up in those results could help you eliminate those results once you search again.
3. Use AND, OR, and NOT (also called Boolean terms) to help you refine your search or expand it. The more you use AND, for instance, the smaller your search becomes, whereas the more you use OR, the wider your search becomes. That's because in using AND, you are saying to the computer, "make sure the results have at least two terms." That is, if you were searching Google for websites that contained lizards AND the Sahara Desert, the Google results will contain links to webpages that contain both lizard and Sahara Desert. A website that only has one of these terms would not show up in the results. In using OR, as in lizards OR Sahara Desert, only one of these terms would need to be on a webpage to show up in the results. Therefore, you would have more results. NOT, on the other hand, acts like the - mark in that it excludes terms from results.
4. Use an asterisk (*), which is also known as a wildcard operator, to replace a word within a phrase inside quotations. This will help you search for variations of a phrase or for a missing word in a phrase.
5. Try using synonyms and words that are similar to the words you first use to write your search query in order to ensure you are finding all that has been written about your subject matter. You may be studying something that people have used other words to describe and talk about. For example, desertification is also known as a type of land degradation. You could try searching using both desertification and land degradation.

Research Your Sources for Credibility and Bias

In the past, you may have heard one of your teachers tell you that you can't use Wikipedia to help you with an assignment. But, did you ever stop to think about why that may be? Perhaps, one way to answer this *why* question is to think about what Wikipedia is. Wikipedia is a wiki, a website that allows people to collaborate, write, revise, and edit together. There are all sorts of wikis online, from wikiHow to WikiLeaks, that cover a wide range of subject matter. Because Wikipedia is an online encyclopedia that is written, edited, and updated regularly by virtually anyone who owns a computer and has access to the site, it creates fluid, changeable texts.

Whether or Not We Realize It, Technologies Influence the Way We Think About the Validity of Information

Information on a wiki may not carry as much clout as a textbook because we have been conditioned to believe that if anyone can edit it at a moment's time, then the information in it might not be reliable. Simply put, we have been conditioned to think a fluid, changeable text or fluid, changeable information created by anyone could be unreliable. Remember, when books became copyrighted, people began to see the printed word, and thus the fixed word, as an authority, one that must be credible given it went through a publication process, one that most likely included reviews by experts and peers.

However, the people who work for the Wikimedia Foundation, the nonprofit organization that oversees Wikipedia, along with the thousands of people in the public who do write on the site, in some regards, represent how knowledge is created, shared, and contested in public spaces in the first place. When someone writes something on Wikipedia, others chime in, offering their own ideas, debating and challenging the information they do not agree with, or rewriting it to make sure that the information is relevant for today's purposes. This happens until a consensus is met for the time being and the information set forth is deemed "correct" until it is negotiated again. This is very much like the publishing process of printed material. When someone writes a draft, they send it to a publisher, who sends it to reviewers, who debate and challenge the information they do not agree with and form a consensus on the information they do agree on.

Wikipedia uses crowds of people to build its resource for the public. To some extent this is a good thing, as this process reflects a society's ability to write and share its knowledge together, to agree on what is acceptable and what is not. Today, many companies use *crowdsourcing*, for example, to gather information from the masses and use that information to build informational guides for their customers. Instead of printed user manuals, companies now may have online support communities that are created by customers themselves who write the information needed to operate, troubleshoot, and maintain a company's products.

Crowdsourcing resources like Wikipedia can be a place to start your research if you need to get a general idea about something, but you should do so cautiously. Not all crowdsourced information is representative of everyone. When information is crowdsourced, it isn't always clear who is a member of the crowd and who is not. Wikipedia, for example, claims to be edited by everyone, but the demographics of those who actually do write articles reveal that the majority of the writers for Wikipedia are males either in their mid-20s or retired. Such writers could have certain dispositions or biases that other writers would not have, and thus, their writing might reflect certain ideologies. Likewise, when certain people are the only ones writing, revising, and editing wiki entries, their voices may be more privileged than others. In the end, always look at a wiki's authors to determine whether or not you should rely on them.

Discussion Questions: Crowdsources

Discuss the following questions in relationship to crowdsourced resources and technologies, such as Wikipedia or an online help manual:

1. Who writes for these? Why?
2. Should such resources and technologies make clear who writes for these and what their biases, ideologies, and preferences are? Why or why not?
3. Who is not writing for these? Why?
4. What information is left out as a result of who writes for these, and why?
5. Should you trust the information you gather from these? Why or why not?

Moreover, it might be a good idea to consider whether or not the wisdom of a crowd is always right to begin with. Crowds of people use to believe the world was flat until someone was brave enough to challenge this belief and sail beyond the horizon. A lot of inventions we have today, after all, are the result of people thinking differently from the crowd and challenging popular beliefs.

If you can't always trust crowds, then you may be wondering: where do you go for reliable information? In the past, you may have heard your instructors say that you should rely only on peer-reviewed resources because those resources are reviewed by experts in the field. Experts use their expertise to deem information credible. But consensus among a few is not always a good thing, either. History is abundant with stories where consensus among experts failed. There was a time when town officials in New England burned people at the stake because they believed those people were witches. Those few town officials were supposed to be trusted authorities, experts at knowing what was best for townspeople, but they ended up making horrible decisions because they didn't consider other perspectives beyond their own.

One strategy, then, is to think rhetorically about information and the technology used to write and distribute it. Perhaps now more than ever, there is a need for rhetorical skills when researching information, especially when technologies can spread fake, biased news stories and narrow opinions. Consider thinking rhetorically about your research, where your information is coming from, who you will then share it with, and why. Choose sources of information only after critically examining them.

However, critically examining information is not an easy task. For one thing, it can be exhausting and time consuming. Yet, it is important nonetheless, and here's why.

News sources are some of the sources we might turn to when we want to know what is happening in our world. News organizations, though, are businesses, run by big corporations that have their own interests in mind, interests that may conflict with your own, or that present only information that confirms the news organization's particular point of view and leaves out information that doesn't. This can be especially true when it comes to presenting political information to the public. News organizations don't necessarily report differing political viewpoints fairly, something people around the world have noticed. In fact, in 2018, the Pew Research Center surveyed people in 38 countries worldwide regarding news media and found that "Large majorities in nearly every country surveyed say that their news media should always be unbiased in their coverage," yet "publics around the globe give the lowest ratings for reporting on different political positions fairly" (Mitchell et al.). Indeed, news organizations have their own biases, and often these biases are reflected in their stories. Be aware of these and develop ways of actively seeking out a multitude of sources so that you can make informed judgments.

Assignment: Examine Your Sources

While technologies can sometimes make it easier to find out more about our sources, as you learned about earlier in this book, we need to do more than just read a news organization's "About" page online. For this activity, research a TV news or newspaper organization's history and, in doing so, try answering the following questions:

- How and when was it created?
- Who created it?
- How has the writing and presentation of information changed over time with this organization?
- What technologies are used to produce, write, and read information you find with this organization?
- What kind of information is shared by this organization?
- What impact does that information have on society?
- What political biases does the organization have, and does the technology you use to get information from these sources make that political biases clear?
- Does the organization fairly present all political issues by representing all voices in their stories?
- Do they endorse (directly or indirectly) political leaders, and if so, does this shape what information they share?
- Whose voices are front and center in their stories? Whose are left out?

You may start your investigation online, but perhaps you could visit and interview the news organization in person, finding out more about the people who work there. Share your findings with your class.

Organizing Information for Your Own Use

Once you have tried out a few strategies in searching for information, you may want to think next about what to do with that information. Say you have gathered a number of ideas from different sources. How, for instance, do you organize information in a way that is helpful to you?

Think back to a time when you studied for a history test. How did you study the information? Did you make notes on note cards? Did you use a notebook, arranging the information in chronological order? Did you highlight key terms? Perhaps you listed important people involved in key events. Did you study maps of places involved in these events? Did you study photographs? Timelines? Now, think about a time when you studied for a science test. How did you study the information? Did you make notes on note cards? Did you use a notebook, arranging the information in chronological order? Did you highlight key terms? Perhaps, you listed important people involved in key events. Did you study diagrams, charts, tables, lists? Did you draw out formulas?

At any point when you were studying for these tests, did you think about the technologies you were using? Did you think about the fact that your notes were written on note cards? Did you think about the blue pen you used to write the notes? Did you think about the computer? The book? Unless there was a problem with them, you probably did not pay much attention to them. But, imagine if you didn't have these technologies. If you grew up during the time of Pheidippides, how would you have remembered information? Would you have recited it out loud over and over again, hoping to commit it to memory?

If you were a student in ancient times, memorizing was an important skill due to the fact that most communication was done orally. Students recited poems, speeches, and stories rather than wrote them down. With the help of technologies today, it might not be as necessary to memorize so much information when we have technologies at our fingertips that can store information in easily accessible spaces for us. However, if that is the case, what are necessary are the skills needed to help sort through information, organize it, and access it in ways that are most helpful to the tasks we undertake? **Organization** is a complex process that may involve structuring, labeling, grouping, separating, and presenting information in a way that is accessible, usable, and findable. Organization often depends on our abilities to understand information but also on the technology we use to structure, label, group, separate, and present information. We can organize information in notebooks with headings, paragraphs, and pages. We can organize information on computer screens by using folders and files. We can organize information in infographics using colors.

As a first step to figuring out what are the best ways to organize information for our own uses, we can study the organizing, the structuring, and the labeling that technologies and their various tools and affordances enable us to do or prohibit us from doing. We can do so by comparing all the technologies we use and asking ourselves: What are the differences, the similarities, the advantages and disadvantages of each technology when it comes to organizing information?

For writers, it is important to think about the ways in which technologies organize information for us, since those ways are what we use to understand information. Those ways of organizing information, in other words, influence what and how we learn and what we don't learn. Consider what ways you currently use technologies to organize information and whether or not those ways really do help you learn information.

Activity: Assess Your Organizational Habits

To assess your organizational habits related to your schoolwork, answer the following questions, making sure to explain with examples:

1. Do you think your ability to organize using specific technologies is helpful to your schoolwork? Why or why not?
2. Does one way of organizing information lead you to certain conclusions over other conclusions that you might have reached had you organized the information in another way? Why or why not?
3. What would happen if you tried different technologies and thus different organizational systems?
4. In what ways are your decisions for organizing information influenced by the technologies you use?
5. Do you prefer to use certain technologies over others when organizing information? If so, why and how do those technologies limit your ability to organize and then make sense of such information? How do they aid your ability to organize and then make sense of such information?

Sharing Information With Others

Organizing information for your own purposes is one thing. Sharing information with others is another. Rick Tierra is a medical researcher at a well-known research university in the United States. He is a member of a lab that is working on a cure for diabetes. In one of his lab experiments last year, Rick garnered significant results that he later published in a well-known scientific journal. His work was well received since the journal's audience, comprised of other members of the field, was already familiar with his research, not to mention up-to-speed on the latest techniques, procedures, and scholarship related to the kind of work Rick conducts in his lab. Thanks in part to journals like the one Rick published in, other scientists and researchers can build upon existing research (like that of Rick's) in the hopes of one day curing diabetes.

However, while Rick did share his findings in a journal for a scientific community, there are times when Rick must communicate with those who are outside of his field. As such, many fields (the medical field included) often have to educate those outside of their fields about what takes place within their fields in order to secure the funding, resources, and support needed to carry out their work in the first place. Sharing information with those outside of your field can be tricky, though. The field of science, for instance, has been criticized for not being able to effectively communicate their research to those outside of the science field for a number of reasons. Often when scientists convey information, they do so dryly, using technical and scientific language that people outside the field just don't understand. In some cases, scientists have been said to lack an awareness of the kinds of language, texts, communication strategies, and so forth that could engage those outside their field. As a result, sometimes securing the much-needed support is slow and unsuccessful.

Whether or not you will be working in a lab like Rick, one thing is for sure: there will come a time when you will need to explain what you do to those outside your career field. Your work may even depend on how well you communicate information about your field. But, even outside of your career, you may find yourself in a position where you may need to explain information to an audience who is unfamiliar with it. So, it makes sense, then, to develop effective strategies for organizing information and sharing it in a way that will make sense to your audience. To help your audience search and navigate your information, you could pay close attention to your naming and labeling of ideas when organizing it, which often happens through language. Having multiple ways to help people locate information within your texts can also help to ensure your texts reach the largest audience. If you were in Rick's shoes and had to communicate research to those outside the medical field, using only technical and scientific language would render your text inaccessible to a large population of people. Only other scientists and researchers would understand. But, if you were to choose language that more people could understand, you would be able to reach a larger audience.

So, one way you can approach organizing information is to think about the role language plays in the organizing of that information. You should think about the language you use to create categories of information and the messages this language sends to your audiences. If you were to think carefully about your audience and use one word as opposed to another, for instance, you would need to think about the impact it will have on the way your readers will interpret the information within that category.

In a later chapter, you will further consider issues of accessibility when it comes to writing. Here, you might prepare for that chapter by considering all the possibilities for organizing information. These key questions can help prepare you to share information:

- In what order do you want your audience to encounter your information?
- What reading path should they follow?
- How will you help your audience move through the information?

- If you are working with data, for instance, are words, paragraphs, headings, and/or pages an effective way to explain this data?
- Are there other modes you could use to organize information, and if so, how?
- What combination of modes should you use?
- Should you use images? Should you use colors? Should you use symbols? Should you use sounds?
- What are the advantages and disadvantages of organizing your text in the way you plan to organize it?

Whether you choose to organize information chronologically, alphabetically, sequentially, or spatially, or whether you chose to organize it in order of importance, grouping like ideas together, or listing it from general to specific (or vice versa), will require some rhetorical thinking on your part. You can begin to determine which way to organize based on your answers to the questions just outlined, but you may also think of organizing as a way of designing the visualness of your text. The way it will look may mean that you will have to lay out your ideas for organizing ahead of time to see how your text will look. Practice different ways until you find one that looks good, that is, will be effective for your audience. Keep in mind the design suggestions and writing examples that you read about earlier in this book. Notice how the examples organize information, and think about whether or not they were successful.

Using Multiple Modes Can Help Express Information Differently

No matter what career field you go into, you will most likely need to communicate a variety of information in a variety of ways. After his lab experiment and the publication of his results, Rick needed to secure funding for his next research project. To that end, he contacted a well-known nonprofit organization that was devoted to curing diabetes and asked to give a presentation to the board of directors. Rick hoped this presentation would lead to the necessary funding. Because the people involved in the organization were not experts in science, but rather were experts at running a nonprofit, Rick thought rhetorically about the modes he could use to best educate this audience during his presentation.

Instead of presenting this audience with the kind of text that would appear in a scientific journal, Rick decided that he would need other kinds of texts, such as an infographic that outlines why diabetes research is so important and how his lab could make progress in the next experiment. The infographic featured a number of modes working together to make a clear argument. Likewise, Rick created presentation slides that outlined a clear agenda for his experiment that he displayed during his talk. Then, to drive home his points, he provided a handout to the directors with a summary of his needs. Three weeks after his presentation, the board of directors called with good news. They would provide the needed funding.

Rick's use of an infographic is one of many ways in which information can be visualized. Indeed, there are a variety of visual texts that can help make organizing, keeping track of, and sharing information effective. People use visual texts all the time, from maps (like the examples in this book), to flowcharts, to project plans, to spreadsheets. One day, you may work for a company that uses visual charts to display the various steps for a project you will work on. Or, you may be in charge of creating a portfolio of graphs, outlining your company's finances. Or, you may need to provide an infographic of your research to people who will decide whether or not to fund your future projects. Understanding the various kinds of visuals that you can create and use to communicate information is a good place to begin when trying to figure out how best to reach a specific audience. Table 8.1 provides some examples of different ways you can communicate information visually. Take the time to practice using these when seeking out the best ways to convey information given your rhetorical situation and the technologies you have at hand.

In truth, we do have a number of technologies at our fingertips that can help us create such visualizations in a matter of seconds. Try using wordclouds.com to see for yourself. Type in words or paste words from a document you have already written into the free online platform and watch how fast the platform visualizes your use of those words, making the words you use most often larger and the ones you use least often smaller.

Yet, as you are by now aware, not all of these technologies are created equally. As a writer, you have to think rhetorically about how and when to use such technologies to visualize information. That's because technologies can be limited in their abilities to help you visualize information, and they can also lead you to misrepresent information, or to represent information in a way that perpetuates stereotypes. For example, if you are working with data on people and you decide to use an image to represent these people, be careful not to perpetuate stereotypes by using technology that provides limited options for designing your texts. Perhaps it automatically uses the colors pink for females and blue for males. Those colors might not be sensitive to all people. Likewise, visualizations can also hamper some in your audience from understanding what you are trying to communicate. People who are color blind, for instance, would have a hard time reading color. So, when using technologies, always consider your audience's needs and abilities when creating a visualization.

TABLE 8.1 List of Visual Ways to Organize Information

Bar chart	Map
Pie chart	Infographic
Line graph	Storyboard
Spread sheet	Tables
Project plans	Illustrations

Final Thoughts

This all might seem obvious, but it is important to remember that technology helps or hinders our ability to write, organize, and understand information. Technology itself is a system whose parts are organized in a certain way. Its system arranges information in a certain way, and that way tells a certain story. That story may limit your understanding of the world as a result. It could make it difficult for you and also for your audience to consider all possibilities for understanding information. As you are making decisions about how you will use technology to write a story—that is, to present information—think about all possibilities for writing that story, that information, and choose the one most appropriate to your situation.

Additional Discussion Questions

1. Gutenberg's printing press represents one technology that changed the way people learned and shared information. Think back throughout history. What other technologies changed the way people learned and shared information? What impacts did they have, and why?
2. What technologies do you use to get information today, and how do these technologies shape that information through their organizing of it? Do you believe that the way in which these technologies organize information helps or limits your understanding of information? Explain your answers.

Additional Activities

1. Data Visualized: Take existing data from a published study (you can find data sets online) and create a visualization, such as an infographic, chart, pie graph,

IMAGE 9.3 Pine Trees in County Parks

etc., to represent this data. Such visualizations aim to make information easily understood by visually representing it. As you create yours, think creatively but also rhetorically. If you were doing research on the number of pine trees in the parks in your county, for instance, could you represent this number using tree icons like in the visualization in Image 8.4?
2. Organizing Information in Many Ways: Collect a variety of texts that organize information in a variety of different ways. Compare and analyze the various ways and determine if they are successful (or not) in communicating the information effectively. To do so, you will need to think rhetorically about the kind of technologies used to create such texts. You will also need to think about their affordances for organizing information and how those affordances enable or prohibit effective communication. You will also need to think about the audiences for these texts and how they will use such texts.

Additional Assignments

1. Organize for Others: Gather information about a local place, like a park, a mall, a restaurant, etc. Then create a text that organizes this information for a particular audience who would be interested in this place. As you create this text, you should consider the following questions:

    - How should you organize and curate this information for others?
    - What drives your decisions to organize in this way?
    - What technologies can help you organize this information in a way that is most helpful to others?

    Share your text with your fellow classmates.

2. A Look at Organizational Elements: Investigate the use of an organizational element such as a heading, label, bullet point, table, etc., throughout history. In other words, find examples of how different writers (and thus their texts) throughout history used such an element and explain how it was used and for what purposes. For instance, if you investigated the use of headings in books and looked back through time at a variety of different books, how were such headings used, and for what purposes? How have such headings changed over time? How have they not? What impact does the use of headings in books have on us and our ability to understand?

Works Cited

Baron, Dennis. "From Pencils to Pixels: The Stages of Literacy Technology." University of Illinois, n.d., www.english.illinois.edu/-people-/faculty/debaron/essays/pencils.htm. Accessed 14 May 2018.

Bodle, Robert. "Predictive Algorithms and Personalization Services on Social Network Sites: Implications for Users and Society." *The Ubiquitous Internet: User and Industry Perspectives*. Edited by Anja Bechmann and Stine Lomborg. Routledge, 2015, pp. 130–145.

Grieco, Elizabeth. "More Americans Are Turning to Multiple Social Media Sites for News." *Pew Research Center*, 2 November 2017, www.pewresearch.org/fact-tank/2017/11/02/more-americans-are-turning-to-multiple-social-media-sites-for-news/. Accessed 10 April 2018.

Mitchell, Amy et al. "Publics Globally Want Unbiased News Coverage, but Are Divided on Whether Their News Media Deliver." *Pew Research Center*, 11 January 2018, www.pewglobal.org/2018/01/11/global-publics-want-politically-balanced-news-but-do-not-think-their-news-media-are-doing-very-well-in-this-area/. Accessed 13 May 2018.

"Total Number of Websites." *Internet Live Stats*, n.d., www.internetlivestats.com/total-number-of-websites/. Accessed 28 March 2018.

Wikipedia. "Wikipedia: Who Writes Wikipedia?" *Wikimedia Foundation Inc.*, 5 May 2018, https://en.wikipedia.org/wiki/Wikipedia:Who_writes_Wikipedia%3F. Accessed 12 May 2018.

World Wide Feb Foundation "History of the Web." *World Wide Feb Foundation*. 2018. https://webfoundation.org/about/vision/history-of-the-web/. Accessed 29 March 2018.

PART 3 READING

The Disappearance of Technology

Toward an Ecological Model of Literacy

Bertram C. Bruce and Maureen P. Hogan

Copyright (1998). From *Handbook of Literacy and Technology: Transformations in a Post-Typographic World* by Reinking, David et al. Reproduced by permission of Taylor and Francis Group, LLC, a division of Informa plc.

Diverse voices have outlined the advantages or disadvantages of technology as they have emerged within classrooms, businesses, communities, and families. Enthusiasts vaunt technological changes, which they contend can effect a more equitable distribution of power. They invoke issues such as empowerment, equality, access, speed, efficiency, liberation, and the development of a global community in support of a pro-technology agenda. As an example, Rheingold's (1993) account of the growth of electronic communication in the Bay Area is framed in terms such as *grassroots groupminds* and *new electronic villages*, terms that call forth the potential of new technologies to support a renewal of community. Going further, some proponents promote a form of technological determinism in which new tools or media alone are seen as bringing about a better world.

More cautious observers warn that technologies can be used to reinscribe existing inequitable power relations. They see technology implicated in the loss of jobs, and poor working conditions . . . surveillance, and regimentation, and caution us about censorship and unequal access. They note that even well-intentioned tools can be used to forward an antidemocratic agenda and that some new technologies support abuses by their very design. Ellul (1980) sees the overall process of technicizing society as "the end of man [humanity]." Technology, he says, "disintegrates and tends to eliminate bit by bit anything that is not technicizable" (p. 203). The result goes far beyond the subordination of humanity to technology.

Thus, we are often faced with a choice between a typically positive, technological determinism and a more negative, social determinism (Bromley, 1997; Bruce, 1993). Rather than conceptualizing the debate via these mutually exclusive and equally deterministic structures, we examine how prevailing ideologies construct the meaning of technologies in different situations. In fact, when technology is used to accomplish specific goals, for certain individuals, in a particular setting, it can be used to liberate or oppress. That is why situated studies of how literacy technologies are used in classrooms, workplaces, or homes and reveal more about these issues than do analyses of technologies or social relations alone (Bowker, Star, Turner, & Gasser, 1997).

We tend to think of technology as a set of tools to perform a specific function. These tools are often portrayed as mechanistic, exterior, autonomous, and concrete devices that accomplish tasks and create products. We do not generally think of them as intimately entwined with social and biological lives. But literacy technologies, such as pen and paper, index cards, computer databases, word processors, networks, e-mail, and hypertext, are also ideological tools; they are designed, accessed, interpreted, and used to further purposes that embody social values. More than mechanistic, they are organic, because they merge with our social, physical, and psychological beings. Thus, we need to look more closely at how technologies are realized in given settings. We may find that technological tools can be so embedded in the living process that their status as technologies disappears.

The Disappearance of Technology

As technologies embed themselves in everyday discourse and activity, a curious thing happens. The more we look, the more they slip into the background. Despite our attention, we lose sight of the way they give shape to our daily lives. This disappearance effect is evident when we consider whether a technology empowers people to do things that would be difficult, or even impossible otherwise.

Consider for example, the telephone. As it comes into use, it is initially considered a novelty that permits new and interesting, but hardly necessary actions. Later, as it is used more widely, the actions it affords move from novelty to habit, the tool becomes commonplace. Soon it is treated as part of daily activity. We might say, "I talked to my friend today," without feeling any need to mention that the telephone was a necessary tool for that conversation to occur. Through this process, we move from looking at the technology as an addition to life to looking at life through that technology. The embedding of the technology in the matrix of our lives makes it invisible. In fact, the greater its integration into daily practices, the less it is seen as a technology at all.

Thus, writing is no longer viewed as a technology; instead, only its newest manifestations take on that role. Each literacy technique—quills, movable type, ball-point pens, typewriters—passes through phases of technology to tool, from unfamiliar to familiar, and from visible to invisible. Already, word processing, once a new technology, is now considered to be just the way people write. Webpage writing conceived as a new technology ability today, will not be so in a few years.

Further, as a tool becomes embedded in social practices, our conception of the ability required for an individual to use that tool changes as well. In the early stages of use, disability is counted as a flaw in the tool: We say that poor design of the technology makes it difficult to use. Later, the disability becomes an attribute of the user, not the tool. We say that the user needs more training, or worse, is incapable of using the tool. Once the status of the tool as technology has fully merged into daily practice, the disability to use it becomes an essential attribute of certain people.

For example, stairs are an architectural technology that empower people to move easily from one floor of a building to another, floors themselves being a technology to increase the ratio of floor space to land and building surface area. But ordinarily, we do not consider floors, or even stairs, as technologies; their ubiquity makes them invisible. Operating invisibly, stairs empower some just as surely as they disempower others.

People who use wheelchairs can move easily within a single floor, but they become disabled by the presence of stairs. The stairs construct wheelchair-ness as a disability. Even if one insists on characterizing wheelchair-ness as a brute fact, a fixed property of the individual, the consequences of that fact are radically altered by the architectural technology. Consider how the addition of elevators to a building reconstructs wheelchair-ness as a minor disability. The important point is that the ambient technologies can alternately able or disable an individual many times in the course of a single day.

This process is one of the crucial ways in which all literacy technologies—slate tablets, typewriters, word processors, networks, computer interfaces, databases, the Web—are ideologically embedded. Effective use of the dominant reading and writing technologies then becomes the defining characteristic for new forms of literacy (Bruce, 1995). Lack of such ability can be conceived as an inherent disability, located in the individual, which might or might not be alleviated through various measures, such as providing more time, easier texts, skill training, tutoring, help features, donations of equipment, and so forth.

But if we recognize that these tools are constructed, we begin to see how design choices create ability and disability. Lack of English fluency, for example, has now been constructed as a literacy disability with respect to the Web, because so much of the Web content and even the Web software tools are in English. Not owning or being able to use a computer is constructed as a disability for attaining a college education. A competent writer may be locked out of an editing job for lack of desktop publishing skills. Thus, new literacy abilities, and consequently, disabilities are continually reconstructed. In this sense, discussion about participation in any literate society must be referenced to that society's current and emerging literacy technologies.

One implication of this is a lack of choice. We cannot simply choose our tools (i.e., to write longhand, use a typewriter, a word processor, or e-mail) in order to be literate participants. Instead, the technology chooses us; it marks us as full, marginal, or nonparticipating. Haas (1996) makes a similar point in her call to consider the materiality of literacy, how its various manifestations over time have always been linked to specific bodily and physical realizations. An obvious implication is that teachers of literacy must consider how new technologies help to reconstruct reading and writing processes for their students.

Students and parents increasingly expect convenient access, explicit instructions, and the use of computer technology in the classroom. Similarly, teachers expect students to have computers at home. Thus, computer use is becoming an integral aspect of academic achievement. The promise of learning more through new technologies is becoming a premise, a requisite for success. A danger is that the mere presence of computers may signal that all is well when little has actually changed in the reading and writing ecology.

The disappearance of technology is more than a metaphor. We cannot see most microprocessors because they are now hidden in artifacts such as telephones, fax machines, cars, dishwashers, and even athletic equipment. Such hidden microprocessors have been called *embedded systems* because they are not obvious in these devices and their function may be invisible to the user. Thus, the infrastructure of the larger world is becoming infused everywhere with software. Soon, General Motors will sell more microprocessors than IBM, because microprocessors will control speed, navigation, braking, suspension, climate, and airbags (Fiddler, 1996).

Embedded systems may entail a loss of control in one sense. Fewer people will be able to fix their own cars or any number of household appliances. They will need to rely more on experts, and they will need to pay for that expertise. On the other hand, these systems can create a more user-friendly world, what some have called "soft technology" (Norman, 1993). Their overall effect will depend on the social conditions and power relations that surround their use.

Similarly, literacy tools are becoming embedded systems. For an increasing number of people, writing means typing on a personal computer, reading means browsing a newspaper on the Internet, and researching means accessing a library database via modem. If a computer hard drive crashes while using today's literacy tools, most people will need to rely on an expert to fix it. Literacy today is becoming dependent on embedded systems that are invisible to the user.

One implication of this embedded technology is that we need to look more carefully at how technology is affecting our lives even when we cannot see it directly. Literacy means not just reading and writing texts, but "reading" the world, and the technological artifacts within it.

An Ecological Model for Literacy Technologies

Awareness of how technologies merge with daily practices leads us to view technology and literacy as constituent parts of life, elements of an ecological system (see also Bromley, 1997; Latour, 1988; Law, 1991). This viewpoint gives us a basis for understanding the interpenetration among machines, humans, and the natural world. Lemke (chap. 17, this volume) has a similar conception of literacy, which he describes as part of an ecosocial system:

> Literacies cannot be adequately analyzed just as what individuals do. We must understand them as part of the larger systems of practices that hold a society together... if we think the word *society* means only people, then we need another term, one that, like *ecosystem*, includes the total environment: machines, buildings, cables, satellites, bedrock, sewers, farms, insect life, bacteria.

Thus, literacies, and the technologies of literacy, can only be understood in relation to larger systems of practices. Most technologies become so enmeshed in daily experience that they disappear; that is, they are no longer seen as technologies. They become the ordinary; in order to see them, we must make the familiar strange. As T. S. Eliot (1943) in "Little Gidding" expressed it, "And the end of all our exploring/Will be to arrive where we started/And know the place for the first time" (p. 59).

Eliot's words resonate for us as literacy educators because we have the responsibility to make the familiar strange—not only to rethink the uses of technologies, but also to know it again for the first time as we consider where our students may be starting. We must recall what it is like to be a novice or to be less privileged. We need to critically examine what has become commonplace, normalized, and even invisible. In some cases, we may need to depend on our students to navigate the voyage because they may be more expert.

A question often arises in the technology debates: Do we use technology, or does technology use us? Idhe (1990) rejects both alternatives, and instead sees people as living within a technologically textured ecosystem. The relations between humans and technology are both sensory and contextual. Because kinesthetic perception is always part of the process of using technology, we can imagine our bodies as extended through artifacts, forming hybrids. Idhe says a technology is not simply a tool, but an artifact with intentionality. In Latour's (1988) terms, technologies are actors in social systems, as are texts, maps, physical spaces, and artifacts of all kinds.

If we assume that technology is necessarily embedded in cultural practices, it is only one step further to see people as caught within not just specific technologies, but in "technology," a process Heidegger (1977) calls *enframing*. He argues that we must understand technology as an activity that surrounds us, as in his famous assertion, "everywhere we remain unfree and chained to technology, whether we passionately affirm or deny it" (p. 311). The essence of technology lies in the way it "comes forth" or reveals itself in human activity. Heidegger wants us to understand technology as an inescapable part of our social world and ultimately, of our basic values. The crucial question then becomes: What is the essence of technology? He warns us that we may perceive all entities in the life world, in the ecology, as a "standing reserve," simply as resources to serve technology. Technology provides a way to order, and then, more ominously, the way to be ordered.

Social Relations and Technologies

People write social relations through the languages of technology, constructing hierarchies and fields of inclusion or exclusion through silicon chips, wires, and video displays. The sentences we write with technologies describe our social life, as surely as the cave paintings of Lascaux or the Mayan calendar tell tales of earlier social worlds. However, technologies also serve to prescribe, to turn social intentions into tangible realities. Latour (1991) encapsulates this point as, "technology is society made durable" (p. 103).

How can this be? How is it that a plastic box full of electronic components can tell the tale of social relations? According to Selfe and Selfe (1994), interface designs are geopolitical borders, a sort of cultural contact zone. They encourage English teachers and students to critique its politics. Such a critique might start with their observation that standard "computer interfaces do not . . . provide direct evidence of different cultures and races that make up the American social complex, nor do they show much evidence of different linguistic groups or groups of differing economic status" (p. 486). They argue that these interfaces, with desktop metaphors, Eurocentric icons, and English language defaults, are markers of capitalism and class privilege. A corporate ideology becomes its primary orientation, which promotes the commodification of information. Information as commodity then translates into big business for commercial networks. Selfe and Selfe also propose that the interface maps the kind of knowledge imbued with hierarchical values characteristic of Western patriarchal cultures rather than knowledge as bricolage—a more intuitive, associative, organic, and perhaps feminine process. The interface, then, is a political, ideological and epistemic borderland where we in fact "write our lives" with technology.

We need to disentangle this complex in order to see how ideology is woven through it. In the sections that follow, we explore how technologies function as ideological tools, focusing on four intertwined themes. First we examine how ideology influences the design of technologies. Second, we examine the distribution of technologies, including questions of access. Third, we consider ideological aspects of using technology. Finally, we look at how we interpret the effects of technologies.

Design of Technologies

One arena for ideology to operate in is the design of technologies. New information technologies are often designed to forward democratic ideals through interaction, collaboration, and sharing of information. A familiar example is local area networks that allow multiple users to share folders as part of their collaborative work. Shareware and groupware programs (such as the synchronous[1] program InterChange) allow real-time conversations among multiple users for collaborative writing (Bruce, Peyton, & Batson, 1993). Such programs can facilitate equal access as they are designed to give voice to many participants. As Beach and Lundell (chap. 6, this volume) show, computer-mediated communication can "create an engaging dialogic forum for social literacy practices."

In a similar spirit, the Internet, what McChesney (1995) calls "society's central nervous system" (p. 14), with its millions of users, can foster new relationships and even build new communities based on shared interests and information (Rheingold, 1993; Spender, 1995). These relationships and communities can be far-reaching, relatively inexpensive, and increasingly multilingual, multicultural, and global (see Garner & Gillingham, chap. 13, this volume). In principle, the weblike design of literacy technologies can offer a more equitable distribution of information than any technology we have previously known.

At the same time, both hardware and software design can disrupt the democratic process and the community-building ideals. For example, InterChange does not erase power hierarchies. Users of these programs still understand who has the authority to initiate, lead, direct, and silence discussions. Furthermore, the texts are controlled by a teacher, administrator, or technologist who can easily monitor students' exchanges without their knowledge or permission. Similarly, within corporations, groupware has become attractive to managers in part because it furthers their ability to monitor and control employees.

Other authors have voiced concern about how epistemology is embedded in the design. Could it be that militaristic ways of knowing and masculine desire are buried in the design of certain technologies? Sofia (in press), drawing on insights from psychoanalysis and semiotics, suggests that the design of the contemporary computer recalls its militaristic male-centered history, a history that has helped further a view of the computer as fetish, which in turn may exclude females' attitudes. As she explains:

> Computers seem to embody the very essence of rationality, working as they do with principles of digital code and processing, and formal logic. Educationalists who believed technologies were neutral ... were surprised by the rapidity with which patterns of masculine domination and female exclusion emerged with the introduction of computing in schools.

Sofia (in press) claims that computer technology, with its connection to one subgenre of science fiction fantasy, with its attendant notions of control and domination, speaks especially to adolescent males. Militarism, formal logic, and science fiction contribute to what is largely a male computer culture, which some females may find uninviting. The result is that computer culture reproduces negative attitudes toward computer use among women. To offset this trend, Sofia recommends that feminists appropriate computers in their own way, rejecting the "informatics of domination," fetishism of the "androcentric science fiction culture," and fantasies of the computer as "second self."

It is important to be careful here: The notion that interfaces or digital codes enforce any one set of values teeters toward the technocentric view, beyond which the tool determines social practice. Nevertheless, the discussion of gendered technologies points to yet one more way that ideology can be embedded in the design of technology.

Distribution of Technologies

A second arena for ideology to operate through technology is that of distribution and access. Consider the case of people who are blind or visually impaired: With older technologies of text, many individuals accommodate to dominant literacy practices, for example, by using Braille or audiotape. New technologies pose a new array of opportunities but also the need for new accommodations. To a certain extent, the wide availability of Internet resources and technology such as speech generation and recognition promise greater access than ever before. However, reliance on graphical interfaces, the abandonment of support for older technologies, and limitations in access time or training can exclude the same individuals from the global information community. Thus, the deployment of computers and how they are used bears on the degree to which visual impairment functions as literacy disability.

In a similar fashion, people in other groups find their access to literacy limited in new ways. Technology, of course, is not free and it is no surprise that those with the most money have the best technology if they want it; those within the lower socioeconomic brackets, as well as racial minorities and females, have less access than other groups (Sutton, 1991).[2] Access is thus partial, restricted, and stratified. With so much rapid change so quickly, new hardware and software are quickly developing to meet consumers' needs. Even technophiles have difficulty keeping up with the trends. To have access to technology, people have to be aware of it, have the means to purchase it, and have the knowledge to use it. Awareness, means, and knowledge can be restricted and privileged. For many, the promise of technology is still remote; for others it is a premise—something that is a normal and already invisible part of everyday life.

Research by Michaels, Cazden, and Bruce (1985) supports the theory that unequal access to technology operates at many levels: "As is so often the case with new technologies, computer use is more apt to reinforce existing patterns rather than change them" (p. 36). In schools, for example, there are inequalities in the ratios of computers to students in software usage and in classroom use. Even when schools have computers, poorer schools often have less sophisticated software. Use may be limited to drill-and-practice software rather than to the Internet and to the problem solving that is more likely to be emphasized in affluent schools. Even when adequate hardware and software are available, schools may implement the technology in ways that further exacerbate inequality; for example, by limiting access to students who are pulled out of regular classes.

In higher education, access to technology can also accentuate economic difference: Many schools now require students to purchase computers. The University of Illinois Law School now requires new students to have a computer.[3] Associate Dean Colombo explained that "for lawyering in the twenty-first century, law students are just going to have to have computer skills—a wide variety of them" (Wurth, 1996, p. A-1). Besides using computerized databases to do legal research, the students may also use document assembly programs, e-mail, and the Web when they are finally hired by a law firm. Also, the law school is hoping that students will receive more one-on-one attention with their law instructors through e-mail communication and electronic exercises.

For those students who can barely afford law school, the addition of the requirement to purchase a computer can be a burden. Thus, the requirement illustrates the presumption that those without technical expertise and the means to afford technology will probably not succeed as lawyers in the 21st century. Thus, computers now delimit the potential for academic success, even before a student considers applying to law school.

As information technologies merge with communications technologies, what can be done with a computer now depends on the quality of network connections. New computers are quickly linked into local area networks and the Internet within organizations and at least to some extent through the telephone in homes and schools. With an inexpensive connection, a user can transmit and receive ordinary text albeit at a slow rate. Faster connections allow the transmission of audio, pictures, and video. This means that "being on the Internet" varies tremendously depending on the kind of network connection one has. Those with faster connections can gather and transmit more information, and in short, do more with their computers. As information becomes increasingly accessible for some but not all citizens, network speed becomes an index of power in society.

In the 21st century, computer literacy means not only being familiar and comfortable with computers, but also having access to information. Network speed therefore becomes an indicator of literacy practices, just as the possession of a quill pen once was. As Table 1 shows, more powerful affiliations have access to more information.[4] The more access they have to information, the more powerful they become within an information-based economy. In this sense, then, power relations are reinforced rather than equalized.

One could think of network access as being analogous to having a membership card for a huge library. The 3,000 times difference in speed means that some members have access to thousands of books, as well as graphics, audio, video, and large data sets; it is as if these members have carte blanche to the Library of Congress. Others, however, are restricted to a limited number of plain text materials; it is as if these members can only go to a community bookmobile. Differences in access become even more significant to the extent that graphics, audio, video, virtual reality, and other media become standard means for representation. Thus, different network speeds differentially construct ability.

TABLE 1 Network Speed, Media, and Users

Type	Speed	Text in 1 Minute	Other Media in 1 Minute	Typical Users
14.4 modem	14.4 kb/s	25 pages	1 black-and-white diagram	School
28.8 modem	28.8 kb/s	50 pages	1 color picture	Home
56 modem	56 kb/s	130 pages	Audio	
ISDN-64	64 kb/s	1 book (150 pages)	Compressed, small window video	Consultant
ISDN-128	128 kb/s	2 books	10 pictures	Small business, some homes, magnet schools
T1	1.54 mb/s	12 books		Medium-size business
Cable modem	10–30 mb/s	16–48 books		Major corporations
T3	45 mb/s	72 books	Full video	Military, multinational corporations

Again, power relations are shaped both by the technologies and by the existing structures that support social stratification.

An interesting side to the power achieved through network speed is that those privileged social actors, living with an accelerated consciousness (i.e., faster is better) in a product-centered society, may increasingly experience a deteriorating quality of life. Dobrzynski (1996) writes that many American corporate workers are burdened by an excess of e-mail and voice mail messages. Corporate downsizing has meant a loss of support staff, so corporate workers deal directly with communications overflow. Some employees go in early, stay late, or use their weekends to respond to e-mail correspondence. It could also be true that high-technology companies are experiencing more communication, but at a lower level of quality and a higher level of irrelevance. Discussions about retirement surprise parties and theater tickets are flirting for employees' attention, whereas more pressing issues such as market reports and plans for product demonstrations may be overlooked, or at least deferred. Because workers are not talking to each other face to face as much any more, management will need to worry about possible misunderstandings and trivial or recreational material comingling with the important.

Rifkin (1995) thinks that the word *karoshi* will be more than a Japanese cultural phenomenon. The term describes a person's emotional and physical breakdown caused by high-tech stress. In a post-Fordist, state-of-the-art workplace, Rifkin imagines, it will soon be a global, cultural condition. This new kind of stress, which may even change workers' biorhythms as they try to calibrate their biology with computer response time, can lead to chronic fatigue and even a fatal breakdown. *Karoshi* is a clear example of how the technology merges with not only our social, but also our physical beings. Of course, for some employees, the inclusion of more recreational discourse within the workplace and new modes of interaction may mark an improved quality of life. Thus, the same effect may be positive or negative depending on one's perspective, a theme we return to later in this chapter.

Another consideration is that, with respect to access to the Internet which has so much information and so many users, we need to perhaps stop asking what is wrong with texts (a tenet of critical thinking), but rather, what is right with them? Which texts are useful? How do we know? Whose ideas are salvageable? Why? Because much of the information on the Internet is unrefereed, and increasingly commodified, the Internet raises new questions about authority and access to unbiased information. In serious academic journals, for example, the manuscripts are carefully reviewed and the journals themselves are typically free of blatantly commercial advertising, although they may have invitations to subscribe to other journals or professional organizations. The Internet, however, has characteristics of both shopping malls and academic journals (Bruce, 1995; Burbules & Bruce, 1995). Will it evolve into an international coffee shop or a high-tech billboard? Will it foster more global dialogue or more corporate monologue? What do we want it to be? How does it fit in with our democratic ideals? Where do we fit in the process?

McChesney (1995) urges concerned Internet users to fight for the kind of information system that guarantees noncommercial access. If not, he warns, cyberspace could be transformed into a giant marketplace:

> The contours of the emerging communications battle are unclear, but most business observers expect a flurry of competition followed by the establishment of a stable oligopoly dominated by a handful of enormous firms. What is clear is that the communications highway will not be devoted to reducing inequality or misery in our society. In fact, without any policies to counteract the market, the new technologies will probably create a world of information have's and have-not's, thereby exacerbating our society's already considerable social and economic inequality.
>
> (p. 17)

The distribution of high-tech communications information is unequal in a stratified society. Who will guarantee that it will not be constrained by corporate leaders? What kind of policy should ensure that nonprofit, noncommercial, and reliable information has equal access?

Use of Technologies

Regardless of how a technology is designed and distributed, the use people make of it becomes a third arena in which ideology can operate. In some cases, the use is for democratic ideals, perhaps to invite student collaboration and more equitable participation. Or, teachers may encourage students to expand their horizons through electronic chats with students from other communities (see Garner & Gillingham, chap. 13, this volume). These changes in schools can also encounter stiff resistance as Neilsen (chap. 8, this volume) documents. Moreover, technology used for censorship, surveillance, and control, countering the very ideals it can promote.

Recently the spirit of the global community has taken an inward turn, as more people are recognizing ways in which technology can be used to gather information surreptitiously. There is an increased demand for cryptography software. Those with greater technological control, especially government agencies and big corporations, can be interlopers, controllers, and censors. Large companies now establish firewalls to separate their information from the public. Some countries, notably Singapore and China, have discussed creating firewalls between their entire countries and the rest of the world.

Computer systems cannot guarantee privacy, and the amount of personal information in databases is disturbing. An interested party can all too easily access information about a person's credit history, spending habits, insurance claims, and health history. This information, or misinformation, can make one vulnerable to credit card fraud, restricted health insurance, and bothersome marketing ploys. Using MapQuest, one can find the address of nearly anyone in the United States, including a map and directions to their house. If you carry a mobile phone, your whereabouts are tracked continually and stored in a telephone company database, even when you are not talking on the phone. What do potential abuses of technology say about our right to privacy in a democratic society? The information age has ushered in a redefinition of public and private space which we are only beginning to understand.

And what of the right to free speech? According to Browning (1996), the Internet is learning to censor itself. The Platform for Internet Content Selection (PICS), developed by the WWW Consortium, is trying to resolve the moral issues that lie at the core of regulating information on the Net. As Browning puts it, "PICS promises to create a do-it-yourself censorship that will allow everybody both freedom to speak and freedom not to listen" (p. 38). The goal of the rating system is to allay government responsibility for censorship. Instead, users can access self-rating schemes, such as SafeSurf, which allow them to find out information about a website's violence, nudity, sex, and language content. Thus, PICS would provide users with "a vast interlinked system of reference, recommendation and reputation" (Browning, 1996, p. 38). The rating system would necessarily be ideological: How much, and to what degree, are violence, nudity, sex, and foul language acceptable? To what extent does banning so-called immoral content coincidentally ban sites that promote political issues such as gay and lesbian rights or destruction of landmines? How are the categories defined? The creators of the systems such as SafeSurf will devise algorithms based on their own set of values.

What has been referred to as "Netwars" is another way that ideology penetrates the use of technologies. For example, America Online, a commercial service, does not provide access to most White nationalist news groups. Although the popular service is trying to promote tolerance and equality, a democratic ideal, it also limits freedom of speech, another democratic ideal. Ideological Netwars thus summon a whole set of issues about defining democracy in cyberspace.

Interpretation of the Effects of Technologies

A fourth arena for the operation of ideology through technology is the way we interpret its effects. For example, a company's downsizing that becomes possible by reliance on more technology is frightening if you are a worker who could be displaced by a machine. However, if you are a corporate director seeking greater efficiency, you would welcome the same technology. If you are a literature student who needs to find a Shakespeare quote quickly, you could find it easily on the Web. However, from your instructor's point of view, this easy access could be negative if the use of quotes was supposed to be an indicator of deep reading.

One can interpret the technologically based changes in the economy in similar ways. Automation in the context of corporate restructuring is leading to a decrease in human labor, especially in the manufacturing and service sectors (see Mikulecky & Kirkley, chap. 18, this volume). For large, technologically advanced companies, the profit margin increases as production becomes more efficient. However, two negative aspects accompany this greater efficiency. The first is increased unemployment, with workers displaced by automated systems in both manufacturing (e.g., rubber, mining, electronics, textiles) and service sectors (e.g., bank tellers, secretaries). The second aspect, a corollary of the first, is that unemployed or underemployed people cannot contribute much to the economic growth that these products promise. According to Rifkin (1995), the two problems indicate a growing dual, or cleaving, economy for the 21st century. The cleaving, Rifkin warns, will occur both nationally and globally. The first economy, the utopian one, will be made up of highly trained, well-educated knowledge workers in an information-based economy. The second economy, for the reserve of other workers, will be struggling with unemployment, part-time work, and jobs left in the service sector, such as waitressing, construction, automotive maintenance, painting, and so forth.

Thus we find two economies and a growing chasm between them. As Rifkin (1995) suggests, "Ironically, the closer we seem to come to the technological fruition of the utopian dream, the more dystopian the future seems" (p. 56). Literacy no longer means just reading and writing to secure a decent job, even one that does not require much of either. Literacy means reading the technological world, including the relation of technologies to these dual economies.

Conclusion

Despite many differences in conceptions, various scholars (Connell, 1996; Heidegger, 1977; Idhe, 1990; Latour, 1993) have pointed to a consensus regarding the study of technology: The more we examine technology, the less we find it useful to focus on its technical attributes per se, and the more we see the need to understand the ways in which ideology is embedded within it. To understand what a technology means, we must examine how it is designed, interpreted, employed, constructed, and reconstructed through value-laden daily practices. Following this line of argument, the concept of situated evaluation has been proposed to evaluate changes as new technologies are adopted (Bruce, Peyton, & Batson, 1993; Bruce & Rubin, 1993).

A social setting produces an ideological matrix that includes both laudable and deplorable realizations of technology. What does this mean for the transformation of literacy in coming years? The ecological model suggests understanding literacy technologies as embedded throughout social practices, often in invisible ways. There is as much reason to be cautious as to be celebratory. Although it is clear that technology can enhance literacy by providing motivation, access to information, new worlds to students, faster communication, and real-time communication with peers, using technology in educational settings requires continuing critical analysis.

The 21st century occasions new ways of conceiving and teaching about literacy. Because of the increasing generation of information through new recent technology, teachers need to consider, perhaps more than ever, how they will teach students to select and critique texts, especially those on the Web. Additionally, literacy teachers need to be ready to handle a wide range of student familiarity and ability with writing and researching technologies. They need to recognize that a computer is a tool, but also a symbol that indexes privilege (Bromley & Apple, in press; Stuckey, 1991). Teachers will need to assess how technologies relate to students' positions in the dual economies, thus expanding the meaning of critical literacy (Muspratt, Luke, & Freebody, 1997) to encompass new means of representation. They may also need to revise their conception of text, as students learn how to read and write hypertexts, graphs, charts, mathematical equations, pictorial models, and even virtual realities.

An important part of literacy education now is to consider a range of options for learning, including a wide range of technologies. One-on-one conferencing and peer editing are still fine ways to teach college writing. This can be done via e-mail or through office visits and peer editing workshops, and in different settings. Reading exercises that celebrate multiple interpretations can be done with or without computer assistance. An ecological model of literacy helps us to visualize the whole, and to see a range of options as part of the whole, neither dismissing nor naively accepting technology wholesale.

Finally, researchers need to do more situated studies that detail the complexities of literacy within an ecological model, and to see how ideology operates within situations where literacy, technology, and humans interact. We may then approach a more rounded understanding of how technologies can either promote or forestall equality.

Notes

1. Synchronous programs support real-time conversation in written form, unlike email, which is usually used asynchronously.
2. Based on a review of research on equity and computers in the schools throughout the eighties in K—12 classrooms.
3. Other law schools such as the University of Richmond, Stanford, Duke, New Mexico, and Oregon have similar requirements.
4. Some of the numbers in the table are approximate. For example, cable modems are shared among users, so the actual transmission rates can be much lower than 30 mb/s. Also, different types of data compression, image size and so on markedly affect how much can be transmitted; there is a clear trade-off between document quality and quantity. Nevertheless, the general pattern shown in these examples still holds: Common transmission rates vary by several orders of magnitude and that has qualitative consequences.

References

Bowker, G. C., Star, S. L., Turner, W., & Gasser, L. (1997). *Social science, technical systems and cooperative work: Beyond the great divide*. Mahwah, NJ: Lawrence Erlbaum Associates.

Bromley, H. (1997, Winter). The social chicken and the technological egg. *Educational Theory, 47*(1), 51–65.

Bromley, H., & Apple, M. W. (in press). *Education/technology/power: Educational computing as a social practice*. Albany: State University of New York Press.

Browning, J. (1996, September). The Internet is learning to censor itself. *Scientific American, 275*, p. 38.

Bruce, B. C. (1993). Innovation and social change. In B. C. Bruce, J. K. Peyton, & T. W. Batson (Eds.), *Network-based classrooms: Promises and realities* (pp. 9–32). New York: Cambridge University Press.

Bruce, B. C. (1995, November). *Twenty-first century literacy* (Tech. Rep. No. 624). Urbana: University of Illinois, Center for the Study of Reading.

Bruce, B. C., Peyton, J. K., & Batson, T. W. (Eds.). (1993). *Network-based classrooms: Promises and realities*. New York: Cambridge University Press.

Bruce, B. C., & Rubin, A. (1993). *Electronic quills: A situated evaluation of using computers for writing in the classroom*. Hillsdale, NJ: Lawrence Erlbaum Associates.

Burbules, N. C., & Bruce, B. C. (1995, November). This is not a paper. *Educational Researcher, 24*(8), 12–18.

Connell, J. (1996). Exploring some of the educational implications of Idhe's philosophy of education. *Educational Foundations, 10*, 5–12.
Dobrzynski, J. (1996, April 28). @wit's end: Coping with e-mail overload. *The New York Times*, p. A2.
Eliot, T. S. (1943). *Four quartets*. New York: Harcourt Brace.
Ellul, J. (1980). *The technological system* (J. Neugroschel, Trans.). New York: Continuum.
Fiddler, J. (1996, April). *Embedding the information revolution* (Computer Science Colloquium Series). Champaign—Urbana: University of Illinois.
Haas, C. (1996). *Writing technology: Studies on the materiality of literacy*. Mahwah, NJ: Lawrence Erlbaum Associates.
Heidegger, M. (1977). The question concerning technology. In W. Lovitt (Trans.), *The question concerning technology and other essays* (pp. 311–341). New York: Harper & Row.
Idhe, D. (1990). *Technology and the lifeworld*. Bloomington: Indiana University Press.
Latour, B. (1988). Mixing humans and non-humans together: The sociology of a door-closer. *Social Problems, 35*, 298–310.
Latour, B. (1991). Technology is society made durable. In J. Law (Ed.), *A sociology of monsters: Essays on power, technology, and domination* (pp. 103–131). New York: Routledge.
Latour, B. (1993). *We have never been modern* (C. Porter, Trans.). Cambridge, MA: Harvard University Press.
Law, J. (Ed.). (1991). *A sociology of monsters: Essays on power, technology, and domination*. New York: Routledge.
McChesney, R. (1995, July 10). Information superhighway robbery. *In These Times, 19*, 14–17.
Michaels, S., Cazden, C., & Bruce, B. (1985). Whose computer is it anyway? *Science for the People, 17*, 36, 43–44.
Muspratt, S., Luke, A., & Freebody, P. (1997). *Constructing critical literacies*. Cresskill, NJ and Sydney: Hampton Press and Allen & Unwin.
Norman, D. A. (1993). *Things that make us smart: Defending human attributes in the age of the machine*. Reading, MA: Addison-Wesley.
Rheingold, H. (1993). *The virtual community: Homesteading on the electronic frontier*. New York: Addison-Wesley.
Rifkin, J. (1995). *The end of work: The decline of the global labor force and the dawn of the post-market era*. New York: Putnam.
Selfe, C., & Selfe, R. J., Jr. (1994). The politics of the interface: Power and its exercise in electronic contact zones. *College Composition and Communication, 45*(4), 480–504.
Sofia, Z. (in press). Computers, gender and technological irrationality. In H. Bromley & M. Apple (Eds.), *Education/technology/power: Educational computing as a social practice*. Albany: State University of New York Press.
Spender, D. (1995). *Nattering on the nets*. North Melbourne, Australia: Spinifex.
Stuckey, J. E. (1991). *The violence of literacy*. Portsmouth, NH: Boynton/Cook.

Sutton, R. E. (1991). Equity and computers in the schools: A decade of research. *Review of Educational Research, 61*(4), 475–503.

Wurth, J. (1996, June 2). Personal computer on UI school supply list. *The News Gazette,* pp. A1, A10.

Reading Questions for *The Disappearance of Technology: Toward an Ecological Model of Literacy* by Bertram C. Bruce and Maureen P. Hogan

1. What do the authors mean by the disappearance of technology?
2. Do you agree with the authors when they say that literacy today is becoming dependent on embedded systems that are invisible to the user? Why or why not?
3. Why should we look more carefully at how technology is affecting our lives even when we cannot see it directly?
4. Why is viewing technology and literacy as parts of an ecological system helpful to our understanding of relationships between people, machines, and the natural world?

PART 4

Technology Is Embedded

Technology doesn't exist in a bubble and doesn't happen in isolation on its own. Technology is in this world, is about this world, and is shaped by this world. It is always connected to something, whether it is our bodies, our communities, or our environments. As a result, when using a technology, we must be critical of how the technology came to be in a specific place at a specific time and by specific people.

In Part 4, therefore, you will consider the implications of technology as embedded in our world and in our societies. To do so, you will look at specific technologies, writing included, and examine how they are situated as part of a larger system of things. Writing is a social activity, one that we do collaboratively with the help of others, and is always situated within a particular location at a particular moment in time. That particular location and that particular moment in time shape the way you and others write.

Key Questions

1. How are technologies embedded in our societies and how do societies shape technologies?
2. Why is writing situated?
3. In what ways does "embeddedness" impact what can and cannot be written?

Key Terms

Chapter 9
1. system
2. interface
3. backend operations
4. frontend operations
5. label
6. algorithms
7. search engines
8. data
9. binary form
10. bit
11. byte
12. database
13. Boolean operators

Chapter 10
1. assemblage
2. kairos
3. augmented reality
4. virtual reality
5. gamification
6. space
7. place
8. GPS
9. stakeholders
10. infrastructures
11. connected
12. hyperlink
13. sharing
14. collaborating

Chapter 11
1. rapport
2. subject line
3. greeting
4. content
5. closing
6. ISP
7. Universal Design

CHAPTER 9

Technology Is a System

Contents

What You See and Don't See 211
Translating From One System to Another..214
Your Role in a System 215
Language in a System 217
Can You Trust Systems? 222
Search Engines 224
Data, Data, Data 225
Searching Data 228
Using Data to Make Writing Better 229
Too Many Systems at Work at One Time 229
Hacking the System 230
Final Thoughts 231

What You See and Don't See

Imagine for a moment that you are lucky enough to score two tickets to see your favorite band play at a local stadium. When you and your friend go to that stadium, most likely printed on your ticket is the multimodal information you need to find your seats. The stadium probably helps, too, with its signs, maps, and ushers, all there to help you navigate the area. And, since the rows are lettered and the seats are numbered, you are able to find your seats easily. That's because long ago you learned your alphabet and numbers and since then you've had lots of practice navigating places that organize their seats using letters and numbers.

Before you got to the stadium and your seats, you had to rely on several other technologies. In the first place, if you bought your tickets online, you relied on several computer systems, some of which you paid attention to and some that worked behind the scenes, so to speak. Perhaps, if you wanted to see your favorite band, you began with a Google search, entered in "my favorite band's name," and pressed enter. In less than a second, Google returned several results. From there, you scanned through the results until you found StubHub, a site that lets you purchase concert tickets. On StubHub, you next moved through an interactive map of a stadium until you located the perfect seats. You added those seats to your shopping cart and then checked out. Once the purchase was made, StubHub sent you an email that allowed you to download and print your tickets at home.

As you can see, the experience of going to a concert did not happen without the help of systems at work. In the previous paragraph alone, there were multiple connected systems that helped you purchase concert tickets in a relatively short amount of time. In purchasing your tickets, however, you probably thought less about the technology you were using and more about how great of a time you would be having at the concert. You probably didn't think about how exactly those technological systems were operating, what they were doing, and when they were doing it. Unless, that is, there was a problem along the way. If your printer didn't work, you probably took notice. Certainly, when systems work smoothly, we often don't pay attention to them, mainly because they are not in our way. But, when they do break down, those systems come into view more readily.

In this chapter, however, you will learn that even when systems don't break down, it is essential to think about how systems operate, our roles and the roles of others in those operations, the role that writing plays in those operations, and how those systems operate in our world. In buying concert tickets, you probably didn't realize that a lot of things were happening. You probably didn't realize that Google and StubHub were gathering data about you through their systems. You probably didn't realize that these companies will use this data later on for business purposes. You also probably didn't realize the politics involved in operating such businesses, the financial decisions companies make to provide their services, the social consequences your actions have as you use such systems, the writing you did in order to find the concert tickets you desired, and so on. You probably didn't realize just how big technological systems really are.

Technology Is Undeniably a System

A *system* can be thought of as a series or set of things that connect together to make up a complex whole. In terms of systems like Google and StubHub, you could also think of a system in terms of procedures or steps that must be used in order to ensure something gets done. When you enter in search words and click enter, those systems process a series of steps in order to complete a task, which, in your case, was to find information for you about seats at a concert.

Google and StubHub are but two examples of systems. There are certainly plenty of others. In fact, Google and StubHub don't work in isolation. These two systems work within and in conjunction with many other systems. Google and StubHub, for instance, have to be able to operate on a variety of computer systems, from PCs to MACs to mobile phones. They also are created within economic and social systems that operate worldwide. In these systems, they have to make money and abide by social rules.

Did You Know? System Development Life Cycle

Oftentimes a system is developed according to a specific process that involves planning, analyzing, creating, testing, and revising. Such a process refers to the system development life cycle (SDLC). When a system is developed, it is most likely done in distinct stages (in other words, according to a life cycle). Developers use such stages to ensure that a system is fully developed. While there are several variations of SDLCs, the following presents one that is useful to consider when thinking about how a system is developed.

> Stage 1: A problem exists and an idea is born to solve it in the form of creating a new system. A problem could refer to a need or opportunity to improve upon something.
>
> Stage 2: Analyses are done to assess whether or not the proposed new system will work.
>
> Stage 3: The plans and designs for the new system are made.
>
> Stage 4: The new system is developed and made reality.
>
> Stage 5: The new system is tested and revised.
>
> Stage 6: The new system is used and maintenance is performed over time.
>
> Stage 7: The new system is finally evaluated for effectiveness.

While Google and StubHub operate on a variety of computer systems, not all systems are related to computers. Computer systems are just one type of system in a world of many. Language is a system of letters and meanings. A museum is a system of artifacts. The Dewey Decimal System is a system that helps people classify and find library books. Even our bodies are made up of systems: the nervous system, the digestive system, and the circulatory system, to name a few.

As you read this chapter, keep in mind that a system is embedded in a variety of places, both artificial and natural, and part of a larger network of systems. By looking at a system as embedded in a network of systems, we are able to see the relationships between technologies, humans, writing, and our environments. In this respect, we have to keep in mind that we should think rhetorically about our role and the roles of others within a system, how those roles enable or limit our capabilities, and how our actions have consequences.

We do play roles in systems, whether active or passive ones. While we create them, operate them, direct them, and manipulate them, we are also shaped by them. They change the way we think. To demonstrate, when you type a search query into Google, it uses predictive technologies to offer you suggestions as you type, which can in turn change the way you might think about what you are searching for.

Translating From One System to Another

Systems of writing make for good examples of the complex nature of systems as they operate in this world. Such a complex nature can lead you and others to think in different ways, sometimes enriching our understanding of things while at other times making it more difficult for us to communicate with one another. We can understand how communication works or doesn't work when moving from one system to another. Translating information from one system to another, for instance, doesn't always work and can make communication between cultures and diverse groups of people more difficult. Although both share similar rules, the English language is one system, while the Spanish language is another. Each has its own history shaped by social, political, and cultural influences. In English, cultural rules as well as rules for syntax and grammar dictate how to write this sentence:

   Michael arrived at John's house.

The cultural rules as well as rules for syntax and grammar for the Spanish language, dictate that this sentence should be written like this:

   Michael llegó a la casa de John.

In the Spanish language, the noun "house" comes before the owner, John. In the English language, John, the owner, comes before his house. In English, the sentence could be written as "Michael arrived at the house of John," and that would be syntactically and grammatically correct. But, how often do you say a sentence like this in English? Probably not often since it would go against cultural norms. Therefore, "John" becomes possessive in the sentence and appears before "house" as in "John's house."

This simple example of a sentence about Michael and John shows how ordering words and how translating them from one system to another could potentially pose problems. In a simple sentence like this one, the reader most likely understands the information in the order he or she reads it. In the English example, a reader reads "John" before "house." In Spanish, the reader reads "la casa de" ("the house of") before "John." What comes first and what comes second might not be such a big deal in the context of these two sentences. People who read these sentences would understand that the house belongs to John and that Michael arrived there regardless of whether they read the sentence in English or Spanish.

However, if these sentences were part of larger works, say 200-page textbooks about real estate and home ownership laws, word choice and the order of information would have greater impacts for both language systems. Because the two language systems operate differently and have different words to mean different things, a reader of an English textbook and a reader of a Spanish textbook might not have the same understanding. Some ideas could be interpreted differently depending on the order of information and the words used in each textbook. The information could also be understood differently because the systems are embedded in different cultures that make meaning in different ways. Words in one language could mean one thing, and in another, the same word could mean something else.

As a writer, you must realize how your writing operates in multiple systems but also how it operates for people who are also embedded within different cultural, political, and social systems. Likewise, you have to keep in mind what systems are at play when your audience reads your writing using a variety of technologies. When you write a document for an online audience, will all your audience members access and read it in the same ways? Probably not. That's because they could potentially access it through a number of different technologies. If you were to write a Microsoft Word document and post this to a website, your audience might try to open that document from a PC, a phone, a MAC, a tablet, and so forth. Each of these has its own operating systems and programs that have to read and translate that document into its own languages. In some cases, information can get lost or misinterpreted.

Although we are certainly surrounded by systems, and although not all of them work together, luckily there are technologies that are working to bring systems together. For instance, say that you want to connect your smartphone's system with your computer. If you are using Apple products, this might be easy to do. That's because companies like Apple, for example, often pair their products for customers automatically. That way, the systems that you use when you use Apple products all speak to one another, making it easier for you to work seamlessly with multiple technologies. But, when you are not using technologies that can be so easily paired with one another, you have to be willing to acknowledge the differences in those systems and to realize how to make them work together in a way that is most effective.

Your Role in a System

Moreover, you should not think of yourself as just a passive builder and user of systems. In reality, you are an active participant in the systems you work within, whether or not you realize it. Every day, as you navigate, gather, sift through, and create information, you do so by shaping and creating your own systems for doing things as well as contribute to those systems built by others. When you use a system such as a search engine, such a system could be monitoring your uses and collecting data on when, how, and why you are using such a system. The people who operate that search engine then make changes to their system as a result.

Take your computer's *interface*, for example. This is the place in which you interact with your computer. You see this interface via the computer's screen as you navigate and access your computer's files, folders, icons, and functions. The interface is the go-between for the *backend operations* (the processing that takes place behind the scenes with the help of computer programming) and the *frontend operations* (what we do with the computer when we use it). This go-between is one that we can customize (within our computer's limits) to suit our own needs and uses, like when we create files, folders, and documents.

If you were to compare your computer screen with those of your classmates, you would see that their interfaces may differ from yours. That's because in using your computer and its systems, you arrange and organize information in a way that makes sense to you. You make the things you want to use prominent on the interface. The things you don't want to use, you hide.

Take a moment and think about your computer's interface. The way you organize your interface is in part influenced by your past bodily experiences, your knowledge, your habits, your preferences, and your learning abilities.

Discussion Questions: Interfaces

1. What does your interface say about you in terms of how you operate a computer system?
2. How do you arrange and organize your icons, your files, your folders, and so on?
3. How much of this organization reflects the ways you organize information in your brain?
4. What are some limitations that a computer might have when it comes to the organization of the interface?

In many ways, your experiences with interfaces are unique even when interfaces are designed to be the same on every computer. That's because the ways in which people interact with them can differ. Take an app as an example. While an app has a finite number of ways to interact with its interface, people can choose their own paths in which to interact. Paths are driven by personal needs, by tasks to be completed, and by rhetorical thinking. While you might choose one path, another person might choose a different path.

Technologies can offer us many different ways to develop a system for organizing information, too. A program like Microsoft Word has built-in tools that make creating headings, lists, tables, and tabs in particular ways within a document. A program like iTunes has other tools for organizing in particular ways, from labels to date stamps.

A program like a course management system has yet other ways of organizing, from pages to modules. As a writer, when using a technology, you must contemplate what consequences arise from such uses, that is, such ways of organizing within a system. Your uses affect not only your understanding of the information, but also your audience's understanding. Although you will learn more about these consequences in the pages to come, for now, let's consider ways in which you can create a system for organizing. While systems exist that automatically organize information, there are times when you will have to develop your own system for organizing.

Activity: System Investigation

Investigate one system you use to find information. As you investigate the system, answer the following questions:

- What paths do you take within this system to find information?
- How does the system organize information?
- What are the advantages and disadvantages of organizing information in this way?
- How do you navigate these paths?
- How do you shape the system when you use it?
- In what ways does the system shape you and your writing?
- How do cultural, political, and social influences shape the system?
- What other systems are connected to the system you are investigating?
- How do those other systems work with and against the system you are investigating?

Language in a System

Language, itself a technology and system, is often used by people working with a variety of technologies to help organize those technologies in ways that help those technologies operate smoothly. Likewise, as technologies utilize language, they often do so in an organized way. In other words, they use language to organize a technology's information. In effect, we can think of a technology as a system of organized information.

With such a system, then, we can create our own systems of organized information. For starters, organizing information may likely mean that you need to rely on developing a good labeling system (categories, groups, common characteristics) for your information based on language. Designing a good labeling system, from headings to subheadings to file names to folder names, requires that you pay close attention to the various parts within the system and choose your words carefully. A label, after all, is a name or marker that provides information about a part and its location, place, and/or purpose for a larger whole.

When we try to make sense of information, our brains often rely on organizational techniques, many that utilize technologies. Say that you are writing a book using the word processing program Microsoft Word and that you have 20 chapters saved to your desktop as 20 separate .doc files. If you title those .doc files with the labels "Chapter 1," "Chapter 2," "Chapter 3," "Chapter 4," and so on, you would know which file to open when you want to work on Chapter 3 and which file to open when you want to work on Chapter 8. Labels such as Chapter 1, Chapter 2, and Chapter 3 are recognizable labels for anyone who has read a book. In this example, such a labeling system has a long history, one shaped by many cultures and many people over time. If you pick up a book at the library, most likely you would expect to find that it contained chapter labels such as these.

Now, let's say you haven't worked on the book in a while and when you sit down at your computer to work on writing it again, you can't remember what each chapter is about. The label "Chapter 3" and the label "Chapter 8" don't do much other than tell you they are the third and eighth chapters in the book. To know what is in these chapters, you would need to open each .doc file and read or scan each chapter's contents. That might take a bit of time if you have 20 chapters.

If you had a better labeling system, however, one using more language in effective ways, you could save yourself some time. Using the labels "Chapter 3: The Storm" and "Chapter 8: The Rescue" for your files, for instance, may give you enough information to remember what is in those files. Likewise, the addition of just two more words in each label provides a reference about each chapter, making it easier for you to understand how the book progresses, making it easier for you to navigate back and forth between the files you are working on. The language you use to label these files makes sense, too, since it summarizes the most important moments in the chapters. If you were to pass your files onto an editor or publisher, they would understand what each chapter was about based on such labels as well.

Choosing your labels carefully doesn't mean you have to have long titles for such labels. Sometimes a word or two can suffice, as in the Microsoft Word example. Sometimes one or two words is the only choice. The Microsoft Word example is just one example of how technologies influence the way that we organize and arrange things. To label a .doc file using Microsoft Word on your computer system, you have to do so within certain limitations. You are limited to using certain characters on your keyboard for your titles. You can't, for instance, use an entire paragraph to label your file. You could try, but it would make arranging your files on your computer's interface a bit difficult.

Even with no limitations, you have to think about how to make your labels helpful. In other words, label information to help you and others organize, group, search, find, and understand information effectively and efficiently. Know that labels are often created based on (1) technological affordances (what the technology can and can't do), (2) practical purposes (how it is helpful), (3) cultural norms (what your audience is accustomed to), (4) genre conventions (how other texts like it are organized), and (5) our experiences in the past with other labeling systems (how you've been successful in the past using a similar approach).

Whereas we might not so much see it with this simple example of labeling Microsoft Word files, our labeling practices and thus our organizing practices in using technologies do have broader consequences. That is, they affect people and places. The language used to label these files "Chapter 3: The Storm" and "Chapter 8: The Rescue" would be acceptable, but these labels would no doubt influence the way an editor or publisher understood the contents of the files. The editor or publisher would expect to read a story about a storm and a rescue. They would visualize ahead of time what they might expect to find in each chapter based on previous understandings of storms and rescues.

While it may be true that the more information there is, the bigger the system you have to create, this simple example sheds light of how naming and organizing files works and shapes the way people understand. But, what happens when we have to develop more names and larger organizational systems for things other than Microsoft Word files about book chapters? What happens when we must use systems and language to organize people, for example? When we organize and label people by putting them into a group or category, what are the consequences? Do we contribute to such things as stereotypes, racism, classism, etc.?

Our language choices become more important when our uses of systems have greater impacts on others. As an example, think about all the applications you have ever filled out, either for a job, for a school, or for a scholarship. Those applications collected information from you that was then organized within a system, perhaps one built on a computer such as a database. Those applications and those technological systems that organize the data operate with the help of language. What languages are used in applications is shaped by the technologies themselves. An application for a job can have only so many questions, boxes to check, and lines to fill in because that's all perhaps the technology used to create it will allow. Which questions, which boxes, which lines are included on such an application and in such a technological system also depend on larger systems: political, social, cultural, financial, and so on.

When certain languages are used over others in organizing data on people, there are real consequences. Sometimes not everyone can be accounted for. If an online application wanted to know what ethnicity a person was and provided boxes next to a list of several ethnicities, there would only be so many the online application system could put in this list given the limitations of the technological system it uses to operate. In other words, it could not list all the possibilities people could check or belong to, leaving some people to have to choose "other." The use of "other" may not be sensitive to all, and it may discriminate against some. Who would want to be labeled "other"?

Discussion Questions: Labels

1. Discuss a time when you were labeled within a system. Why were you labeled in the way you were? Do you feel this label was fair? Why or why not?
2. What technologies were used to create the labeling system, and how did they shape the labels?
3. What are the social, political, and/or economic consequences of such a labeling system?

Systems Use Multiple Modes

Systems don't rely just on language (which, as a reminder, is multimodal). They also use a variety of modes produced and influenced by a variety of technologies. Take the labels on the package shown in Image 9.1. These labels are but two parts of the various systems that you must use in order to mail a package to someone. The labels covey information in a number of multimodal ways. They combine spatial and linguistic information. They present bar codes that operate on a number system, one that is read by a computer, yet another system. They include images (a broken glass and arrows) that represent a warning that the package is fragile and that the package should remain in a particular position. They use the colors black and white to organize and communicate information in a conventional manner. Most packing labels are black and white, after all.

Modes within systems don't just help get packages from one place to another, either. They can also help get people from one place to another. The map shown in Image 9.2 is a system of representations of real things and real places, including other systems, like a road system, a park system, a transportation system, and so forth. The map organizes a

IMAGE 9.1 Example packaging label. Yes- Royalty Free / Shutterstock

Technology Is a System

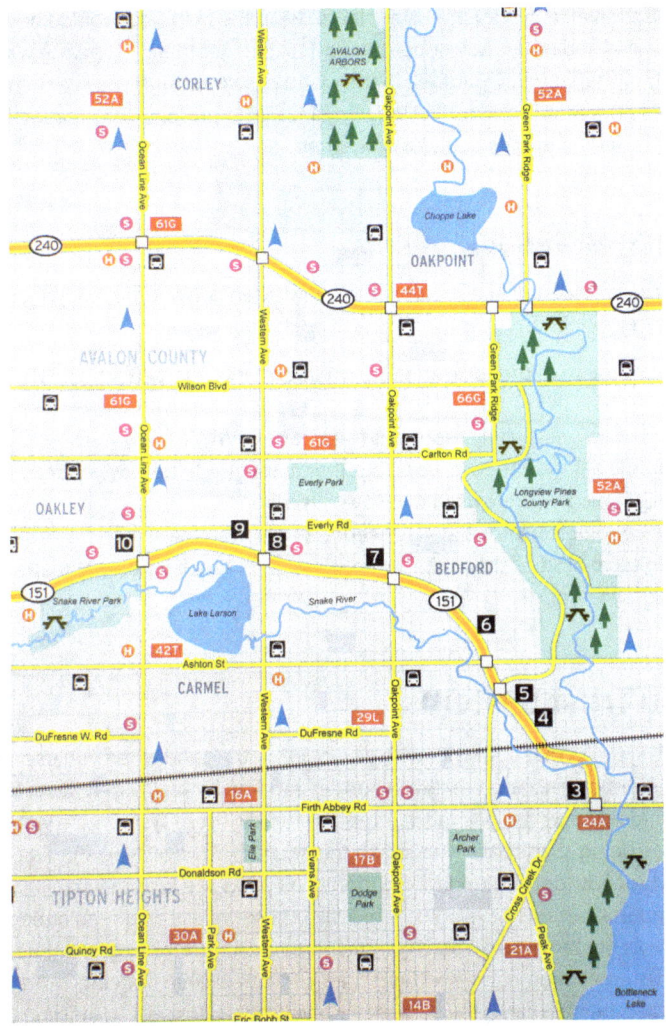

IMAGE 9.2 magnetcreative / iStock

three-dimensional place onto a two-dimensional space using a variety of modes. People learn to read and use a map in order to navigate their world, and they do so in a variety of ways based on their capabilities, knowledge of the world, prior experiences with modes, and access to resources.

Take a moment and examine this map. How would you travel from Lake Larson to the picnic tables at Avalon Arbors? You could take a bus up Western Avenue and walk over to the tables. You could also drive, taking Ashton Street and then Oakpoint Avenue.

221

You could also traverse by foot across the land. Using the map, you would know what direction to head and about how long it should take to get there. Along the way, you would also know what you would see in the world based on what you see on the map. All of this is possible because the technology organizes and presents information in a certain way using a variety of modes that work together.

Activity: Examine a Map

Find and examine a map of a location you know. Then, answer the following questions in a reflection:

1. How does the map organize and present information? Is it effective? Why or why not?
2. Does the map adequately represent the location? Why or why not?
3. How do the different modes work together to influence the way you read the map?
4. What technologies were used to create this map?
5. What technological knowledge is needed to read this map?
6. How do technologies shape the world as a result of their writing of maps that represent the world?

Can You Trust Systems?

When all the systems that you work with all work together, and when you use and create systems of organization that make understanding helpful, it may seem like your life is easy, and you may not pay much attention to how those systems are working and what they are doing as they are working. In this section, however, you should consider exploring why it is important to pay attention to all parts of a system when it is working and what impacts systems have on us, especially those we use on a regular basis when writing. Today, companies use a variety of technological systems to gather information from their customers, sometimes without their customers even noticing, from tracking customers' membership cards to using their online survey answers to utilizing browser cookies. Then, these companies use data mining techniques to search and make sense of this data to help them make future business decisions. And, a lot of this is done through language systems.

Take a moment and think of all the systems you use online. Now, let's return to the example from the beginning of the chapter, to the point you were googling your favorite band and trying to find concert tickets. Chances are, if not for concert tickets, you have used Google at least once in your life. But did you ever stop and think about its impact on you and your society? Did you ever stop and ask yourself the following: How does Google work? Should companies like Google, ones that are big and popular, explain how their systems work? And, more importantly, how does Google shape your and everyone else's ways of thinking?

When you use a system like Google, you input your ideas into its system via a search bar and it, via algorithms, produces results that it believes are best for you. Whether or not they are truly the best for you is up for some debate. How would you know they are the best, after all, if you are unable to see all possibilities but just the ones Google's algorithm thinks are best?

As you search for a concert, you probably wouldn't think about what all has to happen to make Google work. You don't see, for instance, how ad links are determined. You don't see the money trail that businesses create when paying Google for ad space. You don't see Google's employees working behind desks. You don't see the programmers developing code. You don't see how such a large search engine affects the millions of people using it on a regular basis. You don't see the research the company conducts on users. You don't see how other companies and organizations use the data to make business and government decisions. In fact, when you type in a word and click enter, you don't see the system at work or the impact such a search will have on many worldwide. Instead, in the seconds that you used Google, you saw only a simple system, one giving you what you might want, not necessarily one that is complex and connected to many more systems.

Discussion Questions: Systems

1. In what ways do you shape the systems you use?
2. We can do our best to think critically about our actions and those of others within systems, but what happens when companies don't make transparent how their systems work? If a company, like a search engine company, is not sharing their methods for generating results within their search system, can we trust it? Why or why not?
3. What measures can we take to ensure systems are operating ethically?

When systems are massive, like Google is, our job as writers becomes a critical task. The internet connects millions of computers so that we might exchange millions of ideas. When we type words into a search engine, that search engine records those words and uses that data. So our words matter. That's why we have to think about how we protect ourselves when using technologies like search engines, how we protect our information, and how we protect our privacy. We have to think about whether or not we should trust that a system like Google will keep us safe and know what is best for us.

Search Engines

Databases are one type of system (more on these in a moment), search engines are another. Both provide us a lens for which we can think about how we and others operate within systems that are connected to others and are influenced and shaped by a number of factors, such as political, financial, social, and cultural practices. While both use algorithms (a set of exact steps that generate an output), search engines are not exactly the same as databases. Search engines allow you the capability to search the web for information because they use technologies such as crawlers and spiders to search the web for you.

Google works by using software to crawl millions of websites in order to gather data and bring it back to their servers. This data is housed in a search index, one containing every word on every website. Google ranks the websites according to the relevancy and usefulness to your search. Its algorithms work to understand your search terms and your intentions for your search. The results, Google hopes, are what you are looking for. In searching, Google also tracks your searches, creating data on you, such as your whereabouts and when you are searching, which will then be used to shape future search options for you and other users. As Google writes on its website:

> Information such as your location, past search history and Search settings all help us to tailor your results to what is most useful and relevant for you in that moment. We use your country and location to deliver content relevant for your area.
>
> ("How Search Algorithms Work")

In other words, when you use a search engine, like Google, you help write it every time you write in its search box; Google tracks your searches and learns from them as a result.

Check It Out YouTube: For more on how Google works using spiders and search indexes, check out the YouTube video, "The Internet: How Search Works," posted by Code.org.

However, if you wish not to be a part of this system, there are ways in which you can protect your privacy and prevent search engines from gathering information on you. But, though there are measures in place to protect your privacy, you may want to consider how tracking information through search engines can actually help you and others. For starters, tracking information can help you and others make smarter searches. Such information can be used to suggest different ways of stating a query, for instance. Your data could also make the search process faster. Google is fast because it has learned from its users. It has learned what works and what doesn't. Imagine if you never learned from your past. Imagine not drawing on that experience when you undergo a task. Think how long it would take you each time. So, while technology like a search engine might gather information on you, that information could help you.

Discussion Questions: Search Engines

1. How can search engines' abilities to track our information help us?
2. How can it benefit writing?
3. How can it negatively impact us?

Data, Data, Data

Another way of looking at how a system operates in our world is to think of a computer database, a written program that is created in multimodal language and designed to organize information so that it can be searched, analyzed, and changed using multimodal language.

Ciera Nygren is no stranger to databases. That's because her work involves databases and the information they contain. As an educator and speech pathologist working with children who are deaf or hard of hearing, she often gathers data on her clients and their families, data that gets filled out on paper forms and then entered into digital databases that can be used later to make important educational and medical decisions about her clients' future therapy options. Ciera's work is not unusual. A number of professions worldwide rely on databases to make important decisions.

So, what exactly is data? Data is a value that we assign to something or someone. A value could be quantitative (such as a measurement) or qualitative (such as a description). Only when we interpret this data in context does it become information to us. For example, the smallest insect in the world is the featherwing beetle, which measures approximately 0.013 inches in length. In this instance, 0.013 inches is a data point (a measurement) that means nothing by itself. However, when we interpret this number and its relationship to the featherwing beetle (as well as other insects), it becomes useful information. Virtually everything we cross paths with, we assign values to; in other words, data to. Then, we interpret this data within a context connecting it to something. In this instance, that data becomes information.

In computer terms, data is written in binary form, meaning a system of ones and zeros. Your computer operates by processing data, information that instructs the computer how to perform tasks. The smallest unit of data is called a bit, and a bit has a single binary value (0 or 1). A computer byte is made up of eight bits and is what computers use to represent a character such as a letter or number. The word "book" when written in a computer program such as Microsoft Word requires four bytes (one byte per letter) or 32 bits (4 x 8).

One way to think about this is to think of your computer as a container of data. The files and folders you create all contain data. While on the screen in front of you, you might open files and folders and see words like "book" within them, those files and folders are really made up of a system of ones and zeros (data) that the computer reads when processing through the backend operations.

Like a computer, a database is a container for data. A database is also an organized system (often in the form of lists or tables) that stores, organizes, filters, and sorts data within a container. When there is a lot of data, especially in the form of words, the database might consist of multiple tables in order to organize it. The most common type of database is a relational one because it links data in various tables through their commonalities or relationships.

Let's say that you owned a shoe company and had your entire warehouse inventory listed in an internal database so that your employees could readily search the inventory without having to walk through your warehouse. Your database would likely need lots of tables to organize your shoes so that they would be searchable in your database. For instance, you might have one large table for all your shoes (Table 1). You might have one table (Table 2) that lists all shoes that are for walking. You might have another table (Table 3) listing all shoes that are wide, and another (Table 4) for shoes that are brown. If you search your inventory through your database's interface (through the frontend operations where you interact with the data) for shoes that are brown and also for walking, your database on the backend will look for shoes that appear in both Table 2 and Table 4 and return those results to you.

While this example is about shoes, it demonstrates how a simple relational database works. Yet, not all databases are this simple, not when there is a lot of data to be entered by a lot of different people. If 50 employees have access to your shoe database, for instance, and are responsible for entering in shoe data, think about how easy it would be for data to be misrepresented. If one person labels a pair of shoes as navy and another person labels those exact shoes as black, in analyzing that data, people who use the database may find results that are inaccurate. When searching for navy shoes, they may see only one pair in stock when in fact there is another. This might not seem like a big deal when it comes to shoes, but think about databases that are, say, tied to education and medical records as in Ciera's case. What if her treatment plans for her clients are dependent on the data in a database? Wouldn't she and her clients want the data entered in correctly all the time?

When writing and working within a database, consistency can provide a means for ensuring that data is captured correctly. Using consistent language, for instance, when entering in data into a database can help minimize miscommunication among database users, not to mention provide more accurate outputs. The database, when asked for data by its users, searches for word frequencies; in other words, repetitions of uses. If you consistently use different words for the same thing (say you use the words navy, cobalt, and sapphire instead of using just blue), it makes it harder for a database to store this data (it needs more categories) and makes it more difficult for users to work with the data (you would need to search for more words).

In Ciera's case, she collects data about her clients' histories, their medical backgrounds, their bodies, their capabilities, their skill levels, their ages, their ethnicities, their addresses, and so on. From the database in which this data is organized, Ciera and other professionals can extrapolate information that they can use to help clients as well as compare that information with others who work in the field. In this case, the database, its organization, and the language people use to enter and search information is extremely important. Ciera and her clients would want the best course of action, and that is dependent on entering in data as accurately as possible.

INTERVIEW
CIERA NYGREN, MA, CED, PARENT EDUCATOR AND YOUTH SPEECH PATHOLOGIST

Q: What kinds of writing do you do on a regular basis when you work with parents and children who are deaf or hard of hearing?

A: I write all the time including every time I meet with a family, which is often once a week. When a child enters our program, we first do an evaluation to get a baseline of skill level. Based on the test we preform (DAYC and REEL), we then write a detailed report on their skill level. The report contains information about their medical and birth history and if there is any significant medical information that might impact their development. Recommendations on goal setting for the child are also included. We then repeat this annually so we can obtain data on how a child is progressing through our program. Upon exiting our program, we write an exit report with the same information and recommendations for the school district if they are moving on to this setting. When I meet with families, I give them handouts related to my lesson plans for the visit, and I also take lots of notes that help me see whether or not the therapies I am administering are working.

Q: How valuable is it to keep good data on your families?

A: Very valuable since the data we collect and use helps us determine our course of action with our children. The database my program uses is shared with a group of schools that work together on various projects. It is also used to compare growth and program development. So, ongoing, we are always keeping data on our children. We write up lesson goals for each of our visits based on this data. Some children receive services weekly, some just monthly, depending on hearing loss and other medical needs. The lessons typically target a specific goal such as "vocalizing to get needs met" and we will talk about how we can achieve this in the natural home setting. During our sessions, we will take notes on significant information that might be helpful, such as upcoming appointments, new skills obtained, new routines, developmental skills being met, etc. We also keep track of new language skills, such as speech utterances or new words being used. All this data helps us gauge a child's progress.

Activity: Databases

As you think about your future career, think about how databases will be used. Investigate who writes data and who uses the databases in your future career. For what purposes do these databases exist, and how do you think you will be writing and using them in the future? Report your findings to the class.

Searching Data

Long before modern-day search engines and databases were created, scientists, mathematicians, logicians, and philosophers contemplated how people think and organize information in logical ways. Englishman George Boole, a professor of mathematics during the 1800s, developed theories on algebra, logic, and probabilities that we use today when searching for information. You may have used a Boolean operator or two when searching a database. Boolean operators (the words "AND," "OR," and "NOT" that were mentioned previously in the book) are based on Boolean logic: a statement is either true or false, and because so, other statements can be combined with it using the operators. The operators show the relationships between these statements. Because computer databases are complex systems with lots of data and because they have to respond to your input via search queries, Boolean operators help computers sort and retrieve what you are looking for.

In addition, they can also help you manage the information you are looking for within a system. Using the word "AND" can make your search smaller because your search must return data that meets two criteria. When you use the word "AND," as in the query "brown shoes AND walking shoes," the computer database returns all shoes that are both brown and for walking. If a shoe is brown but not made for walking, then the database doesn't include that shoe in the results.

Using the word "OR" can broaden your search. When you use the word "OR" as in the query "brown shoes OR walking shoes," the computer database returns shoes that are either brown or for walking.

Using the word "NOT" can narrow your search because it eliminates terms. When you use the word "NOT" as in the query "brown shoes NOT walking shoes," the computer database returns shoes that are brown but not for walking.

Boolean terms become useful to us when we are searching the web especially. The web contains billions upon billions of information that we can search using language. However, when the results from our searches yield thousands and thousands of webpages, it would be nearly impossible for us to go through all of them. So, when trying to search for relevant information, we need ways in which we can narrow our searches and weed out what isn't useful. Using the different Boolean operators can help us to do so, as they can provide us a means to narrow (or in some cases, broaden) our searches to include more relevant information.

Using Data to Make Writing Better

There are a number of ways that data can help us make writing better. Because many digital technologies are capable of quickly collecting, organizing, and filtering data, people have begun to create many means for using writing data to make their writing better. Learning Boolean terms can certainly help us write better because they make researching more manageable. But there are other means, too. There are technologies that can make your writing better by turning your writing into data, which you can then track and search. For instance, 750 Words (http://750words.com/) is an online writing platform where you can write and track your writing habits at the same time. The platform keeps track of writing habits such as the amount of time spent typing, how many words per minute were typed, and what words were used most often. It also can track your time orientation, primary sense, and mindset. Looking at the data, you could obtain a good understanding of how you write, how you could make changes accordingly, and how you could potentially make your writing better as a result.

Imagine now if every writer were to track his or her writing and then share this data within a database that everyone could search and study. What could we learn about writing? Perhaps a lot. And this information could be used to create curriculum in schools and develop resources, like educational games, that help students improve their writing skills. In some ways, writing like this is already being tracked in school (through tests, for instance). But what about the writing that takes place outside of school? What if all writing could be tracked? What would we learn, then, about our society's abilities to write and how to improve that writing?

> ### Discussion Questions: Tracking Your Writing
> 1. What information about writing should be tracked? And why?
> 2. How could this information be helpful to writers? To schools? To businesses?
> 3. Are there any reasons not to track our writing? Why or why not?

Too Many Systems at Work at One Time

It is clear that systems don't work in isolation as they are always embedded within a larger environment. There are times when we purposively choose to work with multiple systems at one time. Given your use of technology on a daily basis, you may even believe that you are capable of using multiple systems at the same time effectively. Because we live in a busy, technology-enriched world, we may feel at times that we must multitask in order to get things done.

But, too many systems at work at one time may not be beneficial to us and to others. Research suggests that our brains are not capable of moving back and forth between tasks. The more systems we work with, the more complicated and complex our thinking must become. Cynthia Kubu, a neuropsychologist, and Andre Machado, chairman of the Neurological Institute at the Cleveland Clinic, say that successful multitasking is a myth and isn't even possible for most of us. Instead, when we think we are multitasking, we are in fact quickly moving back and forth between tasks. They argue this movement significantly impairs "our ability to function at our finest" and has serious consequences. They contend that "our tendency to divide our attention, rather than focus, is hampering our ability to perform even simple tasks" which impacts such things as attentiveness, learning, and mindfulness.

As you think about your daily habits, perhaps your studying and writing habits, think about whether or not you multitask and work with a number of systems at one time. For example, when writing a research project, do you listen to music, use your computer, monitor your social media sites, and text messages with friends all at the same time? Consider what impacts doing all these things at once could have on your ability to learn and write effectively.

Hacking the System

Throughout this chapter, you have been prompted to critically think about systems. For this final section, you will consider what it means to hack a system. Hacking and hackers have a bad rap, for good reason. While laws have been slow to keep up with changes in technologies, anytime someone hacks a system in order to manipulate it or modify it for malicious purposes, such as to gain unauthorized access, is inappropriate to say the least.

However, not all hacking or hackers are bad. Lots of companies, such as security companies, hire "white-hat" hackers who are good at computer programming. Their job is to find weaknesses in their companies' systems. That way, companies can work to ensure they don't have data breaches, giving access to those who shouldn't have it.

Hacking too can enable people to learn about and improve systems. Through acts of hacking, people learn how the different parts of those systems work, what the potentials are for those parts, and what prevents those parts from working. Hacking can also be a useful way of learning to write computer programming language since it involves critically examining this language from the backend of a system.

At iHub in Nairobi, Kenya, people regularly gather to participate in hackathons, events where people gather to hack. In 2010, Erik Hersman created iHub as a coworking space for technologists and entrepreneurs, programmers, and the like. It has since grown into one of the more prominent tech communities in all of Africa. One of the hackathons now held there is Random Hacks of Kindness (RHOK), a global community event where programmers gather together to create sustainable and usable software as well as solve computer programs for good causes that benefit nonprofits and social organizations.

Assignment: Hacking

Research specific hackers, both good and bad. Walls, Schopieray, and DeVoss define hacktivism as "the art and practice of hacking in opposition to a damaging or restrictive ideological or political power" (275). Find out what hackers did to hack and what the consequences were. What impacts, for instance, did their acts of hacking have on the world and particular organizations, places, and technologies? What impacts did they have on the writing of systems?

Final Thoughts

By now, you should have a clear picture of how and why technology is a system. It is a system because it always involves parts working together to create a functioning whole. By now you should also understand why it is important to be critical of systems, especially when it comes to your role in shaping them and the roles that systems play in shaping your experiences and knowledge. Systems do not operate in isolation, and as such they can shape other systems and technologies, like writing, as well as be shaped by those other systems and technologies. In the next chapter, you will continue to think more carefully about how systems are embedded and connected to other systems in our world. As you do, keep in mind what systems you use on a regular basis and how you shape and are shaped by them.

Additional Discussion Questions

1. Choose a specific system. What are the social, political, economic, and cultural impacts that this system has? Who created this system? How does this system shape its users? How do its users shape it?
2. In what ways could tracking data on your writing habits help you as a writer?
3. In what ways could tracking data on the writing habits of members of a society help that society make writing better?

Additional Activities

1. Google and You: Google your name and examine the results. Then, write a reflection that answers the following questions:
    - What do the results say about you?
    - How do you feel about being a part of a worldwide public system?
    - Who or what is responsible for what you found about yourself?

- Do you think you should be responsible for what you find in the search and thus system?
- Can you delete what you find? If not, why not? If so, why?

2. Infrastructures: Looking at a system necessitates an examination of the infrastructures that help or get in the way of a system's ability to work smoothly. Think about a particular system's infrastructure and write a reflection that answers the following:
   - What policies govern it and the places where it operates?
   - Who owns, manages, fixes, and uses it?
   - What cultural practices shape its uses?
   - When can it operate?
   - Where can it operate?
   - Who can operate it?
   - How is it used?
   - What uses are privileged and which ones are not?

Additional Assignments

1. Data and You: Situate yourself in a body of data and visually represent this data with you in it. In case you can't find data sets on your own, you might start with these links:
   a. Data.gov allows anyone to see the government's data.
   b. Murder data (www.murderdata.org/), hopes sharing data will help officials solve cold murder cases in the United States.
   c. GitHub (https://github.com/awesomedata/awesome-public-datasets#healthcare) provides links to a wide variety of datasets on a wide variety of topics.

2. Tracking Your Writing: Track your writing using a writing tracking technology such as 750 Words over the course of two weeks. Use the data to write up a report that reflects on your writing habits and what changes you could make based on the data.

Works Cited

"How Search Algorithms Work." *Google*, n.d., www.google.com/search/howsearchworks/algorithms/. Accessed 16 July 2018.

Kubu, Cynthia, and Andre Machado. "Why Multitasking Is Bad for You." *Time*, 20 April 2017, http://time.com/4737286/multitasking-mental-health-stress-texting-depression/. Accessed 11 July 2018.

Walls, Douglas M., Scott Schopieray, and Dànielle Nicole DeVoss. "Hacking Spaces: Place as Interface." *Computers and Composition*, 26, 2009, pp. 269–287.

CHAPTER 10

Technology as Situated

Contents

Reading the Technological World	234
Gaming in the Technological World	236
Writing Impacts Places and Spaces	239
Places and Spaces Impact Writing	240
Stakeholders and Infrastructures	241
Connected Online Spaces	243
Tracking Time, Place, and Space	244
You Are One Writer in a World of Many	246
Final Thoughts	249

IMAGE 10.1 Pressmaster / Shutterstock

Pablo Calvog / Shutterstock

Reading the Technological World

If you were to read a hardbound printed version of *Little Women* by Louisa May Alcott, and if you were to read an online digital version of *Little Women* by Louisa May Alcott on your computer, would you be reading the same story? If you were to base your answer on the actual words you read, perhaps you would be inclined to answer yes. But, if you were to base your answer on the physical experiences you would have using the technologies of a hardbound printed version and an online digital one, you might be inclined to answer no. Because of their physical natures, *where* you encounter these texts (that is, the locations of these texts) and *how* you encounter these texts (your bodily actions) are in fact different. In other words, the very technologies that you use to read the two versions of *Little Women* (the hardbound printed book and the computer) provide different reading experiences. As a result, your brain interprets these experiences in specific ways that are unique to each.

With a hardbound printed book, you can see and feel the pages with your body in ways that are different with a digital version. When you read the hardbound printed book, you know that you have to use your hand to turn a page in order to move through the story. You know that you have to focus your eyes on the top left of the page and read left to right and down the page. Your brain interprets these actions in specific ways. When you read a digital version, like the one provided by literatureproject.com, you may have to use your hand to click or select chapters via hyperlinks in order to move through the story. You may have to use your eyes to scan the screen much like you do when you read other digital texts. Reading a screen is different from reading a printed page.

One such reason as to why there are differences in these two experiences has to do with our bodies, and another has to do with our history and the moment in time we are reading. Yet another has to do with the social and cultural influences brought about by the people we encounter in our lives. Our experiences with technologies, in other words, are situated in a number of ways. Reading a hardbound printed book means drawing on past experiences reading other hardbound printed books. As a result, we have learned a behavior, a proper way of doing so. The hardbound printed book has a history and conventions that have been shaped by our society. So too does the online digital version. It is also situated in time and place. It is situated among people in a particular culture. It also has a history that shaped how the text came to be.

While the example here has to do with reading *Little Women*, the same can be said of writing. Writing is an assemblage of things at a particular moment in a particular place. This assemblage tells the story of writing beyond the text itself. When we write in different places on different surfaces among different people, we have different experiences that are shaped by the very places and surfaces and people we write in, on, and among, respectively, and those experiences in turn shape the very texts we write. Our writing can never be untied from our previous experiences, because our bodies are shaped by our past experiences and our bodies are what we use to write. Moreover, when we write, our writing is always tied to our biases, ideologies, cultural upbringings, social positions, and our physical bodily relationships with technology.

To be successful in our writing, that is, our assemblages, we need to have a rhetorical awareness of what is assembled, for whom it is assembled, and why it is assembled. Knowing our bodies, biases, ideologies, cultural upbringings, social positions, and physical bodily relationships with technologies can help us to be more critical of the ways in which we communicate with diverse audiences who have different bodies, biases, ideologies, cultural upbringings, social positions, and physical bodily relationships with technologies. We cannot and should not assume that we are like everyone else. If we do, we may fail to communicate effectively with those who are different from us.

Activity: Technology in Culture

Technology is embedded, or situated, in our culture, and thus it impacts our culture in many ways. Likewise, our culture impacts writing in many ways. For instance, technology influences our culture's languages. So many people used the word google as a verb to mean to search for things on the web that it became an acceptable word and is now in our dictionaries. Google, in other words, was so pervasive and common in our society that we regularly used it to conduct searches. Rather than use the word "search," we began using the word "google." Look back through history and do a report on words that have found a way into our culture because of the fact they are based on embedded technologies, technologies that have become so prevalent in our cultures that they changed our culture's habits, thoughts, beliefs, and so forth.

Time, place, and space, as this chapter will demonstrate, play important roles too in effective writing, as do the people among whom writing takes place. In previous writing classes, you may have learned about the concept of kairos. Such a concept will be useful to this chapter. While kairos literally means "timeliness" or "the right time" in Greek, rhetorically speaking, it refers to doing what is most appropriate for the given situation, the given moment in time, the given place, the given people you write for. In other words, writing the right thing at the right time. In the pages to come, you will further explore this concept by looking at a number of writing technologies and how such technologies are situated. Particularly, you will consider video games, hyperlinks, and data trackers.

Gaming in the Technological World

Like the comparison between a hardbound printed book and a digital book, games (in particular, video games) provide a good lens for thinking about technology and writing as happening within multiple places and spaces, at various times, and among different people. According to the Entertainment Software Association, as of 2017, two-thirds of American households and 2.6 billion people around the world play video games (Gallagher). They do so for a lot of different reasons. For one, video games are written texts that are interactive with audiences in ways other texts are not. They provide experiences that are both entertaining and educative. They often rely on stories. And, they help people develop a variety of skills, including communicative ones.

So, it is appropriate to include gaming in a book about writing and technology because we can learn a lot about writing by examining gaming and how it is situated in our world. How writing helps learning, for instance, is particularly evident in gaming. Video games are written by 1) computer programmers who code as well as 2) those who play video games. Together, the programmers and the gamers learn to create stories in and around games.

This learning is done via multimodal language. In order to play games, in order to understand them and operate within their stories, one must navigate through virtual spaces, interact with features (words, sounds, motions, gestures), and collaborate with other gamers before, during, and after playing. Indeed, there are gaming communities that connect gamers to one another, there are gaming magazines that inform gamers about the world of gaming, and there are movies and books that turn games into other forms of entertainment. There are all sorts of games, too, from simulations and competitions to choose-your-own-adventures and role-playing games (RPG), and there are a number of resources that can help people learn to play such games. Let's Play (LP) videos, for instance, feature gamers playing through video games while providing commentary on their playing.

Furthermore, gaming also provides an opportunity for augmented reality and virtual reality. Augmented reality refers to an interactive experience that happens in the real world but is augmented by a computer in some way. In other words, augmented reality creates a hybrid space where a connected digital device shapes people and places in the physical world. The popular game Pokémon GO is an augmented reality game that lets players catch Pokémon in the real world. Players do so by traveling through locations in the real world and using a computer (such as a smartphone) that contains a map of those locations, but with additional stuff, such as a Pokémon located on it. A player moves close to a Pokémon on the computer map by moving in the real world.

In virtual reality, players interact with 3D computer-generated simulations and environments by physically moving controllers, gloves, helmets, or other electronic equipment. The player is part of the virtual world, usually via an avatar, and can perform a variety of actions from climbing mountains to flying a spacecraft. Today, virtual reality is used for a number of other things besides gaming, such as education and therapy.

Activity: Virtual Reality and Writing

Try out virtual reality by creating an avatar in a virtual reality platform. As you do, think about the role writing plays in the platform. Then, think about what skills a person can learn through virtual reality that could be relevant to writing texts. Write a reflection of your experience and share it with your classmates.

Video games and games in general are technologies whose features have seeped into other aspects of our lives with the intention of making our experiences better. Gamification means applying elements that are characteristic of game playing to non-game contexts with the intention of garnering engagement. In order to sell their products or improve their employees' happiness, many companies create experiences in which customers or employees can earn points and rewards through a series of challenges or games. Health and wellness apps often feature challenges that reward users with points for completing healthy activities like meditating and exercising. The Achievement app is one such example, as it enables users to earn money for walking, biking, swimming, and other exercises that they track via the app. Users can earn up to 80 points per day for exercise activities and six points per day for healthy social activities. The app then pays users $10 for every 10,000 points they earn. In this example, the game (a technology itself) is used by people who are embedded in a particular place and time. In order to use the app, one must draw on previous experiences, including those that involve writing.

Today, gamification has become tremendously popular, and for good reason. In their study of gamification and user engagement of a gamified knowledge-sharing website, researchers Ayoung Suh, Christian Wagner, and Lili Liu found that "different game dynamics contribute to increasing users' needs satisfaction in different ways;" for example, "rewards increase competence and autonomy" and "competition increases competence and relatedness" (209). They conclude that, indeed, gamification of a non-game context, such as a website in their study, improves users' engagement.

Technology Is Embedded

Like games, writing happens in a particular place at a particular moment in time with the help of others. When we write effectively, we pay attention to the *where* and *when* and *who* of writing, just like we would pay attention to the *where* and *when* and *who* of gaming. The connection between writing and gaming is an important one because we can transfer skills from gaming to writing situations as evidenced by Tina Arduini's study on digital gaming. In her study, she found that writing students who played games (especially via the use of a variety of technological devices) were equipped to make well-informed rhetorical decisions in the writing classroom. Not only that, their playing of games helped them to develop 1) technological skills (gaming leads to the ability to examine and troubleshoot software and hardware), 2) multimodal skills (gaming leads to the ability to see multiple media operate within a text), and 3) collaborative skills (gaming doesn't happen in insolation; gamers rely on other players). All of these skills are vital to writing.

When writing, a writer must think about her text rhetorically, thinking about how a text is relevant at a particular moment in time to a particular audience in a particular place. A video game is a text that is played somewhere for some time by someone. In order to play a game effectively, in order to write a text effectively, a player or writer must rely on previous experiences, such as previous bodily actions, his or her ability to find connections to others and navigate them, and his or her ability to listen to others. They also must have a good sense of timing and know what course of action is best given the situation at hand.

Assignment: Create Your Own Video Game

Create your own video game. A number of platforms can help you create your own game. Unity and GameMaker, for instance, provide game platforms online (https://unity3d.com/unity and www.yoyogames.com/). Try out a few different technologies until you find one that suits you and your purpose for creating a video game. As you work on your video game, test it out with your classmates. Find out what they like about it and what they don't. Then, think about the role writing plays in your game and about what skills a person can learn through playing it that could be relevant to writing texts. Finally, consider how time and place shape your game. Write a report of your experience and share it with your classmates.

Check It Out YouTube: If in addition to what you read in this section, you feel inspired to create your own video game and have the patience to learn a new program, try using the Construct 3 platform. This platform gives you simple options to create a basic video game. "Construct 3 Tutorial [01]—Making Your First Game (Binding-of-Isaac-Like)," posted to YouTube by action Cancel, is a good tutorial for beginners of this platform.

Writing Impacts Places and Spaces

Joddy Murray writes that "The world is text because we read the world as symbols, and, in turn, create symbols to be read" (12). We do literally write this world. We put down concrete on the ground and write on it. We cut words into a cornfield with tractors. We carve initials into tree trunks. In the classroom, we write on the walls. We write on a whiteboard. We write on a computer screen. Some of this writing can then be converted into digital notes that students can access, edit, and save on their own personal devices (iPads, smartphones, tablets) in places such as folders and files. Outside the classroom, we write on buildings, on cars, and on clothing. We hang signs from trees, from bridges, and from landmarks. When we do this writing on the world, we shape this world, revising places and spaces along the way.

In the context of this book, space is generally used to refer to open and more abstract areas (like online spaces that are hard to determine their starting and ending points), and place is generally used to refer to more specific locations or positions within spaces (a room is definable by its walls, the rules that dictate what can and cannot happen there, the interactions that occur there, and the stakeholders who built it). It is important to think about space and place and how our writing impacts them because, as Jason Farman writes, "Our concepts of culture, identity, and agency all spring from our understanding of bodies' relationships to the spaces they exist in and move through. Such understandings are conceived out of the various ways space is represented and visualized" (279). If we think back to the two versions of *Little Women*, the places and spaces in which we encounter them have much to do with our past bodily experiences and the cultures we reside in.

Likewise, discussions of place and space are necessary when thinking about technologies because they enable us to examine how technologies are embedded in our societies within networks and systems. A map is one such technology for which we can think about places and spaces, especially when we think about a digital map that utilizes GPS. GPS (Global Positioning System), a satellite-based radio navigation system developed in the United States, gives us an idea of where we are on the planet in relation to other people and other things with the help of geolocation and time information. We can think of a map as a technology in the world about the world and one that can shape the world, too.

We can use words in technologies that utilize GPS (as in entering in the name of a place in Google Maps) to help us locate a place on Earth in a matter of seconds. We can read the map, zooming in and out, toggling between street view, satellite view, etc., and making note of what is in those places. We can read the land, the buildings, the streets, making decisions as to how we will get to and from places. Once we locate ourselves on a digital map (usually represented as a dot or person icon on a screen), we can see that we are but a small part of a larger environment, one that changes with our actions. When we use a digital map to obtain directions to a place, it will often tell us the routes we can take, usually giving us the quickest route from point A to point B. If we take that quickest route, our movements will impact the places that route takes us. If we and thousands of others use that same route again and again, the impact is much greater: roads need to be widened, habitats are lost as a result, pollution builds up due to an increase in traffic, noise levels rise, and so on.

The digital map itself is a written system for which we navigate. The map is part of a larger system, too, a computer system, networked and controlled by governments and companies like Google, which also have their own systems. Our uses help write digital maps each time we use them to get somewhere, locate some place, and to look at things within spaces. And when we do use them, we change the histories and physical natures of the places we search and travel to.

Places and Spaces Impact Writing

Close your eyes and think about a specific place where you write, perhaps at the kitchen table, perhaps at a coffee shop, or perhaps in the library. Think about what this place is. What is in this place? Where are you within this place? Now think about how the place in which you write shapes your writing and why this place is designed the way it is.

In thinking about this place, hopefully, you realize that you do not write in complete isolation from this world. Indeed, you write your texts somewhere in some place. That somewhere is shaped by a number of factors: stakeholders who maintain and own that somewhere, political, social, cultural, and financial decisions that determine what can and cannot happen in that somewhere, the bodily actions that can and cannot occur there, and the very histories that create expectations for how we move there.

Certainly, you may write in a number of places and spaces throughout your lifetime. Take a classroom, for example, a place on a university or college campus that is supposed to be designed for teaching and learning. Sometimes classrooms are called workshops. Sometimes labs. Sometimes studios. Sometimes there are four walls. Sometimes more. Sometimes there are computer stations. Sometimes desks. Sometimes tables. Sometimes there are projectors and whiteboards and cabinets. Perhaps no two classrooms look the same. But, what is common among all classrooms is the fact they are still tied to and shaped by a society and its concept of what classrooms should be.

Likewise, what and how you write in a classroom is shaped by the classroom itself. When you write, you do so in a public place. There are others in the classroom with you whom can see. Most likely there is nowhere in the classroom where you can hide. When you write in this classroom, you have to sit or stand somewhere among other people, perhaps in a desk, at a podium, or at a table depending on your institution's concept of a classroom, a concept driven by political and financial decisions. After all, classrooms are valuable commodities among stakeholders on campuses. What happens in this place and how you act are determined by the physical layout, too. Is there enough room to move around? Too much room? Do the technologies get in the way or facilitate your writing?

When designers design classrooms, we not only hope they keep in mind what should happen there (teaching and learning), but we also hope they design such places so that these places will help or enhance such teaching and learning. We hope they will choose the correct lighting to help us see when we write. We hope they will use acoustic systems to help us with our hearing and speaking. We hope they will place technologies within the rooms to make an impact on our cognition. We hope they will use a layout and design that best shapes teacher-student and student-student relationships. We hope they will use a layout and design that is accessible to all.

We learn from a young age what is socially accepted behavior in a classroom. We know based on years of experience what we should and should not do in a classroom. Ed Nagelhout and Carol Rutz write that, "The classroom is an ideologically charged place of 'learning' and represents an educational system designed to reproduce acceptable social behavior. That behavior, we contend, is conditioned and contextualized by socially constructed beliefs about and images of the classroom" (6). As you think about your past experiences in classrooms, think about your behaviors during these experiences. Why did you do what you did? Was it because you learned from society that these behaviors are appropriate in a place deemed a classroom?

Assignment: Investigate a Place

Research the history of a place on your campus in which writing occurs and investigate how such a place shapes writing. Think about the stakeholders, the institutional policies, the rules, the physical limitations, the financial constraints, the social dynamics, and the technological capabilities that play roles in the design, maintenance, and use of this place. Based on what you find, design your ideal place for writing on campus. Write a reflection and share this with your classmates so as to compare your findings and ideas.

Stakeholders and Infrastructures

Who designs the classrooms on your campus? Who manages and maintains them? Who assigns them? Who pays for them? Who uses them? Among the answers to these questions are architects, builders, facilities managers, administrators, deans, department chairs, teachers, and students. In other words, stakeholders are those who affect or are affected by classrooms and their designs. As Deborah J. Bickford notes, such stakeholders "often come from different university subcultures, speak different languages, and have conflicting perspectives, needs, and desires" (44). When this is the case, sometimes some stakeholders have more authority and more power to determine what goes on and in a classroom as well as the ability to determine who can use a classroom. These stakeholders may or may not have other stakeholders' best interests in mind. As such, stakeholders sometimes do draw on their own needs first and make decisions about classrooms based on those needs before they consider others' needs. In doing so, they may make rules and policies that protect their stake while making it difficult for others.

Classrooms are just one part of a larger college or university infrastructure. Stakeholders work within this infrastructure and are influenced by it. **Infrastructures** are the basic underlying structures or frameworks of an organization or system created and shaped by the ideologies, mission, and goals of the people who work there. These structures could include buildings, policies, politics, and economics, which are all influenced by bodies, race, and gender. Ideally, infrastructures should be built and maintained with the help of all stakeholders involved. When this does not happen, infrastructures can fail to serve all stakeholders. For example, if one stakeholder needs to secure a grant in order to maintain a job, that person must think about what consequences that grant could have on other stakeholders. If the stakeholder received grant money to build computer stations in a classroom, that person would need to make sure that the stations were accessible by all the stakeholders, including teachers and students, who would use the room. That means, for example, that the stations would need to have wide enough rows so that everyone, including a person in a wheelchair, would feel welcome. Trying to maneuver between narrow stations with a wheelchair would be difficult, after all.

Often, infrastructures become most visible when they don't work the way we want them to. When this happens, we are forced to examine them with a critical eye and to question how to make them better. Sometimes, that means we must think carefully about the rules and policies that stakeholders create and that govern infrastructures, and how those can prevent people from freely using the places and spaces. Sometimes, the more rules and policies in place, the harder it is for people to move freely.

Discussion Questions: Classrooms

Take a moment and think about a classroom you have written in. Then think about the following questions to determine if that classroom was a place that was designed for all:

1. Who designed this classroom, and did they have your best interests in mind?
2. What rules or policies governed this classroom?
3. What consequences did these rules and policies have on you and the other people in the classroom?
4. What message or messages do these rules or policies send?
5. What social norms dictated what could and could not happen in that classroom?
6. Did the design of the classroom help or hinder you in your writing abilities? If yes, why? If no, why?

Connected Online Spaces

So far in this chapter, you have considered physical places such as those we traverse when using a digital map and those we write in such as classrooms. Let's turn now to online spaces and how we navigate and write for them to better understand how technology is situated and connected. To be clear, connected here means to be in a relationship with, to be tied to, and/or to be dependent upon something else. A webpage is connected to the web and thus connected to people who use the web.

To do so, let's examine the technology of a hyperlink. A hyperlink, a link within a particular space online that connects and leads users to another space online, requires the use of multiple modes in order for it to work. These include: (1) the words ("click here") or images (such as an arrow) on the screen that provide the opportunity to create a gateway to another space (these are on the interface in which a user engages the hyperlink, usually via a mouse click or finger press), (2) the markup language (HTML) that makes it possible for a user to go from one space to another (this happens on the backend computing process), and (3) the temporal space, the time it takes to move from one space to another.

Hyperlinks are embedded in digital texts and provide users different understandings of such texts. For instance, hyperlinks give people the chance to choose their own unique reading path. Your use of hyperlinks in an online text might lead you to understand the information in one way, and someone else's use may lead to a different understanding. Instead of choosing to read in a linear way, you can choose to experience a text nonlinearly. You can choose the order of information you read by picking and choosing which hyperlinks to follow and which ones to ignore, and in what order you wish to do so.

> **Did You Know? Hyperlinks**
>
> Modern-day hyperlinks grew out of several ideas and technologies in the 1900s. Vannevar Bush, who headed the Office of Scientific Research and Development during World War II, is a significant player in this history. After the war, he recognized that scientists needed a way not only to keep track of scientific publications (indexes at that time were not helpful), but to search and connect ideas and textual knowledge from these publications via associations. To solve this problem, he developed the idea of a memex,
>
>> a desk that combined a microfilm reader, screen, special electronic tubes, and a keyboard—that would allow any user to insert code to link any point in a microfilmed document to any other point. The reader could retrieve those connections at will, pass it along to anyone else with a memex, and buy knowledge with prerecorded linkages (Turow 2).

The memex, Bush believed, would allow users to create an associative trail of related information by linking two pages of information. While his idea for the memex never came to realization during his lifetime, it did inspire others who would go on to create actual hyperlinks and the World Wide Web, including Ted Nelson, founder of Project Xanadu and a technologist who came up with the name *hyperlink*. Nelson was the one who thought about applying Bush's ideas to a worldwide computer network. At the same time Nelson was working on his ideas, Douglas Engelbart was working to create actual hyperlinks, "first (in 1966) by connecting items on a single page and then (in 1968) by implementing a way to jump between paragraphs in separate documents" (Turow 3). When the World Wide Web was created many years later, hyperlinks became a crucial and important feature of it, helping millions of people connect ideas in a matter of seconds.

Because hyperlinks are comprised of multimodal information, when writing a text that contains hyperlinks, you must think rhetorically. You must think about how they organize information, provide people with further knowledge, and connect people to one another. Online spaces are shaped by how people use hyperlinks. A person who runs a business may rely on how many people share the link to that business's website with friends on social media. A person who does PR may rely on how many people click a "like" button (a hyperlink itself) on social media. When writers use hyperlinks in digital texts, they give readers options for reading and understanding the texts in multiple ways.

Tracking Time, Place, and Space

Let's next think about how time plays a role in our writing and the use of technology within places and spaces. Tracking technologies gives us the ability to track our writing over time and in places and spaces. Microsoft Word's Track Changes feature can help people, for instance, keep track of the changes they have made to a document by utilizing different colors of font, underlines for additions, and strikethroughs for deletions. Other technologies can keep track of changes over a period of time by time-stamping changes. Wikis are an example of this. Most wikis, like Wikipedia, keep track of when changes are made.

We measure the passage of time in many ways. As discussed earlier in this book, calendars do this in days, weeks, and months. In other aspects of our lives, we may do so differently. Comedic timing can be represented by a pause or the picking up of pace, placement of the punch line after the buildup, or the rise of the climax in a joke. In a book, a passage of time could be indicated by space. An extra amount of blank space between paragraphs tells us there has been a jump in time in the story. Timing in video games is often crucial to being successful. Knowing when to jump, shoot an opponent, slow down, or speed up can mean the difference between winning and losing.

In writing, timing is important. We must realize what the right actions are at the right moment in time. In other words, we must think about kairos. Texts operate in time and are shaped by time. We learn and come to expect uses of time for specific technologies. The time it takes to do a Google search is .0002 seconds. If it were much longer, people might not be as likely to do it. A commercial is usually 30–60 seconds. If it was much longer, people might not be as likely to keep watching it.

Discussion Questions: When

To write effectively means to think carefully about the *when* of your writing, and to do so, you should think rhetorically about this *when*. Answer the following in regards to the writing you do for this class:

1. When do I write for this class, and why?
2. How does this *when* shape my writing?
3. How long does my writing take given the technology I use? In other words, does the technology help me write in a timely manner?
4. When will my readers read my writing, and how does the *when* shape their understanding?

Imagine the future of tracking time. In Chapter 9, you considered how data about writing could possibly help you become a better writer. Let's return now to that point but consider how time, places, and spaces play valuable roles in such data. To begin with, think about *when* you write, for how long, and in what places and spaces. If you were to examine the times you write and the places and spaces you write within, would you spot any patterns? In some respects, while there are technologies that can keep track of time and place and spaces as we write, imagine the future of writing if what we write can always be treated as data, data that is created in time and located at particular places and spaces. In what potential ways can we use this tracking of our writing at various times to improve our writing as individuals and as a society? For starters, imagine if your entire class's writing (from when it takes place to where it takes place) was tracked from the beginning to the end of the semester. Imagine if your writing was tracked from your first day of college until your last day of college. What could be learned by this data?

As mentioned previously, in some cases, your writing already is being tracked. You may take an entrance and exit exam, you may submit papers for teachers to use to assess curriculum, you may fill out surveys, or you may put together portfolios; these all provide a measure of your progress (or not), and they all provide data that institutions can use to improve their curriculum. But, they tell only part of the story. They capture only a few specific times when you wrote and are often the end products of a very long writing process that spanned a lot of time. What if, instead, everything you wrote was recorded from start to finish? Imagine if your brainstorming, your outlining, your sketching, your prototyping, and your researching with classmates and librarians, every little thing you did to create every draft, was recorded as data? Imagine what it would mean if not only the things you did on the actual texts were recorded, but *where* you did these things (i.e. on a computer, in a dorm room, at a library) and *when* you did these things (i.e. in the evening, right before class, for hours, for minutes) were recorded as data, too. Now imagine if this data were compared to other students' data. What might this data say about writing? What potential uses could this data have? What potential worries should we have about this data?

If we look at a word in this book and think about that one word as one part of a larger writing system, we can see again how time, place, and space come together. If we think about the word "book" in the previous sentence, we can see that time and place play important roles in our understanding of the sentence. If it came before the words "we look" and before "If," the sentence would not make much sense. If you are reading this book as an online ebook, then the word is situated in a space on the internet. The word "book" is the ninth word in the sentence. It follows in time (how many seconds it takes a reader to read it) and place (or position) after the previous eight words. The word "book" comes ninth because of a system of language governed by rules and people's uses. That system of language is shaped by other systems, too, as has been discussed, including social, political, economic, and cultural systems. Your understanding of "book," for example, is shaped by how your culture values books and the conventions they have shaped that govern what a book looks like and consists of. It is also shaped over time with your past experiences of books.

You Are One Writer in a World of Many

While writing can be a private endeavor, such as when you write in a journal, it is also a social one. If you think about all the writing you do, most of what you write is probably seen by others. In fact, in school and on the job, most likely you will share a lot of your writing. When you do share, others help shape it. You may revise based on what those others say about your writing. Furthermore, most likely you will also collaborate with others when writing. So, not only do you write *for* others, but you also write *with* others. Therefore, in the remainder of this chapter, you will learn the various roles that writing and technologies play in sharing and collaborating with others. Beforehand, it is vital to note that there is a difference between sharing and collaborating. Sharing simply refers to giving someone else your writing, while collaborating refers to actually working together to write with others.

Sharing can happen in many ways, especially in online spaces. What and how you choose to share should be something that all writers take seriously, especially when it comes to online technologies. While sharing can be both helpful and empowering (more on this in a moment), it can also, at the same time, be dangerous. You may share your writing and with it, it's possible, your personal information, through email, through social media, through chats, and so on.

LinkedIn is a worldwide professional networking service available through an online website and on a mobile app. The service provides a place where employees and employers can connect by sharing their credentials, such as information about themselves and past work experiences. By creating profiles and links to other users, people can build a professional network within the site that can lead to business and employment opportunities. According to their website, today the service has "more than 562 million users in more than 200 countries." But, like all online spaces where people share information about themselves, LinkedIn has faced a number of challenges to ensure that its users' information is not shared with just anyone, that it is shared only with other users. This challenge was most evident in 2012, when hackers accessed the LinkedIn network, stole millions of LinkedIn users' information, such as their emails and passwords, and made this information public by sharing it on an online forum unbeknownst to LinkedIn's users.

LinkedIn users had thought that their information was safe and secure within LinkedIn's system, but it was not. The truth is that no information online is safe, even information that is password protected. When sharing information online, you should assume that it could be potentially read by everyone, and thus you should proceed with caution.

Yet, not all sharing of information is bad. When it comes to writing, for instance, sharing your work and ideas with others can provide an opportunity for feedback, it can help you ensure that you have adhered to genre conventions, that you have paid attention to the needs of your audience, and that you made smart rhetorical decisions. Despite the times when sharing could be dangerous, sharing can sometimes mean less work, and can also be helpful and empowering. When you write content that is shareable across platforms, for example, you can end up doing less work because you don't have to start from scratch each time you move to a new platform.

In terms of being empowering, sharing can help people see that they are not alone. A hashtag such as #yacancer, which stands for young adults with cancer, can help connect millions of people. No longer feeling alone, some young adults fighting cancer might feel compelled and empowered to also share their stories with others who have gone through the same experiences.

Discussion Questions: Sharing Online

1. What writing do you share online, and why?
2. Do you believe that it is safe to share your writing online? Why or why not?
3. What are the consequences of sharing your writing online?

Just like sharing, writing collaboratively can also happen in many ways. Writing a wiki, for example, can mean that anyone who has access to a computer, the internet, and the wiki site can write the wiki, whether or not they know the other writers writing. At school, you might work with a classmate by talking through your ideas in person while at the same time working online on a Google doc to complete your writing task together.

There are plenty of ways in which people collaborate using a variety of technologies. Wynwood, a neighborhood north of downtown Miami, wasn't always the vibrant place it is today. Nearly ten years ago, it was just a warehouse district when Tony Goldman came up with the idea to use graffiti and street art to transform the walls of the buildings located there. Since then, Goldman has invited artists from all over the world to share their work with others by painting the walls.

Now, Wynwood features painted murals that represent all sorts of things, from portraits to calligraphy to the more abstract. The response to the walls has been profound, and Wynwood has since grown to include the surrounding areas of the original walls, where even more artists have created artwork. Wynwood represents years of collaboration and years of evolving texts situated in a community. These paintings are relevant to today's world, too, often communicating timely messages. Indeed, the texts of Wynwood—that is, its walls—are always changing as new artists come to paint. And, these walls are never done in isolation; they are always connected to people and to other texts. That is, in order for the walls to be as effective as they are in communicating their messages, many people have to collaborate.

From spray cans to scaffolding, the artists employ a variety of technologies to make the walls mean something and to spread their messages. While a single painting carries meaning on its own, together with other paintings at Wynwood, that single painting has yet other meanings. Each artist brings his or her own unique talents and artwork to Wynwood. But, only through the collaboration of all who are involved at Wynwood does Wynwood work to affect those who visit. This collaboration also includes visitors. They leave messages for the artists, and the artists listen and collaborate on what the exhibits should entail in the future.

Collaborating using technology has many advantages besides revitalizing neighborhoods, though. To demonstrate, let's look at another example. Hypothesis (https://web.hypothes.is/) is a collaborative online reading extension that allows you to annotate, discuss, and read webpages with others who also use Hypothesis. Through the process of collaboration, Hypothesis can help you see different connections between ideas by reading what others have annotated on the same online texts. Your reading of an online webpage may be different from someone else's, after all; but when you combine your annotations with someone else's, you may be able to see connections between ideas that you didn't see before. In this case, your collaboration with another reader to annotate a text led you to new understandings of the text. In this case, readers of online texts with annotations reap several benefits, benefits that would not happen without the use of technology.

Yet, collaborating using technology has many more advantages. For one, people all over the world can easily collaborate together thanks to technologies that can connect them.

Before modern-day digital technologies, if someone in China wanted to collaborate on writing a text with someone in Germany, they would have to do so through phone conversations, mail, and telegraph and would have to piece together a draft that would have to be shared back and forth, perhaps through mail, which often demanded lots of time. Today, those two people could get online and, in a matter of minutes, have a draft written together.

While writers can benefit from collaborating as they use technologies, there are some disadvantages they should be aware of. Technology, at times, can get in the way of collaborating effectively. If writers are trying to work together to produce a text, they will need to make sure that they organize and share their work in effective ways so that it can be accessed, completed, and protected by everyone in the group. Everyone most likely will be using a variety of technologies at different times throughout the project. If a group doesn't utilize technologies effectively, the group members may run the risk of having multiple versions of drafts, losing content due to a lack of organization, being unable to open up the correct draft on specific technologies, and exposing drafts and information to people outside the group. Some technologies may even pose barriers to members of a collaborative team. Making sure that everyone has equal access to the work, therefore, is an important step in successful collaboration when using technologies.

Final Thoughts

As was discussed in this chapter, technology, and therefore writing, does not happen in isolation. When we use technology to write, we do so somewhere and at some time. This somewhere and sometime influences what it is we write and how we write it. It is important, then, to remember that writing rhetorically means that we must think carefully about how the *when* and *where* of writing influences our decisions to use technologies. This is particularly evident when we think about sharing and collaborating using technologies. In sharing and collaborating, we have to think wisely about *when* and *where* what we write will be shared with others.

Additional Discussion Questions

1. How do technologies help or hinder collaboration? Come up with examples to discuss.
2. Think about a time when you wrote collaboratively. What technologies did you use, and in what ways did they help or hinder you in your collaboration? What might you do differently when writing collaboratively in the future?
3. What advantages and disadvantages are there to sharing your personal information online? Do you believe the advantages outweigh the disadvantages?

Additional Activities

1. Examine Community Maps: Examine maps that represent your community in different ways. Then, choose one of those maps, travel to a place that is represented by that map, and compare the physical location to that of the map. For instance, perhaps your campus has a map that you can use to locate buildings, or perhaps one of the buildings on your campus has a map to help people navigate that building. Compare the two experiences (looking at the map and looking at the actual location) and write a reflection to share with your class that answers the following:

   - How is the physical place represented as a 2D text?
   - What is and is not adequately represented by the map?
   - What is missing from this map? Who would this map not help?
   - What would you suggest the writer of the map do differently, and why?
   - What impacts do the map and the writing of it have on the actual place it is supposed to represent?

2. Remember that Writing Is a Technology: Think about how place influences your writing. Analyze the room you are in. In what ways does the design of the room shape the way you write? Think about the physical dimensions of the room, the location of furniture, and how the positions of those dimensions and those pieces of furniture shape your body. Think about who had a hand at designing and maintaining such a room. Write a reflection on how a place influences and shapes your writing.

Additional Assignments

1. Photo Essay of a Place: Try representing a place in your writing by creating a photo essay in which you tell a story about this place to someone who has never been there. In doing so, think carefully about how you will represent this place, what features will you highlight, and why such an audience would appreciate these.
2. Video Game Comparison: Analyze and compare several popular video games to find out what role writing plays in the creation and playing of them. Consider how such games are embedded in our society. Write a report that details your findings.
3. Tracking Your Writing Over Time: Track your writing over a period of time (for example, over a month) to find out the role time plays in your writing. As you track your writing over this period, make sure that you make note of when you are writing and for how long. Then think about how your findings are related to how successful you were with your writing. Write a presentation about your findings and share it with your classmates.

Works Cited

"About LinkedIn." *LinkedIn*, 2018, https://about.linkedin.com/. Accessed 29 August 2018.

"About Wynwood Walls." *Wynwood Walls*, 2018, www.thewynwoodwalls.com/overview. Accessed 12 January 2018.

Arduini, Tina. "Cyborg Gamers: Exploring the Effects of Digital Gamin on Multimodal Composition." *Computers and Composition*, 48, 2018, pp. 89–102.

Bickford, Deborah J. "Navigating the White Waters of Collaborative Work in Shaping Learning Environments." *New Directions for Teaching and Learning*, 92, 2002, pp. 43–52.

Farman, Jason. "Mapping and Representations of Space." *Mobile Technologies: Critical Concepts in Media and Cultural Studies*, edited by Gerard Goggin, Rich Ling, and Larissa Hjorth, Routledge, 2016, pp. 279–298.

Gallagher, Michael D. "An Exceptional Year of Growth, Impact, & Innovation." *Entertainment Software Association. 2017 Annual Report*, 2018, www.esaannualreport.com/a-letter-from-michael-d.-gallagher.html. Accessed 28 June 2018.

Murray, Joddy. *Non-Discursive Rhetoric: Image and Affect in Multimodal Composition*. State University of New York, 2009.

Nagelhout, Ed, and Carol Rutz. "Introduction: The Spaces of the Classroom." *Classroom Spaces and Writing Instruction*, edited by Ed Nagelhout and Carol Rutz, Cresskill, 2004, pp. 1–12.

Suh, Ayoung, Christian Wagner, and Lili Liu. "Enhancing User Engagement Through Gamification." *Journal of Computer Information Systems*, 58, 3, 2018, pp. 204–213.

Turow, Joseph. "Introduction: On Not Taking the Hyperlink for Granted." *The Hyperlinked Society: Questioning Connections in the Digital Age*, edited by Joseph Turow and Lokman Tsui, University of Michigan, 2008, pp. 1–18.

CHAPTER 11

Writing Messages

Contents

Messages Can Help Save Lives 253
Choosing the Right Text and Technology for Your Message..........................256
Email Messages 258
Suggestions for Writing Emails 261
Emails Serve Lots of Purposes...263
Why Email Is Not Always the Best Way to Communicate.............................266
Text Messages...267
Think about Accessible Messages 268
Final Thoughts 270

Messages Can Help Save Lives

In 2006, the Smithsonian Institution Traveling Exhibition Service (SITES) and the National Museum of the American Indian (NMAI) co-produced a traveling exhibition titled *Native Words, Native Warriors* to honor American Indian Code Talkers. The exhibition told of their story fighting in the U.S. Armed Forces during World War I and World War II.

According to the U.S. Marine Corps Manual of Military Occupational Specialties, a "code talker" is "one who transmits and receives messages in a restricted language by radio and wire" (National Museum of the American Indian). Especially during World War II, American Indian Code Talkers used their native languages to send messages via radio. In so doing, they developed a coding system that included different types of codes to outsmart the enemies, mainly Type One Codes and Type Two Codes. For Type One Codes, each letter in the alphabet was paired with a word in the Navajo language. For instance, the letter C was paired with the word *Moasi*, which, when translated into English, means *cat*. Table 11.1 displays the U.S. Navy Navajo Code Dictionary alphabet section from June 15, 1945.

TABLE 11.1 Navajo Code Talker Dictionary Alphabet Section, revised June 15, 1945, and declassified in 1968 under the Department of Defense Directive 5200.9.

ALPHABET	NAVAJO WORD	LITERAL TRANSLATION
A	WOL-LA-CHEE	ANT
A	BE-LA-SANA	APPLE
A	TSE-NILL	AXE
B	NA-HASH-CHID	BADGER
B	SHUSH	BEAR
B	TOISH-JEH	BARREL
C	MOASI	CAT
C	TLA-GIN	COAL
C	BA-GOSHI	COW
D	BE	DEER
D	CHINDI	DEVIL
D	LHA-CHA-EH	DOG
E	AH-JAHA	EAR
E	DZEH	ELK
E	AH-NAH	EYE
F	CHUO	FIR
F	TSA-E-DONIN-EE	FLY
F	MA-E	FOX
G	AH-TAD	GIRL
G	KLIZZIE	GOAT
G	JEHA	GUM
H	TSE-GAH	HAIR
H	CHA	HAT
H	LIN	HORSE
I	TKIN	ICE
I	YEH-HES	ITCH
I	A-CHI	INTESTINE
J	TKELE-CHO-G	JACKASS
J	AH-YA-TSINNE	JAW
J	YIL-DOI	JERK
K	JAD-HO-LONI	KETTLE

Writing Messages

ALPHABET	NAVAJO WORD	LITERAL TRANSLATION
K	BA-AH-NE-DI-TININ	KEY
K	KLIZZIE-YAZZIE	KID
L	DIBEH-YAZZIE	LAMB
L	AH-JAD	LEG
L	NASH-DOIE-TSO	LION
M	TSIN-TLITI	MATCH
M	BE-TAS-TNI	MIRROR
M	NA-AS-TSO-SI	MOUSE
N	TSAH	NEEDLE
N	A-CHIN	NOSE
O	A-KHA	OIL
O	TLO-CHIN	ONION
O	NE-AHS-JAH	OWL
P	CLA-GI-AIH	PANT
P	BI-SO-DIH	PIG
P	NE-ZHONI	PRETTY
Q	CA-YEILTH	QUIVER
R	GAH	RABBIT
R	DAH-NES-TSA	RAM
R	AH-LOSZ	RICE
S	DIBEH	SHEEP
S	KLESH	SNAKE
T	D-AH	TEA
T	A-WOH	TOOTH
T	THAN-ZIE	TURKEY
U	SHI-DA	UNCLE
U	NO-DA-IH	UTE
V	A-KEH-DI-GLINI	VICTOR
W	GLOE-IH	WEASEL
X	AL-NA-AS-DZOH	CROSS
Y	TSAH-AS-ZIH	YUCCA
Z	BESH-DO-TLIZ	ZINC

Using the dictionary, try writing a phrase in English and translating that into a code. For example, a phrase like "send more troops" might be the following: Dibeh-Ah-Jaha-Tsah-Be Tsin-Tliti-A-Kha-Gah-Ah-Jaha D-Ah-Gah-Tlo-Chin-Tlo-Chin-Cla-Gi-Aih-Dibeh.

While Type One Codes involved using Native words to represent English letters, Type Two Codes involved translating complete phrases into Native languages. A phrase like "send more troops" would be literally translated into a Native language. However, Native languages didn't always contain a word for the English word when Code Talkers tried to translate, so the Code Talkers had to create new words in their language to account for this. For instance, the Navajo used the word atsá for a transport plane. In Navajo, this word means *eagle*.

Native languages, particularly the Navajo language, proved valuable to the U.S. war efforts. If the messages were ever intercepted, enemies could not understand them. As with a lot of Native American languages, the Navajo language was not a written language and therefore had no records that enemies could use to decipher the codes.

Throughout history, people have found efficient and effective ways to communicate messages for a number of purposes. The Code Talkers are but one example. In Chapter 2, you learned about one kind of message, A&C Industries' organizational update. That update was just one type of message Mike Butler writes on a regular basis as a supply chain manager and engineer. In this chapter, you will consider other types of messages and how writers can make smart choices when creating them, especially when they are aware that they are shaped by technologies that are embedded in our society.

Chances are you write messages all the time. Contemplate what you did in the past two weeks. Did you send someone a message? If so, what kind of message? Was it a text message? An email? A note? A letter? In the last chapter, you read about what it means to think of technology as situated. In this chapter, you will consider that again, but you will also contemplate the many different types of messages you can write and the situated technologies needed to create such messages. While you do so, you will also reflect on why thinking rhetorically about writing such messages can help you to be effective in your communication. In particular, you will reflect on your audiences for your messages and their role in the writing process.

Choosing the Right Text and Technology for Your Message

When insurance salesperson Marcia Hicks makes a sale, she handwrites a thank-you note and sends it to her clients to let them know she appreciates their business. That doesn't sound like a big deal until you consider that Marcia makes hundreds of sales each year. But, Marcia knows the value of a personal touch, so instead of sending a form thank-you letter generated on her computer or a generic email that would have saved her time no doubt, she believes handwriting thank-you notes pays off and makes her a successful businessperson. She believes her clients love her personal touch and recommend her to others, garnering her even more business.

Every day, people around the world handwrite messages, from waiters taking orders in a restaurant to students passing notes in a classroom. Take a few moments and think again about the past two weeks. How many handwritten notes did you write to others or even to yourself? Why did you handwrite them? What purposes did they serve? Were they effective? If you didn't handwrite any notes, why not? Why did you use other options for communicating your messages?

Determining the right text and technology for your message means you need to think rhetorically about your audience and the messages you want to write. Marcia chooses to handwrite messages to her clients because she knows her audience appreciates the personal touch. Keeping her clients happy keeps Marcia in business. To think about your audience, then, is to think about rapport. **Rapport** means to have a good understanding with others while those others have a good understanding of you. In other words, rapport is a two-way street. Both you and your audience establish a good, working relationship. Your writing and the texts you create say something about you, the writer. It helps you establish your ethos. Marcia has had a positive experience, and her notes indicate to her clients that she cares about them.

However, texts and technologies can also have effects that are not as beneficial as was the case with Marcia's handwritten notes. Choosing an inappropriate text and/or technology for your message could indicate to your audience that you are unprofessional and lack audience awareness. In business, that could be bad. Remember that not all texts and/or technologies are appropriate for your messages. Using a text message to explain to your boss your research on implementing a new system at work probably wouldn't be ideal. Text messages tend to be short, informal, and read on the go. If you want your boss to seriously consider implementing a new system, you would probably want your boss to sit down and read your message thoroughly. Perhaps even take some notes. When you think about your message, you might consider how your technology can help or add to your message, when it will be read, and where it will be read. In this scenario, a text that is very long would not help you get your boss to implement a new system. It could, however, frustrate your boss, since there are other ways to communicate your message about the system that would be better for your message and for your boss.

In addition, different cultures use different technologies to communicate messages. If you are writing a message for international audiences, it would be a good idea to research which technologies are used most often and for what purposes. For instance, according to a recent Pew Research Center study, "WhatsApp is popular in Latin America, and this popularity also extends to Latinos in the United States" (Smith and Anderson). If you worked for a company or organization that was trying to reach this population of people, you might consider how you could use WhatsApp to communicate your messages.

Not Only Do Different Cultures Use Different Technologies, but They Also Write Differently Based on Their Cultural Practices

There are a number of resources online that can help you learn about different cultural expectations for writing. Crafting your messages according to your audiences' cultural expectations for writing would help you be more successful in your communication. In the example in Chapter 2, Mike Butler did this when writing his message to his fellow employees and clients abroad.

Assignment: Learn More About Your Audiences

The Cultural Atlas, a project developed by SBS, International Education Services, and Multicultural NSW in Australia, is a free online resource that can help you research various cultures around the world and their customs, including those for communication. For this activity, try doing the following:

1. Check out their website at https://culturalatlas.sbs.com.au/.
2. Pretend that you are in charge of organizing an online event that will bring awareness to a good cause like recycling or cleanup efforts. In addition to raising awareness, you hope to sign up volunteers for future in-person events in countries around the world. Because you want global participation, develop a message that you can send out to a volunteer organization in at least two other countries. As you do, make sure to tailor each message for that particular country's culture. You can use the Cultural Atlas as a guide.
3. Choose a technology that is appropriate for your audience and your message.
4. Compare your messages and note the decisions you made for writing to account for cultural differences in each message.
5. Share your project with your classmates.

On the other hand, while it is important to be sensitive to differences, another strategy for writing messages to various audiences is to think about what those audiences have in common and build your texts around that. Many countries share similar expectations for writing. Building on these similarities could help you establish a relationship with your reader based on their familiarity with your writing choices. Building on similarities can also help prove to your audience that you are thinking globally.

Email Messages

Later on in this chapter, you will further consider different technologies and reasons why you should pay close attention to cultural differences when writing. For now, let's consider a specific type of messaging technology: email. While in the example in the previous section, Marcia prefers to handwrite her thank-you notes, there may be times in your life where handwriting messages just doesn't make sense or is inappropriate. Most likely, once you graduate from college, you will find that you have to write emails for the company or organization you work for on a regular basis. It is hard to tell if in 1971 Ray Tomlinson, the person credited with sending the first ever email, had imagined that nearly 50 years later, billions of people would be sending emails every day. In fact, in 2017, the Radicati Group estimated that there were 3.7 billion email accounts worldwide and that an average of 269 billion emails were sent each day (qtd. in Tschabitscher).

Today, companies and organizations expect their employees to write professional emails. Such a skill is important to your future career indeed, but learning to write a professional email isn't just a skill you need on the job. In your civic and personal life, writing a professional email can provide you a means to communicate effectively with a variety of audiences. There will be times, perhaps, when you have to write the government or your local community members. As a result, you may need to rely on email to express your concerns, your approval, your needs, and your rights.

So, what does it mean to write a professional email? What does being professional look like? Examine the two email examples in Images 11.1 and 11.2. Which of these two examples would you consider to be a professional email message?

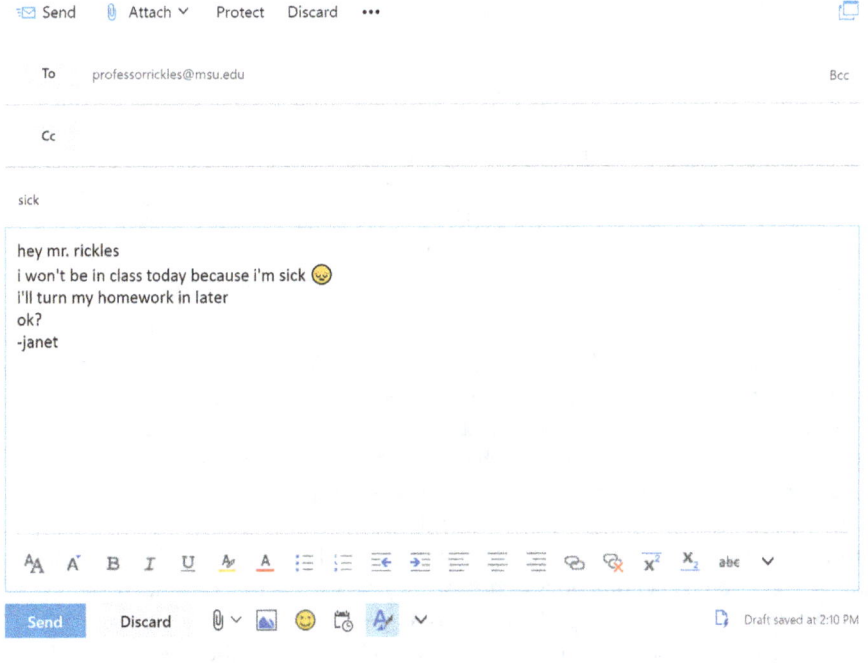

IMAGE 11.1 Example A

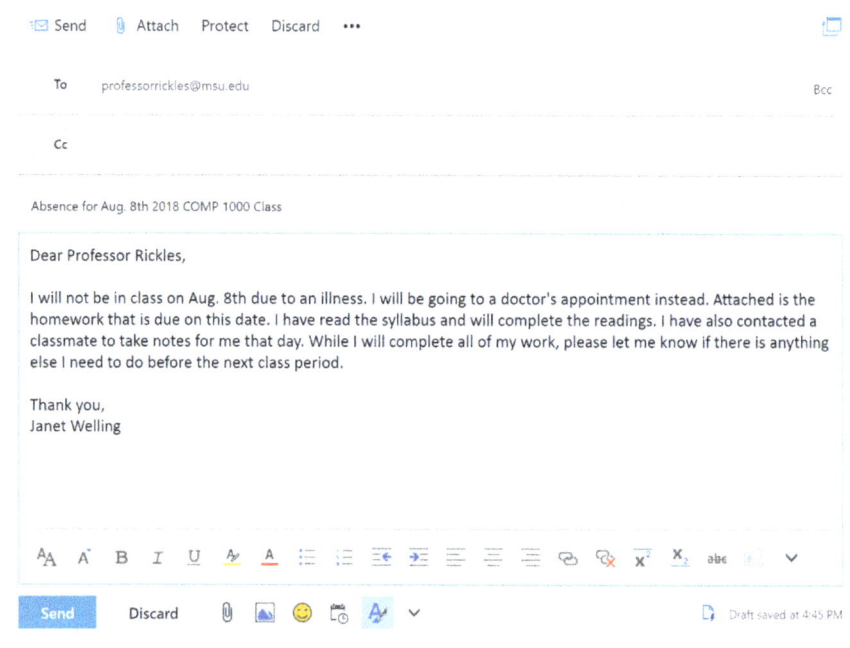

Example B

Most likely, you thought that example B was the professional email. But, why? What about it makes it professional? Breaking down the email into its parts may make it easy to see what makes example B more professional than example A. We can start by looking at the subject line and thinking about who Janet is writing to. Janet probably isn't Professor Rickles's only student this semester. Most likely Professor Rickles teaches several classes and has lots of students. So, using a subject line that indicates the class (in example B) is a good idea on Janet's part. It lets the professor know what the email is regarding.

Next, if we look at the greeting, we can see that she chose "dear" to begin the email. This language choice could be influenced by a number of things: Janet's situated role as a student at an institution and her knowledge of polite customs. It shows that Janet is aware of the professional conventions that her university supports and perhaps feels it would be respectful to her professor if she began this way. After her greeting, she then uses complete and grammatically correct sentences to explain why she will not be in class. Again, this language choice shows that she is aware of her audience, her professor at an institution who probably expects students to write in this manner. Finally, she ends with a "thank you." In her situation, such an email makes sense; that is, it shows that Janet paid attention to her situation and acted accordingly. She didn't text her professor or send a letter. She chose to use an email and wrote it in a way that she believed would be professional. She didn't use emojis or slang, which would have been considered informal.

Suggestions for Writing Emails

To emoji or not to emoji? That is the question. Writing an effective email to your professor might not seem like a big deal, but when you are employed, your emails will be reflections of the company or organization you work for. Perhaps, if you don't get in the habit of thinking rhetorically about writing professional emails while you are still in college, you might not be prepared to write them when working on the job, where an email could mean the difference between landing a deal or not, hiring an employee or not, or securing a promotion or not. In any case, you should think carefully like Janet did in the second example. In that example, Janet used her rhetorical skills, making language and technology choices based on her situation and audience.

To help you make choices like Janet did in the second example, you will find suggestions below for thinking rhetorically about writing an email message. When to use these suggestions does depend on your audience, though. Make sure to pay attention to their needs and adjust your strategies accordingly.

Suggestion 1: Catch Your Reader's Attention

When sending out an email, one that contains important information you want your audience to read, think about the two purposes of a subject line: (1) to explain what the email contains, and (2) to get readers interested in reading the email. A good subject line is important for a number of reasons. If you think about all the emails a person receives every day, chances are they might not want to read all of them. In a lot of cases, a subject line is the reason people choose to read or not to read the email. In Janet's subject line, she accomplished both purposes, choosing to let Professor Rickles know that her email was regarding her absence on a particular date in a particular class.

Suggestion 2: Say Hello Appropriately

After developing a good subject line, next determine the greeting (or how to say hello) that is appropriate for your audience. Janet chose "dear" since it is a formal, professional way to greet her professor. If she were writing to friends and family, though, such a greeting might seem a bit too formal. A "Hey" or "Hi" might be better in those cases. To determine how you will greet your audience, you might consider your rapport with your audience and choose accordingly.

Suggestion 3: Substance Matters When You Write the Content

Of your email's content, that is the body, think again about to whom you are writing, as every culture writes differently. In certain Asian cultures, for example in Korea and Japan, people tend to prefer indirect statements over direct ones, as their cultures value community over individuals, putting the needs of others first. How much explanation is needed depends too on culture. People in particular cultures may expect a lot of detail, or not a lot at all. They may expect a formal explanation, or one that is more informal. As such, try not to use slang or colloquialisms, as they could be unfamiliar to your audience. Be conscious and respectful of different religious, economic, political, and social beliefs. Do your research by studying the texts from those cultures to whom you are writing.

Knowing little things about a culture can make a big difference. In some cultures, the date is written in this order: day, month, year. In the United States, the date is typically written in this order: month, day, year. This might not seem like a big deal, but when you consider writing about an important date or deadline, your audience may find your way of writing a date to be confusing. So, in doing your research, pay attention to things that may seem at first insignificant to you, as they could end up being important to your ability to communicate your messages effectively.

Suggestion 4: Think Audience

Next, think again about rapport and make smart choices about language use and tone of voice. If you read both the example emails from Images 11.1 and 11.2 out loud, you can hear that the tone of voice in each is different. The first seems a bit too informal, while the second seems just right. Choose your words and tone carefully.

Emails in the United States tend to be concise, meaning that every word has to count. Using long-winded paragraphs in an email might not be the most appropriate way to communicate a message via email in the United States and similar cultures, especially if those paragraphs contain unnecessary words and phrases. If you think about how many emails a person receives on a daily basis in such a culture and the nature of that culture (fast-paced, every bit of time matters), you would know that readers wouldn't have a lot of time to read a very long email. So, it might be best to get straight to the point like Janet does in her email in example B.

Suggestion 5: Say Goodbye Appropriately

Finally, you should choose a closing (or how to say goodbye) that is suitable to the situation and reread your email before sending. Just as you did for the greeting, you should think about your audience and your relationship with them in choosing a closing. In addition, before you hit the send button, read your email out loud and make sure that you have included everything you need to say in a way that you feel is most appropriate to the situation. Surprisingly, a lot of mistakes can be caught simply by rereading your writing out loud.

> ### Activity: Email Your Professor
>
> Write an email to your professor in which you explain your goals for the class and how you will accomplish them. Think carefully about your language choices using the suggestions in this section as a guide.

Emails Serve Lots of Purposes

Businesses spend millions of dollars trying to get people to open their emails and read/use their content. That content could include such things as coupons, discount codes, flyers, invitations, transaction receipts, and much more. As chief editor of her school's student literary magazine, called *Digressions*, Nicole Chavannes believed it would be a great idea to create a digital newsletter for her writing staff and send it via email. Doing so on a regular basis would keep her staff motivated and informed, especially since each digital newsletter issue would feature updates on the magazine, important deadlines, and links to additional information; highlight a magazine editor; and share stories about the publication process.

The example in Image 11.3 is Nicole's email newsletter for the launch of the latest issue of *Digressions*. This newsletter was distributed through email just as many digital newsletters are. For the subject line, Nicole chose "Successful Launch! Mags Now Available."

IMAGE 11.3   Nicole Chavannes's Digital Email Newsletter

In doing so, Nicole meets the two purposes of an effective subject line (lets readers know what the email is about, and gets readers to read). The rest of the email contains her digital newsletter right in the body of the text. It's not attached, and that's a deliberate decision. She wanted to increase the chances of her audience reading her newsletter. Because viruses are sent through email, people are hesitant to open attachments. In addition, opening an attachment requires readers to perform extra steps (clicking on the attachment, downloading it, and opening it). Putting the newsletter in the body eliminates those extra steps, saving readers time by allowing them to see the content immediately.

Besides a good subject line, Nicole used many of the suggestions in the previous section for writing an email: concise language, an appropriate tone of voice, and so forth. Below, in an interview, Nicole talks at length about the many decisions she made when creating her email newsletter. As you read through her interview, pay attention to the rhetorical skills she used.

INTERVIEW
NICOLE CHAVANNES, STUDENT AND EDITOR-IN-CHIEF

Q: What technologies did you use to create the newsletter and why?
A: I used MailChimp, a free online service, to create the newsletter because it provides templates to work off of and is user-friendly. The site allows you to edit and manipulate templates to create the newsletter that best fits your purposes, and allows you to see certain statistics such as how many people opened or viewed your newsletter.

Q: What rhetorical decisions did you make when creating your newsletter, and why?
A: I wanted to create both an aesthetically pleasing as well as informative newsletter; instead of bombarding the readers with text, I chose to chunk it up into bite-size sections. I created a section for news as well as recurring sections like "Digressions in History," "Staff Member of the Month" and "Monthly To-Dos" to keep the content both informative and interesting. Stylistically, I chose to keep the tone of the newsletter somewhat conversational while remaining professional.

Q: Why did you design the newsletter in the way you did? For example, what made you choose the colors that you did? The font that you did? Etc.
A: Since the newsletter was for *Digressions*, NSU's student-run literary magazine, I chose to use the magazine's logo as a header and create the rest of the aesthetic around that. I kept the color scheme within the same palette as the logo, deviating only when I added photos. I used blue accents that complemented the logo when separating sections and adding buttons to keep the design consistent. I chose the fonts I did to make the newsletter as readable as possible. I stayed away from script fonts because those can be difficult to read in large blocks of text, and it would have clashed with the logo's font as well.

Q: When you were designing the newsletter, how did you imagine your audience would use it?
A: Ideally, this newsletter would be a monthly recap for the *Digressions* staff to stay informed on recent happenings as well as understand their responsibilities for the upcoming month. This newsletter would replace long group emails with long blocks of text that can be difficult to read, and would instead allow the staff to (a) be informed on all the latest news, (b) learn more about *Digressions'* past (if interested), (c) feel appreciated, and (d) know their responsibilities for the month. If the staff members were in a hurry, they could simply read the most pertinent sections.

Q: Did you get feedback on your design as you were creating it? If so, how, and was this feedback helpful?
A: Initially, I chose to use part of an old *Digressions* cover as the header of the newsletter, but the feedback I received was that (a) it wasn't consistent with other *Digressions* marketing materials (since it wasn't the official logo), and (b) it complicated the design. I chose the official logo instead because of its calming color palette that allowed for a cleaner, more streamlined design.

Q: What writing advice would you give a student who wants to design newsletters?
A: Newsletters are meant to be recaps, something easily read on the go to stay informed without being bogged down by long blocks of text and unnecessary information. Be selective with your words and details; keep the information relevant. Also, know your audience, and shape the tone of your writing into what's most appropriate for that audience.

In the future, you may be tasked with creating all kinds of content for email messages. You will need to think strategically (that is, rhetorically) like Nicole did when doing so. It would be a good idea to get in the habit now of writing effective emails so that when you do land your future job, you are prepared to write such emails. For practice, check out the assignment in the box below.

Assignment: Writing Email Content

Create an email newsletter like Nicole did for a specific international population. The subject matter of your newsletter will depend on your audience and what you wish to inform them about. As you develop your newsletter's content, though, pay attention to the culture you are writing it for. Study examples of text from that culture to determine what is expected of texts. Share your assignment with your classmates and discuss what you learned by researching your audience.

Why Email Is Not Always the Best Way to Communicate

Although it is highly likely that you will write many emails in your future for a variety of purposes, email and the technologies people use to write, send, and receive them have evolved over time, in good ways and in bad. Originally, email was designed to send messages, but technology companies and everyday users have since created new uses for it. Email accounts, for instance, have become storage spaces for messages between people and messages to oneself. They record business, provide a means to make reminders, and enable users to sync calendars and phone numbers with a number of computer devices, such as smartphones and tablets.

Yet, while the above examples demonstrate what could be considered good uses of email, email technologies have also become dangerous. People have used email to develop spam, cheat others out of personal information or money via scams, and transfer viruses that are harmful to computers. In addition, there are times when writing down certain messages might not be a good idea. When written, the message is a record, stored in an online, connected space, one that other people can hack.

On the job, you might work for a company or organization that monitors its employees' email accounts. Depending on which country you live in, most likely that company or organization owns those accounts and can legally view your uses, making sure that you are using your email ethically, responsibly, and according to their policies. It might be a good idea to remember that when you pursue your career, use your job's email account in a manner that won't compromise your job or personal information. If you don't want your boss to read your personal business, you shouldn't use your job's email to write about it.

> ### Activity: Email Privacy Laws
>
> Around the world, governments are busy creating new laws and updating existing ones to keep pace with the ever-changing technologies their citizens use. However, this task is enormous and at times slow going. Research current laws that are supposed to protect citizens' uses of email. Write a reflection that answers the following:
>
> Are these laws up-to-date; that is, do they account for the ways in which people use email today? If so, how? If not, what are the steps the government should take in order to protect citizens' uses of email?

Even still, it might be a good idea to think carefully about your personal email accounts and the information you send and store there. An email account is provided by a third party, an ISP (internet service provider) that stores your account, most likely on a server. Once you click "send," that ISP has a record of the email and either sends it on to your intended recipient or returns it back to you. While your account is password protected, and while the ISP also enacts measures to keep your account secure, your information could still become available to people you didn't intend it to. For instance, the person you sent your email to could potentially (or even unintentionally) share it with others. Even the ISP (depending, of course, on the laws in place) could potentially be court ordered to share your emails. It is best to be cautious about what you share in an email. Sharing a note of encouragement to a friend would be safe. But, sharing your credit card information with your friend may not be. Even though you trust your friend, you never know who might end up seeing the email with that information.

Text Messages

In a lot of ways, a text messaging system operates in a similar manner as an email messaging system. Both enable users to write, send, and receive messages. Both record messages. Both are used for a variety of purposes, and both have similar conventions. Yet, there are some significant differences between them, and in this section, you will consider what it means specifically to write text messages. Before we tackle rhetorical strategies for writing effective text messages, however, let's first reflect on how texting has had an impact on our society and our writing.

Over the years, the kind of writing that people do in text messages has evolved. Because people use text messaging on the go, timing plays a significant role. Often that means messages are short and as a result don't follow the same "rules" as the kind of writing you do in other kinds of texts. For instance, in texting, people may use shortened words, replace numbers for letters, and use acronyms, abbreviations, and emoticons, things that wouldn't be used in a formal letter or research paper. Writing out every word and every letter in a text message isn't always necessary, as readers can understand what we mean given the context of the situation.

Like with all technologies we use, our uses of text messages have consequences, both good and bad. One such negative consequence has to do with the *when* of texting. Using a phone while driving (such as texting) is dangerous, yet people still do it. According to the U.S. National Highway Traffic Safety Administration, "During daylight hours, approximately 481,000 drivers are using cell phones while driving. That creates enormous potential for deaths and injuries on U.S. roads." In fact, the report states, "teens were the largest age group reported as distracted at the time of fatal crashes."

> **Discussion Questions: Texting While Driving**
>
> 1. How has texting while driving impacted our society?
> 2. Why do you suppose people do it even though they may know it is against the law in some places as well as very dangerous?
> 3. What are some ways in which we, as a society, can effectively educate people about the dangers of texting while driving?

Like emails, you have to think carefully when texting. On the job, text messages could make or break an important deal, relay important information about deadlines, provide reminders for clients, and so on. Choosing *when* along with *where* and *how* becomes crucial to writing texts successfully. You might start by carefully contemplating how you would answer the following questions:

- When should I write and send my text message?
- What will my readers be doing when they receive it?
- Where will they be?
- How will the *when* and *where* shape my writing and my readers' understanding of my writing?

Think about Accessible Messages

Now that you have considered a few different types of messages, mainly emails and text messages, you might want to take a step back and think about choosing the right technology for all your messages (not just emails and text messages) so as to ensure you are able to reach all of your intended audiences. When writing and communicating messages with others, you can start with Universal Design principles to help you think carefully about making your messages (and thus the texts you create) accessible to all. In other chapters of the book, you will learn more about accessibility principles specifically for designing in online spaces such as websites. For now, you can use these principles for all messages and texts you create. There are many organizations, colleges and universities, and governmental agencies and committees working worldwide to ensure everyone has access to texts of all kinds. For the purposes of this book, the following is a useful way of understanding Universal Design, one that considers access via environments. According to the Centre for Excellence in Universal Design:

> Universal Design is the design and composition of an environment so that it can be accessed, understood and used to the greatest extent possible by all people regardless of their age, size, ability or disability. An environment (or any building, product, or service in that environment) should be designed to meet the needs of all people who wish to use it. This is not a special requirement, for the benefit of only a minority of the population. It is a fundamental condition of good design. If an environment is accessible, usable, convenient and a pleasure to use, everyone benefits.

In this definition, understanding environments plays a key role in designing for everyone. As was discussed earlier, writing is not only situated in environments but is also a major part of them. Humans are certainly part of these environments, too, and you should always put people first; that is, you should think about what makes each of us unique, from our physical bodies, to our mental capabilities, to our interactions within cultures and environments. There is no such thing as a "normal" body. Your goal, then, in creating accessible messages is to create them in ways so as to reach as many in your audience as possible. At times, this may mean that you must provide multiple formats that utilize a variety of modes (verbal, written, images, etc.) and that those formats are accessible to those you intended; for in the environments they will be interacting with them. For instance, if you were to create a message for a person who relies on an assistive technology (such as a screen reader), you would need to make sure that in using such assistive technology they can in fact read your message.

As an example of how to write a message for the widest audience possible, think first about organization to ensure everyone can access it: (1) use headings to signal to readers what your message content is about, (2) break up longer messages into more manageable and memorable chunks of information, and (3) use lists to help readers keep track of the information in your messages.

In addition to these, you must also think about how you will share your message and what technologies you will use to do so. For example, if you are to include images in a digital message, make sure to include alternate text for those images and to identify the language you are using in the document. Not all computers work the same, so you need to think about how your audience will download and use your messages in a variety of formats.

Finally, when writing messages, think about how your information is presented. If it is too complex, some information may present a barrier to someone. Remember that not everyone learns in the same way. Some people have a hard time focusing their attention. Some people are more visual learners. Some are more aural learners. If you provide multiple types of texts that feature a variety of modes, you may be able to reach a much wider audience. Say you were a volunteer for your local community and you wanted to get the message out about an upcoming event. Using different kinds of texts (a flyer, a radio commercial, and a video on your community's website) may help you reach more in your audience and result in a larger turnout. And, that way, people can choose which messages they feel more comfortable accessing.

Activity: Make an Accessible Text

While Nicole's email newsletter was embedded in the body of her email, there will be times when you need to send an email with an attachment. To give all your readers a better chance at accessing such an attachment, it would be a good idea to use the principles of Universal Design. Even though many writing programs (Microsoft Word, for instance) offer accessibility checkers that help you create accessible texts, it is a good idea to begin writing your documents with the suggestions covered in this chapter in mind (using headings, chunks of information, lists, etc.). For this activity, design an accessible email attachment in Microsoft Word regarding an upcoming event on your campus. Consider this attachment as something you would email students on campus. When you are finished, conduct an accessibility check by testing it or running it through a computer program that checks for accessibility.

Final Thoughts

In the future, while you may not find yourself in a position where you will need to become a code talker and learn to write coded messages in hopes of winning a war, you will, no doubt, need to communicate messages on a regular basis. To this end, you should keep in mind that to effectively communicate messages means thinking rhetorically and choosing appropriate technologies to do so. As this chapter has demonstrated, there are a variety of technologies you can use to write messages. But, choosing the right technology for your message is easier said than done. Be critical and think carefully about how the technology you will use for your message will impact not just the message itself but also your intended audience. Your audience will play a big part in your choices to write your messages. Reaching everyone in your audience will require you to think about how to make your messages accessible to all.

Additional Discussion Questions

1. Discuss what you would need to do in order to write a message to your mayor voicing your concern for unsafe road construction in your neighborhood. Discuss the following questions:
   a. What kind of rapport do you have with your mayor?
   b. What impression do you want to give your mayor?
   c. What kind of text would be most appropriate for this message, and why?
   d. What technology would you use to create it?
2. What considerations does a writer need to make when writing messages that will be accessed using a screen reader?
3. What considerations does a writer need to make when writing accessible images?

Additional Activities

1. Communication of a Problem: Working in a group with classmates, think about a problem in your community that you would like to bring to the attention of your local government. To communicate this problem to the mayor of your city/town, you decide to write a text. Which of the following texts would you choose, and why? What technologies would you rely on, and why?
   a. a letter
   b. an email
   c. a song

d. a video posted on social media
   e. a speech given at a rally
2. **Different Messages:** Write a message to your parents, your teacher, your boss, a president of a company, and a charity to tell them about your qualifications or concerns in order to gain their support for something that you would like to pursue. Analyze the writing of all of these and write a reflection that answers the following:
   a. What media did you choose, and what technologies did you rely on for each? Why?
   b. What modes did you choose for each message, and why?
   c. What language did you choose for each message, and why?

Additional Assignments

1. **Analyze Your Email:** Every day, companies around the world send out millions of emails to current and potential customers. From selling new products to providing customers with policy updates, companies rely on emails to generate and maintain business. In May 2018, when Amazon increased their membership fee, they sent out emails to all its customers informing them about the change. Customers could not reply to Amazon's email because it was sent from a notification-only email address that could not accept incoming email. If customers had an issue with the change in membership, they would need to find another way to reach Amazon.

   For this assignment, analyze your emails. Write a report that considers the following questions:
   a. How many emails do you get from companies on a weekly basis?
   b. What are those emails about?
   c. Do you find that you read them often?
   d. Why do you get those emails?
   e. Do those emails allow you to reply? Are they notification-only emails?
   f. Do those emails change your relationship with those companies?
   g. How much spam do you receive from companies?

2. **Inappropriate Texting.** In this chapter, you read about texting and driving. Investigate other incidents or times when texting would be inappropriate. Develop a presentation that informs your classmates on why these situations would not be ideal for texting with others. Use examples from your investigation and suggest ways in which your classmates can make smarter decisions when texting.

Works Cited

Centre for Excellence in Universal Design. "What Is Universal Design." *National Disability Authority*, 2014, http://universaldesign.ie/What-is-Universal-Design/. Accessed 13 May 2018.

National Highway Traffic Safety Administration. "Distracted Driving." *United States Department of Transportation*, n.d., www.nhtsa.gov/risky-driving/distracted-driving. Accessed 16 June 2018.

National Museum of the American Indian. *Native Words, Native Warriors*. Smithsonian and the National Museum of the American Indian, 2007, www.nmai.si.edu/education/codetalkers/html/index.html. Accessed 26 April 2018.

"Navajo Code Talkers' Dictionary" Revised 15 June 1945, *Naval History and Heritage Command*, 4 April 2017, www.history.navy.mil/research/library/online-reading-room/title-list-alphabetically/n/navajo-code-talker-dictionary.html. Accessed 2 January 2019.

Smith, Aaron, and Monica Anderson. "Social Media Use in 2018." *Pew Research Center*, 1 March 2018, www.pewinternet.org/2018/03/01/social-media-use-in-2018/. Accessed 10 April 2018.

Tschabitscher, Heinz. "The Number of Emails Sent Per Day (and 20 Crazy Email Statistics)." *Lifewire*, 20 April 2018, www.lifewire.com/how-many-emails-are-sent-every-day-1171210. Accessed. 15 June 2018.

USMC. *Navajo Dictionary*. 15 June 1945.

PART 4 READING

Predictive Algorithms and Personalization Services on Social Network Sites

Implications for Users and Society

Robert Bodle

Copyright (2015). From *The Ubiquitous Internet: User and Industry Perspectives* by Anja Bechmann and Stine Lomborg. Reproduced by permission of Taylor and Francis Group, LLC, a division of Informa plc.

As we face an online environment of ubiquitous surveillance, it is worth noting the commercial forces that have provided the rational[e] for tracking users, combining databases, and personalizing the web. Personalization is when online content conforms to the prior actions of the user in an algorithmically generated feedback loop. Examples of personalization include Google's personalized search, behavioral advertising, featured recommendations on Amazon.com, taste preferences on Netflix, headlines on Yahoo! News, Twitter Trends, and Facebook's News Feed rankings. The personalized web can provide convenience, efficiency, interestingness and relevance to users who are served with content that they themselves help to generate. However, there may be unintended consequences, biases, and costs including social discrimination, political polarization, coercion, and the erosion of personal autonomy and human volition. The chapter uses a political economy approach to identify operational logics and unintended consequences for users.

Social network sites (SNS) are ideal sites of inquiry for assessing the developing dynamics of personalization services, which include opaqueness (the black boxing of technological processes), algorithmic-human interfacing and enactment, the reliance on big data including data trails and user-generated content, and the role of advertising as a driving factor. Facebook is particularly important as the dominant SNS and a strong indicator of industry trends that can migrate to other sites. A critical examination of the ubiquity of personalization services provides an important and valuable contribution to the understanding of the underlying logic of interconnectivity, the economic processes of value-creation, and the human rights and democratic implications of personalization.

Looking at personalization services on Facebook as a case study, this chapter will analyze advertising trends on the network, examine the role of predictive algorithms and their implications for users, and arrive at conclusions to help formulate user empowerment and agency.

The Personalized Web

The personalized web uses extensive customer data and predictive algorithms to conform content to the prior actions of the user; one's digital past is used to personalize new online experiences in real time. The personalized web includes Google's Personalized Search, behavioral targeting (e.g., when a specific ad appears on a variety of websites by tracking the user with cookies placed on their computer), locative mobile ads (Delo, 2013), Sponsored Ads and Suggested Posts on Facebook, and Promoted Tweets on Twitter. Technological, social, and cultural factors contribute to an online ecosystem that tracks and collects user data to serve personalized search results, ads, and entertainment. Cloud applications, web cookies, and Open APIs (application programming interfaces) such as social plug-ins (e.g., the 'Like' button) enable third parties to track people's activities from site to site, and from desktop to mobile device (Bodle, 2011). Social media sites encourage social behavior by rewarding participation with increased visibility and attention (Bucher, 2012; Bosker, 2013), that, in turn, produces a trail of data harvested as secondary information products shared, traded, and sold for personalization services.

The collection of valuable user data has given rise to a rapidly growing surveillance industry that includes digital advertising networks and marketing firms, data-brokers, as well as data-mining, tracking, and optimization companies (e.g., Acxiom, RapLeaf). These companies help amass and sort through big data in order to identify people's browsing, viewing, and purchasing habits used to predict behavior and personalize content in real time. They also help comprise 'digital dossiers' (Solove, 2002) that are used to make inferences, correlations, and predictions about future behavior. Although personalized services curate content that is deemed relevant to one's prior interests and activities, the algorithms also decide what is irrelevant for the user, and filters out content.

Google's personal web search demonstrates the filter in-filter out dynamic of personalization services. In December of 2009, Google introduced personal search results based on a user's semantic history (search terms run and results selected), location, time of year, language, and linked social networks (Notess, 2012, p. 43). Personal web search can provide timely and relevant results, but it can also limit one's exposure to information outside of one's range of knowledge and experience. In a recent Pew Internet & American Life Project survey (2012a), approximately 65% of respondents thought that it was 'a BAD thing if a search engine collected information about your searches and then used it to rank your future search results, because it may limit the information you get online and what search results you see' (Pew Research Center's Internet & American Life Project, 2012a, p. 2).

Personalized search has proven to be successful for Google's ad business that sells 'personalized audiences' (Feuz, Fuller, & Stadler, 2011, p. 7) to advertisers (AdSense for search, AdWords for syndicated texts, and DoubleClick for graphics) generating $30 per user, towering well above Yahoo at $7 and Facebook at $4.39 (Manjoo, 2012). Research suggests that personalization services benefit advertisers more than users, actively furthering a commercial agenda by pushing users toward 'criteria predefined' by the company (Feuz, Fuller, & Stadler, 2011, p. 7).

Approach

This chapter looks at the development of Facebook's advertising practices—from simple visual display ads in 2009, to the algorithmic personalization of the News Feed—to identify potential implications and unintended consequences for the user. This work draws on industry press reports as well as empirical observation of how advertising is integrated and personalized on the site. Algorithms used for personalization are proprietary and prevent access and a perfect understanding of their underlying technological processes (Beer, 2009; Feuz, Fuller, & Stadler, 2011; Bucher, 2012). Thus, this study examines general processes and their implications. Although it is impossible to break open the black box of Facebook's algorithms, this limitation is a clear indication of asymmetrical power relations between Facebook, its advertisers, and its users; selective insights about users are shared with advertisers and brands, but not with the users themselves. Realistically, advertisers and third party data brokers also do not have total access to Facebook's analytics and databases (Peterson, 2012). Maintaining a power differential is not uncommon in ad-dependent industries when 'Marketing is a war of knowledge, insight, and asymmetric advantage' (Nichols, 2013, p. 8).

Applying a political economy of communications (PEC) approach helps to identify unequal power relationships and critique them (Greenstein & Esterhuysen, 2006). PEC examines the 'underlying social relations' and potential conflicts of interest between market logic and user needs. Analysis of asymmetrical relationships between online services, advertisers, and users suggests a process of commodification of social labor where personal information is turned into product, reconfiguring social relations as a result (Wasco & Erickson, 2009; Mosco, 2009; Terranova, 2000). 'With its focus on institutional structures and practices,' offers Bettig (1996), 'the political economy of communications is poised to help explain the forces driving these processes and to offer up predictions about their implications' (p. 1).

Information advertising on Facebook is the primary means of revenue for Facebook and drives the company's privacy policies: 'we may use all of the information we receive about you to serve ads that are more relevant to you' (www.facebook.com/legal/proposeddup). If information is the new currency, the underlying market logic of personalization is to learn as much about people, in order to monetize them. This is accomplished by providing user data that enables advertisers to place finely tailored ads on one's Facebook page and to pay a premium for it. General knowledge of how algorithms work will also provide context for a critical discussion of the power of personalization.

The Politics of Algorithmic Power

Recent interdisciplinary work in software and information studies helps explain the sociotechnical dynamics of algorithmic decision-making processes (Beer, 2009; Kitchen & Dodge, 2011; MacKenzie, 2005; Mayer-Schönberger & Cukier, 2013). Algorithms are used to make sense of (infer, filter, and correlate) big data for a wide range of purposes: to personalize cultural production (music, literature, film scripts; Steiner, 2012), regulate incivility on blogs (Morozov, 2013), shape social behavior (Bucher, 2012), target advertisements (Turow, 2011), guide public opinion (Sunstein, 2009; Pariser, 2010), predict future crimes (Mayer-Schönberger & Cukier, 2013), and screen terrorist threats (EFF, 2013). Although Web 2.0 rhetoric celebrates an era of disintermediation, predictive algorithms have been interposed as society's new gatekeepers, information filters, social shapers, and causal agents (Mayer-Schönberger & Cukier, 2013). New empirical and theoretical work from social science and communication studies proposes how seemingly neutral and inscrutable machine processes have political effects that reveal corporate agendas (Bucher, 2012; Gillespie, 2013). Algorithms are not neutral or 'a-political' prediction engines, suggests McStay (2011, p. 137). They are 'codified politics' (McStay, 2011, p. 137); ideological formulations about social relations embodied in code, insulated from political debate, about which most people are unaware' (Bucher, 2012, p. 1171) and 'an important terrain upon which political battles are being fought' (Gillespie, 2013). A better understanding of the politics of algorithmic power can help inform user participation and agency.

Research in behavioral advertising also provides insight into the data-sharing relationships between third parties (i.e., data brokers and tracking companies) and digital intermediaries (SNSs, search companies, user generated content sites, e-tailer sites, etc.) (McStay, 2011; Turow, 2011). Empirical research into other forms of personalization, especially personal web search, helps point to new methodologies for assessing the value, benefits, and ambiguities of personalization for users (Feuz, Fuller, & Stadler, 2011). Political critiques based in liberal democratic theory are used to examine the gate-keeping, censoring, and ideologically polarizing function of personalization (Bollinger, 2010; McChesney, 2013; Morozov, 2013; Pariser, 2010). Other studies cited indicate the harm of racial discrimination as a result of social sorting and personalization services (Gandy, 2003; Lyon, 2003; Nakamura, 2002; Sweeney, 2013). And theories of digital labor exploitation, human rights, and ethics lay out a framework to speculate on user empowerment (Ess, 2009; Fuchs, 2012; La Rue, 2013; Tavani, 2010; Terranova, 2000).

The Rise of Personalized Advertising on Facebook

Advertising on Facebook gradually proved more effective after the SNS learned how to use user data to personalize ad content and better integrate ads within the user experience. Facebook collects information about its users from its social network (clicks, likes, shares, posts, comments, check-ins, RSVPs, apps used, friend activity) and from data-brokers (offline information), creating aggregate profiles that enable advertisers to more accurately serve ads to members on the site. In keeping with broadcast-era advertising strategy based on return on investment (ROI), ads are considered more cost-effective if they can reach the right viewer; corresponding to existing tastes, preferences, and habits of viewers. Personalized ads help provide more ROI for advertisers, support an ad-funded social media industry, and benefit users as well. Finely targeted ads help people find what's relevant to them and reduce clutter.

Facebook initially abstained from advertising (unlike its failed competitor MySpace), instead growing its service's functionality with open application programming interfaces (APIs), and building its user base. The company then leveraged this audience commodity to help commercialize the site. Today, the publicly traded company is heavily dependent on advertising with 85% ($1.24 billion) of its Q1's total ($1.46 billion) earned from advertising revenue (Delo, 2013) and is under intense pressure to grow its ad revenue, while mitigating the over-commercialization of its site and services (Manjoo, 2012). As a result, advertising on Facebook has grown increasingly sophisticated, nimble, and nuanced by visually integrating advertisements into the page layout and by serving real time personalized ads based on user data and inferences made by predictive algorithms. With over one billion members, Facebook harvests 2.7 billion likes, shares, and comments posted daily on the SNS (Manjoo, 2012). These interactions feed an adaptive News Feed algorithm that learns how to encourage more interaction and has, in fact, 'increased people's likes, clicks, and comments by 50%' (Bosker, 2013).

Facebook's growing ad business benefits from blurring the lines between paid advertisements and social status updates, which can minimize awareness of the distinctions and provide a persuasive social context to view ads, Facebook's first social advertising services began in 2009 with 'Marketplace ads' featured on the right hand margin of its homepage. These direct-response ads that were based on click-through rates (CRTs) performed 'about half as well as traditional banner ads' (Wasserman, 2011). In 2010 the average click-through rate for Facebook ads was 0.051%—'half as much as the industry standard of .1%' (Wasserman, 2011). Facebook responded to criticism of poor CRTs by partnering with Nielsen Co. to create a new rating system based on 'gross rating points' that uses 'mixed-media modeling' methods to measure the combined metrics of sales, awareness, and reach (Wasserman, 2011). The underperforming 'Market-placed ads' were gradually replaced by 'Sponsored Stories,' 'Page Post ads,' and 'Premium ads' (May, 2011), which provided greater targeting options and more closely resembled friend's posts in both design and functionality, enabling interactions (the ability to comment, share, and like) and deeper engagement with the ad. The next development is brand pages that encourage people to share ads with their social graph (in exchange for coupons, discounts, and prizes), and allows brand access and reach to 'fans' and 'friends of fans.' The 'Reach Generator' feature enables advertisers to use Facebook's analytics to place ads, which the company claims can reach 75% of a page's fans (as opposed to the 16% without ads; Cohen, 2012). 'Page Post ads,' 'Premium ads,' and 'Sponsored Posts' occupy the right hand margin of the page. It is important to note that 'Sponsored Stories' (now called 'Suggested Posts;' Sept. 2013) are placed upon users' News Feed, appearing in the center column alongside friend's photos and status updates. [Although] ads in the right hand column average 0.04%—0.05% (McDermott, 2012), ads placed within the News Feed earn 1.0%—7.0% CTR, with mobile CTRs earning higher than desktop only (McDermott, 2012). Thus, the enhanced integration of advertisements within social production spaces appears to be successful.

Facebook reports that the increase in advertising is not alienating users (measured by sentiment and satisfaction), however, anecdotal evidence on Twitter typifies a concern: '#Facebook, there are too many freakin ads on my news feed! fix that . . . ' (Bosker, 2013). And discontent with how the company shares member's 'likes' on ads in 'Sponsored Stories' resulted in a class action lawsuit (Facebook settled for $20 million; Fraley, 2012).

Personalization tools and analytics are used to help the company further enhance its advertising efforts while preventing the alienation from over-commercialization. An advertisement is far more likely to make a favorable impression when it is targeted because it conforms to the relevant needs and interests of the user and therefore predicts what the user will want. Facebook provides brands with filtering tools—'selected targeting parameters that are as relevant to your product or service as possible' (Facebook, 2012a), which includes: location targeting (country, city, IP address, and zip code—within the US), age and birthday, interests (likes, interests, and topics), education (college, university, major, graduation year), and connections and/or friends of connections. A brand or ad placement company can use these criteria to broaden or narrow the level of personalization, and reach existing and/or potential buyers. Facebook also provides third party access to members' aggregate user data obtained outside the SNS. The drive to gain perfect knowledge of the user suggests the more information known about a person the more likely to predict that a personalized ad will result in a future purchase. With the development of analytical services based on predictive algorithms Facebook pushes personalization beyond predicting to shaping 'what people want or don't want even before they realize it' (Simonite, 2012, p. 7).

Facebook's Personalization Services and Predictive Algorithms

Algorithms are a digital mode of statistical analysis (McStay, 2011) and are programmed with an adaptable set of procedural inputs, instructions, and rules used to draw meaning from large data sets. Algorithms are not 'cameras' but 'engines,' in that they 'performatively enact' (MacKenzie, 2005) results based on the 'intentions of the programmers' (Introna & Nissenbaum, 2000). Facebook's predictive algorithms are used to select and tailor posts on one's News Feed and thus determine visibility on the social network—who/what is seen and who/what is made invisible. News Feed algorithms rank users' interaction and engagement according to three criteria or three procedural inputs (among others): affinity (popularity), weight (relevance), and time decay (recency). However, these three factors have grown quite sophisticated; there are now multiple weight levels, categories and subcategories of affinity, and Facebook now bends 'decay' rules by keeping older posts alive if they continue to generate interactions (McGee, 2013). Although 'the exact workings and logics . . . include more factors than is publicly known' (Bucher, 2012, p. 1172), the company provides a glimpse to advertisers with the 'Insights API' to conduct real time tracking of 'News Feed Post Performance' (clicks, likes, comments, and shares), 'Virality' (organic propagation), and 'Negative Feedback' (unlikes and hides; Constine, 2012).

Facebook's News Feed algorithm processes are perhaps the most comprehensive collection of offline and online data 'assembled on human social behavior' (Simonite, 2012, p. 3); 'a previously unimaginable trove of information about what consumers see and do' (Nichols, 2013, p. 1). This 'trove' includes all information shared with Facebook, data garnered from user activity external to the SNS through social plug-ins (e.g., the ubiquitous 'Like' button) and cookies (e.g., Facebook Exchange), combined with offline data provided by data mining (e.g., Datalogix) and tracking companies (e.g., BlueKai). The algorithm analyzes personal and public information such as 'names, addresses, phone numbers, and details of shopping habits' (EFF, 2013). Facebook's predictive algorithms discern relevancy, importance, and 'interestingness,' but is also modeled on 'anticipated or future-oriented assumptions about valuable and profitable interactions' (Bucher, 2012, p. 1169). The underlying purpose of personalization is to identify and exploit the cause and effect relationships between advertising and purchasing, referred to by marketers as 'war gaming' (Nichols, 2013, p. 1). In this way predictive algorithms can increase the value of the social audience commodity (Smythe, 1981). 'Contrary to the laws of economics, information increases in value with greater supply; 'The more information you provide to companies, the more value they can extract from it' (Cochran, 2013).

Personalized advertising that includes both the social integration of ad messages and the analytic targeting of users drives the company's privacy practices as well as the company's control over how information is disseminated on the social network, with unintended consequences for user privacy, autonomy, and freedom.

Implications of Predictive Algorithms and Personalization Services

Insights into the operational logics of Facebook's algorithm reinforce an understanding of the company's underlying business model that is predicated on tracking users and amassing data tied to fixed identities. Close examination of Facebook's data-driven personalization practices reveals the fundamental inequality between members, advertisers, and the company. Recognizing Facebook's asymmetrical algorithmic power can provide insights into the implications of personalization for privacy, civic engagement, diversity, and freedom from discrimination.

Informational Privacy and Personal Safety

Although Facebook provides real time insights to advertisers and brands to stimulate engagement, the company does not provide the same to members, revealing an important power differential. Access and control of one's own data is an integral component of autonomy and without it self-determination is relinquished (Tavani, 2010). Withholding what information is known about users and how it is used prevents people from anticipating potential consequences and making informed decisions. For example, recent revelations by NSA contractor Edward Snowden reveals an alliance of internet companies and the US government (e.g., PRISM), where tracking of user data for advertising purposes can also be used to identify enemies of the state. Predictive analytics can undermine user privacy; the unintended consequences are difficult to predict. However, they can include threats to one's personal safety.

Facebook enforces a 'real-name only' policy in order to fulfill a business model, predicated on tracking users and amassing data to fixed identities. The SNS also prevents pseudonyms in order to identify users, but also to provide safety and security for the social network: 'We take the safety of our community very seriously. That's why we remove fake accounts from the site as we find them' (Facebook, 2012b). Facebook's strategic adherence to real-name only norms, however, also prevents anonymity, which is a universally acknowledged extrinsic good of privacy and a fundamental prerequisite to achieving safety and protection from reprisal for expressing one's political beliefs and for freedom of association (UDHR, 1948).

Facebook, along with Twitter, YouTube, and other major platforms, have become critically important means to reach a global audience and to access information. For example, information about Gezi Park protests in Istanbul was not televised by Turkish media but disseminated via social media (Tufekci, 2014). Yet, Facebook's real-name only policy puts the internet's most vulnerable people at risk, including political dissidents, whistleblowers, people holding minority views, people oppressed for their religious beliefs and sexual orientation, and victims of abuse. The Facebook fan page 'We are all Khaled Said,' instrumental for organizing the protests that led to the ousting of Egyptian President Mubarak (January 25, 2011), was suspended due to the page administrator's violation of its real-name attribution policy. The Pew Research Center's Internet and American Life survey, 'Social Networks and Politics,' found that people are discouraged from expressing political views when their real names are attached (2012a). Indeed, the attributes of anonymity, including minimal accountability, disinhibition, and deindividuation, can permit the freedom to speak freely and provide safety from reprisal (Bodle, 2013).

Facebook claims that it does not share the names of people whose data is used to target them. Turow (2011) suggests, however, that 'when companies simply strip the name and address off of data that is sorted and labeled and combined with a telephone number—its claim that you are anonymous is meaningless' (p. 190). If advertisers can use predictive algorithms and social network data to identify and track its users, so can state security forces. Not knowing what personal data is available and how it is used can have a chilling effect on freedom of expression due to an internalized threat of discipline and punishment. Freedom of expression is also undermined through predictive algorithms that filter opposing views.

Algorithmic Gate-Keeping and Deliberative Democracy

Algorithmic filtering on social network sites like Facebook can prevent exposure to a diverse array of competing and contradicting views. Pariser, in *The Filter Bubble* (2010), puzzles over the fact that the political views of his conservative friends don't appear in his Facebook News Feed alongside the views of his liberal friends. In fact, conservative views are censored and made invisible to him. According to deliberative democracy theory (Dryzek, 2000), public deliberation is most likely to occur when citizens are exposed to diverse and antagonistic sources of information, not only views and information that merely confirm one's preexisting opinions and knowledge base. Access to a wide range of competing views can encourage an active and informed citizenry by creating the preconditions conducive to robust, wide open, and uninhibited dialog and debate (Bollinger, 2010). One potential benefit of algorithmic filtering is the censorship of incivility such as 'violence, racism, flagrant profanity, and hate speech' (Morozov, 2013, p. 164). However, First [A]mendment protections in the US provide a high tolerance for incivility as a means to protect unpopular forms of political speech.

Algorithmic filtering can polarize debate by narrowing one's perspective and entrenching it through 'confirmation bias—the tendency to believe things that reinforce our existing views, to see what we want to see' (Morozov, 2013, p. 86). Vaidhyathanan suggests that when 'using Facebook or Google, we're more likely to come across like-minded posts from like-minded people. A republic works better when we make the extra effort to engage with a variety of points of view' (2012). The impact of algorithmic gate-keeping can be far reaching in shaping how people think and come together to solve problems. Exposure to more diverse information, suggests Benkler (2001), can make us freer because we are presented with the options of what is possible. As our options become limited, so does our ability to shape our world and ourselves.

Algorithms are not the only means to filter news and information. With the rise of audience fragmentation and selective exposure, people deliberately fine-tune their political and cultural information flows. A Pew survey revealed that users were likely to block, un-friend, and hide someone who posted political opinions and views that they disagree with or otherwise found offensive (2012b). Zuckerman, co-founder of citizen reporting network Global Voices, laments homophilic tendencies on the internet, and endorses global bridge-building and xenophilia to widen one's views online and to help solve global problems.

Homophily, Social Segmentation, and Intolerance

Facebook's personalization algorithms filter diverse views, including political ideology that can reinforce homophily or the tendency to seek similarity in one's friends. Homophilous online environments provide networks of mutual support and familiarity. But they can also discourage users from seeking diverse opinions and diversity in friends, which can reinforce sociological trends offline as 'physical communities are becoming more homogenous' (Pariser, 2010, p. 66). Personalized ads can deepen social divisions based on differences of race, ethnicity, class, age, education, location, and political ideology. Increased social segmentation is likely to result in a less tolerant society, where stereotypes, prejudice, suspicion, and hatred of the other can flourish. Stereotypes can also shape personal identity; people may feel pressure to filter out their own differences in order to assimilate within homogenous online communities. As the global internet expands the reach of dominant social network sites like Facebook, homophilous tendencies have far reaching implications for cross-cultural interaction and respect. Perhaps the increased emphasis on visual self expression (selfies, vine, video chat) within SNSs, may provide bodily engagement and experiential appreciation of irreducible differences, a precursor to mutual respect (Ess, 2009).

Discrimination and Coercion

Algorithmic guesses or inferences used to target people can reinforce traditional patterns of discrimination in the market place. Predictive analytics can make the same damaging correlations about demographic groups and reinforce cultural stereotypes used to discriminate against people as a result (Nakamura, 2002). For example, studies have found 'statistically significant discrimination in ad delivery based on racially associated names,' including search results that associate names with criminal arrest records (Sweeney, 2013). Such predicted results can hurt one's ability to get a job, complete a rental application, apply for a loan, and make new friends. Personalization services can also result in price discrimination. For example, Orbitz guides Mac users to pricier hotels (Mattioli, 2012). Online stores such as Staples.com charge more for people who are browsing with zip codes that have fewer rival stores (Angwin, 2014). Calo (2011) suggests that in the future, companies will adjust prices according to when people are most vulnerable.

Racially targeting advertising can be used to guide media consumption that draws on feelings of in-group accountability and 'reinforce a consumer's identification with a commodity' (Gandy, 2003, p. 5). Market segmentation can reinforce boundaries between social groups—including macroscopic traditional identity categories (gender, race, class, nationality, and sexuality; McStay, 2013; Terranova, 2004), and reinforce disparities as a result. Consistent with a political economy critique, this serves the interests of advertisers; to interpolate subjects as distinctly segmented markets narrowly defined as 'consumers' rather than citizens, who assume power from consumption rather than from concrete political gains.

Discrimination can result when predictive algorithms infer inaccurate notions about who people are; online profiles can be flawed, incomplete, biased, and dead wrong, with harmful results. Predictive analytics might also overlook the relevancy of one's aspirational self, which entails one's dreams goals, ideals, and notions about the good life. Perhaps someone who is striving and aspiring to have a different life than their present demographic data and online browsing habits reveal. Can we trust algorithms to make the best decisions for who we want to be?

Weighing the Disadvantages and Advantages of Personalization

Facebook has the algorithmic power to make decisions about people's online environments, to reinforce patterns of inclusion and exclusion, and to set social agendas. The social network has enough data on members' desires and interests to tailor online experiences in ways that can manage interactions and guide outcomes. Certainly personalization services, including personalized ads and News Feed analytics, can be framed as user empowerment—people are getting more of what they want, interacting more with who they want to interact with. Indeed, personalized services on social network sites can be incredibly efficient and convenient, saving one precious time [weeding] through irrelevant posts. People can also easily reach a focused social circle by creating a specialized group on Facebook. Rather than lessening political engagement, their 'Likes' on posts related to Network Neutrality, for example, ensures that the topic will likely continue to maintain high prioritization in their News Feed. Instead of being entrenched in one's viewpoint, they actually become more expert, engaged, and committed.

The convenience and familiarity of personalization services on social network sites should be weighed against their disadvantages, which includes ongoing surveillance, loss of informational privacy and self-determination (McStay, 2011). Certainly personalization services reflect people's choices and preferences, however these choices become structurally determined as the results of predictive algorithms can super[s]ede the user's intentions.

Conclusion

This chapter discussed the implications of personalized services on Facebook, primarily the role of predictive algorithms and user data to personalize ads. The asymmetrical access to both one's data and the analytics for serving content, alters the relations of power between users, companies, and advertisers. I have suggested how the market values and business logic embedded in personalization services can mitigate against user autonomy, privacy, and freedom of expression. Moreover this analysis suggests that algorithmic filtering can prevent one's exposure to difference, undermine respect for diversity, discriminate against categories of historically vulnerable populations, and discourage deliberative democratic participation where people's exposure to differences of opinion can support a robust public sphere.

Research is inconclusive as to whether consumer attitudes toward personalized services are generally positive or negative. Perhaps if more people gain a greater understanding of the implications and constraints of personalized information services, they will reject them. Greater transparency of Facebook's tracking and filtering processes can help build critical awareness of the analytic mediation of 'human knowledge practices' (Gillespie, 2013, p. 2). People should have greater control over their data, a better understanding of how their information is used, and the choice to opt out of personalization altogether by default. The domestication of algorithms could prevent greater scrutiny as they grow commonplace, are naturalized and given neutral status as mere machine processes. Algorithms are human-machine hybridizations encoded with the values, interests, prerogatives, and priorities of programmers to produce desired outcomes; with ad-driven personalization outcomes oriented toward primarily commercial ends.

We must explore ways to restore and protect human agency to account for the power asymmetries between companies, advertisers and private citizens. Companies can embed human rights defaults into their sociotechnical systems, including the rights to privacy and informational self-determination.

Snowden's revelations about PRISM suggest that pervasive and systemic monitoring of private information by state-corporate cooperation requires strong privacy protections that are necessary and proportionate to the need for security. Consumer protection laws (such as HIPAA) should be passed to regulate internet and advertising industries to protect personal data. International principles on the application of human rights online, can also guide the design, use, and regulation of personalized services, including all facets of social media, advertising, and big data industries.

Because predictive algorithms are social shaping technologies, consisting of uses as well as the values and affordances embedded in the technology, they can be designed to reflect non-commercial outcomes that enhance intercultural collaboration, social movement building, diversity of information, and robust political discourse. It is yet to be seen if ethical algorithmists, 'new professionals in computer science, mathematics, and statistics' (Mayer-Schönberger & Cukier, 2013), can encode procedures that promote non-commercially based outcomes while respecting the digital rights of users. Perhaps the community design and architecture of the next global peer-to-peer distributed social network might opt out of algorithmic gate-keeping, filtering, and monitoring all together (Bodle, 2010). By restoring informational privacy, autonomy, and self-determination, people might be empowered to make their own decisions, to broaden their lives online rather than to narrow them.

References

Angwin, J. (2014). *Dragnet nation: A quest for privacy, security, and freedom in a world of relentless surveillance*. New York: Times Books.
Beer, D. (2009). Power through the algorithm? Participatory web cultures and the technological unconscious. *New Media and Society, 11*(6), 985–1002.
Benkler, Y. (2001). Siren songs and Amish children: Autonomy, information, and law. *New York University Law Review, 76*(23), 23–113.
Bettig, R. (1996). *Copyrighting culture: The political economy of intellectual property*. Boulder, CO: Westview Press.
Bodle, R. (2010). Assessing social network sites as international platforms: Guiding principles. *Journal of International Communication, 16*(2), 9–24.
Bodle, R. (2011). Regimes of sharing: Open APIs, interoperability, and Facebook. *Information, Communication & Society, 14*(3), 320–337.
Bodle, R. (2013). The ethics of online anonymity or Zuckerberg vs. "moot". *Computers and Society, 43*(1), 22–35.
Bollinger, L. C. (2010). *Uninhibited, robust, and wide-open: A free press for a new century*. New York: Oxford University Press.
Bosker, B. (2013, May). Zuckerberg: Folks on Facebook are happy with all the ads we're showing them. *The Huffington Post*. Retrieved from www.huffingtonpost.com/2013/05/01/zuckerberg-facebook-ads_n_3196195.html.
Bucher, T. (2012). Want to be on the top? Algorithmic power and the threat of invisibility on Facebook. *New Media and Society, 14*(7), 1164–1180.
Calo, M. R. (2011). The boundaries of privacy harm. *Indiana Law Journal, 86*(3). Retrieved from http://papers.ssrn.com/sol3/papers.cfm?abstract_id=1641487.
Cochran, T. (2013, May). Personal information is the currency of the 21st century. *All Things D*. Retrieved from http://allthingsd.com/20130507/personal-information-is-the-currency-of-the-21st-century/.
Cohen, J. (2012). *Facebook's two new promos: Reach Generator, Logouts*. Retrieved from http://allfacebook.com/facebook-reach-logout_b79918.
Constine, J. (2012, April). EdgeRank checker hustles, builds tool just five days after Facebook real-time insights API goes live. *TechCrunch*. Retrieved from http://techcrunch.com/2012/04/25/facebook-real-time-insights-api/.

Delo, C. (2013, May). Facebook: 30% of our revenue now comes from mobile ads. *AdAge Digital*. Retrieved from http://adage.com/article/digital/facebook-30-revenue-mobile-ads/241240/.

Dryzek, J. K. (2000). *Deliberative democracy and beyond: Liberals, critics, contestation*. Oxford, UK: Oxford University Press.

Electronic Frontier Foundation. (2013). *The disconcerting details: How Facebook teams up with data brokers to show you targeted ads*. Retrieved from www.eff.org/deeplinks/2013/04/disconcerting-details-how-facebook-teams-data-brokers-show-you-targeted-ads.

Ess, C. (2009). *Digital media ethics*. Cambridge, UK: Polity Press.

Facebook. (2012a). Disabled: Fake names. *Facebook Help Center*. Retrieved from http://on.fb.me/vdj7JS.

Facebook. (2012b). Targeting options. *Facebook Help Center*. Retrieved from http://on.fb.me/K00daT.

Feuz, M., Fuller, M., & Stadler, F. (2011, February). Personal web searching in the age of semantic capitalism: Diagnosing the mechanisms of personalization. *First Monday*, *16*(2). Retrieved from http://firstmonday.org/article/view/3344/2766.

Fraley v. Facebook Inc., 11-1726 D. U.S. Northern California (2012).

Fuchs, C. (2012). Dallas Smyth today: The audience commodity, the digital labour debate, Marxist political economy and critical theory: Prolegomena to a digital labour theory of value. *Triple*, *10*(2), 692-740.

Gandy, Jr., O. (2003). *Privatization and identity: The formation of a racial class*. Retrieved from www.asc.upenn.edu/usr/ogandy/c53704read/privatization%20and%20identity%20i.pdf.

Gillespie, T. (2013). Can an algorithm be wrong? *Limn* 2. Retrieved from http://limn.it/can-an-algorithm-be-wrong/.

Greenstein, R. & Esterhuysen, A. (2006). The right to development in the information society. In R. K. Jørgensen (Ed.), *Human rights in the global information society* (pp. 281-302). Cambridge, MA: The MIT Press.

Introna, L., & Nissenbaum, H. (2000). Shaping the web: Why the politics of search engines matters. *The Information Society*, *16*(3), 169-185.

Kitchen, R., & Dodge, M. (2011). *Code/Space: Software and everyday life*. Cambridge: The MIT Press.

La Rue, F. (2013, April). *Report of the special rapporteur on the promotion and protection of the right to freedom of opinion and expression*. New York: Human Rights Council, United Nations. Retrieved from http://bit.ly/10IqJna.

Lyon, D. (2003). Surveillance as social sorting: Computer codes and mobile bodies. In David Lyon (Ed.), *Surveillance as social sorting: Privacy, risk, and digital discrimination*. New York: Routledge.

Mackenzie, A. (2005). The performativity of code: Software and cultures of circulation. *Theory, Culture and Society*, *22*(1), 71-92.

Manjoo, F. (2012, April). The morning after: What's next for Facebook? Trying to make enough money to justify that $100 billion valuation. *Fast Company*, pp. 222-223.

Mattioli, D. (2012, August 23). On Orbitz, Mac users steered to pricier hotels. *The Wall Street Journal*. Retrieved from http://online.wsj.com/news/articles/SB10001424052702304458604577488822667325882.

Mayer-Schönberger, V., & Cukier, K. (2013). *Big data: A revolution that will transform how we live, work, and think*. Boston, MA: Houghton Mifflin Harcourt.

McChesney, R. (2013). *Digital disconnect*. New York: The New Press.

McGee, M. (2013, August). EdgeRank is dead: Facebook's news feed algorithm now has close to 100K weight factors. *Marketing Land*. Retrieved from http://marketingland.com/edgerank-is-dead-facebooks-news-feed-algorithm-now-has-close-to-100k-weight-factors-55908.

McDermott, J. (2012). "Amid Criticism, Instagram Reverts to Old Terms of Service". *Advertising Age*. Crain Communications. [Online] http://adage.com/article/digital/amid-criticisminstagram-reverts-terms-service/238895/

McStay, A. (2011). *The mood of information: A critique of online behavioural advertising*. New York: Continuum.

McStay, A. (2013). *Creativity and advertising: Affect, events and process*. New York and Oxford: Routledge.

Morozov, E. (2013). *To save everything, click here: The folly of technological solutionism*. New York: PublicAffairs.

Mosco, V. (2009). *The political economy of communication* (2nd ed.). Thousand Oaks, CA: Sage Publications Ltd.

Nakamura, L. (2002). *Cybertypes: Race, ethnicity, and identity on the internet*. New York: Routledge.

Nichols, W. (2013, March). Advertising analytics 2.0. *Harvard Business Review*. Retrieved from http://hbr.org/2013/03/advertising-analytics-20/.

Notess, G. R. (2012). Searching in disguise. *Online, 26*(1), 43–46.

Pariser, E. (2010). *The filter bubble: What the internet is hiding from you*. New York: Penguin Press.

Peterson, T. (2012, October). Another agency claims Facebook changes. *Adweek*. Retrieved from www.adweek.com/news/technology/another-agency-claims-facebook-algorithm-changes-144405.

Pew Research Center's Internet & American Life Project. (2012a). *Search engine use 2012*. Retrieved from http://bit.ly/yj7QMP.

Pew Research Center's Internet & American Life Project. (2012b). *Social network sites and politics*. Retrieved from http://bit.ly/zrzR0q.

Simonite, T. (2012, June). What Facebook knows. *MIT Technology Review*. Retrieved from www.technologyreview.com/featuredstory/428150/what-facebook-knows/.

Smythe, D. W. (1981). *Dependency road: Communications, capitalism, consciousness and Canada*. Norwood, NJ: Ablex Publishing.

Solove, D. (2002, July). Digital dossiers and the dissolution of fourth amendment privacy. *Southern California Law Review, 75*, 1083–1168.

Steiner, C. (2012). *Automate this: How algorithms came to rule our world*. New York: The Penguin Group.

Sunstein, C. (2009). *Republic.com 2.0*. Princeton, NJ: Princeton University.
Sweeney, L. (2013) Discrimination in online ads delivery study. *Data Privacy Lab*. Retrieved from http://dataprivacylab.org/projects/onlineads/1071-1.pdf.
Tavani, H. T. (2010). *Ethics and technology: Controversies, questions, and strategies for ethical computing* (3rd ed.). Hoboken, NJ: John Wiley & Sons, Inc.
Terranova, T. (2000). Free labor: Producing culture for the digital economy. *Social Text*, 18(63), 33–58.
Terranova, T. (2004). *Network culture: Politics for the information age*. London: Pluto Press.
Tufekci, Z. (2014, February 12). Is the internet good or bad? Yes: Its time to rethink our nightmares about surveillance. *Medium*. Retrieved from https://medium.com/matter/is-the-internet-good-or-bad-yes-76d9913c6011.
Turow, J. (2011). *The daily you: How the new advertising industry is defining your identity and your worth*. New Haven, CT: Yale University Press.
The Universal Declaration of Human Rights. (1948). Retrieved from www.un.org/en/documents/udhr.
Vaidhyathanan, S. (2012, April 17). Voting against the algorithm. *Slate*. Retrieved from http://slate.me/IQpeF0.
Wasco, J., & Erickson, M. (2009). The political economy of YouTube. In P. Snickars & P. Vonderau (Eds.), *The YouTube reader* (pp. 372–386). Stockholm: National Library of Sweden.
Wasserman, T. (2011, January 31). Facebook ads perform about half as well as regular banner ads. *Mashable*. Retrieved from http://mashable.com/2011/01/31/facebook-half-click-throughs/.

Reading Questions for "Predictive Algorithms and Personalization Services on Social Network Sites: Implications for Users and Society" by Robert Bodle

1. What are the benefits for users of a personalized web?
2. What are some disadvantages for users of a personalized web?
3. Bodle argues that "Withholding what information is known about users and how it is used prevents people from anticipating potential consequences and making informed decisions." Do you agree or disagree with Bodle? Explain your answer.
4. Drawing from Bollinger, Bodle also argues that "Access to a wide range of competing views can encourage an active and informed citizenry by creating the preconditions conducive to robust, wide open, and uninhibited dialog and debate." Do you agree or disagree with such an argument? Explain your answer.

PART 5

Technology Is Connected

So far, you have considered how technologies are embedded, that is, situated in particular locations at particular times and how those locations and times affect us and our writing. To further understand embeddedness, we can look at the many connections that result from such embeddedness. In this part of the book, you will examine the various ways within specific contexts that technologies are connected, whether connected to ideas, to people, or to networks, whether those are physical or digital connections, and whether those various ways shape and are shaped by writing. Writing's role in these connections is an important one, as much of our understanding of writing is dependent on our abilities to see such connections and the impacts they have. In the following chapters, therefore, you will discover such connections as you look specifically at three different technologies: social media, websites, and mobile devices.

Key Questions

1. How are technologies connected?
2. How do connections shape and/or are shaped by writing?
3. What impacts do such connections have on our societies?

Key Terms

Chapter 12
1. social media
2. netiquette
3. analytics
4. cyberbullying
5. trolls

Chapter 13
1. computer programming
2. algorithm
3. CPU
4. internet service provider
5. web hosting service
6. web servers
7. URL
8. HTML
9. WYSIWYG
10. analytics
11. accessibility
12. usability
13. user experience
14. utility

Chapter 14
1. mobile device
2. nomophobia
3. personas
4. interaction design
5. mental model
6. wireframing

CHAPTER 12

Writing for Social Media

Contents

A Story of Two People 291
Locally and Globally 293
Writing for Social Media 297
Social Media Impacts More Than Just People 301
Social Media Is a Business 302
Steps to Help With Privacy 304
Final Thoughts 306

A Story of Two People

When Jane Seo, a Harvard graduate, writer for *Huffington Post*, and an avid runner, received her second-place medal for running the Fort Lauderdale Half Marathon on February 19, 2017, she was living a lie. Earlier that morning, as she ran the race, she cheated by cutting the course when no one was looking. However, after she crossed the finish line in a time of 1:21:46, race officials became suspicious. According to the race's splits, Seo ran the second part of the half marathon faster than the first part, an unusual feat in the running world. For long distances, most runners often run the second part of their race at a slower pace. Nonetheless, race officials didn't have any real evidence that she had cheated and awarded her second place anyway.

That was until blogger Derek Murphy, who investigates runners to make sure race results are indeed fair, stepped in and immediately began looking into Seo's performance. Not present at the race himself, Murphy went to work, relying on a variety of technologies including social media. Using Seo's Strava entries, photos from the race, and his own knowledge of running, Murphy was able to piece together what had actually happened during the race.

Strava, a social networking platform for athletes, tracks and keeps records of users' activities by using GPS. Runners can upload their data to the site, track their performance, share their experiences and routes with others, and even compete with others. Strava also allows users to compare different metrics, like running cadence and pace to potentially help runners improve. Seo was an active member of Strava, and shortly after the race, she entered in her race time manually without any GPS data attached to the time. Later that day, however, Murphy saw that Seo made another entry, this time with GPS data. Comparing entries and split times, Murphy noticed that the data just didn't add up.

To confirm his suspicions as well as the suspicions of others, he examined race photos. In doing so, he noticed that Seo was wearing a watch during the race. By zooming in on her watch in a photo taken at the finish line, Murphy was able to read the data on the watch's face. Documenting everything on his blog MarathonInvestigation.com, Murphy concluded again that the data didn't add up. Writing and using images as evidence, Murphy laid out his case for everyone in the public to see. And everyone could see that an injustice had been committed. Murphy immediately began receiving hundreds of comments to his blog post on Seo's less-than-trustworthy performance.

Eventually, the suspicions were too much for Seo. She finally admitted that she had cheated by cutting the course and covering it up by biking the course afterwards and uploading that GPS information to Strava in her second entry. She wrote on her Instagram page later that she had cheated and that she had gotten "swept away in the moment and pretended to run the entire course" (qtd. in Murphy). She accepted responsibility for her actions, saying that she was ashamed and "will face the consequences" (qtd. in Murphy).

Murphy and Seo's story is just one example of how technologies can be used for the good and for the bad and how stories play out over social media in connected ways. On the one hand, Seo tried to use social media to cover up her cheating. On the other hand, several technologies helped blogger Murphy make connections between bits of information and use those connections to investigate the cheating. As a result of those connections, Murphy was able to tell the right story of the race, one that led to Seo's disqualification. In the end, the good prevailed thanks in part to Murphy's drive to make sure runners don't cheat and his ability to utilize social media to find and present the evidence.

Every day, millions of people use social media. While social media is a writing technology, it is also a history keeper, a record of people's behaviors, a platform, an instigator, a journal, and much more. People can study it, learn from it, and use it for many purposes, for instance, to find out what voters will do at the polls, to mine data about participants, and to determine what businesses should sell. There are a wide range of social media technologies, too, from those geared toward the masses and those geared toward small interest groups, from Facebook to Instagram to Twitter to Peach to Wanelo. Some social media are more popular than others in one country and less popular in others. As an example, in the United States, Facebook, Instagram, Twitter, and Snapchat are popular. In

China, its WeChat, Sina Weibo, QQ, and Youku Tudou. In Russia, its Vk (Vkontakte) and OK (Odnoklassniki).

Like with all technologies, however, using social media technologies has its consequences, both good and bad, as demonstrated by this story. Thus, in the pages that follow, you will learn about the various ways that writing on social media can help or hurt us and the roles that writers, tech companies, and the public play in such consequences.

Assignment: Creating a Narrative With Social Media

As was discussed earlier in this book, a narrative is one version of a story. Thanks to social media, there are stories that live solely on the internet, sometimes for hours, sometimes for days. And, they exist on various social media sites. Follow a story as it unfolds on various social media sites, making connections between the bits of information you find as you move from one site to another. Then, write your own narrative of the story, in other words, your version of it as you have found through your investigation. In doing so, consider these questions:

1. How does the story evolve and change over time?
2. What narratives were told?
3. Who are the people involved in telling the narratives and thus the story?
4. How do they tell these?
5. What are the consequences for such narratives and such a story?

Report your findings and your narrative to your class.

Locally and Globally

Writing can be a very social endeavor, and that's because, as you learned in other chapters in this book, it is situated within locations. This is especially apparent when we examine social media technologies, those technologies that enable people to participate in online networks in which they can share content. Such technologies have had an enormous impact on our world on local and global levels because these media are connected to people, places, and things which in turn shape and are shaped by those impacts. For example, they can be helpful to a variety of businesses and organizations as well as the general public in many ways. When the Plantation Women's Soccer Club wanted to raise money for breast cancer research in honor of their friend Dana Wheeler, who had passed away after battling cancer, they decided to hold a soccer tournament at their local indoor field. To spread the word and to get players to register for the tournament, they turned to social media sites like Facebook. Using their network of friends, the club was able to reach hundreds in the South Florida area with the Facebook post seen in Image 12.1. As a result, the turnout for the tournament was good, and the organization was able to raise lots of money for cancer research.

Dana Wheeler tournament   Al-ex Huck

When acoustic guitarist Al-ex Huck released his debut EP, *Be Good*, on the Bandcamp platform, a site that helps artists sell their music to fans, he also turned to Facebook to spread the word. After uploading an image of the EP's design (see Image 12.2), Al-ex wrote on Facebook that the EP was finally available. He included a website URL for his Bandcamp page so that his followers can go immediately to the site to listen and buy his music. His followers can also share Al-ex's post with their friends' networks on Facebook, who can then share with their friends, thus reaching an audience worldwide. Because of social media, people around the world learned about his music in a matter of days, a feat that was nearly impossible for new artists decades ago when such technology didn't exist.

Worldwide, people use social media sites not just to garner participation in events or to sell music. They use it to connect to others in good times and in bad. During emergencies like the bombing at a 2017 Ariana Grande concert in Manchester and during Hurricane Harvey in 2018 in Houston, people used social media to find loved ones who were missing, find and disseminate safety information, raise money for victims, give support to those who were suffering, and coordinate relief efforts. As these writings occurred via social media, social media in turn became a valuable recorder of this history, recording what was said, who said it, when they said it, and where they said it, throughout and after the events.

Writings like these can provide us with a means for studying how people act during times of crisis. In a recent study on the aftermath of a tornado in Ontario, Canada, researchers found that social media sites like Facebook "act as amplification 'stations,' through which information is processed and transmitted" and are useful "for crisis communication during the immediate aftermath of a disaster when information is otherwise scarce and difficult to validate" (Silver and Matthews 1693–1694). Researchers, like the ones studying the aftermath of a tornado, can use the recorded information on social media to figure out the best ways to communicate and provide support to people during future crises. They can determine, for instance, which connections they need to make. Working with government and volunteer organizations, researchers can then share these best practices for communication based on their studies of the information on social media.

In addition to helping in times of crises, social media can also aid law enforcement in their efforts to track down those who commit crimes by making connections with the information written online. Social media, for example, can help law enforcement pinpoint a criminal's location when a criminal uses social media. As well, social media can provide law enforcement with evidence, such as photographs and a timeline of events, that can be used in a court of law.

Researchers also study other behaviors via social media that have led to important insights into social media's effects on class, race, gender, culture, and other social issues. In so doing, they revere those who use social media to enact public change and call into question those who act inappropriately, like those who use social media to perpetuate hate and bullying.

Assignment: Social Media Study

Conduct a study in which you survey and interview a population of people regarding social media's impact on an issue such as politics, consumerism, employment, learning, or fake news. Find out whether or not they feel that the affordances of social media, such as being able to connect with millions worldwide, have positive or negative impacts. To conduct your survey and interview, determine what technologies you will need to utilize. There are a number of online free survey sites that you can use, but you should always think carefully about what you want to accomplish in your research and how such technologies can help you. Check out Part 2 of this book for more help in designing surveys. When you have all your data collected and analyzed, share your findings with your class in a presentation.

As previously mentioned, before social media, people had to wait for news organizations to tell the news. Now, people have access to stories happening around the world a lot sooner thanks to social media. Anyone who has access to social media can report on events, give first-hand accounts, and let us witness events as they unfold across the world via this technology. Before social media, news organizations got to decide what would be reported and how it would be reported. In some cases, some news stories weren't even reported by news organizations, especially in hard-to-reach places. Now, more people have control of stories that news organizations used to only control, giving voices to those who might not have had a voice before. People in hard-to-reach places can tell their own stories rather than waiting for a news organization to send a reporter.

As another example of how social media is used for the good, we can look at nonprofit organizations. Most nonprofit organizations worldwide rely on writing for social media to garner support. Having worked with nonprofits for over 18 years, Rebecca Hahessy knows all too well the power of social media. In her interview below, she talks about the kinds of writing she does and how nonprofits use social media to educate others and get people involved. While you read her interview, consider the impacts the kinds of writing nonprofits have on others.

INTERVIEW
REBECCA HAHESSY, 18 YEARS OF NONPROFIT WORK

Q: Describe the kind of work you have done for the past 18 years.
A: I have worked for a number of nonprofit organizations over the years doing a number of different things from writing standard operating procedures (SOPs) to working on fundraising campaigns to assisting on grants. Currently, I am the director of client services for an organization that provides resources for people who are food insecure. In this position, I am responsible for managing and creating educational resources that can help people develop basic life and job skills. I also manage a staff of people, hire employees, maintain a budget, research current policies and laws, and work with a number of volunteers.

Q: Besides SOPs, what kinds of texts do nonprofit workers write?
A: There are so many texts that they write: procedures, protocols, employee manuals, volunteer manuals, applications, internship manuals, recommendation letters, press releases, articles, website content, and social media posts.

Q: When you are asked to write a text, what are some of the steps you take?
A: I often use examples like, for instance, when I have to write a manual, I'll look at previous manuals so I can learn the verbiage necessary and to also see where I can make improvements. Laws and policies are always changing, so it is important to know how to specifically speak about particular things. There is a lot of research involved when looking at examples and comparing them to what I need to do. After that, I'll create my objectives and outline before I start writing the actual text.

Q: What are some ways in which nonprofit workers use social media?
A: They certainly use it as a platform for fundraising and getting the word out about events. I'd say Facebook, Twitter, YouTube, and Instagram are the ones that are used most. They also use social media to make a call to action and to disseminate information for educational and advocacy purposes. When legislation is put forth, social media can help nonprofits educate people about how such legislation affects their causes. Social media is really important. When I think about its importance, I think about ALS's Ice Bucket Challenge and how successful it was in raising awareness and money for ALS. I think many nonprofits hope to use social media in a similar light to raise awareness and funding for their own organizations.

Q: What other technologies do nonprofits utilize?
A: We use a lot of databases, so many of them in fact. We use them to cultivate relationships with and keep track of donors in order to maintain our funding. For example, in a database, we keep track of when donors give, how much they give, why they give, and how often we contacted them to give. We also have databases for the people we help so that we can keep track of what is working and what is not. Sometimes we are even required to keep track of the demographics of the people we help so that we can show that there is indeed a need to help and to get funding that will meet this need. We also rely on e-newsletters and campaign emails to inform our donors, clients, and the public about what we are doing, about our events, and about how people can help out.

Q: What writing advice can you give someone who wants to work for a nonprofit?
A: I'd say that you have to be a people person and to expect to do a lot of different things including administration work. I didn't realize before I got my first job with a nonprofit how much I would be doing, writing and otherwise. I definitely have to document and write things down constantly and in doing so, I have to be as objective as possible. I also have to keep up to speed on knowing procedures and policies.

Q: Have you worked with international audiences?
A: Yes. I think in general, most nonprofits consider the diverse people that they work with on a regular basis whether locally or globally. I have been a part of organizations that worked internationally. But, even though an organization might not be an international organization in the sense that they have offices or travel or send resources abroad, they still might work with immigrants in their local communities. Anytime we write something, for example, we put it in multiple languages, working with our communication department and staff members who have experience translating. Not everything translates word for word so we make sure to pay attention to our audience and ensure that they understand we are trying to communicate.

Writing for Social Media

While you may write for social media informally for your friends and family, there may come a time when you have to write more formally for the company or organization you work or volunteer for. To understand how to write in such a way for social media, you can begin by studying it closely with a critical eye, investigating how it is used, who uses it, and for what purposes. Social media posts contain a combination of modes that could include words (written or spoken), images (still or moving), and sounds (music and sound effects) to communicate messages. Such uses of modes are driven by rhetorical decisions. In the earlier examples, one about a soccer tournament in honor of Dana Wheeler and one about the release of new music, the writers thought rhetorically and used a combination of modes that worked together to communicate their messages.

If we break down the second example, the one about Al-ex Huck's music, we can clearly see the rhetorical decisions he made when creating the post on Facebook. His purpose is clear: get people to listen to and buy his music. To communicate his purpose, he takes a straightforward approach, choosing to use specific language for his text, "Stream or download my debut EP," followed by a hyperlink to make it easier for his audience to perform such action. Underneath the hyperlink is an image, the cover of his EP album *Be Good*. The image is a child's drawing, conveying the impression that the creator and the music are laid back, less formal, and perhaps even down to earth. This image is the same image that Al-ex Huck Music uses for other promotional items, like stickers and flyers, creating a brand that his audience can identify with and recognize. The words "Be Good" in the image even invoke the feeling of goodness that all should participate in. Thus, all of the modes he uses work together to convey meanings.

As you prepare for your own career, think about the ways in which you will write for social media and how you will do so rhetorically. If you plan to go into business, social media is often used as a means to advertise products and services as well as inform the public about the company itself. Many companies have their own social media guidelines for their employees to follow. Generally, these guidelines focus on netiquette (see Michelle R. Gould's story in the Part 5 Reading section for a definition) as well as specific uses of styles, language, and grammars for various social media platforms. They might also dictate how long posts should be and how often employees should post to social media. Consistently adhering to such guidelines enables a company to create a particular public persona. One day, you may be tasked with following similar guidelines in order to help your place of employment maintain such a persona.

Assignment: Develop a Social Media Ad

Partner with a business or organization and examine their social media platforms, paying close attention to how they use social media to generate interest in the business. Most likely the business or organization will have their own social media style guide that they will want you to follow. In addition, if they are willing to share their analytics with you, determine how you can use them to best create and target potential customers. Then, create a post to advertise a product or service the business or organization produces that adheres to the style of posts the company uses. If you are unable to partner with a business or organization, most universities and colleges have their own social media style guides. Use your school's guide and create a social media ad that promotes an upcoming class, event, or program on your campus. Write a reflection that details your decisions and share your ad with the rest of the class.

In addition, as you think about what you can do to use social media effectively, you should also consider the data you will work with as a result of social media. Lots of companies track their social media users' data. They specifically pay attention to how users interact with their posts, who interacts with them, how often, and for how long. The analytics then help companies ascertain the effectiveness of their writing on social media. **Analytics** refers to the systematic analysis of data. There are many technologies that can do the systematic analysis for you and provide you with information pertaining to this analysis. This information will include data on the people who visited your site, like how often and when they visited, what they clicked on, and so on.

A word of caution

According to a recent study, people spend on "average 2 hours and 22 minutes per day on social networking and messaging platforms" (Salim). While social media can help us study communication, keep in touch with friends and family, and grow businesses, social media can sometimes be harmful and dangerous to us and others. Using social media too much, for example, can lead some people to think negatively about their own bodies and their own lifestyles. In a study on Facebook's influence on body image, researchers found that for college women, "Time spent on Facebook showed a negative relationship with body image" and that "more time on Facebook related to more body and weight comparisons, more attention to the physical appearances of others, and more negative body attitudes after viewing posts and photos" (Eckler, Kalyango, and Paasch 262).

Earlier in this book, you thought about your own writing habits. Contemplate whether or not those included social media. Then ask yourself these questions:

- If your writing habits include social media, how so?
- If not, why not?
- How often do you use social media? Why that often?
- What do you use it for? Why?
- How does your use impact your thinking about yourself and others?
- Would you consider quitting social media? Why or why not?

Writing on social media can lead to far more dangerous consequences. **Cyberbullying**, the act of using electronic communication to intimidate, threaten, or make fun of someone, has led some people to hurt others or themselves. All too often this cyberbullying plays out on social media when people write harmful things about others. People who participant in cyberbullying by provoking fighting and confrontations online and by making fun of other people are called **trolls**. If you participate on social media, make sure that you don't become one yourself. Stand up for those who are being targeted, call out trolls when appropriate, and don't waste your time by giving trolls a chance to speak. There are lots of examples of people shutting down trolls by calling them out on their neglect for human decency. After Neha Dhupia, who has a large Instagram following, was trolled over Indian culture, she posted a message directly aimed at her trolls calling them out for being disrespectful and for wasting their time and energy trying to evoke an unnecessary confrontation (Madhukalya).

Discussion Questions: Yourself and Social Media

1. How much of yourself do you and should you share on social media?
2. Is what you share an adequate representation of who you are?
3. Why do you share what you share with the people you share it with?
4. What are some consequences, both good and bad, of sharing yourself on social media?

Your writing on social media has lots of consequences, some of which you may realize while others you may not. You may believe that because social media technologies are free, they are not governed by any rules, and that laws don't necessarily pertain to what you are writing. However, this is not true. In fact, many social media companies monitor their users' activity, censoring it or taking down posts that directly violate the law, encourage violence, and/or pose a threat to the safety of others. Likewise, governments have also created legislation to help prevent the harmful impacts of social media. However, the responsibility for social media use should not be solely the responsibility of others, whether companies or the government. In some cases, those institutions don't have an easy job considering millions of people use social media worldwide and thus can be slow to catch up to how people use it. In the end, you play an important role in the writing and usage of social media, too.

As Michelle R. Gould argues in the Part 5 Reading, you can't just upload anything you want to your social media accounts without it having an impact on others. In her story, she talks about how doing so could potentially infringe upon copyright laws and how uploading another person's work without giving them credit is unfair. As you think about your own uses of social media, read Michelle's story, and consider what impact you will have on others. In addition to the ways social media use can infringe on copyright law, there are a number of other ways in which your uses could impact others.

So, be hyperaware of your uses. Be aware too of the companies that own social media and what they are doing with your information. In 2014, according to a report by CBS's Lesley Stahl, Aleksandr Kogan developed an app for Facebook that people could download and then take a personality quiz on it. Thousands of Facebook users downloaded it and participated in the quiz. However, when they did this, unbeknownst to them, Kogan collected data on millions of their Facebook friends, people who didn't download and use the app themselves. Kogan then sold that data to the data firm Cambridge Analytica. Just by using an app in Facebook, users impacted how their friends' data could be shared with others without their friends even knowing. So, it is imperative to consider how your actions, whether you are sharing a post, playing a game, or downloading an app, could potentially lead to the sharing of other people's data.

Activity: Viral Posts

While it might seem like a good idea to spread information to as many people as possible, as in the case of the Plantation Women's Soccer Club's effort to garner support, sometimes a viral post is not a good thing. Investigate instances when a viral post has had negative consequences. Write a reflection that considers what these negative consequences were and what they had on people. Use these questions as you reflect:

1. Are viral stories good or bad?
2. When you post to social media, do you want everyone to read it, share it, and talk about it?
3. If you participate in the reading and posting of content that goes viral, what responsibility do you have?
4. In the viral post you found for this activity, what were the negative consequences?
5. Could these have been prevented?
6. Who was impacted?
7. What actions can those who were impacted by these negative consequences take?

Social Media Impacts More Than Just People

Social media can lead to other bad consequences, such as those that impact our environments, ones you may not even realize. If you post an Instagram photo of yourself standing beside a beautiful lake along a hiking trail in a national park with the hashtag #beautifullake, what are the consequences? For starters, your followers may like such a photo, your photo may show up with other photos of lakes with the same hashtag, and others may share that photo with their friends. You may feel good that your friends liked and shared your photo, and you may want to take more like it in the future.

What you might not realize, though, are the consequences to the actual location in which that photo was taken. If you included the actual location of the lake on Instagram, how many people will go there as a result? In the last few years, natural sites, such as parks, lakes, and trails, have seen heavier foot and car traffic due to popular social media posts that feature photos of them. Before social media, those places might have been known to only a few, and the impact those few made on those natural places might have been minimal. After social media, though, those places have seen an increase in the amount of people who don't necessarily have the right knowledge or experience in natural environments and who may accidentally hurt themselves and/or damage those environments, which are home to a number of plants and animals.

Not all is lost, however, as many places, such as parks, have begun to use social media as a tool to educate people about proper behavior in the wilderness, such as to be respectful of nature and not post things that would be harmful to it. Yellowstone National Park, as an example, developed the #YellowstonePledge campaign to educate visitors about being safe in the park and being respectful to the environment there. At the top of the list of practices supported by such a pledge is one that educates visitors about taking safe selfies that don't involve getting close to animals to do so, protecting both humans and wildlife in the process (National Park Service, Department of the Interior).

Whether or not you plan to post on social media about your adventures in the wilderness, it is always a good idea to think about the impact your social media posts have. Posting your photo of a store in a town that has a sale could also impact the environment in that town in ways that are similar to and different from those that would impact a natural environment. So, always think carefully before you post.

Social Media Is a Business

Tech companies have developed savvy ways to use social media as a way to lure people into engaging in it by offering them something in return that they cannot get anywhere else. In 2018, Major League Baseball signed a deal with Facebook giving Facebook the sole right to broadcast 25 of its games in the United States, meaning fans who wanted to see their teams play would have to do so by watching the games on Facebook since no other company in the United States could broadcast those particular games.

Social media companies like Facebook, Twitter, Instagram, and Snapchat are businesses that make money based off your communication practices. Over the past decade, social media companies have also made it easier for other businesses to make money through social media by targeting their potential consumers, selling your personal information, and profiting off your behaviors, such as your habits for liking and disliking content.

In a 2018 *Wired* article, Zeynep Tufekci writes that digital platforms like Facebook and Twitter are ad brokers. She contends,

> To virtually anyone who wants to pay them, they sell the capacity to precisely target our eyeballs. They use massive surveillance of our behavior, online and off, to generate increasingly accurate, automated predictions of what advertisements we are most susceptible to and what content will keep us clicking, tapping, and scrolling down a bottomless feed.

In other words, as ad brokers, these companies tailor ad posts designed specifically to tap into our particular interests, and they are doing so to make money. In fact, in 2017, Instagram had two million advertisers using their platform to reach Instagram's 500 million daily users (Etherington).

Social media companies gather data not just about your devices, their operating systems, hardware, and software, but they also gather data on your locations, the time you use social media and for how long, how you connect with others, the events you are interested in, the videos you watch, and the credit cards you use to make purchases through their sites. They sell this data to advertisers who in turn use it to target consumers via their ads on social media.

Indeed, social media has changed global business practices as a result. Yet, even though businesses make money off our data, there are times when social media users have been able to influence businesses. In fact, users have relied on their writing on social media to change many local and global business practices in several ways, such as giving people a place to demand better customer service, influencing how physical places where business happens are created, and providing opportunities to engage with people who might benefit from services offered. When people take to social media to demand change, businesses listen and quickly respond. For example, when Tina Gable's flight to London was delayed for ten hours due to routine maintenance, she took to Twitter voicing her complaints for missing her friend's wedding. Others chimed in, sharing stories of their flight delays by the same airline. Within 48 hours of Tina's initial post, the airline reached out and tweeted their response, offering to make it up to Tina and to rethink their practices for routine maintenance in the future.

Activity: Social Media Activism

Does social media activism bring about real change in the public? Research examples of how a social media campaign has led to significant changes in public policy. Report your findings to the class.

Even the physical places of businesses have been shaped with social media in mind. Restaurants wanting to make it easier for customers to upload their food pics to Instagram have designed their places with good lighting in mind. These pics in turn act as advertisements for the restaurant. As another example, stadiums have rethought their seating designs and have created social spaces where people can gather and socialize as a result of the behaviors brought about by social media. Even colleges have capitalized on social media to recruit students and to make current students happy. They use social media to find out what students really want in a college and then work to ensure the necessary changes take place to meet those needs.

Did You Know? Selfie Museum

Social media is no stranger to the selfie. Today, millions of people upload selfie pictures to various social media daily. In fact, it is estimated that the "average millennial could take up to about 25,700 selfies in his or her lifetime" (Glum). According to *Time*, Makati City and Pasig, Philippines are the number one places in which people take selfies, followed by Manhattan and Miami (Wilson). Selfies, portraits of oneself, are not a new phenomenon. Actually, history shows that throughout time, people have tried in many different ways to capture images of oneself. However, the proliferation of selfies and the sharing of them, it could be argued, is greater today than thousands of years ago thanks to the convenience and ease of technologies like camera phones and social media. In the spring of 2018, Tommy Honton and Tair Mamedov highlighted this proliferation when they opened The Museum of Selfies. Their museum, a two-month pop-up engagement in Glendale, California, featured interactive exhibits where visitors could take their own selfies, explore the history of self-portraiture, and engage in critical examinations of selfie culture.

Steps to Help With Privacy

To end this chapter, it would be a good idea to discuss how to protect your privacy when using social media. This discussion will particularly call into question how social media policies, such as user agreements, are lengthy, drawn-out texts that are written for the masses in a language that is sometimes hard to understand and therefore is often ignored as a result. But they should not be ignored. The *first step* you should take when you use a social media platform for the first time is to read and question the policies, the user agreements, and the terms of use that the platform's company puts in place, even when it's hard to do so. Box 12.1 contains a few of the user's rights from Instagram's Terms of Use.

Box 12.1 Example from Instagram's Terms of Use "Rights Section"

1. Instagram does not claim ownership of any Content that you post on or through the Service. Instead, you hereby grant to Instagram a non-exclusive, fully paid and royalty-free, transferable, sub-licensable, worldwide license to use the Content that you post on or through the Service, subject to the Service's Privacy Policy, available here http://instagram.com/legal/privacy/, including but not limited to sections 3 ("Sharing of Your Information"), 4 ("How We Store Your Information"), and 5 ("Your Choices About Your Information"). You can choose who can view your Content and activities, including your photos, as described in the Privacy Policy.
2. Some of the Service is supported by advertising revenue and may display advertisements and promotions, and you hereby agree that Instagram may place such advertising and promotions on the Service or on, about, or in conjunction with your Content. The manner, mode and extent of such advertising and promotions are subject to change without specific notice to you.
3. You acknowledge that we may not always identify paid services, sponsored content, or commercial communications as such ("Terms of Use").

At the time this book was published, these rights were just the first three of ten rights listed and came after a list of 17 basic terms and a list of 10 general conditions explained by Instagram. Take a moment and read them. What do these three statements say to you? If you look closely at these rights, you can see that as part of their terms, Instagram has the right to use the content you post on their site. Is that okay with you? Are you okay that Instagram could take what you post and use it for their own purposes?

Instagram is also telling you they have the right to place "advertising and promotions on the Service or on, about, or in conjunction with your Content"; how they do this is subject to change without notice to you. Is this okay with you? In addition, they point out that they don't have to identify "paid services, sponsored content, or commercial communications." Are you okay with not knowing exactly who these advertisers are?

The *second step* is to educate yourself about the privacy settings offered by social media so as to limit how much you share with others. Recent studies suggest that participating in privacy training can be helpful in maintaining a higher level of privacy. According to a team of researchers who conducted a study on Facebook privacy training, adults show an increase in concern over their privacy and are more vigilant about what they are disclosing on Facebook when they are trained on Facebook privacy (Smith, Méndez Mediavilla, and White 250). The study also suggests that training can lessen risks and make your social media environment safer (Smith, Méndez Mediavilla, and White 250). If you wish to educate yourself, as part of this step, you should consider participating in training. Your university may offer workshops or courses that can train you, but you can also find training videos online.

In conjunction with the first two steps, the *third step* is to learn more about how social media actually works. Do your research on the technology itself. To guide you in this research, think rhetorically about who owns social media, who uses it, and how they use it.

Activity: Investigating Social Media

Write a reflection that answers one or more of these questions:

1. How does sharing, posting, and liking on social media translate into companies making money off of people's social media behaviors?
2. Are the social media companies transparent about how they use the data they collect from you? If so, how? If not, why not?
3. What privacy settings do social media companies offer their users, and how can you use them to their fullest extent? If you use social media, do you use such settings? Why or why not?

As a *fourth step*, find out what companies know about you by downloading your data from your social media accounts. In other words, you can find out about the data companies have collected about you. As of the printing of this book, Facebook offers a feature on the account settings page that enables users to download their information, from their posts to their photos to their comments—that is, most of their information that Facebook has collected on them. On the same account settings page, users can then manage this information.

As a *final step*, you might want to speak with others and with experts about what other measures you can take to keep your information private. Your instructor, your technology department on campus, and your fellow classmates are valuable resources that can help you understand more about social media. Beyond your institution, you can find forums and advocacy groups that work with people on a number of levels to help ensure social media use is ethical.

Check It Out YouTube: If you are interested in more ways to protect your privacy online, watch Techlore's YouTube video, "Becoming Anonymous: The Complete Guide to Maximum Security Online."

Final Thoughts

You may not realize just how much your writing of and use of social media can impact other people as well as environments until you actively engage in critical thinking about social media. This chapter has hopefully helped you to do so by prompting you to think about your actions and the actions of others who use social media for various purposes. Moving forward, you should always think twice before writing and engaging in social media so that your writing and engaging of social media will have positive rather than negative impacts on you and others.

Additional Discussion Questions

1. In what ways does writing on social media impact (in good ways and in bad ways) the following?
    a. our behaviors
    b. our relationships
    c. our uses of time
    d. our ways of thinking
    e. our societies

2. How much of our social media writing is influenced by the following, and in what ways?
    a. past writing experiences with other technologies
    b. our culture
    c. our politics

Additional Activities

1. Social Media Journal: If you are a regular user of social media, take a break for one week. Using a journal during this week, record your thoughts and feelings about the absence of social media in your life. At the end of the week, imagine what

your life would be like had you not known social media at all or if you gave it up for the rest of your life. What would that be like?
2. Social Media Impacts: In the beginning of this book, you learned that technologies can change writing and likewise that writing can change technologies. This is particularly true of social media. Social media technologies have changed the way we write, but the way we write has also changed social media. How does social media change technology (including writing) and vice versa? Research examples and share with your class.
3. Protect Your Privacy: Follow the five steps above about educating yourself about social media and protecting your privacy when using one social media platform. Write a reflection that considers what you learned in following such steps.

Additional Assignments

1. Social Media and Your Career: Study your future career field's use of social media. Create a presentation to the class that discusses what you found.
2. Social Media Around the World: Find out how other cultures or countries are using social media. Create a short presentation that outlines your findings for your classmates.
3. Data Download: Perform a social media data download (such as the one described earlier in this chapter) to find out what data a social media company is collecting on you. Write a report in which you reflect on the findings.

Works Cited

Eckler, Petya, Yusuf Kalyango, and Ellen Paasch. "Facebook Use and Negative Body Image among U.S. College Women." *Women & Health*, vol. 57, no. 2, 2017, pp. 249–267.

Etherington, Darrell. "Instagram Now Has 800 Million Monthly and 500 Million Daily Active Users." *TechCrunch*, 25 September 2017, https://techcrunch.com/2017/09/25/instagram-now-has-800-million-monthly-and-500-million-daily-active-users/. Accessed 9 June 2018.

Glum, Julia. "Millennials Selfies: Young Adults Will Take More Than 25,000 Pictures of Themselves during Their Lifetimes: Report." *International Business Times*, 22 September 2015, www.ibtimes.com/millennials-selfies-young-adults-will-take-more-25000-pictures-themselves-during-2108417. Accessed 7 January 2017.

Madhukalya, Anwesha. "8 Times Internet Trolls Were Brutally and Beautifully Shut Down This Year by Indian Celebs." *HuffPost*, 20 December 2016, www.huffingtonpost.in/2016/12/16/8-times-trolls-were-brutally-and-beautifully-shut-down-by-celebs_a_21629193/. Accessed 9 June 2018.

Murphy, Derek. "Runner Disqualified After Claiming 2nd Place in Fort Lauderdale Half Marathon." *Marathon Investigation*, 21 February 2017, www.marathoninvestigation.com/2017/02/runner-disqualified-after-claiming-2nd.html. Accessed 10 April 2018.

National Park Service. "Take the Yellowstone Pledge." *National Park Service, Department of the Interior*, 13 April 2018, www.nps.gov/yell/planyourvisit/yellowstonepledge.htm. Accessed 1 April 2019.

Salim, Saima. "How Much Time Do You Spend on Social Media? Research Says 142 Minutes Per Day." *Digital Information World*, 4 January 2019, www.digitalinformationworld.com/2019/01/how-much-time-do-people-spend-social-media-infographic.html. Accessed 5 April 2019.

Silver, Amber and Lindsay Matthews. "The Use of Facebook for Information Seeking, Decision Support, and Self-Organization Following a Significant Disaster." *Information, Communication & Society*, vol. 20, no. 11, 2017, pp. 1680–1697.

Smith, Karen H., Francis A. Méndez Mediavilla, and Gary L. White. "The Impact of Online Training on Facebook Privacy." *Journal of Computer Information Systems*, vol. 58, no. 3, 2018, pp. 244–252.

Stahl, Lesley. "Alexsandr Kogan: The Link Between Cambridge Analytica and Facebook." *CBS News*, 2 September 2018. www.cbsnews.com/news/aleksandr-kogan-the-link-between-cambridge-analytica-and-facebook-60-minutes/. Accessed 1 April 2019.

"Terms of Use." *Instagram*, 2018, https://help.instagram.com/478745558852511. Accessed 9 June 2018.

Tufekci, Zeynep. "It's The (Democracy-Poisoning) Golden Age of Free Speech." *Wired*, 16 January 2018, www.wired.com/story/free-speech-issue-tech-turmoil-new-censorship/. Accessed 1 June 2018.

Wilson, Chris. "The Selfiest Cities in the World: TIME's Definitive Ranking." *Time*, 10 March 2014, http://time.com/selfies-cities-world-rankings/. Accessed 7 January 2018.

CHAPTER 13

Writing for Websites

Contents

The World Is Online	310
Computer Programming (the Backend)	311
Suggestions for What You See (The Frontend)	316
The Consequences of Design	321
Making a Website Usable and Accessible	322
Final Thoughts	325

IMAGE 13.1 puhhha / Shutterstock

The World Is Online

To begin this chapter, you will need to log on to a computer, open up a browser, and go to International Volunteer HQ's website at http://www.volunteerhq.org/. International Volunteer HQ is a nonprofit organization that helps connect volunteers with opportunities around the world. According to their website, this organization is guided by four values. See if you can find information about these four values on their website before proceeding to the next paragraph.

After you find information on the four values, take a moment and reflect on how you found that information. What steps or actions did you take when searching the website for the information? Perhaps you clicked on one link or several. Perhaps you scrolled through text, scanning the headers and subtext. Perhaps you connected ideas on several pages until you understood. As you were locating the information on the four values, did you think at all about how this website was designed? Did you think about the person or persons who designed it? Did you think about the coding that it required? Did you think about the computer programs used to create it? How about the design decisions that most likely several people made? Did you think about how this website exists on the internet and is connected to other websites? Did you think about accessibility issues or whether or not the website adheres to user experience principles? Did you think about how your computer processes a code and then presents the website to you on your computer screen?

Chances are in the matter of minutes (perhaps even seconds) that it took you to find the four values (responsible, innovative, trusted, and awesome) and information on them, you didn't think about many of these things. You just searched for the information and that was it. Yet, whether you realized it or not, in finding the four values, you relied on several technologies and your knowledge and previous experience of them as well as your ability to connect ideas via the design of the website.

Breaking down the steps in finding these values can provide one way to think about how we write and use websites, building connections between people, places, and things. In this chapter, you will learn about web design from the perspective of the frontend operations (in other words, what users see on their screens) while thinking also about the backend operations (what goes on behind the scenes). Everything you see on the computer screen in front of you is written in code on the backend. That code enables information to be shared from one computer to the next over a network. The International Volunteer HQ's website, in a lot of respects, looks not only like other volunteer websites, but other websites in general, in that it contains common features found on websites, like links, headings, chunks of texts, images, colors, alignment of elements, and so on. While not everyone is going to graduate school and become a computer programmer, having a basic understanding of how computers work and how programs are written and used, can impact the ways in which you write and interact with websites and other online spaces. Chances are, in some aspect of your future job, you will utilize websites, whether reading, using, or writing for them.

Computer Programming (the Backend)

In Chapter 9, you learned about bits and bytes and how data is stored in binary form. A computer is a device that inputs, processes, stores, and outputs data using a variety of systems comprised of hardware and software. As you know from reading this book, there are various types of computers, from smartphones to desktops to tablets. In simplified terms, *computer programming* is a systematic process that begins with a task to be completed. To understand this process, let's return to an example from earlier in the book. Say you owned a shoe store, and you wanted to create a program that could help you and your employees search your inventory quickly. To develop this program, you hire a computer programmer named Suzanne. To create the program, Suzanne identifies the task: to build a database that can store and search inventory. Suzanne then analyzes and studies this task before writing sequential instructions or steps. In other words, she will write an *algorithm*. The algorithm is next translated into source code using programming language. The code enables the central processing unit (*CPU*) to work successfully through the task until it is finished. Suzanne then tests the entire new program for bugs before turning it over to you. Once it is operating smoothly and you clearly understand the program's interface, you train your employees to use it at your store. All of what you and Suzanne did can be considered the basic steps in computer programming.

Did You Know? Steps in Computer Programming

Computers can't do everything, but they can help us solve many problems. Working with data is one such problem that computers can help us with. For example, if you were working with a lot of different data and you wanted to make thorough comparisons, using a computer to do the work for you would save you lots of time and energy.

So, here are the steps you can take to program:

1. Identity a problem a computer can solve (this is the task).
2. Analyze and study the problem in order to identify a plausible solution.
3. Write out instructions in English for the solution to the problem (this is what the computer will do to complete the task).
4. Translate those instructions into a source code using programming language.
5. Test and fix any bugs.

Today, programmers use many different programming languages to get their computers to do what they want them to do. In fact, there are hundreds. Some of the more common programming languages include the following:

JavaScript (used for dynamic elements like multimedia on websites)

Java (used to build Android apps)

Swift (used to build Apple iPhone apps)

Python (web development and scientific computing)

C (one of the oldest languages, still used for computer operations and systems)

PHP (usually runs on a web server and is used for web development and general programming)

Ruby (used in general programming)

C++ (used in general programming)

CSS (stands for cascading style sheets, used for building a website's style, which could include things like background color)

HTML (stands for Hypertext Markup Language)

When building a website, you need to know or work with someone who knows computer programming language to get your website up and running online. In Chapter 8, you learned about the internet and the web where websites operate and live. Let's take a closer look at these before thinking about how to design websites. In order to access the internet and therefore a website, you have to use an internet service provider (ISP), a service that connects you to the internet. These don't publish your websites. While you can build your website offline using various programs, to publish a website, you would need to utilize a web hosting service. A web hosting service has the ability to host a person's website (usually for a fee). They provide a space for your site so that people can connect with it in exchange for your money. Web hosting services have the money and resources needed to own web servers, powerful computers that are connected to the internet. To connect with a website on a server, you need a browser and the address or URL (Uniform Resource Locator) of the page on the website. To access International Volunteer HQ's website, you would use the following address: http://www.volunteerhq.org/. The "http://" in the address is a typical protocol, and the "www" refers to the World Wide Web. These pieces of information within the address help the browser connect you with the right place on the internet. Once on the website, you can connect with other sites through various means including hyperlinks.

The good news is that you don't have to know all of the programming languages in the world in order to take advantage of what you can do with programming knowledge. Instead, a better strategy would be to learn basic characteristics of programming that apply to all languages. If you are going to be working with websites, for example, knowing basic HTML can help. HTML (the most recent version being HTML5) is not necessarily a programming language like the rest of the languages mentioned earlier. Rather, HTML contains all the tags necessary to dictate the display of the text on a computer screen. In other words, HTML is a markup language in that you mark up a document with it using specific language and tags that the computer then translates into a webpage. In addition, learning the basics of HTML and how it works can provide you with a basic understanding of how other programming languages work. A lot of programming languages have similar characteristics, grammars, key tags, syntax, and formats similar to HTML.

To show you how the simplest webpage can be created using HTML, let's look at an example that you can do on your own. Open up a text editor. If you are working on a PC, you can use the program Notepad. If you are using a MAC, try using TextEdit. Type into a document the HTML code contained in Image 13.2, making sure to write these three lines of text exactly as the image shows.

Click "Save As" when you are finished, making sure to save this document to your desktop using the file name "index.html" and the encoding type "UTF-8." Close your text editor and open your newly created file "index.html" in your browser. You now have a webpage that looks like Image 13.3.

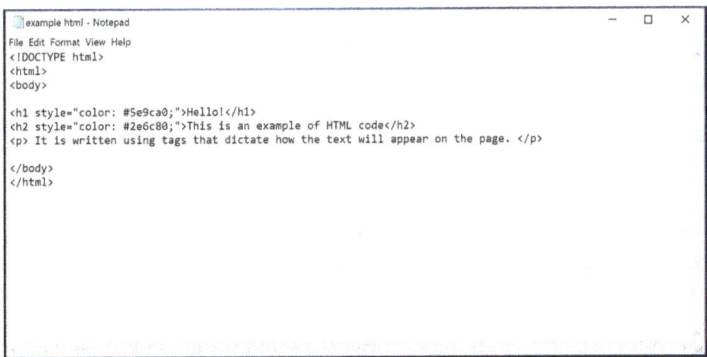

IMAGE 13.2

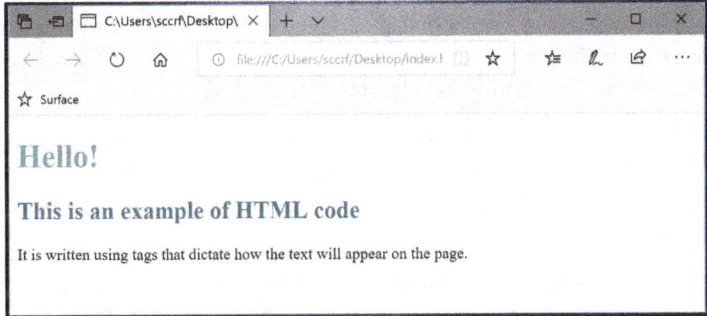

IMAGE 13.3

In Chapter 1, you learned about syntax. Syntax is used in programming language as it provides the set of rules that define how the language is structured. In addition to syntax, programming language must be written in a specific format so that the computer can read the language. All programming languages have key terms and symbols (also known as operators) that have specific meanings that a computer understands and acts upon. The reason why this simple example of a webpage looks the way it does is because you used tags in a particular order to help the computer process what parts you wanted your webpage to contain. The tags used in this example include the following tags and symbols:

The code starts with:

- the document type declaration <!DOCTYPE html>
- the html tag <html>
- and the body tag <body>

The tags for the first header are <h1> and </h1>

The tags for the second header are <h2> and </h2>

The tags for a paragraph are <p> and </p>

The code ends with the </body> and </html> tags

In this example, you can see that the tags begin and end the string of information. The more elements you add into your webpage, the more tags you would need. If you are interested in learning more about HTML and standard practices for using it, check out www.w3.org/TR/html51/.

HTML often works in conjunction with some of the other computer programming languages listed earlier. For instance, in this example, color is coded using CSS embedded in the HTML. For the first heading, the color is written in code this way: <h1 style="color: #5e9ca0;">. The tag <style> lets the computer know that it should use CSS to style the subsequent text "Hello!" in a particular color denoted by the numbers and letters assigned to this color. The numbers and letters are actually a hex triplet, a six-digit, three-byte hexadecimal number that represents colors in HTML and CSS.

Much like CSS, other languages can be embedded into HTML, too. If you see a tag such as <script>, the computer would know to use another scripting language, such as JavaScript. If you are interested in learning more about CSS and the standard practices for using it, check out www.w3.org/Style/CSS/.

Check It Out YouTube: If you want a beginner's tutorial on HTML, check out Traversy Media's "HTML Crash Course for Absolute Beginners." This video will walk you through step by step how to write using HTML.

Writing for Websites

As you know from using the web, webpages are much more complicated than the simple example just outlined. They can feature many more elements including images, sound, hyperlinks, shopping carts, and maps. One way to see just how complicated writing code can be is to look at an existing website's code. You can do this by opening up a browser, going to a website, and then using your browser's features to view the source code. In Chrome, you can do this by clicking on the three dots icon, selecting "more tools," and then selecting "developer tools." This will open up a window pane containing the source code. As you will find, that source code will most likely be much more complicated than the example outlined earlier.

You may not need to program a website entirely on your own in the future. But, perhaps you may find yourself at least working with others to create one. And, even if you are not going to become a computer programmer, most likely you will work with computers no matter what career field you enter. While you don't need to know everything there is to know about programming language, having some basic knowledge and skills can help you be a better writer who may find yourself having to communicate a clear message via a website. To do so, you need to know how to write for the frontend of the website (what users use and see) which is written in code in the backend through programming.

You may one day work for a company or organization that may have access to a particular website building program that allows you to create your website using one of their templates. For the most part, this might enable you to do what you want. There are a number of website builders (such as Weebly or Wix) that operate drag-and-drop-style programs that have made it seem like knowing code is unnecessary. These "what you see is what you get" (WYSIWYG) programs help you create professional-looking websites without having to see and use code, unless you want to. Website builders basically enable you to drag and drop website elements (such as text, images, video, and hyperlink buttons) onto a template as the builder builds or writes the code for you behind the scenes.

However, there may come a time when the template you are using doesn't enable you to do all that you had hoped to when you envisioned your website. Maybe you don't want your website to look like a hundred other websites that all utilized the same program that you are using to build it. Say, for instance, you really want to customize a particular page and image within your site instead. Say you want to use one of your own images on your website, and you want it to be a larger size than the template allows. Looking at the backend and the code for the template, you see that by editing the tag and code for the size of the image, you can manipulate the program to do exactly what you need it to, thus creating the website you envisioned.

If you are trying to reach the widest audience possible for your website, having a basic understanding of HTML and how code works can help you determine if you will be able to reach such an audience. Because people will access your website differently (some may use a computer, others may use a tablet, still others may use a phone), having a solid code in place and clean stylesheets to begin with can help ensure that no matter the technology your audiences use, they will be able to access and understand your website because your programming is written in a way that is responsive to the multiple devices and screen sizes your audience members will use to access your website.

Did You Know? Learning Programming Language

If you are new to programming and want to learn how to do it, one easy and convenient way to do so is to utilize free educational resources online. A wide range of resources are aimed at both young and old audiences. In fact, most programming languages have many sites devoted to teaching both experts and novices on how to use their languages. While a quick search online can help you find these, you can also find free tutorials and courses for programming languages at these websites:

- Codeacademy
- freeCodeCamp
- General Assembly's Dash
- Khan Academy
- w3schools.com

In addition, there are online games (some free and some not) that teach you a programming language as you play along. If you are someone who likes learning by playing games, this might be a good option for you when learning programming languages.

Finally, you can also study websites' source code. Most browsers enable people to view the code. Earlier in this chapter, you were given instructions for doing this in Chrome. If you would like to see code in another browser, you can find step-by-step instructions online.

Suggestions for What You See (The Frontend)

The way a website looks makes a difference in how a user reads and interacts with a website. Therefore, knowing more about how users interact with websites can help you make smarter decisions about the design of your own websites. To begin with, users don't necessarily read everything on a website from start to finish. Often, they scan for important, specific information. Writers of websites can make this process of finding such information easier by making smart design decisions. To that end, here are some suggestions you can consider when writing to ensure your website's frontend works for users effectively:

Suggestion 1: Think First

What people read first should be very informational. In other words, the first information they find on your page should carry meaning, and a lot of it. Information should become less important the more your audience reads on. That's because when people read your website, they are most likely wanting to find what they are looking for quickly. Having to spend more time than necessary can frustrate a user and make them want to move on to another website. So, to help the user out, make sure the most important information on your site is the first information your user will notice. To do so, use signals, styles, headings, alignment, chunks of text, images, and sentence structures, among other things, that help guide users into finding that most important information first.

Likewise, determining how much information should go on your page will require a bit of rhetorical thinking on your part. Typically, the more steps users need to take to find information, the less likely they will remain on your page if they can find what they are looking for quickly somewhere else. If you have a lot of information, you might consider first whether or not that information is quality information. The age-old adage of quality over quantity might be helpful to remember. Writing concisely—that is, efficiently— may help you to ensure that you are not wasting your users' time with unnecessary content.

Suggestion 2: Think Placement

The placement of content on a webpage matters just as much as what is in that content. This suggestion is closely related to the first in terms of what you should present users with first. In fact, the closer to the top of the page the information is, the more likely it is your users will read it. Today, many websites put a lot of their important content above what is called "the fold," the part of the website that is visible to the user without having to scroll. Everything that appears on the screen after a user scrolls is considered below the fold. A 2018 study by the Nielsen Norman Group, an organization that researches user experiences, found that

> the content above the fold received most attention (57% of viewing time); the second screenful of content received about a third of that (17% viewing time); the remaining 26% was spread in a long-tail distribution. In other words, the closer a piece of information is to the top of the page, the higher the chance that it will be read (Fessenden).

If you can, make sure that your important information is above the fold. To help you with this, think rhetorically about the organization of your page. Use examples of successful webpages in your genre and consider how those examples organize information.

Suggestion 3: Think Navigation

Ensure smooth navigation on pages and between pages. There are numerous ways in which people can navigate a website, and as a result, the design of the website can either help or hinder such navigation. One means for helping users navigate is by using headings and subheadings that summarize content throughout. These may actually be the only words your audience reads when visiting your site. Keep them short and to the point. Don't waste time with unnecessary words. Study other sites' headings and subheadings to see why. What are they doing and not doing? To demonstrate, look at the following example.

Example Heading: Rover Travels to Mars
You have four words in this heading. It is active and has one noun and one verb. There are no unnecessary words, and it tells readers what to expect to read about.

In addition to wasting no time in getting to the point, be consistent in labeling things on the same webpage and on multiple webpages within a website. For example, use the same style for your labels. If you use a sans-serif Arial 12-point bold font for your heading on one page on your website, use the same sans-serif Arial 12-point bold font for all your similar headings on all your pages within your site. Doing so allows users to see that the pages on your site are connected through their design and will help users read each of your pages quickly.

Another way to help users navigate is to provide hyperlinks. A hyperlink, as you learned earlier, is the link that provides the connection between these elements. When you click on a hyperlink, you are transported to some other element, whether that be another website, webpage, text, image, or downloadable document. When you look back at the first webpage ever created (see earlier in the book), hyperlinks were not prominent. Over the years, however, hyperlinks have become an expected and useful convention of websites, changing the way people connect with information, but also changing the way people think about order and organization of information. Throughout history, people in Western societies predominately read in a linear fashion, mainly because the texts they read were written in a linear fashion. A book, for instance, is read from page one, chapter one onward; otherwise the story in the book might not make much sense. The advent of hyperlinks challenges this way of reading because it provides people an opportunity to read texts in a nonlinear manner. When reading a website, people can choose the order in which to read information thanks in part to hyperlinks that make going from one element to the next easy.

Think carefully about how and where you create your hyperlinks. Hyperlinks should be more than just the words "click here" or "go" or an arrow pointing in a particular direction. You can take advantage of the various ways in which you can format a hyperlink and provide users with additional information in doing so. A hyperlink such as <u>Sahara Desert animals</u> is much more informational than if a user were to use the hyperlink <u>Click here</u> because it uses words that provide more information.

Activity: Sketch a Website

Think of a website that you would like to create. Sketch out all the elements and features of this website using different pieces of paper to represent the different pages of your website. As you do this sketch, keep in mind your answers to the following questions and how your answers will and should shape your design:

- Is it clear to your audience how they should navigate your website? How so?
- What clues did you give them?
- How long will it take for your audience to understand this navigation?
- Do you have a menu? Is it hidden, prominent, in a place where people would expect to find it?
- Do you use hyperlinks? If so, do you use hyperlinks in a way that is most helpful to your users?
- How will your audience read your site?
- Where will they start?
- What will they read first, second, third, and why?
- What have you done to guide them on this path?
- Can they easily get back to where they started?
- Do you provide consistent menus, links, etc., on all your pages?

Suggestion 4: Think Clean

A clean design makes accessibility easier. By clean design, you should consider the following when creating a website:

a. Avoid overcrowded and cluttered pages. Jamming as many visuals and information as possible into a website will only frustrate your users. You do not want to overwhelm them and force them to work harder than needed to understand your website. Instead, users should be able to understand and orient themselves with your webpages in a matter of a few seconds. If not, they may move on. See www.sphere.bc.ca/test/sruniverse.html for an example of a crowded website.
b. Utilize the same design schemes throughout your entire website. Consistency makes searching your site easy and quick because once users understand your design, they will come to anticipate where information will be located each time they move to a new webpage within your website.
c. Use chunks of information such as block text instead of long-winded paragraphs, and make sure to separate those chunks using enough space. When doing so with headings, this will make finding information easy and quick. As an example, read the following two texts. Then compare how much easier and faster it is to find the answer to the question "What do elephants eat?" with the text on the right.

It is easy to find the information in the text on the right because the text on the right uses short chunks of text (rather than one large one) as well as headings that clearly identify what those chunks of text are about.

d. Make sure your wording is readable, which means you should purposely choose a font style (must be readable by all), font color (must contrast with background color), and font size (not too small, not too big) that are appropriate for your website. Some font styles are easier to read than others. When designing your website, choose two or three font styles, colors, and sizes, but no more, as you will run the risk of having a messy design. Choosing too many can be distracting for your users, too. See Part 2 of this book for more on typography.

e. Finally, use alignment and proximity (see Part 2 as well) to help arrange and group elements on the page that would meet users' expectations. When you go against users' expectations, your users will get stuck wondering why they are stuck instead of looking for what they came to your website for in the first place.

TABLE 13.1 Example of Block Text About Elephants

African Elephants	**African Elephants**
African elephants roam the woodlands, deserts, and forests of Sub-Saharan Africa. Those that live on the savannah can be found in many countries such as Botswana, Tanzania, and Kenya. Those that live in forests can be found in many countries in west and central Africa. Female elephants live mainly in family units that consist of other females and calves. One older female elephant, known as the matriarch, leads the family unit. Male elephants, on the other hand, live alone or with a small group of male elephants. Researchers have found that both male and female elephants are very intelligent and can learn, grieve, and play, among other abilities. In the wild, elephants use their trunks to gather their food. They eat a variety of vegetation including leaves, grasses, roots, bark, and bamboo. Today, there are between 450,000 and 700,000 African elephants in the world. However, their species is threatened by poachers, habitat loss, and climate change.	**Habitat** African elephants roam the woodlands, deserts, and forests of Sub-Saharan Africa. Those that live on the savannah can be found in countries such as Botswana, Tanzania, and Kenya. Those that live in forests can be found in west and central Africa. **Behavior** Female elephants live mainly in family units that consist of other females and calves. Male elephants, on the other hand, live alone or with a small group of male elephants. Both male and female elephants are very intelligent and can learn, grieve, and play. **Diet** In the wild, elephants use their trunks to gather their food. They eat a variety of vegetation including leaves, grasses, roots, bark, and bamboo. **Population** Today, there are between 450,000 and 700,000 African elephants in the world. However, their species is threatened by poachers, habitat loss, and climate change.

Activity: Bad Website

Analyze an ineffective website and come up with a thorough plan for revising it based on what you read in this textbook. Determine, first, why the website is ineffective; that is, why users would have difficulty using it. Then, create a step-by-step plan for revising it. Present your plan to your classmates for feedback.

The Consequences of Design

Technology shapes the way we present information and this is particularly clear online. Websites tend to feature chunks of information, or bite-sized paragraphs, rather than many long paragraphs, for good reasons. Users have lots of websites they can choose from with a click of a button. If they can't find what they are looking for quickly, they move on. If you are the owner and/or creator of a website, you wouldn't want your users to leave, right? Chunks of information, therefore, could be designed to fit on the screen all at once or in ways that mean readers don't have to perform extra steps, like scrolling and clicking too much, in order to read everything. Designers could use fewer words or even shorter words to make this happen. They could make sure that they don't waste readers' time with unnecessary, and therefore, extra words. The information contained in the chunk would be the essential information. Too much, and the reader would perhaps stop reading.

Using chunks of information might seem like a good idea to help readers read. But, after you think about all the information you consume on a weekly basis, you might reconsider this. How much of that weekly information is provided to you in bite-sized chunks? What are the consequences of understanding things via such chunks?

While it is hard to believe that all things could be conveyed in bite-sized chunks of information, imagine your life and your understanding of things if you read only bite-sized chunks of information. What would you be missing out on as a result? What would chunks of information do to your brain's development and abilities? Would you lack the ability to synthesize larger amounts of information? Would you have a hard time thinking about complex things?

The choices that writers make when designing their texts, websites included, have consequences. Writing websites in a particular manner, like using chunks of information, is no different. While you can put only so much on a website, what you put is important as it will certainly impact the people who read it as well as the people, places, and things you write about on your website. If, for instance, you use only short paragraphs to describe a complex problem on your community's website, will your readers really understand the problem and be able to make the right choices to solve such a problem with the information you provided them?

As a writer of a website, you have to balance wanting to get people to use your website—that is, wanting to garner as much traffic as possible—with how your writing of information impacts others. Do you really need short chunks of information, or do you need to consider more information in order to help your readers understand? To get a better handle on this balance, you could start by keeping track of data, getting to know what is working and what isn't on your website. In the process, you could find out who is visiting your website, how they are visiting, and from where they are visiting.

Analytics could help you determine if your website is working and meeting your goals as well as helping your users find what they are looking for. Analytics involves the systematic analyses of data and statistics that lead to important insights and information, which in turn can help you make important decisions about what to change and what not to change on your website. Today, a number of technologies conduct analyses of data and statistics and present these findings to us to use for our own purposes. When it comes to website analytics, a number of free technologies and services are available as well as those you can pay for. These range from providing basic analytics to more in-depth ones. Depending on what you wish to know, you can choose the technologies and services that are most appropriate for your situation.

It might be best to start with some basic analytics first until you get a better understanding of how they work. For example, you might choose an analytics technology that lets you track where in the world your traffic is coming from by looking at the IP addresses. Every computer has a unique IP address, and so you could track whether or not you are reaching your target audience. You can also track how users arrived on your site, how long they stayed on your website, and on what pages they stayed. You can see what devices and browsers they are using to access your site, too. With this information, you can fix problems and track your website's progress over time, but you can also make the best decisions as to how you should write your website. What are your users willing to read? What are they most interested in? For how long are they reading? These are all questions you could answer using analytics, and those answers could help you determine how to write your website.

Making a Website Usable and Accessible

Creating accessible texts is the responsibility of everyone. As a writer, you cannot assume that everyone will connect with your texts in the same ways. Some people may have old computers. Some people may have new ones. Some people may need assistive technologies. Some may not. Likewise, you cannot assume that using technology will magically make all your texts accessible to everyone. Technologies can actually make texts more difficult to access. So, when you think of accessibility, you should think about designing texts that give everyone an equal opportunity to use and understand them. That is why it is imperative that you think carefully about the nature of your text and the environment in which it will be accessed to ensure that you are not creating any barriers for people.

In addition, you should consider Universal Design principles, as they will also help you think more about the consequences of your designs. In writing a website, you will need to consider the many ways people will use the different features of your website and to make sure to present information in more than one way to account for all users. One approach is to think about it in terms of usability and user experience (also known as UX). The Nielsen Norman Group provides a good definition for usability by breaking it down into five important components and the questions writers should ask:

1. Learnability: How easy is it for users to accomplish basic tasks the first time they encounter the design?
2. Efficiency: Once users have learned the design, how quickly can they perform tasks?
3. Memorability: When users return to the design after a period of not using it, how easily can they reestablish proficiency?
4. Errors: How many errors do users make, how severe are these errors, and how easily can they recover from the errors?
5. Satisfaction: How pleasant is it to use the design? (Nielsen, 2012)

The Nielsen Norman Group also believes that in addition to thinking about these five components and questions, writers must also think about utility, meaning they must think about whether or not the functionality of the design does what users need it to do (Nielsen, 2012). No doubt, your audience is a major actor in your design processes from the beginning. Usability testing is more than just your audience testing your text when you have completed a draft or prototype of it to see if it works. Your audience must believe that your website is useful and does what they want it to do.

Earlier in this book, you were introduced to the World Wide Web Consortium (W3C) and its work to ensure international standards for the web. To help you make your website accessible, you should read through W3C's Web Content Accessibility Guidelines (WCAG). Their newest version as of this writing (2.1) contains 13 guidelines organized into four principles. Box 13.1 provides an outline of the four principles as well as the 13 guidelines. For more information and examples on how to use these, visit www.w3.org/WAI/WCAG21/quickref/.

Box 13.1 W3C's WCAG 2.1 Four Principles and 13 Guidelines

Consider how you can use such principles and guidelines as you design your websites in ways that are accessible to as many people as possible.

Principle 1: Perceivable: Information and user interface components must be presentable to users in ways they can perceive.

1. Text Alternatives: Provide *text alternatives* for non-text content.
2. Time-Based Media: Provide alternatives for time-based media.

3. Adaptable: Create content that can be presented in different ways.
4. Distinguishable: Make it easier for users to *see and hear content including separating foreground and background*.

Principle 2: Operable: User interface components and navigation must be operable.

5. Keyboard Accessible: Make all functionality available from a *keyboard*.
6. Enough Time: Give users *enough time* to read and use content.
7. Seizures and Physical Reactions: Do not design content in a way that is known to cause *seizures or physical reactions*.
8. Navigable: Provide ways to help users navigate, find content, and determine where they are.
9. Input Modalities: Make it easier for users to operate functionality through various inputs beyond keyboard.

Principle 3: Understandable: Information and the operation of user interface must be understandable.

10. Readable: Make text content *readable and understandable*.
11. Predictable: Make webpages appear and operate in *predictable* ways.
12. Input Assistance: Help users *avoid and correct mistakes*.

Principle 4: Robust: Content must be robust enough that it can be interpreted reliably by a wide variety of user agents, including assistive technologies.

13. Compatible: Maximize *compatibility* with current and future user agents, including assistive technologies.

Activity: Accessibility

While humans are the best testers, a number of automated programs can help you test your website for accessibility issues. Try out a number of these to ensure that your website is accessible. While a search online will garner you a number of these programs, you might start with the following:

WebAIM: Wave tool: https://wave.webaim.org/
AChecker: https://achecker.ca/checker/
Access Assistant toolbar from https://webaccessibility.com/
SortSite—Accessibility Checker and Validator by PowerMapper at www.powermapper.com/products/sortsite/checks/accessibility-checks/

Final Thoughts

Using analytics and accessibility testing are a few ways to test the design of a website, but they are not foolproof. They won't, for example, necessarily determine if your website is boring and will lead your users in the other direction, that is, away from your website. Speak with people as they test out your website to find out what they like and dislike about it. Then, you can revise accordingly. So, as a final note, when you think about designing a website, always keep people in mind. This can sometimes be hard given that so much of the process of building a website involves the computer, a screen, and a program. But such a process cannot be thought of as humanless. The very point of creating a website is so that humans can connect with it. If they can't, then you wasted your time in building it.

Additional Discussion Questions

1. Why is it useful to learn basic coding?
2. In what ways do you believe a website is connected?
3. Why should you have a clean design for your website?
4. Why is it important to use accessibility checking?

Additional Activities

1. Assistive Technologies: When people are unable to access a text, they may need to rely on assistive technologies. Assistive technologies are tools that people can use to access texts. They can include: screen readers, sign language, CART (communication access real time transcription), magnifying software, keyboards, head pointers, and so forth. Test out these kinds of technologies to learn how they work. Then, write a reflection that considers their impact on your design of texts, including websites.
2. Trace Connections: Working in a group, choose a website and trace its connections to people, places, and things. Report your findings to the class.

Additional Assignments

1. Genre Analysis: Conduct an extensive analysis of a particular genre of website (educational, restaurant, entertainment, medical, etc.) and create a website in this genre based on your findings. Make sure to test it out and share it with your classmates.
2. WCAG 2.1: Find examples of websites that demonstrate the WCAG 2.1 four principles (along with their guidelines) and share them with the class in a presentation.

3. Create Your Own Website: Use the suggestions in this book, and particularly in this chapter, to create your own website. The subject of your website and your audience for your website will be up to you. Keep in mind how rhetorical thinking can help you create it. As your ideas take shape, also consider how your intended audience will access it.

Works Cited

Fessenden, Therese. "Scrolling and Attention." *Nielsen Norman Group*, 15 April 2018, www.nngroup.com/articles/scrolling-and-attention/. Accessed 1 September 2018.

Flaherty, Kim. "Zigzag Image-Text Layouts Make Scanning Less Efficient." *Nielsen Norman Group*, 26 November 2017, www.nngroup.com/articles/zigzag-page-layout/. Accessed 1 September 2018.

Nielsen, Jakob. "Usability 101: Introduction to Usability." *Nielsen Norman Group*, 4 January 2012. www.nngroup.com/articles/usability-101-introduction-to-usability/. Accessed 22 June 2018.

W3C. "How to Meet WCAG 2 (Quick Reference)." *W3C*, 11 June 2018, www.w3.org/WAI/WCAG21/quickref/. Accessed 22 June 2018.

CHAPTER 14

Writing for Mobile Devices

Contents

Mobile Technology to the Rescue 327
What Is a Mobile Technology?. 328
Comparing the Past With the Present. 329
Smartphones and Good Consequences 331
Smartphones and Bad Consequences 331
Writing With a Smartphone 333
Suggestions for Designing Apps 334
The Backend: To Template or Not. 341
Final Thoughts 342

Mobile Technology to the Rescue

Early one Tuesday morning in the fall of 2014, Officer David Cameron of the Campbell Police Department near San Jose, California, put his tech skills to the test to locate a missing woman. Melissa Vasquez had disappeared the day before, and no one knew where to find her. Officer Cameron, however, believed that using Apple's Find My iPhone app would help lead police to her. He believed that if Melissa had her iPhone on her when she disappeared, and if police could locate the phone, they could potentially locate Melissa. According to ABC7News, after obtaining Vasquez's iPad at her home, Officer Cameron went to work cracking its passcode using an educated guess of common numbers people use for passcodes. Once he unlocked her iPad, he was able to use her Find My iPhone app to locate her iPhone. Less than a half hour later, rescuers from the U.S. Coast Guard used the location of her iPhone and spotted Melissa and her car in a ravine outside San Diego. She had been in a serious car accident, thrown from her vehicle, and unable to move. Rescuers quickly airlifted her to a nearby hospital for immediate treatment and recovery.

Melissa's harrowing story is only one of many such stories worldwide that demonstrate how mobile technologies have been crucial in saving lives. Today, first responders use mobile devices in a number of ways, from coordinating rescues to issuing alerts to locating missing people. But, they are not the only ones using mobile devices. Every day, people around the world rely on their mobile devices. With the help of comprehensive data, GSMA Intelligence provides research statistics and data on mobiles worldwide. As of April 2018, their real-time tracker showed that there were 5,057,257,841 unique mobile subscribers worldwide. That number is expected to grow thanks in part to the continuous development of mobile devices.

Mobile devices, particularly smartphones, have changed our world and will continue to do so in the future. Businesses, organizations, schools, churches, clubs, governments, and almost everyone use phones to reach constituents in a variety of ways. Most likely, whatever career you will go into once you graduate, you will need to use a smartphone to communicate with your boss, colleagues, clients, and the public. So, it makes sense to think about the most effective ways to write with and for smartphones and how those smartphones are connected to people, places, and things. It makes sense to think about what exactly mobile devices are, what can they do, how, when, and where people use them, and for what purposes. In other words, it makes sense to think rhetorically.

What Is a Mobile Technology?

When you think of a mobile technology, or device, you may first think about a smartphone. A smartphone is but one type of mobile device. In general, a mobile device refers to any handheld mobile computing device. These can include tablets, wearables, and handheld game consoles, just to name a few examples. In this chapter, we will be looking mainly at smartphones because smartphones and mobile phones in general are used worldwide by millions of people. In fact, we have seen an increase in the amount of people who own mobile phones since their creation. By 2016, "A staggering 82% of adults worldwide personally had a mobile phone . . . according to Gallup's global surveys representing more than 99% of the world's population" (Crabtree and Burchell).

When Alexander Graham Bell first envisioned a telephone, it's hard to imagine he would have envisioned the modern smartphones we have today or the variety of smartphones that exist on this planet. No two smartphones are exactly alike, as there are different kinds of smartphones (Apple iPhone, Samsung Galaxy, Microsoft Lumia, etc.) that utilize different operating systems, iOS and Android platforms being the more popular. Each smartphone enables users to customize its features, from allowing users to download a variety of apps to allowing users to choose any image as a screen saver. Smartphones come in different sizes, too, with different screen sizes and capabilities.

If you own a smartphone, take it out and examine its physical specs. Next, take a look at its features, that is, what it can do. If you were to compare your smartphone to those of your classmates, most likely you would find both similar and different specs and features. You would also certainly find that your classmates have customized their phones in a variety of different ways.

Activity: Daily Phone Use

Write a reflection that critically takes into consideration your daily phone use. The questions below can help guide you in your reflection, but you should also consider how your use and the use of others impact your society. Discuss your reflection with your classmates.

- What are the things you do with your phone daily?
- What do these things say about the kind of person you are?
- Can you do without your phone? Why or why not?
- What kinds of writing do you do with your phone, and why?
- What impacts do your uses of your phone have on you and others?

Comparing the Past With the Present

In previous chapters, you learned about different ways people might use mobile devices (like using smartphones to take selfies, to text, and to engage social media). In addition to the things you learned about, people use mobile devices for a variety of other purposes, which in turn have shaped communicative practices. For example, according to a recent Pew Research Center report, "More than eight-in-ten U.S. adults now get news on a mobile device (85%)" (Lu). A hundred years ago, people read the news in newspapers printed on black-and-white paper, an experience, in many ways, much different from today's reading of the news on a mobile device.

Indeed, a hundred years ago, when people read stories about their fellow citizens, they could write letters to the editors expressing their thoughts about such stories, and they could speak with others about what they learned from reading the news. In some respects, this still happens today. However, a hundred years ago, people couldn't click on a link within a news story to get more information on that news story. They couldn't, with the touch of a screen, read multiple versions of that same story from different news outlets in a matter of minutes. They couldn't share a link to the story, either, or post immediate comments for the whole world to see. That's because news stories on our mobile devices allow for more connections. We can connect the stories to our network of contacts or with the entire world in many different ways. As a result, today's news has changed in some ways beyond just the use of hyperlinks embedded in the stories. Often, news stories are written specifically for mobile devices and are delivered to mobile users via apps. These stories feature not just text, but videos, links, sounds, and much more, things that news stories didn't have a hundred years ago.

In this comparison of past and present, we can see that news organizations have had to adapt their production and dissemination of their stories to reach audiences who are increasingly using a variety of technologies like mobile devices. They've had to change their communication strategies or risk having no impact altogether.

 Everett Collection / Shutterstock
 AkayArda / iStock

Nevertheless, people don't just use their mobile devices for reading the news. They use them to communicate with others via text messaging. They use them to video chat with loved ones. They use them to connect with clients in order to do business. They use them to navigate places as they travel both short and long distances. They use them to photograph events and people, buy goods and services, keep journals, and record voice memos. They use them to listen to music. The list goes on and on. In fact, there are so many things people do with mobile devices that there aren't enough pages in this book to mention all of them.

Activity: Writing and Your Phone

Investigate one feature of your smartphone that enables you to write with your smartphone. For starters, you could consider one of the following features:

- Voice-to-text
- Predictability functions
- Autocorrect
- Wi-Fi connectivity
- Processing speed

As you investigate the feature, think critically about what the feature does, how you use it, and how it shapes your writing. Share your findings with your classmates.

Smartphones and Good Consequences

If you want to be a better writer, someone who takes into account the best technologies for your communicative task, it is always a good idea, as we have learned in this book, to consider the consequences of using technologies. While people have found many uses for smartphones, such uses have consequences, both good and bad. To begin with, smartphones can help locate missing people, as the case of Melissa Vasquez demonstrates. Second, the convenience of smartphones can lead to an increase in productivity. People are able to access information virtually from anywhere on the planet whenever they want. In some remote areas of the world that have been essentially cut off from the rest of the world, smartphones have provided valuable connections and access to information that was impossible to get quickly 20 years ago.

Smartphones have also led to the changing of other behaviors and to bringing awareness to things that were not talked about before. Earlier, you thought about how social media has helped level the field in some regards to covering the news around the world. Whereas before only news reporters were able to share information, now more people can potentially share information about an event with the help of their smartphones. Before, news reporters had to go to the remote places and bring back the news. Today, people in remote areas can send news themselves, and therefore, reporters don't necessarily need to go there. When this happens, the people get to decide what gets recorded and shared, not the reporters. Smartphones and their ability to capture video has essentially forced people, businesses, and governments to have to account for their actions when someone shoots a video of them acting inappropriately and shares it with the world via their smartphone. So, those with a smartphone and the ability to connect feel more empowered in their lives.

Finally, another good consequence has to do with how smartphones make us feel, like feeling empowered. In some cases, even, smartphones make people happier. In a Gallup World Poll study on mobile phone use and happiness, researchers found that happiness is improved when mobile devices bring internet access to those who would otherwise not have it (Crabtree and Burchell). Having such access could be crucial to a person's success. People with internet access have an advantage over those who do not, because with the internet comes access to things such as education, government, and health care experts.

Smartphones and Bad Consequences

In May 2018, tragedy struck in southern Odisha, India, when a man tried to take a selfie with an injured bear. On the way back from a wedding, Prabhu Bhatara spotted the injured bear after the vehicle he was traveling in stopped. Despite pleas from the other passengers in the vehicle warning him not to, Bhatara decided to take a selfie with the bear. As he got close to the bear, the bear attacked, killing Bhatara. According to reports, this is not the first time in India a person has died trying to take a selfie. A study conducted by researchers from Carnegie Mellon University and Indraprastha Institute of Information Delhi reports that during a two-year period, 76 selfie deaths occurred in India (Sharman and Dubey).

Despite the good consequences mentioned earlier, using smartphones (such as using them to take selfies) has led to many bad consequences that have impacted people and the planet in negative ways. For starters, many people have become addicted to their smartphones, so much so that they participate in reckless behaviors, like texting and driving, which put themselves and others in danger. According to the U.S. National Highway Traffic Safety Administration, when driving, "Texting is the most alarming distraction. Sending or reading a text takes your eyes off the road for 5 seconds. At 55 mph, that's like driving the length of an entire football field with your eyes closed." Yet, despite knowing the dangers of texting and driving, some people do it anyway. Indeed, a 2014 study by David Greenfield, a University of Connecticut Medical School professor, found that "98% of those who text every day and drive frequently say the practice is dangerous. Still, nearly 75% say they do it anyway" (Worland). Perhaps they do so because they cannot be without their smartphones at any time.

Nomophobia (which stands for NO MObile PHOne phoBIA) is the word used to describe the fear someone has when they are without their mobile phone (LaMotte). Addiction to mobile phones is real and has had both physical and psychological ramifications. In a recent study, teenagers who were addicted to their phones "had significantly higher scores in anxiety, depression and levels of insomnia and impulsivity" (LaMotte). Like other technologies, smartphones can impact not just our behaviors, but also our brains. We think in certain ways when using our smartphones, perhaps even in ways that are harmful to ourselves (like ignoring our friends when they tell us taking a selfie with a bear is not a good idea).

Take a moment and think about this past week and your smartphone use. As you were using your smartphone, at any point, did you think about how the behaviors you were engaging in might be harmful? Did you think about how such use could change your brain? Now think about whether or not you could live without your smartphone. For a week? For a day? How would that make you feel?

Try taking the Center for Internet and Technology Addiction and Professor David Greenfield's Smartphone Compulsion Test: https://virtual-addiction.com/smartphone-compulsion-test/.

While smartphones can be bad for people, they can also be bad for our environment. For instance, disturbing wildlife to take a selfie forces such wildlife to become defensive and distressed, as was the case with the injured bear. As discussed in other chapters of this book, land, too, can be at risk. When people take pictures with smartphones and post them on social media, the places where those pictures were taken become inundated with more people who also want to take their own pictures, thus changing the landscape.

Finally, the very development and disposal of smartphones can be causes for concern. Think for a moment about what your smartphone is made out of. What materials were needed to make it? How were these materials obtained, assembled, and sold? Do you ever think about the manufacturing processes it takes to build such a device? Do you think about the people involved in these processes? Do you think about the distance your smartphone travels before it even winds up in your hands? Do you think about the trade policies among countries that manufacture them? Do you think about the laws that govern the selling of them? Do you think about what happens to your smartphone once you trade it in or throw it away when you are done using it?

The life cycle of smartphones is often short (perhaps just two years). Yet, such a short life cycle requires energy, labor, resources, spaces, travel, and policies to produce and sell smartphones; all of these contribute to a footprint on Earth. Given the billions of people who have or who have owned a smartphone and given that smartphones don't last long, the environmental costs add up.

Assignment: Life Cycle of a Smartphone

Research the life cycle of your smartphone to get a better understanding of the footprint technologies leave on Earth. Examine the manufacturing processes, the resources and materials, and the labor needed to produce it, the places where it is made, and so forth. As you research this life cycle, consider whether or not your smartphone was built with a sustainable design (perhaps using recyclables) to reduce its replacement cycle. Discuss your findings with your fellow classmates and discuss ways in which technology companies can reduce such a footprint.

Writing With a Smartphone

Now that you have had a chance to reflect on how smartphones impact our lives and our environment, let's turn now to how smartphones can help us write. For starters, let's consider apps. After all, with the rise of smartphone use, there has been tremendous growth in the development of apps, including those particularly designed to help people write. According to digtialtrends.com, "Globally, there were 175 billion app downloads in 2017, and people spent $86 billion in app stores in the same year" (Hill). These numbers are expected to rise in the years to come. Tech companies have created a number of writing apps, each geared toward helping people write.

Take Evernote, for example. The app enables writers to write, copy, and store written notes in a cloud so that a user can access these from any connected device. Even apps that are not designed specifically for writing do require us to write. There are a number of social media apps that are designed for social media purposes. To use them, you must write. In this sense, a lot of the writing we do with apps is public facing, meaning that we are connected to others. It is also either synchronous, meaning that we write instantly to other people who are also writing and using the same apps, or asynchronous, meaning that we write and respond over a greater span of time.

Take a few moments and investigate the apps on your smartphone, paying attention to their features. How do you write with each one of these apps? What do you write with each one? Why do you write with each one?

Another way to think more about how you write with your smartphone is to compare the writing you do with your smartphone with the writing you do without it. Take a few moments and think about the actions you take to write with your smartphone and the actions (physical and mental) you take when you are writing with other technologies, like a laptop or pen and paper. How are these actions similar? How are they different? Most likely, you will see that while there are similarities in how you write with a smartphone and other technologies, there are quite a few differences, too. Perhaps when you write with your smartphone, you rely mostly on your thumbs to type, as opposed to using all your fingers like you do when you type on a computer. Perhaps when you write with your smartphone, you prefer to use a feature like voice-to-text to speak your words into your smartphone's microphone so that your smartphone can then convert your spoken words into written words. Perhaps when you write with your smartphone, you are doing so while moving as opposed to sitting behind a desk.

Suggestions for Designing Apps

Now that we have briefly looked at using apps to write, let's next consider the actual writing of apps. Just like you did in the previous chapter, when designing for smartphones, you have to think about the backend writing and the frontend writing that are necessary for communication to work. Furthermore, you need to consider how people will use and access such writing. Keeping the suggestions in mind from the previous chapter (since they can, in some regards, apply to writing for smartphones), you should consider the suggestions explained in this section as they will provide you with further guidance in making important rhetorical decisions specifically for creating apps for smartphones. Writing a website for use on a computer is different from writing for a smartphone. As you read these suggestions, consider creating your own app for a smartphone. In this way, you will think through a specific writing situation and will be able to see how such writing can differ from the writing you may do for websites or other kinds of texts. Quite a few free online app builder sites can help you do this.

Before you begin, first take a look at the following example. For an assignment in one of her writing classes, Jeweliana Register, a student you met earlier in this book, created her own app called Bujo, an app intended to be used on mobile devices, such as a smartphone. Bujo is short for Bullet Journal, as Jeweliana's goal was to create an app that would allow users to write bullet journals on the go and from anywhere. Bullet journals are creative and customized handwritten lists, journals, diary entries, and sketches. People use bullet journals for a variety of purposes, from planning to remembering dates to making to-do lists. As a fan of bullet journaling herself, Jeweliana wanted to create an app version so people didn't have to carry around a notebook and pen. They would just need their mobile device instead. Images 14.3 and 14.4 are screen shots of the user interfaces for Jeweliana's app, in other words, the screens people use to interact with the app.

Jeweliana created the designs for her app's screens (the frontend that users see) using an online design platform devoted to helping users create all kinds of graphics. Using their templates and their graphics, she was able to create a design that suited her app idea. To code her app, though, she would need to then convert those designs into a code on the backend using computer programing language that could translate the designs into interactive screens.

The process Jeweliana used in designing her app began with the frontend design. This is just one process for designing an app. You could begin with the backend. Likewise, you could work on both the backend and frontend at the same time. Your process will depend on your experience with writing for mobile devices and your familiarity with coding and designing examples. Because Jeweliana never designed an app before, beginning with

IMAGE 14.3 "Home Screen"

IMAGE 14.4 "Journal Screen"

the frontend made more sense to her. In the future, you may find yourself in a similar situation, where you need to design an app from the frontend and then turn over your designs to a computer programming team to write the code. If this is the case, you will want to make sure you have a good design in place beforehand. In the pages to come, you will find a few suggestions to keep in mind as you create the frontend designs for your app. As you do, think about all the connections your app will make with its users, with other people, with other apps, with the environment, with other computers, and with other systems.

Suggestion 1: Think People First

As you read the interview with Jeweliana, you will see that she thought deeply about her audience for her app. In designing it, she thought first about including as many options as possible so as to give as many people an opportunity to use the app for their own purposes. When planning your own app, think about your audience, and think about these key questions when you do:

- Who are they?
- What are their characteristics?
- How can you keep the user experience in mind as you create your app?
- How will they access your app?
- What purposes will they use it for?
- How will they use your app to connect with people, places, and things?

Understanding your audience may require a bit of research on your part, but that research will be a valuable component of your design, as the information you obtain will help you make important decisions about what to include and what to leave out of your app. For example, in researching your audience, you should develop personas. Personas are not specific individuals but are instead groups or types of people who exhibit similar habits, preferences, attitudes, motivations, and characteristics. If you were Jeweliana, you might use creative writers as one persona for an app like Bujo. Characteristics of a creative writer could include being artistic, good at thinking outside the box, and imaginative. Knowing these characteristics could help you then develop features for the app that such a user would want and use to be creative, to think outside the box, and to be imaginative.

As a word of caution, in developing your personas, you will want to rely on authentic characteristics and avoid preconceived biases and stereotypes. If you were Jeweliana and were to research creative writers, you would want to base your persona on what is real about such writers, not what is stereotype. To help you, there are free technologies and resources that can aid in developing personas and keeping track and revising them based on your experience in designing. For example, uxpressia.com, allows users an opportunity to create personas on their platform.

Suggestion 2: Think Cross-Culturally

While it is vital to be aware of cultural differences, when creating an app for a global audience, it is just as vital to pay attention to the cross-cultural practices that enable everyone to use it. Writing scholar Gustav Verhulsdonck contends that using interaction design—that is, a design that employs "common, familiar design elements to help users better understand the purpose of a design quickly"—is helpful in creating an app that is not "intricately bound to particular cultures or contexts" (141). In his view, creating an app that uses interaction design can help you to account for global networks and changing communicative practices.

There are a number of ways to employ interaction design throughout your process for creating an app, but at the beginning, it is important to develop a concept for your app that factors in cross-cultural practices and ideas. For starters, you can think carefully about your app's name and logo. If you are hoping to reach a wide audience, choosing a name and logo that people globally could recognize would be a good idea. Drawing from Donald Norman's *The Design of Everyday Things*, Verhulsdonck recommends using a mental model to develop ideas for mobile apps, saying that "A mental model is a conceptual model designers use to map an individual's understanding of a design's function and purpose" (Verhulsdonck 145). He uses the example of a neologism to demonstrate how an app's name could be recognizable cross-culturally. He writes that Snapchat "uses the understanding of 'snap' and 'chat' for quick social sharing of social photo with a limited window of time in one's private network" (Verhulsdonck 145). Regardless of their culture, people who use Snapchat for the first time would have a pretty good understanding of what the app does based on their knowledge of the words "snap" and "chat" ("snap" means quick while "chat" means to talk) along with their knowledge of how apps operate. When those two words appear together, it is easy to see that the app is for quick talk.

Like always, as you develop your own app, test out your ideas with different groups of people by asking them to guess what your app does (based, for instance, on your app's name and logo). If they have a hard time understanding what your app does, consider revising your concepts so that more people can understand what your app is and how to use it.

Suggestion 3: Think Big

When it comes to the actual design (what your interface will look like), think carefully about all (not just some) of the screens your users will encounter and navigate and how those screens will work together as one cohesive app. Navigation will play a central role in the design of your app as it should help users move quickly throughout your app. How will users smoothly navigate from one screen to the next and back again? Making navigation evident and familiar will reduce the risk of distracting your users from the rest of your app.

To know how people will move through your app, actually draw out a big picture by wireframing your app. Wireframing helps you to visualize your app's structure and layout, and to see that such a structure and layout has met your goals for your app. Think of your wireframes as your blueprints. They will guide you as you build your app. Using either an online wireframing program or just a notebook, sketch out each screen and draw connections between them that represent the ways in which users can move from one screen to the next and back again. Draw where on the app users will make these connections so that you do not forget to create navigational cues to prompt users to move. These could include icons and links. Then, test out your wireframes to ensure you will have an operational flow that is user friendly.

Moreover, go beyond your own app to think big. Investigate other apps like yours and find out what they do or don't do. Take notes and pay attention to how those apps are designed, how users navigate various screens, and how the apps include features and elements. Read the app reviews in app stores, too, to find out what people like and don't like. Compare what you find with your own design concepts. Then, once you build a prototype of your app, test out different navigational schemes with different audiences again to find out if they can navigate smoothly.

Suggestion 4: Think Small

The kinds of reading and interacting that occur with smartphones are indeed different from that which happens with desktop and laptop computers. Partly, this is due to the physical nature of these technologies and our relationships to them. While screen sizes come in many dimensions, relatively speaking, smartphone screens are much smaller than those of desktop and laptop computers. As a result, we tend to hold smartphones closer to our bodies rather than place them on a surface (such as a desk or table) at arm's distance in order to use them. When designing texts for smartphones, keep in mind the smaller nature of a smartphone. Small spaces and places that are cluttered with a lot of information, features, and elements might feel overwhelming to users on a small screen. If you clutter your app, you may run the risk of rendering it useless to your users. Using small chunks of information, headings, and keywords (in other words, keeping your app simple) may help users navigate on a small screen more effectively.

While in her interview, Jeweliana talks about including as many options as possible for her users, in actuality, her app has a finite set of features. What she did was marry her want to give her audience many opportunities with the need to make the app useful, simple to use, and intuitive. Because the screen is small, and because people often use apps on the go, overly complicated apps tend to become useless as people don't have the time and energy to waste on trying to figure out how they work. If you take another look at her user interfaces in Images 14.3 and 14.4, you can see the options users have. On the first screen, the home screen, users have just three options. On the second screen, the journal screen, they have five. All of these options, however, are what users would probably expect to find in an app for bullet journaling. Likewise, all these options are things people can actually do on a smartphone.

With that said, the features you use (such as text and images) should be readable for a small screen. Choosing readable font styles and image sizes are important to maintaining a usable design.

INTERVIEW
JEWELIANA REGISTER, STUDENT, COMMUNICATIONS MAJOR

Q: What rhetorical decisions did you make when creating your app, and why?
A: I wanted the app to be very creative and user-focused since the bullet journal experience is just that. I chose to incorporate as many options as I could think of for each section and personalized it as much as possible. I placed myself in the user's shoes and thought about what I would want in the app. Anytime I am bullet journaling, I find myself searching for inspiration on Pinterest or Instagram, so I thought this app could bring them all together. I decided to focus on these aspects and then offer a way for users to get their designs out into the community. The text-heavy pages are the "how to" and the "FAQ" sections, but there was really no way to get around that. Overall, I just kept in mind what the user would benefit most from and tried to implement that in a clean, simple way.

Q: Why did you design the app in the way you did? For example, what made you choose the colors that you did, the font that you did, etc.?
A: When it came to designing the logo, I knew I wanted the font to be very handwritten and imperfect looking, but still very clean so as not to distract from the actual creativity of the app. I found the perfect font for what I envisioned: the stenciled-on font called "Alberta Stencil." I thought it paired nicely with "Roboto Condensed" because of its simplicity and the fact that it was sans serif, so it did not distract from the stenciled, center stage font. I wanted to keep the app simple and clean so that the design did not distract from the main purposes of the app: the user customizing and designing their personal planning system. I used a mint green, white, and gray color scheme with pops of color on the social feed and the new journal page.

Q: When you were designing the app, how did you imagine your audience would use it?
A: I imagined that the audience would want a fully customized experience. Drawing inspiration and information from the bullet journal community, I knew that users would want blank pages and all the creative freedom.

Q: Did you get feedback on your design as you were creating it? If so, how and was this feedback helpful?
A: I received feedback from my classmates when it came to the app's purpose and the wording for my rationale. I took their suggestions into consideration and implemented them as I saw fit. I was also inspired by the apps they were working on, and it was nice to be able to bounce ideas off of each other.

Q: What writing advice would you give a student who wants to design apps?
A: Avoid feeling overwhelmed. The project can be a bit daunting, but once you get started, you will realize that it is a lot of fun. Don't be afraid to be creative, and always keep the user experience in mind.

Suggestion 5: Think Mobile Friendly

Nowadays, most companies that have a website also have a version of the website for mobile devices. This mobile-friendly version may contain similar information to the website, but it is also different in a lot of ways. If you want your mobile text to be user friendly, you have to design for mobile use. In other words, instead of designing one text that you hope will work for all technologies, try designing a text specifically for the kind of technology it will be used with. That is, instead of designing a website that you hope will work on a phone, design an app and treat it differently than if it were a website. That isn't to say that there are not similarities in designing the two or that the two can't have some of the same content. There certainly are examples of websites and apps that have the same content (after all, having some of the same content can help you save time and money in the design process).

But, if you want your audience to use your text on their smartphone, design your text for a smartphone. With that said, know what smartphones are and can do and take these into account. For example, think about such things as screen size, the various functional and navigational capabilities smartphones have, audience's expectations for using smartphones, and so forth. You would also need to consider the very actions people will perform with your app that might be different from the actions someone would need to use on a website.

Activity: Design Choices and the Ways People Use Apps

As you design an app, consider taking a break to reflect on your choices and how those choices will impact the ways in which people interact with your app. That way, you will be able to think through whether or not your app will work most effectively for the widest possible audience. To help you with your reflection, consider answering the following questions:

- Will users be using their fingers? If so, how many, and what for?
- Are your elements, links, and icons big enough for fingers to touch?
- Will your audience be using a stylus? Their voices? How so and why?
- Will your audience need to write things? Say things? Fill in forms? How will they do so?
- How will you account for all of the ways your users will interact with your app in your design?

Suggestion 6: When and Where Matters

As you think about the nature of smartphones when designing your apps, you must contemplate when and where people will use them. User experience is tied to particular times and places. Your users' experiences are not just on the screen but are also tied to the physical 3D spaces they inhibit, and those spaces are impacted by their histories, their cultures, and their politics. Think rhetorically about your audience and when and where they will use your app. If they were going to be using your app on the go or in a particular location, most likely you would need to create an easy navigation scheme for your app that would help users find information quickly, but also wouldn't put your users or people around them in danger. If you were creating an app meant for a user's car, you wouldn't want your user to use that app when she's driving, possibly distracting her from the road. Instead, you would want to create an app that prevents dangerous behaviors.

The locations in which users will use your app can also be participatory. In other words, the environments in which users use their smartphones could play a part in the user experience, too. When your users go to a physical location, like a restaurant, their smartphones could recognize it through their GPS features. You could create a "check in" feature that is linked to social media that enables users to let everyone know they are there at the restaurant. When a restaurant sees that they have "checked in," the restaurant would have an opportunity to offer users specific services. So, as you design your app, consider how location and time will impact the use of your app. Likewise, consider how your app can be most effectively used at a particular location and at a particular time.

The Backend: To Template or Not

So far in this chapter, you have been mainly considering the frontend design of your app (the place where your users interact). In conjunction with this, you also need to consider the backend design (more on this in a moment). Newer technologies have made creating an app a lot easier. As with website builders, some app builder programs do not require that you know code in order to create an app. There are plenty of programs in which you can drag and drop elements onto a platform to create your app without having to look at the code on the backend. But, just like when you are developing websites, having a working knowledge of what happens on the backend can help you make smarter decisions that can make the frontend more effective. You may be tempted into using an app template, for example, to save you time and money. But, if those templates can't do what you want them to do, you may need to figure out an alternative solution. Box 14.1 provides a list of resources you can use in order to build your own app.

Box 14.1 App Developer Programs and Resources

If you wish to develop and code your own app, it might be a good idea to begin with developer guidelines. You can find guidelines for two different platforms at the following websites:

- Developer Guidelines for iOS: https://developer.apple.com/design/human-interface-guidelines/ios/overview/themes/
- Developer Guidelines for Android: https://developer.android.com/guide/

iOS platforms rely on the Swift programming language and can be developed in the Xcode development environment.

Android platforms rely on the Java programming language and can be developed in the Android Studio.

Programs like Corona SDK (mainly used to build games) and MIT's App Inventor can help you make an app without having to learn too much programming code. There are also quite a few Adobe programs, like Adobe XD, that can help you create your app, too.

If you prefer a simpler WYSIWYG platform, try searching online for a free app builder. Such builders are easy to use and have drag-and-drop features that require no knowledge of coding.

As you work in a program to build your app, you need to make decisions about what kind of app you are building and the type of architecture it will need in order to work. You may need to figure out how your app will collect data on users, how it will send push notifications to users, how your app will integrate with other programs and apps, and how your app will connect to a server. If you are unsure of any of these things, it would be best to speak with experts who can guide you in the right directions.

Check It Out YouTube: If you are interested in learning more about creating an iOS app, check out the first video in CodeWithChris's series on making an app for beginners. His first lesson, "How to Make an App for Beginners (2018)—Lesson 1," walks you through using Xcode.

Final Thoughts

It may be hard to imagine the future without a smartphone. Perhaps, though, like many technologies do, smartphones will evolve into a technology unlike what we have today. Maybe smartphones will not feature apps in the future but some other thing that millions of people will rely on daily. For the time being, at least, apps do play a major role in our smartphone's operations. So, as you think about creating your own apps, certainly consider the suggestions in this chapter as well as the suggestions for writing in the rest of this book. As you do, contemplate writing's role in the process and how you can use your writing skills to make smart decisions while you create your apps.

Additional Discussion Questions

1. In addition to the ones discussed in this chapter, what are some other positive and negative impacts that mobile devices, particularly smartphones, have on people and environments?

2. Should people use their smartphones longer rather than trade them in or throw them away in a couple of years?
3. In what ways can smartphones help us become better writers?
4. In what ways is writing for a smartphone similar to and different from writing for a website?
5. In what ways have smartphones changed the way our society writes?

Additional Activities

1. Take a Smartphone Break: Put your phone away for a week. Write about your experience in a reflection and share it with your classmates.
2. Top Ten Writing Apps: Create a list of top ten writing apps. Then analyze them to find out what they are capable of. How do they help people write? How do they shape writing? What impacts do such apps have on society? Compare your findings with the findings of your classmates.
3. Smartphone Use: Conduct an observational study in which you find a place that prohibits smartphone use. Reflect on people's behaviors in this place. Are people using their phones anyway? If so, why do you suspect they did so?

Additional Assignments

1. Your Smartphone Usage: Analyze how you use your smartphone throughout one week. Pay close attention to the where, when, what, and how you use your smartphone. Then, write a report that explains what you discovered and how your uses impact yourself and others.
2. Build an App: Working with the suggestions in this book, create a basic app using an app builder. Reflect on this experience in a presentation to your classmates.

Works Cited

ABC7News. "Officer Explains How He Used Mobile phone to Find Woman." *ABC Inc., KGO-TV San Francisco*, 15 October 2014, http://abc7news.com/news/officer-explains-how-he-used-mobile phone-to-find-woman/351163/. Accessed 15 April 2018.

Crabtree, Steve and Julia Burchell. "Do Mobile Phones Make People Happier?" *Gallup*, 14 February 2018, https://news.gallup.com/opinion/gallup/226199/mobile-phones-people-happier.aspx. Accessed 19 June 2018.

GSMA Intelligence. "Definitive Data and Analysis for the Mobile Industry." *GSMA Intelligence*, 2018, www.gsmaintelligence.com/. Accessed 15 April 2018.

Hill, Simon. "How Do People Really Use Apps? We Asked an Expert." *Digital Trends*, 24 March 2018, www.digitaltrends.com/mobile/how-do-people-really-use-apps/. Accessed 21 June 2018.

LaMotte, Sandee. "Smartphone Addiction Could Be Changing Your Brain." *CNN*, 2 December 2017, www.cnn.com/2017/11/30/health/smartphone-addiction-study/index.html. Accessed 19 June 2018.

Lu, Kristine. "Growth in Mobile News Use Driven by Older Adults." *Pew Research Center*, 12 June 2017, www.pewresearch.org/facttank/2017/06/12/growth-in-mobile-news-use-driven-by-older-adults/. Accessed 15 April 2018.

National Highway Traffic Safety Administration. "Distracted Driving." *U.S. Department of Transportation*, 2018, www.nhtsa.gov/risky-driving/distracted-driving#16986. Accessed 19 April 2018.

Sharman, Jon and Dinesh Dubey. "Man 'Trying to Take Selfie' Dies After Being Mauled by Bear." *Independent*, 5 May 2018, www.independent.co.uk/news/world/asia/man-bear-selfie-video-mauled-death-selfies-india-odisha-asia-a8335806.html. Accessed 21 June 2018.

Verhulsdonck, Gustav. "From Cultural Markers to Global Mobile: Using Interaction Design for Composing Mobile Designs in Global Contexts." *Computers and Composition*, 38, 2015, pp. 140–150.

Worland, Justine. "Why People Text and Drive Even When They Know It's Dangerous." *Time*, 6 November 2014. http://time.com/3561413/texting-driving-dangerous/. Accessed 4 April 2019.

PART 5 READING

Thank You for Letting Me Share

Michelle R. Gould

Michelle R. Gould writes and manages several popular Facebook pages as well as belongs to several groups of principled page owners who provide education and support for page owners who are just starting out in social media management. From years of experience, she has learned how to write and share ethically online. Her hope is that by reading her story, users and creators of social media content will be more respectful of other people's work by sharing it rather than uploading it. The story was originally published online on the *Wellness Universe* blog as *Public Access Does Not Mean Public Domain* in 2015 and has been adapted for this book.

I didn't know squat about "Netiquette" when I opened my first Facebook Page. I thought sharing meant saving an image I admired, uploading it to my Facebook Page, and tagging it with a shout-out to the Page where I found it. I didn't realize that those acts had negative ramifications. I didn't realize that I should have used the share button instead. The act of "uploading" as I'm using it here means seeing a poster, meme, or image on someone else's Page, saving it to your own computer or mobile device by downloading it, and then uploading that same poster, meme, or image to your own media account whether that be on Instagram, Twitter, or Facebook, as in my case. Your account, the one that you uploaded someone else's work to, receives "credit" for that person's work. On the internet, credit translates to exposure. Exposure generates metrics: analytics detailing the number of likes, comments, and shares received for specific content. These metrics indicate a post's popularity which the Facebook algorithm interprets as engagement. The more engagement there is for a Page's post, the more likely the algorithm will favor that Page in a news feed and suggest it to potential fans.

When I started managing Facebook Pages, I downloaded posters, memes, and images to use as my own and thought, "Well, if someone makes it public, it belongs to the public." However, copyright law doesn't support this position. Nor does Facebook which recognizes copyright laws regarding intellectual property. When a picture, poster, or wording of any idea is expressed in visual form, it attains copyright status. Posting someone else's online work without the URL that links it to the creator's Page is unethical and illegal. Facebook's Help Page is clear: "Generally, copyright does not protect facts and ideas, but it may protect the original words or images that express that idea . . . If you're not certain that you are legally authorized to use the content, do not upload it to Facebook"

(Help Center).

The more research I did on copyright law, social media, and netiquette, the more I realized my own practices had to change. Today, I author three Facebook Pages that are followed by 50K, 23K, and 15K respectively. Because of my success, other Page owners often ask that I share their Page links or their posters, memes, or images, hoping that my audiences will generate traffic to their Pages. The problem is, though, that I often find that "their" posters, memes, or images aren't theirs, but in fact, were taken from the work of other people.

Practicing Netiquette

One way to ensure that you don't violate copyright is to practice netiquette. Netiquette is exactly what it sounds like: internet etiquette. It's about exercising good manners in your online behaviors and communications (Arouri and Hamaidi 85). To learn more about the sort of overall manners you might need on the internet, see the links in Reading Box 5.1. For this article, I am concerned about an area of netiquette that receives less coverage than it deserves: respect for intellectual property. This involves accurately crediting sources, obtaining permission to use material when required by law, and only using what you're legally allowed to use in ways that won't violate someone else's rights.

Box 5.1 More About Netiquette

www.auburn.edu/citizenship/netiquette.html
www.education.com/reference/article/netiquette-rules-behavior-internet/
www.bbc.co.uk/webwise/guides/about-netiquette
www.albion.com/netiquette/corerules.html
https://onlinelearning.rutgers.edu/faq/netiquette
www.education.vic.gov.au/Documents/about/programs/bullystoppers/afnetiquette.pdf
http://online-journals.org/index.php/i-jet/article/view/6424
www.iste.org/docs/excerpts/digci2-excerpt.pdf

You might wonder why this component of netiquette has been overlooked. Unfortunately, popularity can sometimes breed carelessness. There's a reason posters, memes, and images gain viral exposure. When we see an image we can relate to, we react emotionally; we claim it as ours, giving little thought to who created it or who it belongs to. As the saying goes, we want what we want when we want it. Unfortunately, there's no overarching, effective governing body that polices intellectual property theft on social media. Each platform (Facebook, Twitter, Instagram, etc.) has a policy in place, but it's been my experience that misappropriation is so widespread that enforcement is slow, sparse, and inconsistent.

Regulation of intellectual property may prove to be one of the next decade's hot-button topics. So, if we want to be ethical digital citizens, we have to be responsible for our actions (Ribble 31) and for respecting the rights of others (Ribble 35). In today's digital world, it is foreseeable that some aspect of your career will involve writing for or managing social media accounts, perhaps for your business or employer. In some work settings, you may be tempted to compromise your ethics in favor of expedience or popularity. Writer and journalist Julie Schwietert Collazo advises that you should avoid publications that make adjustments to their work to improve "clickability" while sacrificing credibility. Even if you don't plan to be a writer, her words are important to keep in mind as many careers rely on social media in one way or another. As a responsible digital citizen, you should have more than a passing familiarity with netiquette. It should be your standard.

Accountability is of constant concern in an environment that allows expansive participation from a diverse population. Internet accessibility has expanded quickly, faster than a system of digital ethics could be developed and imposed. In addition, the growth of social media has increased global availability of multimedia materials (Demiray 271), giving way to the creation of technologies that can enable people to use other's work both ethically and unethically. As George Albert Gladney and Matthew C. Ehrlich have pointed out, the novelty and availability of image manipulation technologies, for instance, have tempted photojournalists and editors into distorting many magazine images or advertisements (Gladney and Ehrlich 496–498). This proliferation of altered images may have had a role in influencing the average internet user's widespread acceptance of unethical media judgment and behavior.

What Does It Mean to Share?

When you share a poster, meme, or image using the share button in Facebook, your share links back to the Facebook Page that created the original poster, meme, or image. The metrics are credited to that original Page, not yours. On any social media platform, whether you have a personal or business account, each of your posts has its own unique link called a URL (Uniform Resource Locator), whether it's an image, video, or text. When a poster, meme, or image is saved and uploaded to a new Page instead of being shared via the share button, this generates a new URL that links only to the new Page instead of to the Page that created it. Simply tagging the original Page does not negate this process. The tag may link back to the original Page, but the poster, meme, or image does not. If the uploaded poster, meme, or image performs well, it increases the visibility of the Page that stole it rather than the person who created it.

In other words, Facebook supplies Page owners with the aforementioned metrics in the *Insights* tab. When you upload someone else's poster, meme, or image and post it as your own, it counts toward *your* Page engagement, robbing the content creator of exposure. If a post gets shared thousands of times after being uploaded to your Page, the Facebook algorithm responds by increasing your visibility rather than the artist's visibility. Unfortunately, some very large Facebook Pages build their audiences entirely on content they steal from other Pages, ignoring Facebook terms of service and copyright law.

The Creator's Page Name Is on the Poster, Meme, or Image. Isn't That Good Enough?

Nope. Not when you get the credit instead of the person who did the work. A disclaimer in your "About" section doesn't let you off the hook, either. If you didn't create it, it doesn't belong to you. The © symbol doesn't have to be evident. According to the U.S. Copyright Office, notice of copyright is optional and goes into effect upon publication. Publication occurs when an original work is distributed to the public, by sale, loan, or display. Think of it this way: Imagine if you spent months writing a book. You finally publish it online and are excited to connect with readers. Imagine instead that someone downloads your book, makes a few design changes to your cover, then uploads that book to their Page, and builds a following with it. That person gets all the credit for your work instead of you. Sounds unfair, right? That's what happens when you build an online social media following by using someone's else work without permission.

You might think of the difference between sharing and uploading as a key distinction between curating and creating (Babovic 143). We share content we've curated from others. We upload content we've created ourselves. There's not a Page owner on Facebook who objects to sharing. Unfortunately, in their zeal to build a following, fellow social media managers are some of the worst offenders, hiding behind the popular notion that everything we see on the internet is free. Contrary to public opinion, free access does not mean free use. That's why there's a share button, and it takes a lot less time and effort to use it than it does to upload the work someone else spent hours on in order to build an audience on someone else's efforts. There's a responsibility that comes with managing a public Page. Not educating yourself about social media copyright policies, copyright law, and netiquette isn't an excuse for stealing. It's analogous to bootlegging CDs and saying it's okay as long as you tell people who the artist is. In doing so, you've robbed the artist of their livelihood and decreased the value of their work.

Let's Talk Terminology: Debunking Common Misconceptions

Another way to understanding the difference between sharing and uploading work is to think about the term "free." I have seen digital media workers use this term in three contexts that contribute to the confusion: access, cost, and use.

1. **Free access.** Just because it's easy to find and easy to download doesn't mean it's free to use. Take Google Images, for example. Many people working on the internet are under the impression that Google Images is a free image source. It's not. It's a free *catalog*. Think of it the same way you'd think of a library—you can't just take a book off the shelf and walk out with it. If you left-click on the images instead of right-clicking to save, you'll see a copyright notice on almost every image in their repository. Open access literally means just that—access is open to anyone with an internet connection. Depending on how you want to use what you've accessed, you may have to pay for it. Creative artists have the same right to be compensated for their efforts as any professionals. This decision is at the discretion of the creator or publisher. For example, some peer-reviewed open access journals charge a publication fee to recoup costs, though the majority do not (Suber).
2. **Free cost**. Just because you have free access to a website, be it a stock photo website or a photographer's website, that doesn't mean you have the right to use their work without paying for it. That's someone's intellectual property. Someone spent time and money on creating that artwork, and probably invested time and money in training to learn how to design it as well. They have a right to expect credit and payment for their work the same way you expect a paycheck for yours. Changing it in some way doesn't necessarily entitle you to use it, either (see later in this chapter on fair use).
3. **Free use**. Just because social media sites are free to use, that doesn't mean you have the right to save any image you like and use it for your own purposes. Repackaging someone else's artwork with your own flair may seem derivative enough to claim it as yours, but you need the original artist's permission to do so if you want to publish it. There's a public perception that assumes anything on a social media site is "in the public domain." In fact, social media sites have copyright policies built into their terms of service that prohibit the theft of posters, memes, and images. That's why there's a share button. Another misconception is that the copyright symbol is required to establish copyright ownership. The truth is, as soon as a work is published where others can see it, it is copyrighted. The U.S. Copyright Office protects "original works of authorship fixed in any tangible medium of expression" but does not protect ideas, concepts, or processes (Section 102). According to the U.S. Copyright Office's compendium on what is and isn't eligible for copyright, a work cannot be copyrighted once its copyright has expired, and once it is in the public domain (32).

Public Domain is an often-misunderstood term. "Public Domain" simply means that the material is not restricted by copyright and is available for personal or commercial use by the public at no cost. It does not mean that attribution is not required. Unless specifically stated otherwise, sources must be credited (University of Chicago). The same is true of work licensed under Creative Commons open licenses. "Open" does not dismiss the need for attribution. The only images that do not need to be credited and can be used freely and altered freely are images with Creative Commons Zero licensing.

Similar rules apply to textual content. The term that is often bandied about as an excuse for reprinting someone else's words is "fair use." It's important to have a clear understanding of what delineates fair use. According to the U.S. Copyright Office, fair use is permissible without copyright infringement "for purposes such as criticism, comment, news reporting, teaching (including multiple copies for classroom use), scholarship, or research" upon consideration of these four factors:

1. the purpose and character of the use, including whether such use is of a commercial nature or is for nonprofit educational purposes;
2. the nature of the copyrighted work;
3. the amount and substantiality of the portion used in relation to the copyrighted work as a whole; and
4. the effect of the use upon the potential market for or value of the copyrighted work.

These four factors are weighted together but may not all be weighted equally. In other words, meeting some criteria does not necessarily establish the basis for fair use. Determinations of fair use are contextual and require a balanced test of all four factors. You can use short quotes on your posters, memes, or images under fair use in most cases. It is the *expression* of the information or ideas that is copyrighted. We've heard it said that there's probably no such thing as an original idea at this point in history. However, it is the way ideas are presented that is proprietary.

For more detailed information on fair use, see Reading Box 5.2. While in this article I am strictly speaking about U.S. copyright and fair use practices, you should follow the copyright laws in the country the artwork was created. In other words, if an artwork was created in the U.K., for instance, you would follow the U.K. laws on copyright. Each country, too, has its own versions of fair use. In the U.K., their version is called fair dealing.

Box 5.2 Interpreting Fair Use

www.copyright.gov/title17/92chap1.html#107
www.copyright.gov/fls/fl102.html
https://fairuse.stanford.edu/overview/fair-use/what-is-fair-use/
https://copyright.columbia.edu/basics/fair-use.html
www.lib.purdue.edu/uco/CopyrightBasics/fair_use.html
https://guides.library.yale.edu/c.php?g=295868&p=6534485
https://creativecommons.org/share-your-work/public-domain/cc0/

In addition, most "free" stock photo sites require that you credit all contributors. For example, if you use a photo of a statue by Jane Smith that was taken by Joe Baker, and attribution is required, you must *always* credit both Jane and Joe when you distribute this photo. As well, you're supposed to keep a log of any changes you make to the original work, and a record of the original source code of the picture, so it can be traced. If the words *license, author, property, release, model, acknowledgement, requirement, attribute, credits, creative, editorial,* or *use* appear anywhere on the screen, you can't use the picture freely. Reputable "free" stock photo sites charge for most pics, from $0.19 to hundreds of dollars *per photo*, though some sites let you download *one* free photo per week in the hopes that you'll tire of waiting and buy sooner.

Are You Part of the Problem?

This is where Page followers come in. Yes, it is thrilling to Page owners when individual social media users download their work because it speaks to them. But when you upload that work to other Pages, those Pages appropriate and repost them as their own, with or without a Page name on them. When you download someone else's poster, meme, or image to your personal timeline without sharing it, your post doesn't link back to the Page that created it. This is important because the metrics we see on each post tell Page owners what works and what doesn't. We can't please you if we don't know you've engaged with our work. I understand wanting to share something that helped you. Again, using the share button takes a lot less time and effort than downloading and protects the integrity of the work. One day you may be a Page owner of a major social media Page or site and it will mean a lot to you to know that your work can reach your audience. When unscrupulous social media users diminish its value by misappropriating it, that's less likely to happen.

What You Can Do?

I don't assume I'm entitled to the work of the teachers, cashiers, artisans, nurses, utility workers, and scientists I encounter in my life experiences just because I need their skills. I recognize their expertise, and I pay for it. While Facebook Pages are free, Page owners should manage them ethically. This sentiment extends to all social media platforms such as Instagram, Twitter, and Snapchat. When they don't, or when we see others using someone else's work unfairly, we should speak out. Without publicizing the problem, we can't affect change. Many frustrated artists have spoken out. Some strong articles have been published on the subject of recognizing copyrights on the internet. Jonna Ivin, for instance, reported the frustrations of plus-size model Tess Holliday whose images were used without permission to promote an app that lets users create skinny images of themselves. In a furious Instagram rant, Holliday took a stand by calling out the platform for failing to regulate the app's advertisement.

In 2014, the administrator of a large Facebook Group saved one of my posters and attempted to pass it off as his work. The poster featured a poem I'd found in a collection that I then paired with a stock photo. I credited the poem's author and provided the title and ISBN number for the book. The Group administrator cropped off my Page name and replaced it with his Group name. He also covered the author's name with a colored box that matched the background image, making it appear as if the poem had no author. The group members loved it and it was shared hundreds of times. But, I felt horrible because I had done the work. To me, calling out someone who steals someone else's work isn't about ego. It's about respect. Would you pirate a Beyoncé album, hand it to people and say, "Follow my work"? That's what it looks like when a Page owner with an album full of stolen posters sends me a message that says, "Share my Page."

To me, it's also about ethics. There's been a lot of coverage about fake news on social media since Facebook's admission that it was an unwitting but responsible participant in election tampering and privacy violations (Zuckerberg). As an audience, we've reacted with a demand for accuracy. In a sense, uploading someone else's artwork instead of sharing it promotes the inaccurate dissemination of information because you've led the audience to believe you created it.

Whether you're someone whose job will require them to manage a social media account, or you're just a regular social media user with no plans to work in social media as a career, or you're experienced at managing a Page, or you're a student learning about writing for technologies, I hope my story will inspire you to be a responsible digital citizen. As a writer and designer, I'm disappointed to see people build reputations on stolen work. I attract followers to my Pages with quality content that I created. Free access to my Pages ≠ free usage of my work. Uploading posters, memes, or images takes effort, but hitting the share button takes seconds and means the original creators get the credit they deserve.

Thank you for letting me share.

Works Cited

Arouri, Y. M. and Hamaidi, D. A. "Undergraduate Students' Perspectives of the Extent of Practicing Netiquettes in a Jordanian Southern University," *International Journal of Emerging Technologies in Learning*, vol. 12, no. 3, 2017, pp. 84–97.

Babovic, Mihajlo. "The Emperor's New Digital Clothes: The Illusion of Copyright Rights in Social Media," *Cybaris: An Intellectual Property Law Review*, vol. 6, no. 1, Spring 2015, pp. 138–192.

Collazo, Julie Schwietert. "How to Stay True to Your Journalism Ethics in the World of Content Marketing," *The Freelancer by Contently*, 22 May 2018, https://contently.net/2018/05/22/trends/journalism-ethics-in-content-marketing/. Accessed 8 May 2018.

Creative Commons. "CC0," *Creative Commons*, n.d., https://creativecommons.org/share-your-work/public-domain/cc0/. Accessed 8 May 2018.

Demiray, Ugur. "Functions and Roles of Scaffolding and Meta-Communication in Distance Education for Distance Learning Materials," *Proceedings of the 2016 International*

Conference on Information Communication Technologies in Education, 2016, pp. 270–276, www.icicte.org/Papers_ICICTE2016/7.3%20151_Demiray%20ed.pdf. Accessed 8 May 2018.

Gladney, George Albert and Matthew C. Ehrlich. "Cross-Media Response to Digital Manipulation of Still and Moving Images," Journal of Broadcasting & Electronic Media, vol. 40, no. 4, 1996, pp. 496–508.

Help Center. "Copyright," Facebook, 2019, www.facebook.com/help/1020633957973118/. Accessed 1 April 2019.

Ivin, Jonna. "Plus Size Model Tess Holiday Slams App for Stealing Her Pictures and Slimming Them Down," Guacamoley! Get Your Scoop, n.d., www.guacamoley.com/the-scoop/2018/05/26/aAEaN/plus-size-model-tess-holiday-slams-app. Accessed 28 May 2018.

Ribble, Mike. Digital Citizenship in Schools: Nine Elements All Students Should Know. 2nd Edition. Eugene, OR and Arlington, VA: International Society for Technology in Education, 2011.

Suber, Peter. "Open Access: Six Myths Put to Rest," The Guardian, 21 October 2013, www.theguardian.com/higher-education-network/blog/2013/oct/21/open-access-myths-peter-suber-harvard. Accessed 23 May 2018.

@tessholliday. "Pipcamera Time," Instagram, 23 May 2018, www.instagram.com/p/BjHIQNXh3vj/?taken-by=tessholliday.

The University of Chicago. "3.35: Crediting Material in the Public Domain," in Chicago Manual of Style. 17th Edition. Chicago: University of Chicago Press, 2017.

U.S. Copyright Office. "Chapter 1: Subject Matter and Scope of Copyright," Copyright.gov, n.d., www.copyright.gov/title17/92chap1.html#102. Accessed 8 May 2018.

———. "Copyrightable Authorship," The Compendium of U.S. Copyright Office Practices: Chapter 300, 29 September 2017, www.copyright.gov/comp3/chap300/ch300-copyrightable-authorship.pdf. Accessed 8 May 2018.

Zuckerberg, Mark. "Hard Questions: Q&A with Mark Zuckerberg on Protecting People's Information," Facebook, 4 April 2018, https://newsroom.Facebook.com/news/2018/04/hard-questions-protecting-peoples-information/. Accessed 28 May 2018.

Reading Questions for "Thank You for Letting Me Share" by Michelle R. Gould

1. What is netiquette, and what are some ways to practice it?
2. Why is it important to use the share button instead of saving and uploading an image from someone else's social media page?
3. What are the differences in actions between curating and creating?
4. What are the differences between free access, free cost, and free use?

PART 6

Technology Is Embodied

While technologies are situated within particular locations and as a result are connected in more ways than one to people, places, and systems, it is important to remember that they do not operate on their own. Their very existence is reliant upon human bodies and what those human bodies are and are not capable of. So, when we think of technologies, like writing, we must think about ourselves and our bodily relationships with them. As Nye reminds us, "technologies are not just objects but also the skills needed to use them," and that when our bodies interact with technologies, when we use them, we develop a feel for them (4). Technologies are always bodily experiences, and in this final part of the book, you will examine the various ways your body shapes and is shaped by them. In particular, you should consider the many modes that we write with as each, with the help of technologies, require certain bodily experiences.

Moreover, technologies represent the ideas of those that create and use them. They represent the cultures and histories of people who create and use them, too. They also represent what can and cannot happen in our world. In this final part, you will think more about how our bodies use modes and technologies to write. Yet, it is equally important to consider how the embodiment of our ideas in technology shapes our world and our writing. Some might equate technology as the embodiment of progress, of success, of evolution. While others might think the opposite, that technology embodies exclusivity, an otherness that is not accepted by society, that it represents what some bodies are not capable of.

Therefore, as you read this final part, you must not lose sight of what such embodiments of technology mean to all people. Not all people can and do use technologies in the same ways. Likewise, what technologies mean to people varies. In one culture, technology might embody one thing, and in another, something else. In thinking rhetorically, we can see that cultural, social, economic, political, and historical understandings of technologies influence what, how, why, and with whom we write. More than anything, though, technological embodiment speaks to how we live our lives. How do we operate in this world? How do we communicate? How do we learn? How do technologies make our bodies, and how do our bodies make our technologies?

Technology Is Embodied

Key Questions _____

1. How is technology embodied?
2. How do our bodies shape technology and writing?
3. How do technologies shape our bodies?

Key Terms _____

Chapter 15

1. physical actions
2. social actions
3. cognitive actions
4. technological actions
5. past actions
6. voice-to-text
7. sound
8. rhythm
9. feelings
10. emotions
11. podcasts
12. Audacity
13. destructive editing
14. real-time editing
15. TED

Chapter 16

1. resolution
2. dpi
3. raster graphic
4. vector graphic
5. rule of thirds
6. power points/crash points
7. focal point
8. angle
9. timing
10. signposting
11. trail guide

CHAPTER 15

Feel, Hear, and Speak

Contents

Embodied Actions 358
Textures in a Technological World 361
Sound in a Technological World 363
Analyzing Sound: Music and Emotions 365
Suggestions for Creating Podcasts 368
Creating Sound: Public Speaking. 373
Final Thoughts 375

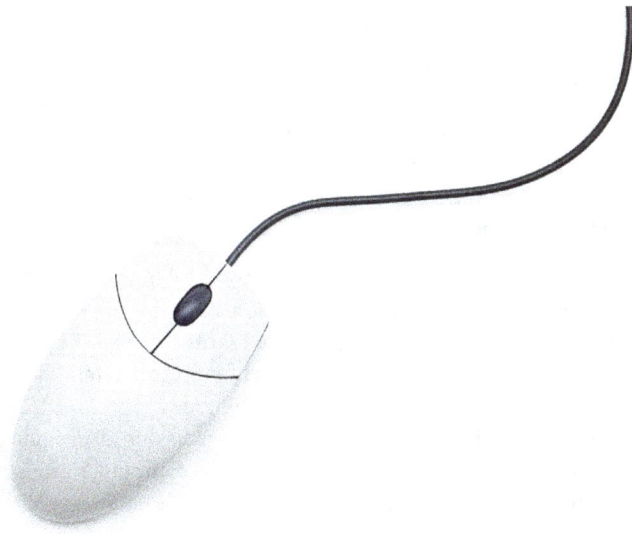

IMAGE 15.1 swinner / Shutterstock

Embodied Actions

Understanding technology as being embodied requires us to examine the various parts that make up a technology and how those parts are designed and shaped based on bodily experiences with them. If you were to take apart the basic computer mouse, like the one featured in Image 15.1, you would see that it is made up of the following parts:

1. a left button that is linked to the pointer/cursor that appears on your screen
2. a right button that when clicked, brings up a menu on your screen
3. a wheel between these buttons to aid users in scrolling
4. a trackball or sensor to detect movement of the mouse on a surface
5. a USB cable to connect to the computer
6. wires that transfer the signals

Together, these parts create a system. Earlier in the book, you learned that systems consist of parts working together and that systems involve people and places, and the policies, rules, and regulations that govern them. Systems also include the movements we perform with our bodies. In this example of a mouse, a system enables the mouse to turn our hand motions into signals that appear on and control our computer's interface. Using the mouse, we have the ability to click on icons, open and close files, move our cursor, highlight text, and so forth. Our hand, our wrist, our eyes, our brain, and our body all perform these actions to make the mouse work.

Remember what Nye said: "Technologies are not just objects but also the skills needed to use them . . . To know such a tool it is not enough merely to look at it" (4). The actions we take with the mouse are many and are learned over time through our bodies. There are the physical actions. We learn to grip the mouse based on our experiences with similarly shaped objects, understanding the mouse's shape, and its contours. We learn by getting a feel for how the mouse is cradled in our hand as it glides across a surface, understanding just how fast and how far we should move our hand. We learn this in conjunction with using our eyes to follow the cursor on our computer's screen while our brain makes the connections between the actions.

In addition, there are the social actions. We learn by watching other bodies use the mouse in particular contexts to perform particular tasks. There are the cognitive actions. We learn by drawing on past bodily experiences that have been stored in our memory. We then think through the present situation and determine how we want to use the mouse for the task at hand. There are the technological actions, too. The mouse's parts (the trackball, the wires, and the sensors) are all designed with our bodies in mind so that they may work together with the computer's processing actions to translate the movements onto the screen. Finally, there are the past actions that led up to the very moment we use the mouse. Those past actions could include the prototyping of the mouse (testing it out with bodies), the manufacturing of the mouse (bodies working to produce the technology), the selling of the mouse (bodies profiting), and so on.

In this chapter, we will consider the many bodily actions we and others take when writing and operating technologies and the implications such actions have on ourselves and others. Scholar Christina Haas's words best explain why a focus on the body is important in order to understand how writers use their bodies. She contends that

> Writers use their bodies, and the materials available to their bodies via the material world, to both create and to interact with textual artifacts. Writers' bodily movements and interactions are evident in the conduct of everyday literacy activities: Writers pick up and chew on pencils, they rest their hands on keyboards, they move closer to their texts in some circumstances, push back from them in others; readers hunch over manuscripts with pens, stretch out with books under trees, move through on-line texts by pushing keys or clicking buttons.
>
> (Haas 226)

Our bodies shape technology, and our bodies are also shaped by technology, as Haas's words demonstrate. Over time, our ability to use a mouse improves (perhaps the repetitive bodily movements get smoother each time), so much so that we almost ignore the fact that we are using the mouse when we use it. How often do you think about using your mouse as you are using your mouse? How often do you think of your hand as you are using your hand to control the mouse? Perhaps, the mouse becomes an extension of our hand, and therefore our body, making it feel natural to move it.

Today, there are a lot of variations of the computer mouse from the wireless to the flexible. People choose which computer mouse to use based on a variety of reasons: comfort, convenience, speed, affordability, access, and the actions they wish to perform. All of these options weren't always available, though. As you have learned, technology evolves over time, shaped by users who use it for different purposes in different contexts. The computer mouse is no different; it has evolved over time, too, and this evolution is tied to our bodily actions.

While Douglas Engelbart is credited as having invented the computer mouse in 1968, his invention was a combination of the innovation, improvement, and modification of previous technologies, all too based on bodily actions. In 1968, computers were not ubiquitous; students didn't have a desktop computer at home or in their dorm room. As computers became smaller, more affordable, more dynamic, a means for bodies to access and interact with the computer became apparent. A mouse provided one such means.

But, the mouse is but one technology in a long line of technologies that our bodies now use to interact with a computer. Think about the stylus pen and its likeness to an ink pen; think about how it operates in both similar and different ways as a mouse, enabling us to perform a number of tasks on a screen. Think about voice and touch technologies that allow us to use our voice or finger on a screen to make things happen. In part, those technologies enable us to perform actions that are similar to that of a mouse. When given a hyperlink button on a website, for instance, we can press it by tapping the mouse, we can press it by tapping the stylus pen, or we can press it by tapping our finger. We can also use voice commands to activate the button, too.

Activity: Actions and the Design of Technology

Choose a specific writing technology in your classroom, such as a mouse. Think rhetorically about how it is constructed, what purposes it was constructed for, what audiences it was constructed for, what contexts it was constructed for, and so forth. Then, think about the actions you can perform with the technology.

- How are these actions learned?
- What are the impacts of these actions?
- Who might not be able to perform such actions?
- How do these actions shape your writing?

Finally, think about how the writing technology shapes your body. Write a reflection on your findings and share with your classmates.

Likewise, the computer mouse, like other technologies, has given us possibilities to imagine more uses, more ways of doing things with our computers. However, while over time, the mouse has evolved, has changed shape with the adding and deleting of features to account for the diversity of bodies, such a technology, like many technologies, has also excluded some bodies. Not everyone has the physical or mental capability to use a mouse. As a result, not everyone has the same experiences with such a technology. To experience a computer, someone who cannot use a mouse must use some other means. That some other means may present a number of challenges. That some other means might identify a body as being different from other bodies. That some other means might make it more difficult to access certain programs, features, and uses of the computer, limiting that person's understanding, and thus shaping their bodily experiences in different ways.

Different bodily experiences with technology mean different bodily understandings. When we write, we cannot assume that everyone will access our writing through the same means and therefore have the same understandings of our writing. We cannot assume everyone develops their writing using the same technology in the same ways either.

Take a moment now and do this experiment: Write the same paragraph three times, only each time use a different technology, say a crayon on a piece of paper, a voice memo on a mobile device, and a word processing program on a computer. Think about the physical nature of these technologies and the actions they involve. Think about how you use your body as you perform the movements required. Compare your experiences with each of the technologies. How are they different in terms of bodily movements? How might each change the way we understand such writing? Now imagine if you went your whole life writing with only one of these technologies. In what ways would this limit your ability to write as well as your understanding of the world?

Technologies very much shape our bodies. To use a computer mouse, one must hold the arm at the side of the body with a hand out front. The elbow must be at an angle, the wrist in a flexed upward position, and fingers curled around it. As we use it to write, our brains make specific connections between our movements and our bodily positions, connections not created when using other technologies.

Yet, our bodies are not passive consumers of technology. We do have some agency in the shaping of technology with our bodies. And, in the remainder of this chapter, you will think more about the different bodily actions you perform when writing in multiple modes using technologies. Remember, modes are actions, after all. For starters, our senses (sight, smell, hearing, taste, and touch) provide one lens for which to think about such actions as they highlight what bodies are and are not capable of doing.

Textures in a Technological World

As mentioned earlier, the computer mouse is operated in part by our sense of touch in conjunction with our other senses. We develop a feel for the mouse based on our sense of touch but also our sense of sight (seeing the pointer on the screen) and hearing (the click sound we hear when we press the mouse and the scrolling sound we hear when we move the mouse). When we develop a feel for the mouse, the material textures of a mouse play an important role, too. The mouse's outer surfaces are smooth and rounded, helping us to grip it. Our body reads these textures in ways that help our abilities to use such technology. A mouse that is not smooth and rounded would perhaps not be comfortable. Imagine using a mouse that was designed with an uncomfortable rough texture. We would probably notice the mouse each time we used it.

> ### Did You Know? Touch Screens
>
> Today, we don't have to solely rely on a mouse to interact with a computer. Indeed, in order to operate many of the digital technologies that we use, such as our mobile phones, our computers, and our tablets, we can rely on other means such as the use of touch-screen technology. That is, in order for us to interact with the interfaces of such digital technologies, we can touch our fingers or a stylus to the devices' screens

(in other words, a responsive glass panel) and perform various actions. We may not realize it, but touch screens have been around for some time now, having been invented in the 1960s and developed further in the decades to come for such things as air traffic control displays, computers, gaming, Palm Pilots, and ATMs. Modern touch screens work by registering our touch. Namely, when we press our fingers or our stylus pens to the surface of the screen, that touch alters the physical state of the screen which the device recognizes. When this happens, the device records the location of that touch and that location is translated into a command for the device to carry out. When, for example, we read a digital book and in doing so, we press a finger to the right side of the screen and then move that finger across the screen to the left, the device recognizes the altered state of the screen, senses the locations of our touch, and knows to turn a page.

Our writing and the texts we produce are also textured, inviting or inhibiting the bodies we write for. Those textures are created through materials. That is, they are produced by the materials we use in writing. As a writer, your choices in textures and thus materials do matter. As an example, think about the writing of a resume. When you write a resume, you are writing to obtain a job, and you are writing to impress and persuade someone into hiring you for that job. While you may fill out online applications, and while you may attach a digital copy of your resume to it when applying, the time still may come when you will need a physical printed copy of your resume (say for an in-person interview, job fair, or networking event). If you were to give a printed copy of your resume to that someone you wish would hire you, most likely you would want to do so on a thicker and heavier (perhaps 24 or 32 lbs.) paper than the kind of thin, ordinary paper you get from most copy machines. Not all paper is weighted the same, and not all paper has the same texture as it is made of different materials. A thicker and heavier paper made out of linen and cotton, for example, has an interwoven texture that feels durable, giving the impression of strength. Someone who feels a resume printed on such paper may understand your ethos as being strong.

Moreover, we perceive texture not just through our sense of touch. Texture is also known through other senses. We can see a rough texture. We can say that a sound has a rough texture, too. Textures do indeed convey messages. In the resume example, the texture of a thicker and heavier paper may convey the message that the person applying for the job is professional, is courteous, and takes the time to ensure things are done right. Textures also convey meanings based on the very materials they are made of. If we return to the example in Chapter 3 of Nikki Gomez choosing her materials for her informational table at the local community fair, we can see that her choice in natural materials for her messages about the park helped convey meaning. She felt choosing digital materials would not be as effective as choosing more natural materials. People who stopped by her table could feel the handmade recycled materials and their textures.

Activity: Textures

Investigate a texture in the world and report your findings to the rest of the class. As you conduct your investigation, consider the following questions:

- Where and how is this texture used?
- By whom is it used?
- What is its history, its politics, etc.?
- What messages does the texture convey in a particular culture?
- How are these manufactured?
- What technologies are needed to produce them?
- How are these textures used to write?

Sound in a Technological World

Examining the modes of sound (in conjunction with other modes) can provide yet another way to understand the complexity of writing in a technological world. To say that sound belongs in a writing classroom is not a novel idea. A look back at history shows that many cultures used sound in all facets of education. In some cultures, for instance, integrating oratory, speeches, declamations, and music alongside or in lieu of the creation of handwritten texts was an important part of the curriculum.

Take a moment and think about the sounds you hear, feel, and create daily. Think about the technologies you use to listen to, feel, and create them, from the websites you visit to the apps you use on your smartphone. Today there are a number of ways people can create and share texts that contain sound. Voice-to-text technologies, for instance, can help us write as they translate what we say verbally into a written text. You may have used your phone's voice technology to write a text or email or message to yourself or someone else. Other technologies, like the Amazon Echo, are mainly operated via voice. People can use their voices to do a number of things besides translate speech or talk with Alexa. They can order products, turn on the news, pay for music, and find answers to questions they may have. According to a recent Pew Research Center survey, "Voice-controlled digital assistants are being incorporated into a wide range of consumer products, and nearly half of U.S. adults (46%) say they now use these applications to interact with smartphones and other devices" (Olmstead).

Before we consider specific types of sounds and how to create them, let's first think about what sound is. To think of sound only in terms of what we physically hear through our ears would be a naïve way to understand sound as sound is much more as the examples that follow will demonstrate. Sound is multimodal. It involves physical vibrations that we understand not just with our ears, but with our entire bodies. We rely on several actions to understand it. There is the feeling of the vibrations, the emotions that they invoke, the brain connections we make, and our awareness of what and where this sound is in relationship to our world.

Technology Is Embodied

Cartoon 1. jesadaphorn / iStock   Cartoon 2. nadia_bormotova / iStock

In the two cartoons shown in Images 15.2 and 15.3, the physical energy, the vibrations that produce sounds, do not exist when we read these cartoons. That is, those vibrations are not moving through the air. They don't travel to our ears. So, when we read the cartoons, we might not actually hear the sounds of clapping, and we might not hear the word "Yes" being spoken with our ears. However, we do hear these sounds nonetheless. As we read these images, we hear the sounds within our minds, sounds triggered by our reading of moving hands in the first cartoon and a word bubble in the second. We perceive these sounds, and we do so because we have learned these sounds through similar past bodily experiences. Because we perceive these sounds, we ascribe meaning to them. We believe that the man clapping is satisfied, impressed even. In our past experiences, when we heard hand clapping, that clapping occurred during a particular context, one in which people were satisfied and impressed. We believe the man saying "Yes" is also happy as past experiences have led us to realize an exclamation accompanied with the word "Yes," a thumbs up, and a smile equates happiness.

The technologies that were used to create these cartoons play a role in our understanding of their meanings as well. The organization and positioning of lines, color, space, and so forth help us to recognize that we are looking at people who are performing specific actions that produce specific sounds. To understand sound in these cartoons, we need to know what a cartoon is and we need to perform actions to help us understand them, like reading the lines, the color, and the space with our eyes and interpreting them with our brains.

Now, take another moment and compare these cartoons to the actual listening of hands clapping and a person speaking "Yes!" Have someone clap and have someone say the word "Yes!" out loud as you listen. How are these experiences of sound similar or different to your experiences reading the cartoons?

Activity: Radio Station

Visit a radio station or recording studio. Explore the various ways in which people use these to produce sounds. Interview those who produce sounds, from DJs to singers to producers. As you do, think about how such people use sounds to write. Write up your observations and report your findings to your class. Then, discuss how you can use what you learned from this activity to write with sounds in your own texts.

Analyzing Sound: Music and Emotions

On an everyday basis, we encounter a variety of sounds. Sounds provided through music can serve as a good example of how we can write sounds with our bodies. In addition to telling stories, music gives us a way to see bodies in motion as well. In writing and listening to music, our bodies perform actions: we create emotions that produce feelings, we move our bodies to rhythms and beats, we visualize a story based on lyrics, and so on. To help us think about what it means to create sound through music, let's look more closely at one particular bodily action, the production of emotions. The role of emotions in writing and listening to music is an important one, as it makes people feel and connect their bodies to worldly and spiritual experiences. Throughout history, music has been a prominent part of societies around the world. Think about your own society. Can you even imagine this society without music?

Music can evoke emotions in a number of ways, through words, rhythms, melodies, cadence, timbre, pitch, harmony, texture, pulse, meter, and tone. Read the following lyrics from the song "Holding These Regrets" that Al-ex Huck, the songwriter introduced to you earlier, performs with his acoustic guitar and harmonica. This song is about what happens after someone breaks off a relationship with a loved one.

> I keep on getting this pain in my chest
> And I don't know if it's from you or something else
> Like some undiagnosed condition
> That will leave me dead at 27
> No I can't die
> Holding these regrets
>
> I keep on getting this pain in my head
> And I don't know how it started

> But I wish it would end
> Cause I keep getting my tongue-twisted
> And I keep feeling like I'm missing
> Out on part of my life
> Holding these regrets
>
> I keep on getting this pain in my bones
> And I think it's just from always being alone
> If I could find my way off this couch
> I would probably meet someone else
> Then I won't die
> Holding these regrets
>
> No I won't die holding these regrets.

In reading the lyrics, you can see and feel a rhythm at work. Rhythm refers to a strong repetition or arranged pattern of movement or sound. As one example, Al-ex uses a repetition of wording ("I keep on getting" and "holding these regrets") at the beginning and end of a verse to establish rhythm. This rhythm carries meaning and draws on a listener's past experiences. The second time a listener hears these words, they are reminded of the first time they heard them.

Before we move any further, it might be best to distinguish between emotions and feelings. To understand the difference, you should think of feelings as associated with your mind and emotions with your body. That is, feelings are what happen when our brains (and thus our minds) experience emotions with our bodies. Emotions are those physical responses to something that happens externally. Our bodies experience emotions first, and then we have feelings that are influenced by previous experiences that we have had before. To give you an example, let's say you win a soccer game. In the moment your team scores the winning goal, your body experiences joy (this is an emotion, a body's reaction). After which, you feel elated (your mind draws on the previous experiences you had where your body reacted in a similar way). Though, you should realize that it is possible to think about a feeling and that thought can trigger a bodily emotion.

Activity: Music Listening

Create a feelings journal as you listen to several songs from different genres of music. As you reflect, consider the following:

- What about each song brings about these feelings?
- How did you learn to identify these feelings?
- What role does writing play in evoking these feelings?
- What role do feelings play in your own writing of texts?

Knowing the difference between emotions and feelings can help you think carefully about how you write a text, perhaps a text with sound like Al-ex wrote, to evoke your audience's emotions and feelings. Al-ex certainly thought about different ways he could make his audience feel something. For more on this, check out his interview below.

INTERVIEW
AL-EX HUCK, SINGER AND SONGWRITER

Q: How do you write a song?
A: Every song that I write starts with the lyrics. I'll come up with a line in my head and I'll develop the lyrics around that one line. I'll ponder on the words for a while. I'll write them down in a notebook or sing them into my phone. When I have a full verse, I'll put guitar chords to them.

Q: Can you talk about your inspiration for songwriting?
A: I studied poetry in college and that influences my songwriting. I'm fascinated by rhythm schemes, which is what you see in poetry. Rhyming to me is so important, but it has to make sense, and it can't be cliché.

Q: What roles do emotions play in your music?
A: Every one of my songs is based on a real-life experience, like a breakup that I've had, so emotions play an important role. "Botox on B Road" is a song about an ex-girlfriend of mine that lived on B Road. I tried to convey the fear of change and sense of sadness for something that had been lost in that song. The road itself cuts through an old farming community and leads up to newly built wineries and spas. It's the perfect example of old versus modern. It was a quiet road once, but now a bunch of wealthy drunk people go by on trolleys and buses. The song is about how the road will never go back to what it was before and how it could even be worse in the future. There's a feeling of hopelessness of the people that live on that road because there is nothing they can do.

Q: How do you record your music?
A: I first record a demo on my phone using the voice memo feature. Then, a friend of mine has a studio. I'll send him the demo and figure out what to do with it. When I get to the studio, I record the guitar part of the song first with a microphone in a soundproof room. I listen back to that while I am singing the words in my head to get the rhythm right. I don't want it too fast, but also not too slow. Then, I will record the vocals just in the same fashion on a microphone in the soundproof room. After that, I add in instruments separately if I need them, and then my friend puts it all together to make a rough mix. He will email it to me as a wav file when he is done so I can listen to it. I'll make notes and send them to him so that he can make changes. This is the production part of the process, really. I'll say add in this effect here, fade out at there, add sound effects here and there. He'll do those things and then I'll get another mix. I'll listen again and send more notes. We'll do this back and forth many times until I get a mix I'm comfortable with. That's when I'll send it to friends and other musicians to get feedback on it. They will give me some pointers that I'll send back to the studio. When it is finally finished, I'll get it ready to distribute. For this EP, I uploaded my songs to Bandcamp.

Q: How and why did you design your EP cover in the way you did?
A: I got my inspiration from people in my life. I released this EP in January. The cover design is actually a drawing my nephew gave me to be around Christmas time. It is supposed to be me wearing a hat. I thought it was great and I was fascinated by it. I was thinking that the next time I release music, I'll have him draw another portrait of me. That way fans can see how I evolve over time. The title on the other hand comes from a friend of mine. He used to say to me, "Be good," instead of saying bye. It was his unique saying. I like the fact that it isn't grammatically correct because people can relate to it. Nobody says "Be well." In songwriting, you don't have to be grammatically correct.

Suggestions for Creating Podcasts

In recent years, there has been tremendous growth in podcasts. Podcasts are digital audio files that people can download online and are usually available as a series. Such growth can be credited in some ways to the development of listening and recording technologies. According to PodTrac, a company that measures the audience analytics for podcasts worldwide, in March 2018, NPR's podcasts had the most global streams and downloads at a whopping 130,826,000. What makes podcasts so appealing to their listeners could be attributed to a number of factors, one being the ability to listen to the podcasts whenever and wherever. Such a factor is important to think about when creating a podcast (more on this in a moment). Encountering sound while moving through the world provides a layer to the places people are when listening. When visiting a park, for instance, if you were to listen to a podcast about hiking while you are on a trail, no doubt this listening experience would impact your experience of the park.

Discussion Questions: Podcasts

NPR's various podcasts shows are some of the most popular shows worldwide. Discuss the following:

- What other companies are responsible for the most popular podcasts worldwide, and what does this say about the content of these podcasts, the people who listen, and the technologies used to produce and distribute them?
- Why do you think they are so popular?
- What impact does listening to a podcast have?
- What role does writing play in podcasts?
- What role does sound play in podcasts?

So, one way to understand writing sound is to actually do so. While there are many ways to do so, for this chapter, you will consider writing for a podcast. In addition to thinking about when and where a podcast will be listened to (more on this later), here are some suggestions for creating podcasts:

Suggestion 1: Listen and Study

If you are unfamiliar with what it takes to produce a podcast, you might start by listening to a variety of podcasts and study their basic nature. If you are planning to create a podcast in a particular genre (for example, say you were to create a podcast devoted to the outdoors), you should listen to podcasts in that genre to get a good sense of what podcasts in this genre do. As you listen, pay attention to your body. How do you feel? What do you hear? What do they make you do? What do they make you think about? Take notes that reflect on your listening experiences so you can use them as guides for your own creations.

Activity: Active Listening Exercise

Listening is something we do with our entire bodies, not just our ears. Creating sounds is not just creating a text, but it is also about creating an experience with your audience. We can feel vibrations pulsing from a speaker, we can see it in movements, and so forth. In listening to a meadow or field, for instance, you will rely on many senses at once: sight, sound, feel, and touch. You will feel the sun on your skin, you will smell the honeysuckle, and you will feel the smooth underside of a blade of grass. This place and its materials thus shape your experience with sound.

Go out to a meadow or field and listen. Then answer the following in a reflection:

- What sounds do you hear and what makes them?
- How does this make you feel?
- What sounds do you try to block out, and which ones do you try to pay attention to on your way through a meadow or field?

Next, go to a mall or store and answer the following in another reflection:

- What sounds do you hear, and what makes them?
- How does this make you feel?
- What sounds do you try to block out, and which ones do you try to pay attention to on your way through a mall or store?

Compare your reflections. How are they similar and how are they different? If you were to create a podcast, how might you use this activity to create or capture sounds for it?

Suggestion 2: Connect With Your Audience

Another reason why podcasts are popular among their listeners has to do with the creator's relationship with the audience. Often, podcasts are created using an informal, conversational tone of voice, in other words, using language that listeners use themselves. In fact, listeners would expect as much given the nature of a podcast. Podcasts tell stories and are often narrative in nature, even when they feature interviews. A conversational tone of voice makes sense, then.

Along these lines, there are other ways to meet audiences' expectations. This could be achieved through tone of voice but also through other means. If you were to create a podcast on the outdoors, listeners would expect to hear sounds associated with the outdoors: birds chirping, wind hollering, twigs snapping, thunder booming. And, they would expect the host to be discussing outdoor things.

Likewise, to connect with your audience you should include everyone, even those that are non-hearing. When distributing your podcast, provide alternative texts, such as a transcript or a website that can provide written sounds.

Finally, provide for your audience a space to connect with you and other audience members. Doing so will help you get feedback on your podcast and that feedback can help you determine what is working and what isn't.

Suggestion 3: Engage All Senses

As a podcast writer, you will need to think about all the ways in which you can engage your audience's senses so as to make for a memorable and engaging listening experience. Recording a podcast about the outdoors while in the outdoors could provide sensory experiences for the listener that transports them to the outdoors. With the help of techniques (such as recording on location), in some regards, podcasts can enable the listener to imagine themselves in that location, transporting themselves to another place and moment in time. They can enable a listener to feel a certain way as well and to think a certain way, too.

Moreover, there are other ways that you could engage the senses. You could use music as a way to set the mood for your podcast. You could use a speeding up or slowing down of certain parts to portray meaning. For instance, speeding up conveys a sense of urgency and may put your audience on edge. Slowing down conveys a sense of ease and may make your audience relax. As you write your podcast, think of all the techniques you can use to engage people's senses.

Suggestion 4: Plan and Then Practice

If this is your first time creating a podcast, you should consider planning out what you will do in the podcast and then test it out by practicing. This is especially helpful if you will be interviewing someone (a common feature of podcasts). Knowing ahead of time what you will say may improve your chances of creating a smooth podcast. Write out questions ahead of time, reach out to the person you want to interview, and set up a time to do so.

Planning and practicing can also help you access equipment and become familiar with it before you use it. You wouldn't want to show up to an interview with equipment

TABLE 15.1 digital audio file types box

Digital Audio File Types:	Format:	Used For:
MP3 (MPEG-1 Audio Layer 3)	Compressed	Smartphones, iPods
WMA (Windows Media Audio)	Compressed	Windows Media Player
AAC (Advanced Audio Coding)	Compressed	iTunes
WAV (Waveform Audio Format)	Uncompressed	Broadcast CD quality music files
AIFF (Audio Interchange File Format)	Uncompressed	High quality and for editing and mixing

you didn't know how to use. To begin with, know what files you will need in order to share your podcasts (see the chart in Table 15.1) and find out what equipment you will need to do the actual recording and converting of files. Check out equipment from your school or your local library and learn to use it. Find others who have used such equipment, such as your instructor, for guidance. As you practice using the equipment, make sure to practice different techniques for creating special effects in your podcast. For example, if you want to portray a crowded party scene, practice recording and combining the different sounds people would expect to hear from such a scene (people talking, music playing, glasses clinking, etc.). Practicing these techniques can help you plan out the kinds of sounds you will need to capture for your podcast and the effects you hope to achieve in doing so.

You may also find that some of the sounds that you would like to include in your podcasts might be too difficult to record on your own. If you wanted to include a recording of a gorilla in your podcast, traveling to Africa to record it probably wouldn't be feasible or cost effective. In a case like this, you would need to turn to other resources for such sounds. Online resources like freesound.org provide free sounds, while Soundsnap and audioblocks.com offer sounds for a low cost.

Suggestion 5: Edit Effectively

Depending on your podcast, you may have to record the podcast as several parts (instead of all at once), and then combine and edit those parts using editing software to prepare it for distribution. But, even if you record all at once, you may need to edit for quality. Editing should be an important step in your process for several reasons. First, if you have a time limit for your podcast, you will need to either add or cut parts of your podcast to fit this time limit.

Second, as you playback your podcast, you will need to listen for instances where you need to make smoother transitions between the parts of your podcast, making parts that are too soft louder and those that are too loud softer. Listen carefully for increases or decreases in sound quality when doing this. If one part is really loud and one part is really soft, the transition could be jarring and unpleasant for your listeners. You should also listen for distracting background noises, noises that would distract your audience from what you have in the foreground. There may be times when you will need to go back and redo an interview because the background noises are too cumbersome to edit out.

To edit your podcast files, think carefully about the kind of editing you want to do. There are a number of software programs available and they each have different capabilities. Audacity (featured in Image 15.4) is a free open-sourced platform available online that not only allows you to edit sound, but you can record with it, too. Try out different software programs until you find one that you like best and will fit your needs.

However, before you do so, there is one more thing you should do: consider the differences between destructive and real-time editing. Destructive editing refers to a process of editing that modifies/changes the data from the original audio file. When you delete data, such as a particular portion of the audio, that data is deleted from the actual file until you hit the "undo" feature. If you want to make a lot of changes to your audio file, destructive editing may make the process cumbersome, especially if you want to try out different edits. In destructive editing, you can only undo your edits in reverse order.

With real-time editing, on the other hand, you can make changes to the data file at any time and in any order because the file itself isn't changed immediately. Rather, the changes occur when you play back the file. In a real-time editing program, when you

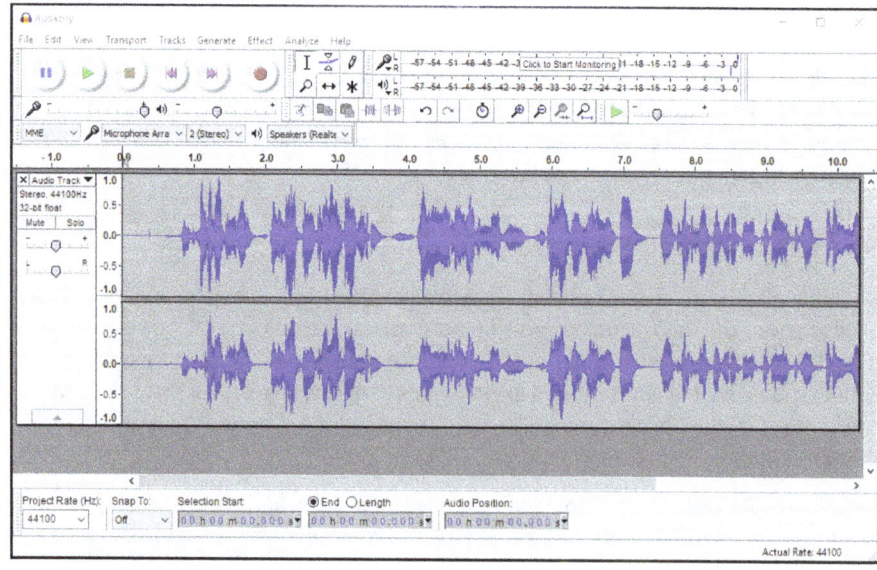

Image 15.4 Audacity Example

make changes, like when you delete a portion of the audio file, that portion isn't actually deleted from the file, but instead is hidden during the playback.

Suggestion 6: Save and Distribute

Once you have edited your podcast and are ready to distribute it to your audience, think about where and how you will save and store your podcast. You will not only want to ensure you do so securely, whether saving files to your hard drive or in a cloud, but you will also need to have easy access to them so as to distribute them.

To distribute your podcast, think again about your audience and how best to reach them. Perhaps you will want to make your podcast available to everyone, choosing an online public platform where anyone can access your podcast. Conversely, if you wish to keep the podcast private and available only to a specific audience, you may need to find other ways to distribute it. Research technologies that can help you achieve your goals in distributing and weigh the pros and cons of using them in order to figure out the best distribution plan.

Check It Out YouTube: For more on how to create a podcast, Pat Flynn's series of tutorials on YouTube videos about podcasting can help. Check out these two in particular: "How to Start a Podcast (2019 Tutorial) Equipment & Software" and "Top Podcasting Tips & Tools for Recording, Interviews & Exporting (2019 Tutorial)."

Creating Sound: Public Speaking

Maybe you will not be a musician, and maybe you will not be a podcaster in the future. Nevertheless, there are other ways in which you will need to think about sound. Take public speaking, for instance. Public speaking is most likely going to be part of your life. There will be times in college, at work, and in your community when you may need to give a speech, a talk, a performance, or a presentation. In those situations, you will need to think carefully about sound and how it operates in those kinds of public speaking genres.

For instance, if you were to make a persuasive speech to a group of fellow citizens with the hope of raising money for a local children's hospital, you would probably want to pay close attention to your tone of voice, making sure you balance your want to secure funds with your want to come across as friendly and passionate. Read the following two sentences out loud and notice the difference in tone of voice.

> Please help me raise money.
>
> PLEASE HELP ME RAISE MONEY!

Notice, that when the second sentence is read, it seems as though you are shouting. If you were to shout your entire speech like this, most likely, your audience would be put off.

There are a number of other ways in which you can think carefully about sound when public speaking. Silence, for example, can help emphasize a point, provide a dramatic flair, or give listeners a chance to reflect. Read the following out loud and notice the impact the silence has when you pause.

> Your donations help children like Mark who is battling brain cancer (pause), or Cindy who was just diagnosed with a rare form of leukemia (pause). Please (pause) help me raise money.

> Your donations help children like Mark who is battling brain cancer, or Cindy who was just diagnosed with a rare form of leukemia. Please help me raise money.

As you think about the role sound plays in your own public speaking, consider practicing different ways of achieving your goals beforehand by using different types of sounds (your voice, the voices of others, special sound effects, and music) and making sounds longer or shorter, higher or lower, and faster or slower. You could test out such sounds as you practice by getting feedback from your classmates, friends, tutors, and instructors. You could also turn to the experts who study sounds to find out which approaches to sounds you should consider in your own public speaking.

The global community known as TED (Technology, Entertainment, and Design) first started as a conference in 1984. Today, the community has expanded to other platforms from live campus talks to online videos, where speakers present on any topic or idea. What makes TED Talks so successful are the speakers, and over the years, researchers have been studying them to get a better sense as to why they are so successful. A lot of the success is a result of speakers' uses of sound. For instance, a study on TED Talk videos found that "The more vocal variety a speaker had, the more views they had. Specifically, vocal variety increased the speakers' charisma and credibility ratings" (Van Edwards and Vaughn).

So, think about how the sounds of your public speaking work with or against other modes to convey your messages. When public speaking, most likely you will need to think about your bodily positions and movements, like hand gestures and facial expressions. If you don't match your gestures and facial expressions with your tone of voice, will your audience become confused? Will they think less of your credibility as a speaker?

Assignment: Research Public Speakers

For this assignment, research successful public speakers to find out how they use sound (as well as other modes) to give speeches/presentations. As you research these speakers, you should watch, read, and listen to several of their speeches/presentations (perhaps you could watch a TED Talk). Take notes as you do, paying close attention to the ways in which they use sounds to convey particular messages. If you can, it would be a good idea to interview them as well to find out more about how they use sound. After you have researched these speakers, create a presentation in which you explain your findings to the rest of the class.

Final Thoughts

When we write with emotion, with texture, and with sound, we must make smart rhetorical decisions about the technologies we use and how those technologies shape the ways in which the diverse bodies of our audiences understand them. We can develop an awareness of how technologies came to be because of our bodies and the bodies of others as demonstrated in this chapter. When our bodies are in motion, they impact the way technologies are used and how they are developed over time. Likewise, we can pay close attention to how technologies help or hinder our bodies' abilities to write. In moving forward, then, it is important to consider your own body as well as the bodies of others and what they are and are not capable of when writing using modes and technologies to do so.

Additional Discussion Questions

1. In what ways do our bodies use technologies to write?
2. In what ways do technologies shape our bodies?
3. How does sound engage all senses?
2. In what ways can sound evoke feelings through emotions?
3. In what ways do different genres of music evoke different kinds of feelings?

Additional Activities

1. Create a Song: Using a music editing program, create a song. As you do, consider what roles writing, technologies, and our bodies play in the creation and understanding of sounds.
2. Sound Collection: Collect sounds on your campus in order to create a sound essay that tells a story about your campus. You can use any sound editor (such as Audacity) to put your sounds together.
3. Written Sound: Collect examples of written sound in a number of different texts (for instance, in cartoons, in magazines, in TV commercials). Bring these to class to share and discuss with your fellow classmates.

Additional Assignments

1. People in Your Community: Create a podcast series that profiles the people in a particular community. Develop a theme for your series (for example, the outdoors people of a community or the volunteers of a community). Consider using interviews as a way to capture what makes these people unique. Also, consider recording locations as a way to further enhance the listeners' understandings of the people featured in your podcasts.
2. Your Campus Community: Create a podcast series for a particular group, organization, or club on your campus. Consider using interviews as a way to capture what makes these people unique. Also, consider recording locations as a way to further enhance the listeners' understandings of the people featured in your podcasts.
3. History of Sound: In the remote mountain village of Kuskoy in Turkey, villagers use whistling sounds to communicate. Create a presentation for your class that traces the history of a particular sound and its importance in a particular culture.

Works Cited

Olmstead, Kenneth. "Nearly Half of Americans Use Digital Voice Assistants, Mostly on Their Smartphones." *Pew Research Center*, 12 December 2017, www.pewresearch.org/fact-tank/2017/12/12/nearly-half-of-americans-use-digital-voice-assistants-mostly-on-their-smartphones/. Accessed 28 June 2018.

PodTrac. "Podcast Industry Audience Rankings." *Podtrac*, 2016, http://analytics.podtrac.com/industry-rankings/ Accessed 12 May 2018.

Van Edwards, Vanessa and Brandon Vaughn. "5 Secrets of a Successful TED Talk." *Science of People*, n.d., www.scienceofpeople.com/secrets-of-a-successful-ted-talk/. Accessed 4 April 2019.

CHAPTER 16

Picture, Preform, and Present

Contents

Images in a Technological World 377
Suggestions for Writing Still Images 379
Suggestions for Creating Moving Images 386
Suggestions for Creating Live Images 388
Final Thoughts 393

Images in a Technological World

Imagine you are walking down the sidewalk in your neighborhood and you see a white truck on the street. As the truck approaches, you realize this is no ordinary truck. It is, in fact, an ice cream truck. You know this because you see the images of ice cream on the truck's side (a picture of a cone, a popsicle, a chocolate fudge bar); you hear a kid-friendly jingle blaring from its speakers; you notice that the truck is moving slowly; you see the driver, a man in a white hat, smile and wave; and you feel happy. Your brain reads the truck against the background of the neighborhood, too. What is a truck like this doing here in the late afternoon? It's here because there are lots of kids that live on your street and school is over for the day. They are outside now and heading over to the truck.

The white truck might not seem like a text, but it is. In this moment, you are reading the truck, its images on its side, its shape, its colors, its driver waving, that familiar happy feeling you feel inside. All of the modes of communication that are at play here are working together to signal to you that this truck is an ice cream truck. And, this truck is but one of the many images you might find on any given street in your community. Everywhere we go, we see images that have been written by someone for someone. Thus, in this chapter, you will consider what it means to write images all the while you consider the rhetorical choices and technological choices writers must make when doing so.

To begin with, images are integral to our way of understanding the world and our way of communicating messages in the world. Rhetoric scholar Joddy Murray's work on multimodal composition, image, and affect shows us how a brain functions through image and how images shape the brain. He writes that

> Many working in the fields of neuroscience and cognitive science agree that image—the multisensual, multimodal, multiexperiential snapshot held in our neural cortex—is fundamental to thought. As such, those who compose in several modes are more likely to be rhetorically appropriate for any given audience ... Rhetors who understand how to compose with image (and, consequentially, affect) also understand how to reach an audience (111).

Think about your experience just now as you read the first paragraph of this chapter. When you were imagining—that is, thinking about—walking down a sidewalk and seeing an ice cream truck, what visual images did you have in your mind to help you make sense of the scene? If you need to, go back and reread the first paragraph. Pay close attention to what you are visualizing in your mind. Do you see a white truck? Do you see an ice cream cone? Do you see a driver in a white hat? Do you see children? Now think about all your senses as you are visualizing this scene. Do you hear sounds in conjunction with what you are visualizing? Do you hear a jingle? Do you hear children? Indeed, when we read images, we rely on many senses that help our brains make sense of what we are seeing. Images are powerful communicators in this regard as they tell us what and how to think by engaging our senses (ignited by our body's remembering of past experiences in specific contexts).

Images can persuade audiences, entertain them, inform them, warn them, delight them, and encourage them. That's because images carry meaning that we make sense of through our bodies. Take Image 16.1 as an example.

IMAGE 16.1 Lightspring / Shutterstock

What does this image of a dove holding an olive branch perched atop missiles and bombs mean to you? How did you arrive at this meaning? To begin with, your body had to read the elements of the image and the relationships between them based on past experiences in the cultures you live in. You had to connect these relationships together in your brain based on what you know about bombs and what you know about a dove with an olive branch. In many cultures, a white dove and an olive branch are symbols of peace. Missiles and bombs are not.

Today, when people use images to communicate with others, technologies often play an integral role in writing these images and distributing them, too. If you think about social media, for example, images that are created with technology and distributed through technology can go viral, reaching millions of people.

Activity: Image Journal

Take a walk on campus or in your city or town. Pay attention to all the images you see along your walk and write about them in a journal. Share your findings with your classmates. Here are some questions to consider as you write about the images in your journal:

- What are the images?
- How would you describe these images?
- Who created the images?
- With what technologies did they create them?
- Why were they created? In other words, what purposes do they serve?
- How do you think they were created?
- Who are the intended audiences for the images?
- Do the images and their purposes meet the goal of reaching this audience?

Suggestions for Writing Still Images

To be an effective writer of images, you will need to think carefully about how to create images for particular audiences and for particular purposes. Murray writes that

> a composed image does more than represent or illustrate something in an essay or hypertext; an image can itself be articulate of its own meaning, can persuade on its own merit; and be comprised of complex layers of meaning and emotion as long as it is composed to do so (177).

So, in this chapter, you will learn about writing still, moving, and live images, whether for videos, performances, or presentations. While presented in separate sections, the suggestions below could apply to all situations involving writing images.

Writing images certainly means thinking rhetorically. But, not every situation will call for an image. Some ideas, perhaps, may be best communicated through other modes. For instance, a long, complicated story might be best communicated through words rather than through one complex image that tries to capture all the complexities of the story at once. In part, your decision to use images will depend on your purpose and your audience. A series of comics might not be the best means for explaining physics to a group of scientists, but it might be appropriate if you were trying to teach kids about a difficult concept like physics. In such cases, you would be using a familiar genre to uncomplicate something so as to help your audience understand. Hence, when writing images, you have to think about your purpose, your audience, and whether or not an image is best for such a purpose and audience. If you decide that truly an image is best, then you have to think about the process for creating an image and what impact your image will have.

Suggestion 1: Choosing the Right Technologies

If you want to work with technologies to create and distribute your images, there are a number of free and low-cost options. You should begin with what you have on your own computer and what you have access to through your school. To determine what technologies are best for your project, you should think rhetorically. Here are some key questions to ask yourself as you decide:

- Why do you need images?
- What genre of text will you be writing with these images?
- What modes of communication will you rely on and why?
- How will you obtain these images?
- Do you need to take your own photographs? Do you need to draw images?
- How will technologies help you? What affordances or limitations will these technologies have?

Producing images: While most computers, tablets, and smartphones have built-in cameras, you might need to consider their quality before choosing to use them. Owning a smartphone is convenient, but if you need a high-quality photograph for your printed text, you might find that the quality of a smartphone photograph, when printed, isn't as great as you had hoped. Digital photographs might look great on a screen but might not look so great when printed. Ask your instructor about your school's resources. You might find that your school allows students to check out or rent camera equipment that can produce better-quality photos.

You can also find programs and resources that contain stock images that you can use for free or for a low cost as well as programs and resources that help you draw and craft your own images from scratch. Don't be afraid to sketch out your ideas and turn them into usable images for your projects.

Editing images: Once you have gathered your images and are ready to transform or edit them, likewise, there are lots of free and low-cost options available online or in an app store that can help you do so. GIMP, for instance, is a free software that works a lot like Adobe's Photoshop in that it lets you edit and create images. Practice editing your images by exploring what each program's and each resource's tools can and cannot do. It may be necessary to use a number of them to edit just one image.

Distributing images: No matter what kind of technology you use, you should think carefully about how your audience with engage with your work. Not all texts created and saved in one technology will transfer correctly to another. For instance, if you create a MS Works text containing images using an Apple computer, will someone who is using a PC be able to read the file containing your text? You also have to think about storage and file sharing capacity. How large of a file will you create, and can this file be distributed digitally without any problems? Finally, because everyone will likely access your images differently, make sure to include alternatives for your images so as to maximize your audience's ability to access your texts.

Suggestion 2: Image File Types

Another consideration when working between dimensions and working with digital and non-digital texts has to do with the resolution of your text's images. Have you ever had an image that you thought looked awesome on your computer screen look not so great when you printed it? One of the reasons this may have happened has to do with the resolution of your image as well as the type of image you are working with. Resolution refers to dpi (dots per inch) that a printer is capable of printing. With digital technologies, there are several ways in which we can create and save an image file. However, not all of these ways have the same resolution. Some file types have higher or lower resolutions depending on the medium. Images for the computer screen don't need as high of a resolution as printed images do to look good. Typically, 300 dpi is a good quality to have for printed images. The web operates on 72 dpi, which is far less than ideal for printing. In fact, when you print out a web image, you can see that the quality is not as good. As a rule of thumb, the higher the dpi, the better the quality for printing.

When creating an image on a computer, you will likely do so as either a raster graphic or a vector graphic. Raster graphics include JPG, TIF, GIF, and PNG files, ones you are probably familiar with. A raster graphic is one that is made up of a bitmap, a grid comprised of a set number of individual pixels or dots that together make up an image. A bitmap is a group of tiny dots. Each dot within a bitmap represents a hue or shade. If you were to enlarge a raster graphic, you would see the jagged edges of the bits that comprise it. Because the bits are a set number, scaling raster images is difficult. Raster graphics work best with photographs and artwork that contain a lot of detail.

A vector graphic, on the other hand, is a graphic that is more conducive to resizing because of its scalability. That's because a vector graphic isn't made up of bitmaps that have a set number of dots like raster images are. They are instead created using mathematic equations that map out geometric points using lines or curves (otherwise known as paths) to create shapes. A vector is best for illustrations and can be saved as a PDF, EPS, AI, or SVG file.

Activity: Toolbox for Still images

Create a toolbox by gathering a number of free and low-cost resources that can help you work with images. You can start by looking at what is on your computer. For example, many computers come with programs such as Paint and tools such as the Snipping Tool that can help you create and edit images. In addition to the ones you find, here are a number of resources that can help too:

> *Resources where you can get images:*
> Wikimedia Commons
> Morguefile
> Creative Commons
> *Resources that can help you edit or create images:*
> GIMP
> Blender
> Comic Life
> *Tutorials that can help you work with images:*
> YouTube
> Lynda

Suggestion 3: Choosing the Right Materials

Not all of the texts that you will produce in school and on the job will be digital texts. You may create them digitally, but they might need to be distributed non-digitally. When that is the case, you should think carefully about the material that you are printing your texts on and what your texts are made out of. One example that demonstrates the importance of choosing the right material is choosing the right paper for printing photographs. For a smoother texture, you might choose a high-glossy finish paper for your photos. For a slightly rougher texture, you might choose a matte finish paper. Your choice in materials is an important one because materials impact the message you want to communicate. If you were printing old photographs of a battlefield to use in a project about a war that took place 100 years ago, a high-glossy finish might make the photos look too modern, whereas a matte finish may make the photographs look more authentic.

Suggestion 4: Focal Point

Earlier in the book, you learned about Meghan Pearson's work as a graphic artist. She designs calendars as well as many other kinds of texts using photographs. While Meghan is an artist, you don't have to be an artist to design effective texts. Knowing a few skills can make all the difference. For instance, when designing a text such as an image or photograph, the rule of thirds can help you capture and create an interesting text. The **rule of thirds** is really a guideline that suggests that you divide your image or photograph (basically what you see within a frame) vertically and horizontally into thirds or nine equal parts (see example 1, Image 16.2).

As you can see in the photograph of the flower (example 2, Image 16.3), there are nine equal parts that divide the photograph. The intersections of the vertical and horizontal lines serve as important positions within the frame. These are called **power points** or **crash points**. In essence, you should make sure to place or position your subject matter so that it aligns with these intersections or comes close to them. The flower within the photograph is positioned along the right vertical line, and its petals touch the two right intersections. Thus, the **focal point** of this photograph to which your eyes are drawn (also known as the center of interest, attention, or activity) is not in the very center of the photograph and is instead located right of center, making this an interesting and well-composed photograph.

Using the rule of thirds and a clear focal point can help you find the right balance of elements within your image. If you were not able to capture the right focal point or to

IMAGE 16.2 Example 1: Rule of Thirds Grid

IMAGE 16.3 Example 2: Focal Point in a Power Point. AR Photoshut / Shutterstock

383

align your most prominent elements with the rule of thirds when shooting a photo, use editing tools to help you crop or enlarge elements to do so. As you work with the rule of thirds and you work for a clear focal point, here are some questions to keep in mind: Do you have the right balance of prominent elements, and are there distractions in the background that might steal the viewer's attention?

For more advice on shooting your own photographs, check out the interview below with another photographer, Akamie Insardi.

INTERVIEW
AKAMIE INSARDI, PHOTOGRAPHER

Q: What kinds of photographs do you take?
A: Portraits.

Q: What strategies do you use to ensure you take memorable photographs?
A: Engaging the client and making sure they feel comfortable with me and in front of my camera. Enlisting a good dose of humor always helps.

Q: What advice would you give writers who want to use photography to create their texts?
A: Photographs and/or visuals can evoke emotions and put the potential reader in the state of mind you are trying to create. As well as transport that same reader to the place and time within your story's setting.

Q: What technologies do you use on a regular basis to edit, save, and share your photographs?
A: There is a mass array of creative programs to accomplish this. My main sources are:

- Adobe Lightroom
- Adobe Photoshop
- An external hard drive
- Pixieset and/or Dropbox to share, depending on the client and the type of portrait session

Q: What role does writing play in your photography business?
A: Writing tends to set the tone for your images. How you want your images viewed and the way your potential viewer should feel.

Q: What role do you think photography plays in our society and people's ability to communicate?
A: Photography is playing an enormous role in our society these days. With the ever-growing popularity of all social media platforms being image based, it is taking the place of the written words and/or captions. Photographs are becoming the new form of communication and creating a lack of conveyance since the viewer has to assume what is meant by the photograph. Photographs are also only a glimpse into the lives of others and can create misrepresentation in all aspects of that person's life.

Suggestion 5: Overused Images

While you may find that your computer comes with free images (such as clip art), you should think twice about whether or not those kinds of images would be the best for your writing. For starters, if you were to publish your work, you'd need to get permission for the clip art. Second, because almost everyone who has a computer has access to those same free images, those images can become overused and even cliché. You have to weigh the costs involved in using such images. Those costs include whether or not you achieve your purpose in communicating. If your goal is to stand out in your writing—that is, to be unique and therefore memorable—then using images that everyone else uses isn't going to help you accomplish this goal. Sometimes it is best to create your own images entirely from scratch.

Suggestion 6: Shapes

When creating your own images, you should think about how you will do so using shapes. Elements of an image, including shapes, carry meaning. Let's say that you were in charge of designing advertising materials for an upcoming children's event in your community. You decide that the mascot for the event will be a friendly dinosaur. To draw the friendly dinosaur, you would need to include friendly features. For example, in drawing the dinosaur's teeth, you wouldn't want to draw jagged, pointed teeth. That would make the dinosaur look like a scary monster, working against your rhetorical purpose and possibly frightening children. Instead, you would want to draw rounded, smooth teeth, perhaps along a curved line that could serve as a smile. Children would read this image as friendly and would be more likely to want to attend. Likewise, using shapes consistently throughout a text can help create a pattern that brings cohesiveness to your text.

Suggestion 7: Placing Images Within Texts

When you are placing images within larger texts, remember that not all images can speak for themselves. In some cases, you will need to explain images using other modes. For example, one way to make a bar graph or pie chart containing different types of data accessible to your readers is to explain how the data is represented in such images and how to interpret it. When you do this—that is, when you explain—it would be a good idea to also place the image and the words you use to explain it close together. That way readers don't have to look very far to find the image you are talking about. When you don't need a lengthy explanation, try using a caption, title, or label for your image that captures the main point of the image and helps readers understand the image quickly.

Suggestion 8: Careful Representations

When using images to represent ideas (like the example of the dove earlier in this chapter), you have to be careful to make sure that the images you create do justice in representing the ideas that you intend to represent. Often, images can be misleading and end up having a negative impact on readers. That is why having a cultural awareness, one in which you are respectful of all in a society, can help you make important decisions as to what you should include and not include in images. You would not what to choose an image to represent an idea if that image would be insensitive to someone.

In addition to thinking carefully about creating images that adequately represent ideas, you also have to think about what is left out of the images you create. Much meaning can be created in leaving out important information in an image. If you are, for example, trying to represent a diverse population of people in your image, you would want to make sure that you do not leave anyone out; that is, you would want everyone in your audience to be able to see themselves in your image. Leaving out someone may express the idea that someone isn't welcome or included.

Suggestions for Creating Moving Images

Now that you have considered a few strategies for developing still images, let's now turn to those images that move, like those in videos. When images move, writers must make a number of decisions when trying to communicate their messages. Writers need to think about timing, sequences of scenes, and order of information, what comes first, second, third, and so on.

Because so many technologies enable people to create videos in a number of ways, you could say that no two videos are the same. If you were to peruse YouTube videos, you would find a number of different kinds of videos in a number of video genres, from how-to videos to advertisement videos to informational videos. If you are tasked with creating a video, you should first think about what kind of video you are going to make and study the features of videos in that genre. Throughout this book, you have learned about conventions and how paying close attention to those conventions can help you create a variety of successful texts. Like with other texts, in creating a video, you certainly need to think critically about conventions. Perhaps the only time you should break a convention is when you have a good reason for doing so and that reason would be appreciated and understood by your audience.

Secondly, when you think about creating a video, you have to think about the modes of a video and how they will work together. How will sound, color, and movement work to create meaning in your video, for instance? Go back to Chapter 2 in this book and use it as a guide to think about the interconnections between the modes of your video. Finally, while some of the suggestions made earlier about still images could certainly work with moving images, here are some additional suggestions you should consider when images move.

Suggestion 1: Angles

Just as a focal point and rule of thirds are helpful to a still image, so too is the camera angle for videos. If you are shooting your own video, say on your smartphone camera, you will certainly want to make sure that you do so with a steady hand and the right angle. Many cameras have guides on their screens (sometimes in the form of gridlines) to help guide you with filming scenes in the right angle. For example, using a grid on your smartphone camera's screen, you could back up away from the action of the scene and then shoot from a wide angle to give viewers a wider perspective of the scene. The grid would provide guidelines that you could align with images in the background of the scene you are shooting, thus making the wide angle a steady, successful one.

An angle does indeed refer to the point of view or perspective that you are creating for a scene in your video. If you are shooting a video from the viewpoint of a child, for instance, you would want to lower your camera's lens to a height of a child, one in which your audience would be looking up at the world just as a child would be. Such an angle would make your video seem authentic and true to the character of the child.

Suggestion 2: Lighting and Sound

Not all cameras are created equally, as they all have different features that afford you different capabilities. You will need to plan ahead and test out your equipment before you begin shooting your video. If you choose to use your smartphone's camera, make sure to test for lighting and sound issues. Some smartphone cameras and their abilities to record lighting and sound are not as good as other recording devices. For example, you could consider using a different microphone for your sound recording, perhaps one that is solely for recording sound. Using a video editing program, you could then merge your video and sound recordings to ensure a high-quality listening experience.

Suggestion 3: Creating Scenes Using Time

Your video most likely will be a series of scenes. Plan these ahead of time by storyboarding so that you know what you will need to do in order to film them. As you plan, think about how timing will be used. While timing can refer to the action of the film and how long it takes for that action to occur, it can also refer to how you present information throughout your video and how you move from one scene to another. Timing, therefore, should be factored into your plans for each of your scenes. As you think of timing, consider these questions:

- How will I transition between scenes, and how will time play role in these transitions?
- How can time help tell the story in my video?
- How long will the action of each scene need to be?
- Do I need to speed up or slow down?
- If I am telling a story, when do I need to have the climax? The resolution?
- If I am telling a story about the past, how will I represent this time period?

Suggestion 4: Direction

Finally, you will also need to consider the direction in which the movement occurs. This is often tied to the angle and the timing of filming a scene. Movement that occurs in particular directions adds meaning to your video and the messages you intend for your audiences. When your movement of elements or characters leads your audience away from the scene, for example, your audience may feel less connected due to the growing distance between them and the elements or characters in your video. Moving forward, perhaps, from the left of the screen to the right of the screen, may indicate an element or character is progressing. Moving the opposite direction may mean the element or character is going backwards.

Activity: Toolbox for Moving Images

If you plan to create a video, you will need to gather resources that can help you. There are a number of free and low-cost options for capturing and editing video that can be done on a digital camera, smartphone, or computer. There are also downloadable software options, too, such as Microsoft Photos or iMovie. If you need to create video that captures your computer screen, you could try Camtasia, Screencast-O-Matic, or Wondershare Filmora. For creating animation, you could use Xtranormal. For an open-source video editing option, you could try OpenShot. In this activity, explore your options and create a toolbox in which you gather video making resources that will help you with your video projects.

Suggestions for Creating Live Images

Now, let's consider images as live experiences. We can do so in the context of performances and presentations. When texts happen live, there are a number of rhetorical choices writers must make. In performing the classical Indian dance form of Kathak, dancers write stories using hand movements, footwork, and facial expressions. This traditional dance traces back to the Kathakars, who were traveling storytellers of northern India. In such a dance, performers combine units of movement with rhythmic patterns in order to tell stories. Such movements include Chakkars (spins) and Hastas (subtle hand gestures or arm movements) and are accompanied by music. In addition to the movements, performers wear costumes and ankle bells that add to the meaning of the performance.

Gestures and bodily movements play an integral role in performing, too. And, as you have been learning throughout this book, they carry different meanings in different cultures. Gestures not only can tell stories, they can reflect emotions and moods. In the Hindu tradition, Kathak dance performers use gestures such as facial or hand gestures to invoke mythology, retelling the stories of Hindu gods and goddesses.

IMAGE 16.4 Kathak Dance. Sujay_Govindaraj / iStock

If you are in a communicative situation that you believe calls for a live performance (such as a dance), keep these key questions in mind as you prepare:

- What will my bodily gestures mean to my audience?
- What is the history of the movements in different cultures, and how can I honor this in my performance?
- How will I include the conventions of performance genre I am using?
- Should I break from conventions, and if so, why?

Activity: Analyze a Dance

A number of YouTube videos feature a variety of dances. Choose one and write a reflection on the movements you see and the meanings they create in conjunction with costumes and music (if any). If you need to do some further research on the history of the dance genre, do so. Then, think about how this history informs what you are seeing in the video. Share your reflection with your classmates.

Most likely, at some point during college or on the job, you will be asked to give a presentation. Before you open a PowerPoint template and start filling in the slides, before you type up a handout, and before you fill a box with props, stop and think about what your goals are for such a presentation. A presentation is a performance, one you should not wait until the last minute to prepare. When creating a presentation, you should think rhetorically about your audience, your purpose for giving the presentation, and where and when you will present. What you say and how you say it are the two most important parts of a presentation because these are what will engage your audience. So, to further help you think about what you will say and how you will say it, consider the following suggestions before you get started on your presentations:

Suggestion 1: Practice What You Say and How You Say It

If you want a chance at succeeding in giving a stellar presentation, you need to put together what you will say and do during the presentation ahead of time. Whether you are using a script or notecards, you should think about the major points you want your audience to remember once your presentation is over and how best to deliver those points during the presentation. Find the right balance of information, making sure you don't give your audience too little or too much. Give the audience a chance to remember your presentation by working into your presentation mechanisms (pauses, handouts, easy-to-read lists, questions, and so forth) that allow for time to reflect, engage, and discuss in purposeful ways. Finally, to ensure success, always practice your presentation ahead of time to get your timing right and make certain you have the right tone of voice.

Suggestion 2: Avoid Information Overload

The purpose of giving a presentation is so that an audience can watch and listen to a speaker and remember this person's points. Sometimes, when speakers use too many slides, props, or handouts, especially when those are crowded with information, an audience can have a difficult time paying attention or following along. That's because the audience's attention gets divided when a speaker relies too heavily on too many things at one time. Too many texts, too many sources of information, could lead to information overload.

Giving a handout, for instance, in the middle of your presentation means your audience will need more time to listen to you speak and read the handout at the same time. The more texts you have for your audience to look at, the more they have to divide their attention in order to understand all that is going on. Earlier in this book, you learned that people can't multitask effectively. If you must have slides, handouts, and props, think strategically about how you will use them. You might find that providing a handout well in advance of your presentation is a better option, as it can ensure people can access your presentation ahead of time and can prepare them for what you will say in your presentation.

Indeed, regardless of whether or not you use slides, you should seriously consider giving audience members a handout or transcript of your presentation to ensure that you reach all audience members. Remember that accessible texts are those texts that everyone has access to, and your presentation should not be an exception. Presentations, with or without slides, are texts. Providing a handout or transcript (ahead of time if possible) is one way to reach more audience members. Those who need more time to prepare questions can do so if they receive the handout ahead of time.

Suggestion 3: Just Say No to Bullet Points (Most of the Time)

Image 16.5 is from a presentation about Sahara Desert animals. Can you guess what kind of technology the presenter used to create this? If you said Microsoft PowerPoint, you would be right. But, how did you guess that? Was it the heading? The colors? The arrangement of information? Was it the bullet points?

In Western cultures, we have reached a point where bullet points have been used way too many times in a presentation and therefore have lost their meaningful effect, perhaps even resulting in boring presentations. While earlier in this book, you learned about conventions, things people come to expect, sometimes conventions are not a good thing, and in a presentation, that could be true of bullet points. There is nothing exciting or memorable about the slide, right? Instead of bullet points in a presentation, you might consider using one image or one concept on a slide as a way to be more engaging to your audience. That way they can focus on you, the speaker, once they understand your slide, which they should be able to do in just a few seconds.

Besides using bullet points, there are certainly a number of other ways in which you can provide a structured presentation that audiences can follow along with. Using a consistent design, layout, and techniques like *signposting* (signaling or cueing audiences) as you transition from the different parts of your presentation or summarizing or repeating key ideas can help make your presentation memorable, too. Use a visual

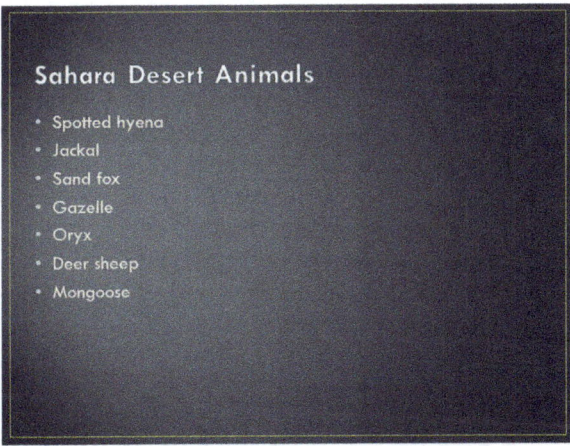

IMAGE 16.5 Example Presentation Slide

trail guide in your slides to help audience members see where they have been, where they are, and where they will be going during your presentation. A trail guide could be as simple as using numbers on your slides to represent the main ideas you would like to share and letting audience members know at the start of your presentation how many main ideas they will learn as you go along.

Check It Out YouTube: If you must use bullet points, save them for a handout that you will give your audience in advance. For more on creating slides for a presentation, check out Pat Flynn's "How to Create an Awesome Slide Presentation (for Keynote or PowerPoint)."

Suggestion 4: Go Beyond a Template

Today, a number of presentation technologies make creating a presentation quick and easy. PowerPoint is one of those. However, just because you have access to presentation technologies like PowerPoint, and just because they may be easy to use due to their premade templates, doesn't mean you have to use them. When everyone uses the same templates, the templates become boring or cliché. It might be best to create your own slides from scratch, making them unique to your presentation and therefore making your presentation more memorable. If you must use a program like PowerPoint, change or manipulate the templates to make them your own.

Suggestion 5: Be Creative

Have you ever sat through a boring presentation, one that you couldn't wait until it was over? Most likely you have, and most likely the reason why the presentation was boring was because the presenter didn't think creatively enough to engage his or her audience.

In their Intro to Business Writing class, Josh and Miguel developed a business plan for a grilled cheese restaurant in their community. When Josh and Miguel presented their plan to their class, they created a handout in the shape of a grilled cheese sandwich. When audience members opened up the sandwich handout before the presentation, they saw what made Josh and Miguel's ideas for the restaurant unique. Their presentation was no doubt memorable. In the same Intro to Business Writing class, Emma, who developed a marketing plan for a nail salon, opted not to pass out a handout during her presentation. Instead, she passed out her presentation transcript along with nail polish bottles that had her proposed logo on them. Throughout her presentation, Emma referred to her business's logo as being representative of her proposed nail salon's core values. No doubt her presentation was memorable, too.

Be creative with a purpose. Going overboard with creativity can backfire, so practice and test out your ideas first. Make them count and make them related to what you are doing. A lot of presentation software programs have various options for including sound effects and animation. Just because a program enables users to include these things doesn't mean you should include them. Using these things in excess can be distracting and take away from the point of your presentation. Everything you do in your presentation should be done so with a purpose, and that purpose should be clear to your audience.

Suggestion 6: Delivery Is Everything

You can prepare all you want for a presentation, but if in the moment, you don't pay attention to how you say what you say, then that preparation will have been for nothing. Delivering a presentation means building a relationship with your audience. You must dress appropriately, wear a friendly smile, and interact with your audience so as to establish a trustworthy ethos. Be charismatic and authentic. No one will believe in someone who is unenthusiastic or someone who pretends to be someone they are not.

You should think about timing during your delivery (saying the right thing at the right moment). But, in doing so, don't let the technology you are using slow you down or get in your way (that is, don't hide behind it). Technology will play a key role in the delivery of your presentation, so it is important to think ahead of time how best to utilize it.

Activity: Past Presentations

Think about the presentations you have attended in the past. What made them great? What made them not so great? Make a list of the things you should and shouldn't do during a presentation based on your past experiences attending presentations. Think about the visuals, the props, the technologies, and the handouts the presenters used. Keep these lists in mind the next time you present.

Final Thoughts

Creating images requires you to use several modes as well as to pay close attention to how they work together. Creating images also demands you think carefully and critically about the technologies you will use to write them. There will be times when technology will help you and times when it will hinder you as you create such images. Be patient. If you test out and practice using a variety of technologies, you will develop the right skills to help you be more successful in writing images in the future. Finally, as you do so, keep in mind that images are representations of our world and therefore should be created in a fair light. Create your images ethically to ensure that you do not misrepresent anyone or anything and thus deceive your audiences.

Additional Discussion Questions

1. Why is clip art not a good idea to use when creating a text?
2. Imagine you are tasked with having to present to a group of college students about climate change. Discuss ways in which you could creatively put together a powerful presentation that persuades this audience to be more aware of their impacts on the environments they live in. What role will images play in this presentation, and what technologies would you use to create them?

Additional Activities

1. Images and Cultures: Investigate how another culture uses images in their texts to communicate specific ideas. Share your findings with the class.
2. Presentations on Campus: Attend an upcoming presentation on your campus. Make notes about the presentation. What technologies did the speaker use? Why and how? What made the presentation effective and what did not? What role did images play? Share with your class.

Additional Assignments

1. Video Creation: Create a video in which you tell a story about your campus. Think about what images and technologies you will need to do so. When you are finished, write a reflection on your experience and share it and your video with the class.
2. Presenting on Performing: Prepare a presentation on a particular style of performing. Deliver your presentation to the class using the suggestions in this chapter. Afterwards, write a reflection on your experience presenting.

Works Cited

Murray, Joddy. *Non-Discursive Rhetoric: Image and Affect in Multimodal Composition*. Albany, NY: State University of New York, 2009.

PART 6 READING

The Voice of Lived Experience

Mobile Video Narratives in the Courtroom

Mary Angela Bock and David Alan Schneider

This article was first published in the journal *Information, Communication & Society* in 2017.

Video is transforming the online media environment. Clips of police encounters dominated news coverage in 2015, granting the public with visual access to scenes such as the fatal shooting of Walter Scott after a traffic stop in South Carolina or a protester in Baltimore being pepper sprayed at close range for defying a curfew during civil unrest. The slogan 'pics or it didn't happen,' reflects the ubiquity of images online and the ease with which video can be recorded, posted, shared and repeatedly re-contextualized. This veritable explosion of clips has overtaken our understanding of how video operates in the public sphere.

This project uses a case study of one criminal trial in the US to explore the nature of video in terms of its unique documentary and narrative value. While video itself is not new, having arrived with the invention of television in the mid-1930s, the ease with which nearly anyone carrying a smartphone can shoot, post and share events is unprecedented. While it has much in common with film and photography, digital video's communicative properties are evolving in unique ways that warrant scholarly attention. Our study starts within the narrative paradigm articulated by Fisher (1984, 1985) and its application in the courtroom setting, but this is largely a grounded, qualitative project that closely examines the way multiple video clips were rendered meaningful in the courtroom setting before proposing theoretical interpretations for our observations.

Background and Theoretical Foundation

The case at the center of this study involves an Austin Texas man, Antonio Buehler, who was arrested after an altercation with a police officer on 1 January 2012. Buehler, a West Point and Stanford graduate and Afghan war veteran, was on his way home from celebrating New Year's eve with a friend when they stopped to fuel their vehicle at a convenience store and witnessed a drunk driving investigation in progress. A woman who was originally not under arrest (Norma Pizana) was pulled from her car by officers and started crying out to bystanders to 'film this.' Buehler did so, taking stills with his camera because he could not get the video function to work. He also shouted at police when he saw what he considered to be overly aggressive tactics being used against the woman. One of the officers confronted Buehler and eventually arrested him on charges of public intoxication, assault (for allegedly spitting on the officer), interference and refusing to obey a lawful order.

Buehler's case made headlines in Austin after it was learned that a bystander had filmed the incident from across the street—which seemed to support Buehler's version of the event. In the months that followed, Buehler would start the Peaceful Streets Project, a police accountability activist organization which (among other activities) regularly patrolled city streets and filmed police activity. Eventually all charges except the misdemeanor of failing to obey a lawful order were dropped—and Buehler opted to go to trial on that charge, alleging that the only reason he was charged in the first place was because he had been photographing police activity on the night in question.

Four pieces of video would be used in the trial: the bystander's clip of the incident, two so-called dash-cam clips from the police department and tape from a rooftop surveillance camera at the convenience store. The bystander's clip was incorporated into news stories by television and newspaper journalists before the trial; the police dash-cam clips and the 7-11 surveillance video were not available to the public until the trial. Each of these clips is described in Table 1 and they are available online via YouTube and the authors' home page.

Theoretical Foundation: the Narrative Paradigm

Fisher (1984, 1985) positioned his narrative paradigm as a foil to what he original dubbed the 'rational world' paradigm and argued that humans make sense of their lives not through enthymemes and logical evidence but through storytelling. We are storytelling creatures, according to the *homo-narrans* argument, who explain ourselves, justify our actions and construct reality with a style of discourse that relates coherent sequences of events in a way that imparts significance. That first dimension of narrative—coherence—is largely the object of study for structural narratologists, whose analyses of plot, character, narrator and narratee are invaluable to the study of filmic representation

TABLE 1 Videos offered into evidence.

	What is seen	What is heard
Dash cam from Officer Oborski	Hill's arrest	Buehler & Officers arguing
Dash cam from Officer 2	Pizana in backseat	Buehler & Officers arguing
7-11 Surveillance video	Parking lot	No Audio
Bystander's smartphone	Altercation	Buhler shouting

(Barnouw, 1974; Chatman, 1978, 1990). The second dimension, what Fisher calls 'fidelity,' is more difficult to examine empirically, and might best be understood as the moral or 'point' of a story, something that is necessarily culturally and socially contingent (Fisher, 1984, 1985; Rideout, 2008).

Fisher's paradigm has been adopted by many fields outside of rhetoric and literature including two that are pertinent to this study: journalism and law. Journalism scholars have used the narrative paradigm to explain how and why certain kinds of news stories appear repeatedly, and how they advance ideology (Bird & Dardenne, 1988; Machill, Kibler, & Waldhauser, 2007; White, 2005). Legal scholars have drawn from the narrative paradigm to show how competing versions of events—i.e., narratives built from a set of facts—operate in a courtroom and compete for juror acceptance. In *A theory of the trial*, for instance, Burns (2001, p. 159) invokes the spirit of Fisher's characteristics of coherence and fidelity when he writes that 'It is through narrative that we remember, and the internal characteristics of a given narrative contribute significantly to its concrete plausibility.' Bennett (1981) studied dozens of court cases and used experimental methods to investigate what makes a courtroom story believable, finding a connection between structural ambiguity and juror skepticism. That is, a story that 'hangs together' without gaps (Fisher's coherence) strikes an audience as more truthful than one with holes in it, regardless of the details of legal facticity. Rideout's (2008) legal analysis breaks coherence into two parts: consistency and completeness, and connects the notion of fidelity to the normative elements of judicial persuasion. He proposed an additional narrative dimension relevant to this study of courtroom video, 'correspondence,' representing the way a story's elements connect to the world outside of it, evoking the semiological notion of indexicality (Barthes, 1977).

Photographs, film and video have long been incorporated into courtroom narratives (Mnookin, 1998). Indeed, law-enforcement institutions adopted the camera for surveillance and criminal identification faster than news organizations embraced photography (Tagg, 1999, 2009). Mnookin (1998) traced the history of photography in the courtroom and argued that judges use an analogy—that photos are like other illustrations or pictures. This allows photos *as part of* witness testimony, but not as independent evidentiary voices, and maintains the court's authority over truth. This also had the effect, Mnookin argued, of protecting the 'reign of words' in the logocentric world of law.

The right to film police action has become a contentious issue in the US in recent years, as smartphone proliferation has made it easier to record events and share clips online. Dozens of websites devoted to so-called cop-watching exist, and a number of groups in the US now regularly patrol high-incidence areas in order to monitor police activity (Hoffberger, 2013). Antonio Buehler, the man at the center of this case, started the Peaceful Streets Project because bystander video made a difference in his criminal defense. The man who shot that video was threatened with arrest by police at the scene, and Buehler contended that he himself was targeted for using his camera during the incident.

Video deserves scholarly attention, therefore, not only for its forensic value as an indexical representation of a scene, but also for its use in the construction of persuasive narratives. If narratives are useful for judicial persuasion, the addition of corresponding, unedited and unmanipulated video might be invaluable. How might these new digital 'texts' help prosecutors and defense attorneys craft competing narratives for the sake of a jury? How might video impart credibility to testimony from individuals in the witness stand? To state our research question formally: How does video shape judicial narratives?

Methodology and Method

Case studies are useful for qualitative exploration and descriptions of phenomena that are either too 'new' for hypothesis formulation and testing, or for situations in which statistically appropriate sample sizes are unattainable (Yin, 2009). This case is appropriate for understanding the role of multiple videos from a variety of sources. The trial represents an unusual intersection of social forces, institutional practices and pieces of evidence. That the case also turned upon a citizen's right to visually document authority with a camera further marks this case as worthy of a deeper analysis about how video and its narratives affect the truth-seeking process.

Method

This case study is based on participant observation in the courtroom augmented by non-recorded interviews with participants, the trial's audio transcript, news stories about the case and other documents. Table 1 lists the videos and their key elements. The trial was held in October 2014 in the municipal court facilities adjacent to the Austin police department. One or both of the authors was in the courtroom for every hour of the four-day trial. Table 2 lists the schedule and key events from the proceedings. The researchers took notes by hand, discussed their observations, re-typed key portions of their notebooks and reviewed the notes to look for themes related to narrative, video, cameras,

TABLE 2. Trial observation(s) 23–31 October.

	Observer(s)	Key events
Thursday, 23 October	Obs 1 am, both in pm	Voire Dire, Opening arguments
Friday, 24 October	Obs. 1 am, both in pm	Buehler on stand
Monday, 27 October	Obs. 1 am, both in pm	Juror excused
Tuesday, 28 October	Court in recess; Judge researches case law re. mistrial motion	
Wednesday, 29 October	Obs. 1 am, both in pm	Buehler acquitted

credibility and authority. On a self-reflexive note: both authors are former television journalists, one of whom once covered the judicial system as a beat. As journalists, we are sympathetic to the First Amendment issues raised by this case.

Findings

Buehler was originally charged with two felonies, 'interference with a police officer' and 'resisting arrest,' both of which were nullified by a Grand Jury. The charge that remained, 'failure to obey a lawful order' is a Class C misdemeanor in Texas, which puts it in the same category as city ordinance and (non-parking) traffic violations. He was accused of refusing to put his arms behind his back when instructed by an officer during the events of 1 January 2013. Buehler faced a maximum fine of $500; no jail time was at stake. Under Texas law he had the right to, and opted for, a jury trial as a matter of principle.

The power of cameras was acknowledged even before the trial started, as those arriving were greeted with a sign on the courtroom door prohibiting photography and video and audio recording (Figure 1). Before calling court to order, the judge warned members of the gallery that recording of any kind, audio or photographic, would not be allowed (though after requests from spectators and journalists, this prohibition was suspended during breaks). Throughout the case, photographs and video were referenced, displayed, created and shared by participants. Table 3 lists the names of key individuals and their roles.

As expected based on previous scholarship, these participants talked about video as they crafted stories for the jury, and it served a documentary function for witnesses when they testified. It also occasionally spoke for itself.

FIGURE 1. The sign that greeted the public for case involving photography prohibited cameras. Photo by author.

TABLE 3 Key participants.

Antonio Buehler	Defendant turned activist
Officer Patrick Oborski	Police Officer who accused Buehler of spitting on him
Officer Robert Snider	Police Officer who accosted the DUI passenger
John Blackbird	Man who videotaped Buehler's arrest
Ashley Hill	Driver pulled over for a DUI (charges later dropped)
Norma Pizana	Passenger in Hill's car who shouted "film this" (charges later dropped)
Millie Thompson	Buehler's defense attorney
Matthew McCabe	City Prosecutor
Hon. Mitchell Solomon	Presiding Judge
Jermaine Hopkins	Former Officer who testified against the Austin Police Department
Ben Munoz	Antonio Buehler's companion on the night of the arrest

Talking About Video

Even before the jury was empaneled, video evidence was part of the courtroom process, and indeed, delayed the proceedings. The presiding Judge Mitchell Solomon called court into session at 8:37 hours and videos were offered into evidence three minutes later. Soon a courthouse employee arrived to set up a video playback system and immediately encountered technical problems because the prosecutor's computer would not play a DVD. Defense attorney Millie Thompson and Buehler vacated the defense table temporarily so that software updates could be completed on their computer to allow video evidence to be played and projected, and one of the clips was briefly played as a test. Attorneys and the judge worked out a system by which the court clerk would have physical control of a switch that allowed the projector to be controlled by either the defense or prosecution tables.

The significance of the specific video clips in this case was first talked *about* in open court during jury selection. Thompson talked to potential jurors about their role as fact-finders and asked what they would consider to be convincing evidence. The first answer, blurted out almost immediately by two potential jurors was 'video.' After some prompting from the prosecutor, other members of the jury pool added 'witnesses' and 'testimony' to the list of evidentiary forms. As jury selection proceeded, Thompson made a pointed reference to the semiotics of a police uniform, asking how jurors might assess a speaker's truthfulness and whether officers, by virtue of their profession, are automatically more credible. At least one member of the jury pool admitted to giving more weight to the testimony of police officers and attributed that belief to 'watching too much television.'

It took about two hours to choose and swear-in six jurors for the misdemeanor panel, and opening arguments proceeded. Almost immediately, video was discussed once again in the hypothetical, as prosecutor Matt McCabe told jurors that he would offer three videos as evidence: two 'dash-cam' recordings and the 7–11 surveillance video. McCabe told jurors the videos were 'pretty boring' but 'get good when Mr. Buehler shows up.' McCabe's opening statement emphasized that the officers would be testifying and that video was only part of what they would use to learn about the case, saying 'I want to give a full context. I want to be able to see what led up to this situation, for today. To give you as an opportunity to see focus on what really happened.'

At the same time, McCabe told the jury that the question of case was merely whether or not Buehler failed to comply with a lawful order, and he reminded them that this was a misdemeanor with no jail time and potentially only a dollar fine at stake.

Testifying With Video

Jurors watched the first video only [a] few minutes after the first witnesses took the stand on day one. Officer Patrick Oborski was armed and in uniform. He looked directly at the jurors when he told them that Buehler was verbally abusive and spat on him. Prosecutors then asked Oborski whether his car is equipped with a VCR (yes) and whether police are able to alter video once it is recorded (no).

Playing back the video entailed procedures that involved the entire courtroom. The lights were dimmed and the jurors were directed to watch a large (approximately six-foot wide) screen on the opposite wall. The judge, lawyers, staff and gallery onlookers joined this ritualistic shared viewing, during which McCabe and Oborski occasionally spoke to explain what was transpiring on the tape. This clip included an audio track that was unclear. Buehler cannot be seen; the altercation occurs off-camera and can only be discerned by the low-quality sound. What is visible on the black and white tape is the gas station, the time-code, and, for several minutes, the back of the woman who was under investigation for drunk driving as she waited to begin her field sobriety test. She can be seen standing, apparently unsure whether to proceed, while audio of the altercation ensues.

The prosecutor backed up the tape several times during this scene in a way that interrupted the audio stream. Oborski's testimony about the video was delivered in a very flat, almost neutral manner, using simple declarative statements with little emotion or elaboration. This contrasted dramatically with what was heard in the audio. Although it was often difficult to understand exact words due to the distortion caused by Oborski's proximity to the microphone and his raised voice, the aural evidence depicted an officer who was agitated, loud and seemingly confrontational.

The prosecution played the second video after Oborski's testimony. This 14-minute clip from the 7–11 surveillance camera is completely silent. This camera was positioned to provide security surveillance of the store's parking lot and gas pumps and the foreground shows parking spaces and foot traffic in and out of the store. The gas pumps and sidewalk are in the background at the top of the frame. The truck Buehler was driving and the traffic stop are partially obscured by the gas pumps and a beam holding up the awning over the pumps. The police vehicles and traffic stop are further in the background. Unlike the previous dash-cam clip, this video depicted the event in a discernible sequence: Buehler and his companion entered the 7–11 parking lot as the traffic stop was in progress and they completed pumping gas and reentered their vehicle as if to leave and then exited the vehicle shortly thereafter. The prosecutor solicited little testimony from Oborski during the playback of this video. The absence of audio in this playback contributed to a quiet in the courtroom that was in sharp contrast to the noise of the first one.

The third video was played after lunch that day during the testimony of officer Robert Snider, who was holding onto Norma Pizana, the woman who cried for onlookers to 'film this' during the incident. Snider's dashboard camera was initially facing the traffic stop but was turned toward the back seat of his car after he took Pizana into custody for disobeying her order to stop using her cellphone. Snider testified that this was done because suspects sometimes 'injure themselves' while in custody. Snider, also in uniform, testified that he felt threatened by Buehler and thought that Buehler had been summoned by the young woman to violently interfere. As in the other dash-cam video, the altercation with Buehler cannot be seen; only roughly and incompletely heard.

The fourth video was not introduced until the very end of the day during defense testimony, recorded on an iPhone by John Blackbird. Blackbird was a private citizen walking along the opposite side of the street who observed the confrontation and started filming because, like Buehler, he was alarmed by the way the officers were treating Pizana. As he put it: 'The way they pulled her out of the car, the way they twisted her, it just didn't seem like anybody should treat a human being like that.' During Blackbird's testimony, Thompson replayed the video in slow motion, which clarified the way Buehler was thrown to the ground while distorting his shouts of 'What are you doing? Why are you doing this?' Blackbird testified that he thought the officer was the aggressor in this incident, and that he was threatened with arrest as well after loudly asking them whether they were proud of their actions.

Throughout the afternoon's events in court, uniformed members of the police force visited the gallery and sat in the back. Some of the officers wore the symbols of higher rank as they watched their colleagues testify. This sort of silent display is common in court settings where matters of police work are involved. In fact, during a different case in Austin, the chief of police prohibited his force from attending court in uniform during the murder trial of a man who fatally shot an officer, on grounds that the jury might be unnecessarily influenced by such a display of blue unity.

Other gallery-watchers sitting behind the prosecutor's table (implying support for that side) were frequent visitors wearing formal suits, who occasionally interacted with McCabe and were likely members of the prosecutor's department. But other than one of Antonio Buehler's supporters who wore a Peaceful Streets T-shirt, spectators sitting behind the defense table had no 'uniform' to identify their sympathies. Members of the press were easy to spot; some wore cameras (out of their hands in order to demonstrate that they were not using them). Other journalists had laptops open for note-taking, and most and sat close to the back on the prosecutor's side, near the authors, a position with a comfortable view of the screen when videos were played.

Video Speaking for Itself

In accordance with typical court procedure, the video clips were consistently used as *documents* in support of witness testimony. Yet video cannot be experienced in the same way as a still photograph, which, while classified as document evidence, might also be experienced as 'object' evidence, pulled out of envelopes, handled and passed from juror to juror. In this case, some photographs (such as the ones Buehler took of Officers Snider and Oborski) were shared with the jury as prints and shown on the screen. The difference in materiality changes the way the images or video are incorporated into the narratives being constructed. With printed images, a juror might spend a few extra seconds examining some aspect of the photo before passing it along; another might give it a cursory look. In this case, jurors were also observed turning the still images to different angles to vary their point of view, an option that is not so easily available with projection on a screen. Video's technological, phenomenological and semiological characteristics lent each clip a certain voice of its own.

In contrast, the videos in this case were experienced in real time, simultaneously, and could not be touched by the jury. Video cannot be ritually handed to jurors to symbolically entrust them with the evidence. Merely setting up the room for the video playback took considerable time before the trial even started. Interestingly, the dash-cam and 7–11 videos were exhibits for both sides but were played back from a DVD copy held by the defense; its validity and accuracy was not questioned as it left the defense laptop and moved to the screen. The validity of each clip was never at issue in this case; each clip was entered into evidence as a raw clip.

The videos enhanced and supported the performative aspects of witness testimony beyond the words they uttered. For example, during his testimony Antonio Buehler used a white board and his own body in order to demonstrate to the jury what happened on the night of his arrest. He mapped out the gas station on the white board and was allowed to leave the witness box to stand and pantomime how he moved in response to Snider's movements. But even with the hand-drawn maps and physical demonstrations, it was hard to envision the placement of the various parts of the scene, the truck Buehler drove, the police cars, the car involved in the DUI, the gas pumps, the street and the store based on discourse alone. The videos subjectively placed jurors into the scene and established the narrative setting with sight, sound and kinesthetic details not possible from the witness stand. The bystander video had the most embodied presence, because it was obviously handheld and moved with Blackbird's hand (and breathing). This video also framed the event itself in a wide shot, unlike the dash-cam and surveillance videos, which were perfectly and mechanically still and never moved in accordance with the event, to an extent that is almost frustrating to anyone who really wanted to understand what happened that night.

Finally, of course, the videos contained basic visual information—both as expected, but with details and symbols that again, were not necessarily communicated by testimony or lawyer statements. The sight of a 7–11 parking lot on New Year's Eve, for instance, is something many of us have experienced, but until we watch it together, it is only a hypothetical parking lot. The sound of an officer saying 'you spit on me,' and the way the tone, inflection and volume of that statement was recorded by video compared with the way the officer repeated it in court gave the jurors and independent marker of what happened, beyond the testimonies of Buehler and Oborski. The presence of multiple points of view in video allowed one to either contradict or amplify what was present in the others. The audio evidence of Buehler allegedly spitting occurred off-camera in the dash-cam version and was not supported by the visual evidence from the 7–11 or from across the street.

Any of these semiological markers, whether the forensic-looking time-code that dominates the frame from the dash-cam video, or the shakiness of the smartphone clip from Blackbird that captured silhouettes of Buehler and Oborski, constituted statements of fact *independent* of courtroom discourse. Thompson called attention to the fact that Oborski's silhouette advances on Buehler's and does not appear to flinch, jerk back or put a hand to its face—in contradiction to Oborski's sworn testimony that he had been spat upon in the face. That the jurors could witness this on their own, from the vantage point of an eyewitness, might well have been the factor that led to Buehler's acquittal.

Discussion: Narratives Layered and Competitive

The question that guided this project asked how video shapes judicial narratives.

Much of what we found reflects finding of previous research on legal persuasion (Bennett, 1981; Cheng & Cheng, 2014; Entner, 1993). The Western trial model is generally described as a system in which two sides compete in narrative construction, and adjudication results from the 'winning' story (Bennett, 1981; Cheng & Cheng, 2014). This project bears that out, but points to the existence of other narrative structures. For in addition to the two competing narratives about what happened the night Buehler was arrested, the videos established their own coherent timeline—though they could not establish the story's fidelity.

We also observed that throughout the case spectators were presented with an additional, overarching narrative: that justice was being served. This meta-narrative was not articulated verbally; it was performed. Law is rooted in language, but justice is experienced: It is visual, body centric and rooted in ritual; from the space in which it is decided and the decor within, the clothing worn by its actors and the multiple controls over what is seen by whom and when (Brion, 2014). Before the jury was even selected, onlookers and jurors were subjected to a visual display of power and the authority of the court. One of Buehler's supporters tested this power on the first day of the trial, by not standing when the court clerk called out 'all rise' at the start of the session.

Antonio Buehler's clothing, short haircut and posture alluded to his standing as a military veteran and financial expert, and contrasted with the long-hair he wore the night he was arrested. Other visual and performative cues included the police officers' uniforms and weaponry, Judge Solomon's colorful shirts under his robe (a lavender shirt on day two marked him, whether intentionally or not, as liberal), benches that resemble church pews, wooden paneling and a high desk that puts the judge above the room. Performances such as the choreography of attorneys before the jurors and the way that supporters from each side entered the room and sat behind a divider that separates the public from what is essentially a stage, support the ritualized performance. Indeed, because onlookers are expected to be silent and subject to the rule of the word (law and testimony) these displays are all the more important.

Video both supports and challenges a courtroom's visual rhetoric. While the four evidentiary clips were only part of the performance of justice in this case, they challenged the power of the court because of their indexical relationship with reality. They were used to support and contradict verbal testimony. Even though no single clip settled the fact, their visual, aural, kinesthetic and temporal information presented a narrative timeline that defied discursive contextualization. Multiple videos from different perspectives were incorporated into competing narrative constructions, preserving the court's authority and the meta-narrative that justice was 'being done.'

Putting Video Into Context (Talking About)

One essential characteristic of this case is that not only were videos used as evidence but the *creation of* videos and photos by citizens was also at issue. Buehler became involved that night by shouting at police and pulling out his camera. Officers confronted him and Blackbird for allegedly getting 'involved.' More than once Thompson asked questions of witnesses regarding the First Amendment right of a citizen to film police working in public.

The truthfulness of raw video was never questioned in court. Instead, much of the prosecution's effort appeared to be trying to construct a narrative that diminished the power of the video evidence while helping jurors to empathize with the officers in order to explain their decisions and actions. The prosecutor and witnesses consistently worked to explain why officers needed to control the situation and why they might want to defend themselves from bystanders in order to justify the conduct the jurors could observe.

Another way attorneys minimized video's indexicality was by pointing out the *constructed* nature of video, such as framing, angle and microphone placement. The fact that there were four videos from multiple angles further emphasizes video as a construction of reality (Brion, 2014; Cheng & Cheng, 2014; Kember, 2003). In this way, much of what we observed in the way video was talked *about* worked to reify the law, containing and controlling video's message (Mnookin, 1998; Sherwin, Feigenson, & Spiesel, 2007). By talking about video as a technology and of cameras as something that might cause concern for police, the power of the clips' content could be mitigated.

Video as Explanation (Testifying With)

The most famous early instance of a police accountability video—of Rodney King's beating in 1991—is also the textbook case on how to undermine such evidence. Prosecutors simply rolled the tape, expecting its documentation of 56 baton strikes and six kicks to make their case, ceding control of the narrative to technology. But the officers were acquitted after defense attorneys showed the jury the video in pieces, re-editing and altering the timeline of the beating (Feldman, 1994). This case shows how much has changed since one tape could be placed in court in 1991. Four tapes from different angles and sources were shown to a jury more accustomed to multimedia, a generation after riots in Los Angeles called attention to the fallibility of police officers.

But the primary lesson of the King case prevailed in this case: that video's voice can be answered with discursive strategies. When the videos were played in this case, witnesses were asked to explain what was happening in real time; in some moments, they even were invited to point to the screen to highlight particular actions. The police officers, for instance, relied on their dash-cam videos to explain DUI arrest protocols, attempting to persuade jurors as to why they would feel threatened by someone pulling an object out of their pocket.

The dash-cam videos, though, were incomplete with regard to the case at hand, since they were focused on the drunk driving investigation and not the confrontation with Buehler. The audio was hard to hear and interpret, and the action of interest was usually out of frame. Snider's squad car camera, for instance, was focused on an apparently inebriated Pizano in the back seat while jurors were expected to focus on the audio from Snider and Buehler, who could not be seen. That audio may have proved to be critical in this instance, however, in the way the profanity and shouting by officers on tape contrasted with their calm accounts in the witness box.

In this way, video undermined the credibility advantage police have traditionally had in court by virtue of their position, uniform and even their familiarity with court regulations and personnel. Video that contrasts with this *performance* might be just as much of a problem as one that represents different facts.

While the clips were occasionally played without comment and the truthfulness of raw tape was not an issue, the video was always mentioned as part of the narrative constructions by one side or another. In this way the clips also were folded into the meta-narrative performance of justice. The court maintained authority over projection and contextualization of the evidence, allowing the jurors to assess for themselves what they saw. Yet even though they were controlled and incorporated into narrative constructions, the video represented a significant challenge to discursive contextualization—largely because of the way the events depicted by the clips unfolded in real time.

Video's Own Narrative Timeline

On first blush one might be tempted to think of video evidence as an extension of photographic evidence. Photographs have been presented as evidence and used for forensic purposes almost since the invention of the camera (Tagg, 1999; Wall & Linnemann, 2014). The essential difference is that photographs contain no inherent story; they are objects, artifacts, frozen moments in time that without context and interpretation are meaningless. As a number of visual scholars have explained, a single image is ambiguous and requires context in the form of language to be understood or rendered persuasive (Benovsky, 2011; Blair, 2012; Hawhee & Messaris, 2009; Messaris, 1997). Their indexical relationship to reality can enable truth-telling and memory but can also be miscast and seductively deceiving (Barry, 1997; Coleman, 2006; Fabos, 2014; Williams & Newton, 2007; Zelizer, 2005). In court, because photographs are material they can be used as props to support the testimony of an individual, handled, examined and then explained.

But video cannot be handled, it must be played and experienced temporally. Raw, unedited video represents a timeline, with technological, phenomenological and semiological characteristics that constitute a narrative structure that *speaks for itself*. More than once during this case, the judge, jury, court staff, attorneys and spectators all shared in viewing a video's projection simultaneously. Because it must be viewed using some sort of device, it exists in its own moment in the courtroom. More than its audio and images (which can be frozen and even printed), video communicates a timeline when it is played back. This timeline is its own evidence and cannot be discursively contextualized the way a single image can.

The phenomenology of the timeline in an unedited, raw clip is what allows video to speak for itself, providing, in a sense, a hard line that the trial's two competing narrative constructions cannot bend. Philosopher Paul Ricoeur (1980), whose work influenced Fisher's, argued that the power of narrative is rooted in its metaphorical connection to human temporal experience. Unedited, raw video mimics this experience in time. That is, we move through the world in a temporal sequence, and this embodied experience lends power to narrative's persuasion.

When tied to the timeline, the visual and aural information in video is especially rich. It can add information that is not communicated verbally and answer questions the jurors did not know they had. For instance, the 7–11 video showed other bystanders in the parking lot and the way they reacted (and did not react) to what was going on near the gas pumps. The dash-cam videos have a forensic style: the camera tends to not move, it has the time-code, it is plain and static, much like the security camera footage. Blackbird's video is connected with his body; it moves according to the action in the frame and as a smartphone lens is more familiar to the average viewer than the wide-angle flatness of the police cruiser. Distant, out of focus, and somewhat shaky, but it still portrayed the backlit shadows of two men. Played back in real time, this unanticipated video from someone who thought to record what he was witnessing better matched Buehler's testimony that he was unnecessarily shoved and pushed to the ground, and at no time showed an officer recoil or wipe spit from his face.

Summary: Coherence and Fidelity

As they constructed their competing narratives, both sides talked about and testified *with* video strategically. The defense sought to explain the video while the prosecution needed to explain it away. At the same time, video's hard-edged timeline spoke for itself, providing structural coherence and completeness for those narratives. Inconsistencies between the police officers' polite answers and harsh audio and their explanations about feeling threatened when the video shows them throw a grown man to the ground, most likely influenced the jurors regarding their decision in this specific case.

In connecting its characteristics to narrative theory, it seems that video fulfills the elements of coherence, as proposed by Fisher (1984, 1985) and expanded by Rideout (2008). Unedited, raw video presents events in sequence—a plot. There is at least one actor, the author or videographer, and a video might also depict other characters who speak and act. Video establishes a setting and places the viewer within that setting. The technology contains the structure of a story phenomenologically and semiologically. What is missing is the very point of the story which in this case, as with other court cases that have relied on the camera's output, was decided by the jury.

The persuasive power of a narrative, as Fisher explained, is in how well it rings 'true' for its audience, and whether actors within a story use 'good reasons' for their actions. Legal scholars have connected this idea to courtroom narrative, noting that the moral component of Fisher's 'fidelity' is largely a matter of how well the story matches the juror's (as representatives of the community) normative ideas about right and wrong. Here, video is not particularly useful in playback. The hard edge of its timeline makes no normative statement. Fidelity is established instead through the creation and use of video by human actors; it is the performance of justice.

The videos in this case were all created as part of human activity, but only one was created directly and with human hands: the one Blackbird shot with his iPhone. Peters's (2001) typology of witnessing is helpful for thinking about how the creation of video in the conduct of witnessing is an embodied activity with moral dimensions. To document an event in order to bear witness on behalf of others, putting one's body on the line in the course of that action, is at the heart of the sanctity of witnessing. Such an act empowers others, and lends what Couldry (2010) calls 'voice' to their concerns as well as those of the video's creator. Blackbird's decision to film the scene, like Buehler's decision to use his camera, was affirmed by the jury. In this way, the act of creating a video, itself a performance, was incorporated into the court's overarching narrative: that justice was done.

Video's role in this case has important implications for public policy. The right to film police in action has been affirmed by several federal court cases (Smith, 2012) but continues to be the subject of debate in everyday encounters. Police departments are investing in the deployment of wearable cameras for officers which would subjectively film their actions automatically (Stross, 2013; Volokh, 2014). Such clips would still only tell part of the story. In this case, while no single clip settled the facts, it was the spontaneous wide shot from across the street, filmed by a bystander who [was] motivated by concern, that likely made the greatest difference in this case.

Spontaneous, citizen-generated videos constitute embodied witnessing on behalf of others that gives voice to their experience and supports individuals as they account for their actions. Buehler's decision to get involved got him arrested, and Blackbird was nearly arrested as well. But based on the way video constitutes narrative coherence and its creation shapes fidelity, it seems better to consider the documenting of police activity as a form of public service that deserves social support and legal protection.

Conclusion

The trial at the center of this case study was hardly the first to introduce video as evidence, nor was it the first case to contend with citizen rights to film police. What was special about this case, however, was the number of videos, their sources and the fact that the right to film police was one of its underlying themes. In 2015, e-marketer estimated that two billion people on Earth had smartphones, and more than 80% of Internet use occurred by way of a mobile device (Srivastava, 2014). As smartphones continue to proliferate along with badge cams, dash cams and other forms of surveillance, it is likely that many more trials will incorporate multiple pieces of video as evidence.

This case study allowed us to explore the way video served and challenged the performance of justice. We observed that video was talked about, testified with and through an inviolable timeline, occasionally spoke for itself. These findings advance the usefulness of the narrative paradigm in the legal setting for the ways that video plays a role in the meta-narrative of justice; the ways it is incorporated into competing case narrative constructions and the way its timeline structure establishes narrative coherence. Video cannot, by itself, convey the moral of its own story, and fidelity remains the discursive job of human actors in the justice system.

As a case study, there are limits to what might be generalized to other instances, but this project serves to illustrate key characteristics of video that distinguish it from other forms of evidence, whether in court or in everyday life. As smartphone video on the web proliferates, it is useful to understanding its narrative requirements, limits and potential. This case exemplified the way multiple angles and storytelling can be harnessed by state authorities and interrogated by the less powerful. The right of everyday citizens to film the activities of police and government authorities, therefore, is essential to establishing a balance of power. Video's power to control the narrative means that its production is likely to be a matter of considerable concern and controversy for years to come.

Disclosure Statement

No potential conflict of interest was reported by the authors.

Notes on Contributors

Mary Angela Bock (Ph.D., University of Pennsylvania) is a former TV journalist. She joined the faculty at the University of Texas at Austin in 2012. Her most recent project (with co-authors Shahira Fahmy and Wayne Wanta) is *Visual communication theory and research: A mass communication perspective* (Palgrave, 2014). Bock is also the author of Video journalism: Beyond the one man band, and co-edited The content analysis reader with Klaus Krippendorff. [email: mary.bock@austin.utexas.edu]

David Alan Schneider is a lecturer in the department of Radio, Television and Film at The University of Texas at Austin. He has more than 20 years experience in television production. He earned his master's degree in Media Studies and Production from Temple University with a film project titled Give Us our Toasters and our TVs: Network and Media Self-Criticism. [email: directordavid@yahoo.com]

References

Barnouw, E. (1974). *Documentary: A history of the non-fiction film* (Vol. 1983). Oxford: Oxford University Press.
Barry, A. M. S. (1997). *Visual intelligence: Perception, image and manipulation in visual communication*. Albany: State University of New York Press.
Barthes, R. (1977). *Image, music text*. New York: Hill & Wang.
Bennett, W. L. (1981). *Reconstructing reality in the courtroom: Justice and judgement in American culture*. New Brunswick, NJ: Rutgers University Press.
Benovsky, J. (2011). Three kinds of realism about photographs. *The Journal of Speculative Philosophy*, 25(4), 375–395.
Bird, S. E., & Dardenne, R. W. (1988). Myth, chronicle and story: Exploring the narrative qualities of news. In D. Berkowitz (Ed.), *Social meanings of news* (pp. 333–350). London: Sage Publications.

Blair, J. A. (2012). The rhetoric of visual arguments. In C. W. Tindale (Ed.), *Groundwork in the theory of argumentation* (pp. 261–279). Dordrecht: Springer. Retrieved from http://link.springer.com/chapter/10.1007/978-94-007-2363-4_19

Brion, D. J. (2014). The criminal trial as theater: The semiotic power of the image. In A. Wagner & R. K. Sherwin (Eds.), *Law, culture and visual studies* (pp. 329–359). Dordrecht: Springer.

Burns, R. P. (2001). *A theory of the trial*. Princeton, NJ: Princeton University Press.

Chatman, S. (1978). *Story and discourse: Narrative structure in fiction and film*. Ithaca, NY: Cornell University Press.

Chatman, S. (1990). *Coming to terms: The rhetoric of narrative in fiction and film*. Ithaca, NY: Cornell University Press.

Cheng, L., & Cheng, W. (2014). Documentary evidence as hegemonic reconstruction. *Semiotica*, 200, 165–184. doi:10.1515/sem-2014-0009

Coleman, R. (2006). The effects of visuals on ethical reasoning: What's a photograph worth to journalists making moral decisions? *Journalism & Mass Communication Quarterly*, 83(4), 835–850.

Couldry, N. (2010). *Why voice matters: Culture and politics after neoliberalism*. London: SAGE Publications.

Entner, R. (1993). *Encoding the image of the American judiciary institution: A semiotic analysis of broadcast trials to ascertain its definition of the court system* (PhD). New York University, OCLC ID: ocm 30772701.

Fabos, B. (2014). The trouble with iconic images: Historical timelines and public memory. *Visual Communication Quarterly*, 21(4), 223–235. doi:10.1080/15551393.2014.987282

Feldman, A. (1994). On cultural anesthesia: From desert storm to Rodney king. *American Ethnologist*, 21(2), 404–418.

Fisher, W. R. (1984). Narration as a human communication paradigm: The case of public moral argument. *Communication Monographs*, 51(1), 1–22.

Fisher, W. R. (1985). The narrative paradigm: An elaboration. *Communication Monographs*, 52(4), 347–367.

Hawhee, D., & Messaris, P. (2009). Review essay: What's visual about "visual rhetoric"? *Quarterly Journal of Speech*, 95(2), 210–223. doi:10.1080/00335630902842095

Hoffberger, C. (2013, August 16). *Seale and Balko visit peaceful streets*. Retrieved June 18, 2015, from www.austinchronicle.com/news/2013-08-16/seale-and-balko-visit-peaceful-streets/

Kember, S. (2003). The shadow of the object: Photography and realism. In L. Wells (Ed.), *The photography reader* (pp. 202–217). London: Routledge.

Machill, M., Kibler, S., & Waldhauser, M. (2007). The use of narrative structure in television news. *European Journal of Communication*, 22(2), 185–205.

Messaris, P. (1997). *Visual persuasion: The role of images in advertising*. Thousand Oaks, CA: Sage Publications.

Mnookin, J. L. (1998). Image of truth: Photographic evidence and the power of analogy. *The Yale Journal of Law & the Humanities*, 10, 1–74.

Peters, J. D. (2001). Witnessing. *Media, Culture & Society*, 23(6), 707–723.

Ricoeur, P. (1980). Narrative time. *Critical Inquiry*, 7(1), 169–190.

Rideout, J. C. (2008). Storytelling, narrative rationality, and legal persuasion. *Legal Writing: The Journal of the Legal Writing Institute*, 14, 53–86.

Sherwin, R. K., Feigenson, N., & Spiesel, C. (2007). What is visual knowledge, and what is it good for? Potential ethnographic lessons from the field of legal practice. *Visual Anthropology*, 20(23), 143–178. doi:10.1080/08949460601152799

Smith, J. (2012, May 14). Christopher sharp v. Baltimore City Police Department et al.

Srivastava, A. (2014, January 23). *Two Billion smartphone users by 2015: 83% of internet usage from mobiles [study]*. Retrieved June 26, 2015, from http://dazeinfo.com/2014/01/23/smartphone-users-growth-mobile-internet-2014-2017/

Stross, R. (2013, April 6). Wearable video cameras, for police officers. *The New York Times*. Retrieved from www.nytimes.com/2013/04/07/business/wearable-video-cameras-for-police-officers.html

Tagg, J. (1999). Evidence, truth and order: A means of surveillance. In S. Hall & J. Evans (Eds.), *Visual culture: The reader* (pp. 244–273). Thousand Oaks: Sage.

Tagg, J. (2009). *The disciplinary frame: Photographic truths and the capture of meaning*. Minneapolis, MN: University of Minnesota Press.

Volokh, E. (2014, May 25). Federal appeals court reaffirms right to videorecord, including at traffic stops. *The Washington Post*. Retrieved from www.washingtonpost.com/news/volokh-conspiracy/wp/2014/05/25/federal-appeals-court-reaffirms-right-to-videorecord-including-at-traffic-stops/

Wall, T., & Linnemann, T. (2014). Staring down the state: Police power, visual economies, and the "war on cameras". *Crime, Media, Culture*, 10(2), 133–149. doi:10.1177/1741659014531424

White, P. (2005). Narrative impulse in mass-media "hard news" reporting. In F. Christie & J. R. Martin (Eds.), *Genre and institutions: Social processes in the workplace and school* (pp. 101–123). London: Bloomsbury Publishing.

Williams, R., & Newton, J. (2007). *Visual communication: Integrating media, art and science*. New York: Erlbaum.

Yin, R. K. (2009). *Case study research: Design and methods*. Thousand Oaks, CA: Sage.

Zelizer, B. (2005). Journalism through the camera's eye. In S. Allen (Ed.), *Issues in journalism* (pp. 167–176). Maidenhead: Open University Press.

Reading Questions for "The Voice of Lived Experience: Mobile Video Narratives in the Courtroom" by Mary Angela Bock and David Alan Schneider

1. What impact do videos have on society, especially in places like a courtroom?
2. Do you believe that videos should be allowed as evidence in a court case? Why or why not?
3. In what ways can studying videos help us understand the ways people write in this world?

Index

Note: **Boldface** page references indicate tables and images. *Italic* references indicate boxed text.

2 Dope Queens comedy duo 153–155
2D texts 49–50, *51*
3D texts 49–50, *51*
750 Words online writing platform 229
2001 (film) 65

accessibility: of information 199–200, **200**; internet and 201, 283, 331; of messages 268–269; of technology 198; of websites 322–323
Achievement app 237
active, technology as 12–13, 69
active voice 130–131
activism, social media 302
Activities: Accessibility *324*; Actions and the Design of Technology *360*; Active Listening Exercise *369*; Additional 18–19, 36–37, 55, 93, 114, 135, 160–161, 188–189, 231–232, 250, 270–271, 306–307, 325, 343, 375, 394; Alignment *108*; Analyze a Dance *389*; Analyzing Your Mail *48–49*; Assess Your Organizational Habits *184*; Bad Website *321*; Daily Phone Use *329*; Daily Technology Use *16*; Databases *228*; Design Choices and the Ways People Use Apps *340*; Different Ways of Brainstorming, Different Ways of Thinking *77*; Editing Log *131–132*; Email Privacy Laws *266*; Email Your Professor *262*; Examine a Map *222*; Examine Your Sources *182*; First Web Pages, The *169*; Hacking *231*; Image Journal *379*; Information for All *170*; Investigate Modes Working Together *32*; Investigate a Place *241*; Investigate Your Own Calendar *151*; Investigating Social Media *305*; Learn More About Your Audiences *258*; Life Cycle of a Smartphone *333*; Make an Accessible Text *269*; Music Listening *366*; No Computer Information *171–172*; Observe Your Draft *122*; Past Presentations *393*; Radio Station *365*; Reading and Experiencing Materials *53*; Research Tool Box *89*; Search Engines *177*; Sketch a Website *319*; Social Media Activism *303*; Specific Ways of Searching *178–179*; System Investigation *217*; Technology in Culture *235*; Textures *363*; The Many Versions of an Event *159*; Toolbox for Still Images *382*; Viral Posts *301*; Virtual Reality and Writing *237*; Writing Technologies *11–12*; Writing and Your Phone *330*; Your Story *157–158*
Adventures of Tom Sawyer, The (Twain) 140
advertising: behavioral 276; click-through rates and 277–278; discrimination in 282; Facebook practices 275–278; market segmentation and 283; personalized 277–278; racially targeting 283; return on investment and 277; social media and 302–303
affordances 32, 43, 50, 78, 184, 218–219, 284
After the Deadline software 129
Albert of Brandenburg 46
Albertus Magnus 61
Alcott, Louisa May 234–235
Alexa (Amazon Echo) 363
Al-ex Huck 294, 297–298, *367–368*
"Alex from Target" 159–160
algorithmic gate-keeping/filtering 281–282, 284–285
algorithms 223–224, 276–280, 283–285, 311
alignment of design elements 107–108
alphabetic draft **118**
alphabets 8, *10*, 138, 144
Amazon Echo (Alexa) 363
America Online 203
analogous color 101, **102**, 199
analytics 275, 278–279, 280, 282–284, 298–299, 322, 325, 346, 368
analyzing data *85*, 345, 368
"AND" Boolean operator 228
angle of moving images 386–387
annotation of sources 92–93
APA citation style 91–92
apps, designing: audience and 336; backend 341–342; Bujo app and 334–336, **335**; culture and 337; frontend 334–338, **335**, 340–341;

413

Index

navigation and 337, 340; overview 334, 342; resources *341–342*, 342; small nature of device and 338; user friendliness and 340; when and where people use devices and 340–341; wireframing 337–338; see also specific name
Aquinas, Thomas 61
Arduini, Tina 238
Ariana Grande concert bombing (United Kingdom) 294
Aristotle 11, 60–61
Arnold, Josh 134
artwork see images
assemblage 235
Assignments: Additional 19, 37, 55–56, 93–94, 115, 135, 161, 189, 232, 250, 271, 307, 325–326, 343, 376, 394; Create Your Own Video Game *238*; Creating and Distributing Digital Texts Non-Digitally *47–48*; Develop a Social Media Ad *298*; Gutenberg's Impact *166*; Research Public Speakers *374–375*; Social Media Study *295*; Technologies and Your Career *34–35*; Writing Email Content 265
assonance 154
asynchronous feedback 120
attribution 91–92, 280, 349–351
Audacity 372, **372**
audience: analytics 368; apps for mobile devices and 336; color and 105; design and 99–100; differences and, attention to 36; email messages and 262; feedback from 121–122; multiple, writing for 35–36; observation of reading 121; podcasts and 369–370; reading path and 99; revising text and 127; text-based videos and 134–135; videos and 134–135; websites and 323
audio/aural mode of communication 25, *26*
augmented reality 236–237
Augustine, Saint 61
automation 203

Babak, Larissa 25
backend computer operations 216, 311–316
Bacon, Roger 61
Baegun (Buddhist monk) 165
Baker, Jamal 168–169
Bandcamp social media platform 294
banning websites 202–203
Beach, Richard 197
Be Good album promotion 294, **294**, 298

behavioral advertising 276
beliefs, people's social/political 32–33, *52*
Bell, Alexander Graham 328
Benkler, Y. 281
Berners-Lee, Sir Tim 169
Best Video Tutorials 76
"be" verbs 130–131
Bhatara, Prabhu 331
Bickford, Deborah J. 241
Bigelow, Jacob 63
binary form 225, 311
binary value 225
Bingham, Betsy *153*
Bi Seng 165
bit 225, 311
bitmap 381–382
Blackbird, John 402, 404, 408–409
Bock, Mary Angela 85
bodily movements 388; see also embodied actions
books 25, 42, 165, 213, 234–235; see also specific title
Boolean operators 228–229
Boole, George 228
Boston Marathon bombing (2013) 155–156
boxing draft **119**
brainstorming 74–77, **75**
brainstorming poster 97, **98**, 99
breaking design rules 112
Browning, J. 202
Brownlee, John 109
Bruce, B. 198
Buehler, Antonio 395–397, 399, 403, 405
Bujo (Bullet Journal) app 334–336, **335**
bullet points in presentation 391–392, **391**
bullying 10
bumper sticker colors 101, **101**
Burns, R. P. 397
Bush, Vannevar *243–244*
Butler, Mike 22–24, 31–32, 33–36, *33–34*, 78, 80, 258
byte 225, 311

C++ computer language 312
calendars 148, **149**, 196
Calo, M. R. 282
Cambridge Analytica 300
Cameron, David 327
"Can We Define Technology" (Nye) 11
Carlson, Katrina 4

Carnegie Mellon University study 332
case studies 398; *see also* courtroom mobile video narratives
Cazden, C. 198
C computer language 312
center alignment 107
Center for Internet and Technology Addiction and Professor David Greenfield's Smartphone Compulsion Test 332
central processing unit (CPU) 311
Centre for Excellence in Universal Design 268
characters *110*
Chavannes, Nicole 263–264, *264–265*
Chicago citation style 92
choose-your-own-adventure games 236
Chrome search engine 176, 315
Cicero 61
citation styles 91–92
citing writing: citation styles 91–92; copyright/fair use and, understanding 89–91; critical thinking 87, **88**, 89; keeping track of/annotating sources 92–93; overview 86
City of Lighthouse Point (Florida) 48
clarity of text **128**
classroom design 240–242
clean design 99–100, 107, 319–320, **320**
click-through rates (CRTs) 277–278
clip art 112, 385; *see also* images
closing/ending email message 260, 262
CMYK color 103, 105
Code.org post 224
Code Talkers 253, **254–255**, 256
CodeWithChris 342
codex 42
coercion 282–283
cognitive actions 358
cognitive automaticity 142, 144
coherence of text **128**
collaborating 247–249
Collazo, Julie Schwietert 347
color: analogous 101, **102**, 199; audience and 105; of bumper stickers 101, **101**; CMYK 103, 105; complementary 101, **102**; contrast and 103; cool **102**; feelings and 100–101; fonts 127; historical perspective 100–101; *Jaws* poster and 101; monochromatic **102**; for organization 103, 105; power of 100–101; red 101; RGB 103, 105; saturation and 103; text placement and 105; types **102**; warm **102**; wheel 101, **102**; working with, knowledge about 101, **102**

comma 131
commodification of information 196
Communia Mathematica (Bacon) 61
communication: crisis 294–295; electronic, growth of 191; modes of 1, 24–29, *26*, *29*, *31*; rhetoric 13; *see also* modes
complementary color 101, **102**
computed-generated materials 41
computer: backend operations 216, 311–316; as database 225; data in terms of 225–226; forensics 155; frontend operations 216, 316–320; language 169, 243, 312–315, **313**, *316*; literacy 199; materials generated by 41; mouse **357**, 358–360; programming 311–316, *311*; source code 311, 314–315
confirmation bias 175–176
Confucius 178
connected/connectedness 15, *26*, 243–244, 289
consistency in text **128**
consumer protection laws 284
content: attribution 91–92; creating 348; curating 274, 348; drafting text and 118; of emails 260–265, 269; fair use of 350; navigation of 318; personalized 174–175, 247, 273–274, 277; placement of on website 317; regulating 202–203; revising text and 127; terms of use and 304–305, *304*; uploading 348; user-generated 179–180, 273, 276; of websites 193, 317; website versus mobile device 340; *see also* information; sharing
contrast 103, 106
conventions 24, *31*, 112
cool color **102**
copyleft 90
copyright 89–91, 167, *168*, 300, 346, 348, 350
Couldry, N. 409
courtroom mobile video narratives: background information 395–398; coherence and 408–409; context of video and 405–406; fidelity and 408–409; findings 399; method 398–399, **398**; methodology of studying 398–404; narratives, discussion of layered and competitive 404–409; overview 395, 409–410; participants **400**; talking about video 400, 405–406; testifying with video 401–403, 406–407; theoretical foundation 396–398; timeline of video's narrative 407–408; trial, theory of 397; video speaking for itself 403–404

415

Index

CPU (central processing unit) 311
crash points 383
creating content 348
Creation of Adam, The (Michelangelo) 118
creativity 112, 392
credibility of sources 179–182
credit for work, giving others 90–91, 350–351; *see also* citing writing
crisis communication 294–295
critical literacy 204
critical thinking 87, **88**, 89, 173–177
crowdsourced information 179–181
cryptography software 202
CSS computer language 312, 314
culture: apps and, designing 337; big picture and 337; diversity and 191; messages and 258; navigation and 337; privacy and 36; storytelling and 151–152; technology and *153*
curating content 274, 348
cursive writing *see* handwriting
cyberbullying 10, 299

dance 388–389
dashboard cameras 396, 402–404
data: analyzing *85*, 345, 368; binary form of 225, 311; in computer terms 225–226; in database 226–227; defining 225; searching 228–229; social media's gathering of 302–303; for writing improvement 229; *see also* information
databases 224–227, 311
deliberative democracy 281–282
delivery of presentation 393
democracy, deliberative 281–282
demo draft **119**
De Natura Deorum (Cicero) 61
design: of apps 334–338, **335**, 340–342, *341–342*; audience and 99–100; classroom 240–242; clean 99–100, 107, 319–320, **320**; consequences of website 321–322; defining 96; identifying technologies for help with 80; interaction 337; observations on, making 96; overview 114; reading path and 97–99, **97**, **98**; of technologies 196–198; Universal 268–269, 323; *see also* design principles
Design of Everyday Things, The (Norman) 337
design principles: alignment 107–108; breaking rules and 112; color 100–103, **101**, **102**, **104**, 105; creativity/imagination 112; defining 100; emphasis 110–111; moving through text 108–109; overall look 113; overview 100; point of view 111–112; proximity 106–107, *107*; repetition 108–109; size 106; typography 109–110; for websites *323–324*
destructive editing 372
Developer Guidelines for Android *341*
Developer Guidelines for iOS *341*
Dewey Decimal System 45, 213
Dhupia, Neha 299
"digital dossiers" 274
digital gaming 236–238
digital maps 239–240
digital texts 43, 46–47, **49**, 54, 234–235
digitaltrends.com 333
dimension 49–50, 109, 221, 338
Dirda, Michael 140–141
direction and moving images 388
direction of visuals 132
discrimination in advertising 282–283
Discussion Questions: Additional 17–18, 36, 55, 93, 114, 135, 160, 188, 231, 249, 270, 306, 325, 342–343, 375, 394; Breaking the Rules *113*; Classrooms *242*; Colors *106*; Comparing Digital and Non-Digital Technologies *46*; Crowdsources *181*; Editing Tools *130*; Fast and Convenient Sources of Information *174*; Interfaces *216*; Labels *220*; Language and Search Engines *176–177*; Online Storytelling *155*; Podcasts *368*; Search Engines *225*; Sharing Online *247*; Stories *154*; Systems *223*; Texting While Driving *267*; Tracking Your Writing *229*; When *245*; Yourself and Social Media *300*
distances, temporal 107, 133
distribution 198–201, 373, 381
diversity and technology 191
Dobrzynski, J. 200
dpi 381
draft: learning method of 127; testing 120–122; of text 118–119, **118–119**

ecological model for literacy technologies/tools 194–196, 204
economics and clothing materials' selection *52*
ecosocial system 195
ecosystem 195
Edison, Thomas 62–63
editing images 381
editing podcasts 371–373

416

editing text: "be" verbs and 130–131; commas and 131; criteria for 128–129, **128**; letting go of unnecessary words 130; as negative process, perception of 128; overview 127–128, 135; sound-based text 133–134; strategies for 128–129, **128**; taking apart text and 121–122; timing of phase 127–128; video-based text 134–135; visual-based text 132–133; word-based text 129–131
efficiency 130, 323
Egyptologists 148
Ehrlich, Matthew C. 347
Elements of Technology (Bigelow) 63
Eliot, T. S. 195
Ellul, J. 191
email messages: audience and 262; closing/ending 260, 262; content of 260–265, 269; dangerous uses of 266; employment monitoring of 266; examples **259**, **260**; first 259; good uses of 266; greeting 260, 261; ISP and 266–267; language in 260; limitations of 266–267; newsletter 263, **263**; overview 258–259, 258–260, **259**, **260**; privacy and 266–267; professional 259–260, **260**; purposes of 263–265; reader's attention and, catching 261; subject line of 260–261, **260**, 263–264; writing 261–262
embedded systems 194
embedded, technology as 14, 192–193, 204–205, 209
embodied actions 358–361, 375
embodied, technology as 15–16, 355
emotional mode of communication *26*
emotions 365–367
emphasis of design principles 110–111, 133–134
enframing 195
Engelbart, Douglas *244*, 359
Entertainment Software Association 236
eotechnic technological complex 64
errors 323
essays, writing 167
ethical choices in writing 93
European Council for Nuclear Research (CERN) 169
Evernote 333
evolution, human 57–58, 60
examples in writing, gathering 81
exclusion and genres 33
exigency 77
expanding search for information 173–177

Facebook: advertising practices 275–278; algorithmic gate-keeping and 281–282; algorithmic power and 276; coercion and 282–283; deliberative democracy and 281–282; discrimination and 282–283; homophily and 282; intolerance 282; Major League Baseball deal with 302; netiquette and 345–346; News Feed 279; personalization services and 278–279, 282; personal safety and 280–281; political economy of communications approach to 275–276; predictive algorithms and 278–280; privacy and 275, 279–281, 352; Reach Generator and 278; real-name only policy 280; revenue of 275–276; social segmentation and 282
Facebook.Live 159
fade-ins 134
fade-outs 134
fair use 89–91, 350, *350*
"fake news" 86
FedEx logo 113, **113**
feedback on text 120–122
feelings: color and 100–101; defining 366; emotion versus 366; music and 365–367; writing and 24–25
file types: for digital audio 371, **371**; for images 381–382
Filter Bubble, The (Pariser) 281
filtering, algorithmic 281–282, 284–285
firewalls 202
First Amendment 281
first-person point of view 111
Fisher, W. R. 395–397, 408
5Ws and How questions 87, *88*
Flag Story Quilt (Ramsey) *153*
flex text 127
Florey, Kitty Burns 140–141, 143
flow of text **128**
flyer, baseball boot camp 29, **30**
Flynn, Pat 373, 392
focal point of image 383–384, **383**
focus group, conducting *82–85*
"fold, the" 317
folktales 152
fonts 109–110, **110**, 127, 338
forensics, computer 155
Franklin, Benjamin 138
Franks, Tammy 72–74, 77–78, 80–81, 120
free access 348–349
free cost 349

417

Index

free use 349
frontend computer operations 216, 316–320
fund-raising memo **72–73**
future and writing/technology 5

Gable, Tina 303
Gallup global surveys 328
gamification 237
gaming 236–238
gate-keeping, algorithmic 281–282, 284–285
gender and technology 64–65
genre 23–24, 29–33, *31*
Gestalt principles *107*
gestural mode of communication 25, *26*, 27
gestures 388; *see also* embodied actions
Gezi Park protests (Turkey) 280
GIMP 132, 381
Gladney, George Albert 347
Global Positioning System (GPS) 239, 292
GNU Project 90
Gomez, Nikki 40–42, 54, 362
Google algorithm 223
Google Maps 45, 123–124
Google search engine 174, 176, 212–213, 224
Google's Personalized Search 274–275
Gould, Michelle R. 300, 345
Graham, Steve 141
grammar *8–9*, 28
Grammarly tool 129–130, **129**
grassroots groupminds 191
Gray, Matt 29
Greek alphabet *10*, 144
Greenfield, David 332
greeting, email message 260–261
groupware programs 197
GSMA Intelligence 328
gustatory mode of communication *26*
Gutenberg, Johannes 46, 165–166

Haas, Christina 8, 14, 193, 359
hacking system 230
Hahessy, Rebecca 296, *296–297*
handouts for presentation 390
handwriting: death of, long-term view of 144; famous authors using 143; Franklin's view of 138; historical perspective 137–144; individualism and 139; Palmer Method of 139, 142; perceptions of good 138–139, 141; printing press and 139; "slow handwriting" movement and 143; Sumerians and 138, 144; teaching of 138–139; typewriter and 140; Zaner-Bloser curriculum 141
"handwriting effect" 141
Harvard Business Review 76
hate speech 281
Hawisher, Gail E. 152
Heidegger, M. 195–196
Help from HowTech 76
help in researching, asking for 85–86
Hersman, Erik 230
Hicks, Marcia 256
hieroglyphs *10*, 11, 24
Holliday, Tess 351
Homa, Richard 105
homophily 282
Honorable Caligula post 8
Honton, Tommy *304*
Howells, William Dean 140, 143
HTML computer language 243, 312–315, *313*
HTTP computer language 169
Hull, Glynda A. 152
Hurricane Harvey (2018) (Texas) 294
hyperlinks *243–244*, 318

ideology 14, 196, 198, 202–204, 282, 397
IEEE citation style 92
iHub 230
images: altering 347; angles and moving 386–387; crash points of 383; direction and, moving 388; distributing 381; dpi of 381; editing 381; file types 381–382; focal point of 383–384, **383**; "free" stock 350–351; function of 378, **378**; Instagram and 4; lighting and moving 387; live, creating 388–393; materials for, identifying right 382–383; meaning of 379; in Microsoft Word, embedding 32; moving, creating 386–388; netiquette and 347; overused 385; overview 393; power points of 383; producing 380; representation of ideas and 385–386; resolution of 381; scenes and moving, creating using time 387; shapes and 385; sizes of 338; sound and moving 387; in technological world 377–379, **378**; technology for, identifying right 380–381; with text, placing 385; viral 159–160, 346, 379; writing still 379–386
imagination 112
Indraprastha Institute of Information (India) 332
infographic project 124–125, **125**

418

information: of accessibility 199–200, **200**; accessibility of 199–200, **200**; bias and 179–182; commodification of 196; confirmation bias and 175–176; credibility of 179–182; crowdsourced 179–181; displaying 186–187, **187**; expanding search for 173–177; multimodal 211–212; multiple modes for expressing 186–187, **187**; narrowing search for 177–179; organizing 183–186, 217–218; overload in presentation 390–391; overview 188; privacy of 280–281; regulation of 202; searching for right 172; seeking 168–172; sharing 164–165, **164**, 184–186; social media for personalizing 175; validity of 180; viral 159–160, 346; visualizing 187, **187**; website 317; *see also* content; data
infrastructures of technological world 241–242
"In Praise of Copying" (Trithemius) 139
Insardi, Akamie 384, *384*
Instagram 4, 87, 89, 159, 292, 301–305, *304*, 351
intellectual property 346–347
interaction design 337
InterChange program 197
interface 216
International Volunteer HQ's website 312
internet: accessibility and 201, 283, 331; communities and, building 197; defining 169; exposure and 345; homophily and 282; hyperlinks and *243–244*, 318; information on 45, 168–169, 171, 173, 198, 201; internet service provider and 176, 266–267, 312; network connection and 199; Network Neutrality and 201, 283; online storytelling and 155–156; public domain and 91; regulation of 202–203, 284; relationships and, building 197; scientific journals on 172; as system 223; user statistics 409; viral information/images and 159–160; *see also* netiquette; searching internet; websites
internet service provider (ISP) 176, 266–267, 312
Interviews: Al-ex Huck *367–368*; Butler, Mike *33–34*; Chavannes, Nicole *264–265*; Hahessy, Rebecca *296–297*; Insardi, Akamie *384*; Nygren, Ciera *227*; Pearson, Meghan *150–151*; Register, Jeweliana *339*
interviews, conducting *82–85*
intolerance 282
ISP (internet service provider) 176, 266–267, 312

Java computer language 312
JavaScript computer language 312
Jaws poster 101
Jikji (Baegun) 165

kairos 236, 245
karoshi 201
Kathak (Indian dance form) 388, **389**
kerning *110*
KERNTYPE game *110*
K'iche' (Mayan text) 152
Kogan, Aleksandr 300
Kubrick, Stanley 65
Kubu, Cynthia 230
Kulab, lord of 143

labeling system 217–220
labels 220–221, **220**, **221**
Lacrae (hip-hop artist) 154
language: computer 169, 243, 312–315, **313**, *316*; in email messages 260; English 8, 193; grammar and *8–9*; literacy and 167; modes and 27; multimodal 236; native 256; Navajo 253, **254–255**; rules for 167; in system 217–221; technology and 8; translating 214–215; writing and 9–10
Latour, B. 195–196
learnability 323
left alignment 107–108
library 45, 213
Library of Congress 199
lighting and moving images 387
Lincoln, Abraham 63
Lindon Leader 113
linguistic mode of communication 25, *26*, 27–28; *see also* language
LinkedIn professional networking service 87, 89, 247
literacy: complexities of 204–205; computer 199; critical 204; ecological model for 194–196, 204; education 204; language and 167; materiality of 193; reading/writing and 167; technologies/tools 193–196
literatureproject.com 234
"Little Gidding" (Eliot) 195
Little Women (Alcott) 234–235
Liu, Lili 237
live images, creating 388–393; *see also* images
live performances 388–393; *see also* public speaking

419

Index

logo 113, **113**
Lundell, Dana 197
Luther, Martin 46–47

McCabe, Matt 401, 403
McChesney, R. 197, 201
Machado, Andre 229–230
macro level 81
McStay, A. 276
magazine genre 32–33
Major League Baseball deal with Facebook 302
Mamedov, Tair *304*
MapQuest 202
maps, digital 239–240
March for Our Lives rally (2018) 42
market segmentation 283
Marx, Leo 63
Massachusetts Institute of Technology 63, 64
materiality of literacy 193
materials: apparel companies' selection of *52*; choosing correct 54; computer-generated 41; defining 51; for images 382–383; of writing 51–52, 54
Mayan calendar 196
media 25, *31*
medieval letter **164**
Medina, Jose 4
medium 25, 29
Melville, Herman 60
memex *243–244*
memorability 323
mental model 337
messages: accessibility of 268–269; culture and 258; importance of 253, **254–255**, 256; organization of 269; overview 270; presentation of information 269; sharing 269; technology for, choosing right 256–258; text 267–268; text for, choosing right 256–258; *see also* email messages
Michaels, S. 198
Michelangelo 118
micro level 81
microprocessors 194
Microsoft Word 31–32, *110*, 216, 218, 225, 244
militarism and design of technology 197–198
MLA citation style 91–92
Mnookin, J. L. 397
mobile devices: apps for, designing 334–338, **335**, 340–342, *341–342*; defining 328; good uses of 327–328; news via 329–330, **330**; overview 342; past versus present uses of 329–330, **330**; popularity of 328; writing with 333–334; *see also specific type*
mobile mode of communication 26; *see also* courtroom mobile video narratives; mobile devices
Moby Dick (Melville) 60
mockup draft **119**
modes: evolving 27–28; as multimodal 26–27; multiple 24; storytelling and 152; types of 1, 24–29, *26*, *29*, *31*; working together 28–29
monochromatic color **102**
morphemes *9*
morphology 8, *9*
motivational poster 97, **97**
mouse, computer **357**, 358–360
movable type 165
moving images, creating 386–388; *see also* images
moving through text 108–109; *see also* reading path
multimedia 25
multimodal: defining 25; information 211–212; language 236; modes as 25–27; redundancy of 27; storytelling 152–155; system 220–222, **220, 221**; technology as 1, 12; texts as 25, 41; writing as 1, 24–28
multiple modes 24, 186–187; *see also* multimodal
multitasking 229–230
Mumford, Lewis 63–64
Murphy, Derek 291–292
Murray, Jody 7, 96, 239, 378–379
Museum of Selfies *304*
music 365–367

Nagelhout, Ed 241
narrative, technology as 13, 144; *see also* storytelling
narrative theory/paradigm 396, 408; *see also* courtroom mobile video narratives
narrowing search for information 177–179
National Museum of the American Indian (NMAI) 253
native languages 256
Native Words, Native Warriors exhibition 253
natural language processing 129
Navajo language 253, **254–255**
navigation 318, 337, 340
negative space 113, 133
Nelson, Mark Evan 152

420

Nelson, Ted *244*
neotechnic technological complex 64
netiquette: accountability and 347; copyright and 346, 348; credibility and 347; crediting use of 350–351; Facebook and 345–346; free access and 348–349; free cost and 349; free use and 349; images and 347; intellectual property and 346–347; practicing 346–347; resources *346*; sharing and 347–348; suggestions for implementing 351–352; terminology 348–350; uploading content and 348
Network Neutrality 201, 283
New Atlantis (Bacon) 61
Newcomen, Thomas 62
new electronic villages 191
New London Group *9*, 25–26
newsletter, email 263, **263**
news, online 158
new technologies 16–17, 78
Nielsen Norman Group 317, 323
Ninety-Five Theses 46
No Child Left Behind law 142
nomophobia (NO MObile PHOne phoBIA) 332
non-digital texts 42–46, 54
Norman, Donald 337
"NOT" Boolean operator 228
NPR podcasts 368
Nye, David E. 11, 13, 57
Nygren, Ciera 225–227, *227*

Oborski, Patrick 401, 403
Ohio Proficiency Tests 142
Oldenziel, Ruth 64
Olfactory mode of communication *26*
one-on-one conferencing 204
Ong, Walter J. 8
online news 158
online sources, going beyond 82, 85
online spaces 243–244
online storytelling 155–156
online writing groups 120
online writing platform 229
oracle bone script (*jiǎgǔwén*) 42
Orbitz 282
"OR" Boolean operator 228
organization: color for 103, 105; of information 183–186, 217–218; of messages 269; proximity for 106–107
organizational update 22–24, **22**, 30–32
Oxford comma 131

paleotechnic technological complex 64
Palmer, A. N. 139
Palmer Method of handwriting 139, 142
paper cutting (*jianzhi*) *43*
Papin, Denis 62
Pariser, E. 281
passive voice 130–131
past actions 358–359
past and writing/technology 5
Peaceful Streets Project 396, 397, 403
Pearson, Meghan 80, 148–149, *150–151*, 383
peer editing 204
penmanship 137; *see also* handwriting
permission to use others' work 91
personalization services 278–279, 282–285; *see also* Facebook
personalization tools 278
personalized information 175, 247; *see also* Facebook
personalized web 274–275
personal safety 280–281
personas 298, 336
Pew Research Center 158, 182, 257, 329
Pew Research Center Internet & American Life Project survey 274, 280
Phoenician alphabet *10*, 138
photos *see* images
Photoshop 132
PHP computer language 312
physical actions 358
piracy 14
Pizana, Norma 395–396, 402
place 239–241, 244–246
planning writing: brainstorming 74–77, **75**; determining purpose and how technologies can help 77–78; exploring new technologies 78; gathering examples 81; identifying technologies for initial research 79; identifying which technologies will deliver text 80; identifying which technologies will help with design 80; overview 74; troubleshooting problems 81; understanding audience 78
Plantation Women's Soccer Club fundraiser promotion 293, **294**
Platform for Internet Content Selection (PICS) 202
Plato 61
Pliny 61
podcasts 368–373
PodTrac 368

421

point of view 111–112
Pokémon GO game 237
political economy of communications (PEC) approach 275
Popol Vuh 152
poster boards 42
Post-it notes 126
power points 383
PowerPoint template 389, **391**, 392
predictive algorithms 277–280, 284–285
predictive analytics 280, 282–283
presentations 389–393
present and writing/technology 4
price discrimination 282
printing press 46–47, 139, 165, **166**
PRISM 280, 284
privacy: culture and 36; email messages and 266–267; Facebook and 275, 279–281, 352; informational 280–281, 283, 285; protecting 176, 223–224; rights 202, 284; search engines and 176, 223; smartphones and 202; social media and 304–305, *304*; technology and 202
producing images 380
propaganda 10
protocols 169
prototype *51*
prototyping draft **119**
proximity of design elements 106–107, *107*
public domain 91, 349
public speaking 24, 373–374, 389–393
punctuation 27–28, 131
Purdue OWL 92, 131
purpose, determining 77–78
purposefully thinking 134
purposeful writing 40–42
Python computer language 312

Qiao Xiaoguang *43*
quality of visual- or sound-based text 132–133
questions: for analyzing data *85*; 5Ws and How 87, **88**; for researching writing 82; for survey/interview/focus group *82–83*; for technology selection *84*; for testing draft 121; for testing technology selection *84*
quilts and storytelling 153
QWERTY keyboard 140

Ramirez, Juan 122–123
Ramsey, Suzanne Kesler *153*
Random Hacks of Kindness (RHOK) 230

rapport 257
raster graphics 381–382
Reach Generator 278
readability 28, 106, 120
reading path 97–99, **97**, **98**; *see also* moving through text
real-time editing 372–373
recursive 74
recycling bins with trash 40, **41**
Register, Jeweliana 124, 334–335, *339*
Remington Arms Company 140
repetition of design elements 108–109
researching writing: asking for help 85–86; conducting survey/interview/focus group *82–85*; going beyond online resources 82, 85; identifying technologies for initial 79; overview 81–82; questioning what is needed 82
resolution 381
return on investment (ROI) 277
revising text 122–127, **125**; *see also* editing writing
RGB color 103, 105
Rheingold, H. 191
rhetoric 1, 13, 235
rhythm 154, 365–366
Rideout, J. C. 397, 408
Rifkin, J. 201, 203
Robinson, Phoebe 153–154
role performance 388–393; *see also* public speaking
role-playing games (RPGs) 236
Royal Society 61–62
Ruby computer language 312
rule of thirds 383, **383**
Rutz, Carol 241

SafeSurf 202–203
safety, personal 280–281
Saloman's House 61
satisfaction, user 323
saturation, color 103
SAT Writing Exam 141
scenes, creating using time 387
Schneider, David Allen 85
science and technology 62–63
Scientific American magazine 63
scribes 47
scripts 42, 138
Script and Scribble (Florey) 140

search engines *79*, 174, 176, 223–224; *see also specific name*
searching internet: data 228–229; expanding 173–177; narrowing 177–179; for right information 172; search engines for *79*, 174, 176, 223–224; *see also* search engines
second-person point of view 111–112
self-determination, informational 283–284
Selfe, Cynthia L. 152, 196
Selfe, R.J., Jr. 196
selfie *303–304*
semiotics 6
senses, podcasts and engaging all 370
Seo, Jane 291–292
Shannon, Susie *153*
shareware programs 197
sharing: danger of 246–247; information 164–165, *164*, 184–186; messages 269; methods of, varied 246; netiquette and 347–348; power of 246–247; uploading versus 348; *see also* netiquette
shirt boards 143
signposting 391, **391**
signs 6–8, **6**
singers/songwriters, storytelling by 154
Sistine Chapel ceiling 18
situated, technology as 233–236, 249
size of design elements 106
sketching draft **119**
"slow handwriting" movement 143
smartphones: addiction to 332; Android platforms *341–342*; connections and 15; dangerous uses of 331–333; disposal of 333; good uses of 327–328, 331; GSMA Intelligence and 328; impact of 328; iOS platforms *341–342*; life cycle of 333; manufacturing of 333; nomophobia and 332; privacy and 202; text messages and 267–268; writing with 333–334; *see also* mobile devices
Smith, Cyril Stanley 62
Smithsonian Institution Traveling Exhibition Service (SITES) 253
Snider, Robert 402–403
Snowden, Edward 280, 284
social actions 358
social beliefs of people 32–33, *52*
social determinism 191
social media: activism 302; advertising and 302–303; awareness in using 300; as business 302–303; consequences of, varied 301–302; crisis communication and 294–295; dangerous uses of 299–301; data gathering and 302–303; on global level 294, **294**; good uses of 291–292, 294–295, 299; on local level 293, **294**; overview 306; personalizing information and 175; popular U.S. platforms 292–293; privacy and 304–305, *304*; selfie and *303–304*; technologies 293; writing for 297–300; *see also specific platform name*
social network sites (SNSs) 179, 273; *see also specific name*
social plug-ins 279
social relations and technology 196
social segmentation 282
Socratica post 178
Sofia, Z. 197–198
Solomon, Mitchell 400
Sombart, Werner 63
sound: Alexa and 363; Amazon Echo and 363; analyzing 365–367; defining 363–365, **364**; file types for digital audio 371, **371**; meaning of, ascribing 364; moving image and 387; music 365–367; podcasts and 368–373; public speaking and 373–374; in technological world 363–367
sound-based text, editing 133–134
source code, computer 311, 314–315
space 239–241, 244–246
spaces after period 27–28
spatial distance of visuals 132–133
spatial mode of communication 25, *26*, 27–29, *29*
special effects 133–134
Spencer, Platt Rogers 139
Stahl, Lesley 300
stakeholders in technological world 241–242
Staples.com 282
Steinmetz, Charles 63
stereotypes 282
still images, creating 379–386; *see also* images
Stonehenge 60
stories 152, 156–160
storyboard draft **119**
StoryCorps (nonprofit) 155
storytelling: "Alex from Target" and 159–160; Boston Marathon bombing and 155–156; calendars and 148, **149**, 196; communities and 151–152; culture and 151–152; Facebook.Live and 159; heritage and 151–152; importance of 151–152; modes and

152; multimodal 152–155; online 155–156; overview 160; Pheidippides's marathon run 164–165; protecting stories and 159–160; quilts and *153*; by singers/songwriters 154; technology and 148–149; tools and, using 59; versions of story and 158; writing stories and 156–158
Strauss, Leo 61
StubHub 212–213
subject line of email message 260–261, **260**, 263–264
subway system image 103, **104**
Suh, Ayoung 237
Sumerians and handwriting –143144, 138
surveillance industry 274
survey builders 79
SurveyMonkey 79
surveys 79, *82–85*
Swift computer language 312, *341*
symbols, 6–8, **7**, 239, 314
synchronous feedback 120
syntax 8, 28, 314
system: computer mouse as 358–359; database 224–227; data for improving writing and 229; embodied actions and 358; hacking 230; internet as 223; labeling 217–220; language in 217–221; multimodal 220–222, **220**, **221**; multitasking and 229–230; overview 231; person's role in 215–217; search engines 79, 174, 224; search engines and 224; searching data 228–229; technology as 211–214, 231; translating from one to another 214–215; trust in 222–223
system development life cycle (SDLC) *213*

tablet houses 138
tactile mode of communication *26*
tags 314
Talese, Gay 143
Tang dynasty and folktales 152
techne 60, 62
Technics and Civilization (Mumford) 63–64
technological actions 358
technological complexes 64
technological determinism 65, 191
technological world: connected online spaces and 243–244; embodied actions and 358–361; emotions in 365–367; gaming in 236–238; images in 377–379, **378**; infrastructures of 241–242; music in 365–367;

place and 244–246; reading 234–236; sound in 363–367; space and 244–246; stakeholders in 241–242; textures in 361–362; time and 244–246; writers in 246–249; writing in 17, 239–240, 249; *see also* technology
technology: accessibility of 198; as active 12–13, 69; as actor in social systems 195; art and 62; audience and, writing for multiple 35; automation and employment and 203; bad uses of 10; collaborating using 248–249; as connected 15, 289; critical thinking bout 173–177; culture and *153*; defining 11–16, 57–65; for design, identifying 80; design of 196–198; digital 41; disappearance of 192–194; distribution of 198–201; distrust of 61; diversity and 191; as embedded 14, 192–193, 204–205, 209; as embodied 15–16, 355; embodied actions and 359, 361, 375; enframing and 195; etymology of word 60, 63; as evolution (not revolution) 165; future and 5; gender and 64–65; German use of term 63–64; good uses of 9–10; human evolution and 57–58, 60; for images, identifying correct 380–381; importance of 1; for initial research, identifying 79; interpretation of effects of 203; language and 8; literacy 193; as medium 29; for messages, choosing right 256–258; misconception about, fundamental 62; as multimodal of 1, 12; as narrative 13, 145; new 16–17, 78, 198; past and 5; power relations and 191–192; present and 4; privacy and 202; purpose of, central 58; science and 62, 62–63; as set of tools 192; as situated 233–236, 249; social relations and 196; storytelling and 59, 148–149; stress involving 201; for survey/interview/focus group *83–84*; as system 211–214, 231; text and 16; for text, identifying 80; tools and 58–59; touch 359–360, *361–362*; types of *31*; use of 202–203; validity of information and 180; value of by ancient civilizations 61; voice-to-text 334, 359–360; writing as 1, 7–8; *see also specific type*; technological world
Technology Matters (Nye) 57
Technology for Teachers and Students post 178
Techquickie 43
TED (Technology, Entertainment, and Design) 374
telephone 192, 328
template 341–342

424

temporal distances 107, 133
temporal mode of communication *26*
Terms of Use for Instagram 304–305, *304*
test/testing *51*, *84*, 120–122
text: alignment of 107–108; clarity of **128**; coherence of **128**; color and placement of 105; consistency of **128**; conventions 112; drafting 118–119, **118–119**; efficiency of 130; feedback on 120–122; flow of **128**; fonts and 109–110, **110**; images with, placing 385; for messages, choosing right 256–258; moving through 108–109; printed copy for revising 127; size of 106; sound-based, editing 133–134; typography and 109–110; unity of **128**; video-based, editing 134–135; visual-based, editing 132–133; word-based, editing 129–131; *see also* design
texting 267–268, 332
text messages 267–268
texts: defining 16; digital 43, 46–47, **49**, 54, 234–235; as multimodal 25, 41; non-digital 42–46, 54; technology and 16; 3D 49–50, *51*; 2D 49–50, *51*; type of 23–24
textures 52–54, 361–362
Themysteriousworld website 174
thinking critically 87, **88**, 89, 173–177
thinking purposefully 134
Thompson, Millie 400
Tierra, Rick 184–187
time 244–246
timing 244–245, 267, 386–388
Tomlins, Ray 259
tools and technology 58–59
touch technology 359–360, *361–362*
touch-typing 143–144
tracking *110*
trail guide 392
transitions in videos 134
translating from one system to another 214–215
Traversy Media 314
trial, theory of 397
Trithemius 139
trolls 299
troubleshooting problems in writing 81
trust in systems 222–223
Turow, J. 281
Twin, Mark 140
Twitter 17, 159, 278, 303
Tycho Brahe 62
typeface 109–110
typewriter 140–141
typography 109–110; *see also* text

Uniform Resource Locator (URL) 87, 347
unity of text **128**
Universal Design 268–269, 323
University of Illinois Law School 199
uploading content 348
URL (Uniform Resource Locator) 87, 347
usability 322–323
U.S. Copyright Office 348, 350
user experience (UX) 323
user friendly 340
user-generated content 179–180, 273, 276
user interface 335, **335**
U.S. Marine Manual of Military Occupational Specialties 253
U.S. National Highway Traffic Safety 267, 332
U.S. presidential election (2016) 86
utility 323

validity of information 180
Vasquez, Melissa 327–328
vector graphics 382
Vergilius Augusteus (Virgil) 42
Verhulsdonck, Gustav 337
VHS video cassette 44, **44**
video-based text, editing 134–135
video cassettes 44
video games 236–238
videos: audience and 134–135; dashboard 396, 402–404; editing text based on 132–133; as evidence in courtroom **396**; impact of 395; of police encounters 395; TED Talk 374; testifying with 401–403, 406–407; text-based 134–135; transitions in 134; *see also* courtroom mobile video narratives
viral information/images 159–160, 346, 379
Virgil 42
virtual reality 237
visual-based text, editing 132–133
visual mode of communication *9*, *25*, *26*
voice, active/passive 130–131
Voice of Lived Experience, The (Bock and Schneider) 85
voice-to-text 334, 359–360

Wagner, Christian 237
warm color **102**
web 169

425

Web 2.0 276
Weber, Max 63
web hosting service 312
webpage 315, 318
web servers 312
websites: accessibility of 322–323; analytics and 322, 325; audience and 323; backend computer operations and 311–316; banning 202–203; clean design of 319–320, **320**; computer language and 312–313, **313**; computer programming and 311–316, *311*; consequences of design of 321–322; content 193; design principles for *323–324*; efficiency of 323; errors on 323; "fold" on 317; frontend computer operations and 316–320; hyperlinks 318; information 317; internet service provider and 312; learnability and 323; memorability and 323; navigation on 318; online world and 310–311; overview 325; placement of content on 317; satisfaction with, user 323; usability of 322–323; *see also* internet; *specific name*
what you see is what you get (WYSIWYG) programs 315, *341*
"white hat" hackers 230
wiki 179–180
wikiHow 180
Wikileaks 180
Wikimedia Foundation 180
Wikipedia 179–180
Williams, Jessica 153–155
wireframing 337–338
Wolf, Maryanne 138, 142
word-based text, editing 129–131
World Intellectual Property Organization (WIPO) 90
World Wide Web 169, 197, 201, *244*; *see also* internet
World Wide Web Consortium (W3C) 169, 202, 323, *323–324*
World Wide Web Foundation 169
writers in technological world 246–249
writing: apps 333–334; as assemblage 235; bad uses of 10; collaborating in 247–248; culture and 258; data for improving 229; defining 137; email messages 261–262; embodied actions and 359; feelings and 24–25; future and 5; goods uses of 9–10; images, still 379–386; importance of 1; language and 9–10; materials of 51–52, 54; with mobile devices 333–334; as multimodal 1, 24–28; past and 5; place and 239–241, 244–246; present and 5; purposeful 40–42; rhetorical 1; signs and 6–7, **6**; with smartphones 333–334; for social media 297–300; space and 239–241, 244–246; stories 156–158; Sumerians and 138; symbols and 6–7, **6**; in technological world 17, 239–240, 249; as technology 1, 7–8; texture and 362; unnaturalness of 138; *see also* handwriting; *specific genre*; writing strategies
writing strategies: citing 86–87, **88**, 89–93; drafting text 118–119, **118–119**; ethical choices and 93; fund-raising memo example 72, **73–74**, 74; overview 72, 93; planning 74–81, **75**; researching 81–82, **82–84**, 85–86; revising text 122–127, **125**; *see also* editing text
Wynwood neighborhood (Florida) 248
WYSIWYG (what you see is what you get) programs 315, *341*

Xcode 342

#YellowstonePledge campaign 302
YouTube resources: "Analog vs. Digital as Fast as Possible" 43; "Beginner's Guide to Google Search Basics and Tips and Tricks" 178; "Construct 3 Tutorial [01]—Making Your First Game (Binding-of-Isaac-Like)" 238; "Evolution of Writing (8000 BC to 2017), The" 8; "How to Create an Awesome Slide Presentation (for Keynote or PowerPoint)" 392; "How to Do Mind Mapping and Brainstorming Ideas Online" 76; "How to Get Better Search Results/Be a Google Pro/Study Tips" 178; "How to Make an App for Beginners (2018)—Lesson 1" 342; "How to Start a Podcast (2019 Tutorial) Equipment & Software" 373; "HTML Crash Course for Absolute Beginners" 314; "Internet Everywhere" 171; "Internet, The" 224; Lacrae performances 154; "Pedagogy of Multiliteracies, A" 25; "RGB-HexColors Explained" 105; "Synchronous vs. Asynchronous Communication" 120; "Top Podcasting Tips & Tools for Recording, Interviews & Exporting (2019) Tutorial" 373

Zaner-Bloser handwriting curriculum 141
Zuckerman, Ethan 282

For Product Safety Concerns and Information please contact our EU
representative GPSR@taylorandfrancis.com
Taylor & Francis Verlag GmbH, Kaufingerstraße 24, 80331 München, Germany

www.ingramcontent.com/pod-product-compliance
Lightning Source LLC
Chambersburg PA
CBHW050525300426